CRIMINAL PROCEDURE FOR THE CRIMINAL JUSTICE PROFESSIONAL

THIRD EDITION

CRIMINAL PROCEDURE FOR THE CRIMINAL JUSTICE PROFESSIONAL

THIRD EDITION

By
John N. Ferdico, J.D.
Member of the Maine and Massachusetts Bars

Former Assistant Attorney General
and Director of Law Enforcement Education
for the State of Maine

West Publishing Co.
St. Paul • New York • Los Angeles • San Francisco

COPYRIGHT © 1975, 1979 By WEST PUBLISHING COMPANY

COPYRIGHT © 1985 By WEST PUBLISHING COMPANY
50 West Kellogg Boulevard
P.O. Box 64526
St. Paul, MN 55164–0526

Library of Congress Cataloging in Publication Data

Ferdico, John N.
  Criminal procedure for the criminal justice
professional.

  Rev. ed. of: Criminal procedure for the law enforcement
officer. 2nd ed. c1979.
  Includes indexes.
  1. Criminal procedure—United States. I. Ferdico,
John N. Criminal procedure for the law enforcement
officer. II. Title.
KF9619.F47 1985   345.73'05   84–29092
ISBN 0–314–85234–4   347.3055

Preface

Criminal Procedure for the Criminal Justice Professional is an update and complete revision of *Criminal Procedure for the Law Enforcement Officer*, the most recent edition of which was published in 1979. The change in the title reflects a broadening of perspective and an attempt to provide a deeper understanding of the basic principles underlying the law of criminal procedure. Whereas *Criminal Procedure for the Law Enforcement Officer* was primarily directed toward providing guidelines for the law enforcement officer on the legal aspects of his or her daily duties, this new edition goes a step further and attempts to provide a basic understanding of the reasons behind the rules. It is hoped that this new approach will enhance the value of the book for the criminal justice student, whatever career in criminal justice he or she chooses, while still maintaining the book's value as a practical field guide for the law enforcement officer on the beat.

Among the highlights of *Criminal Procedure for the Criminal Justice Professional* is an entirely new Part I entitled "A Framework for the Study of Criminal Procedure." This new part is the primary vehicle by which the book attempts to provide the underlying bases for the many complex rules and procedures under which our criminal justice system functions. Chapter 1, "Individual Rights under the United States Constitution," after presenting a brief history of the Constitution, discusses each provision of the Constitution dealing with individual rights, such as freedom of speech, press, and religion, habeas corpus, and the right to jury trial. The chapter includes introductory materials on the Fourth, Fifth, and Sixth Amendments, to which the remainder of the book is primarily dedicated. The main thesis of this first chapter is that the law of criminal procedure is the result of the continuing efforts of courts and legislatures to balance the need to protect individual rights against the need for more effective law enforcement.

Chapter 2, "An Overview of the Criminal Court System," is an update and revision of former chapter 13 in *Criminal Procedure for the Law Enforcement Officer*. The chapter deals with the rules and procedures that govern the course of a criminal prosecution beyond the investigatory stage, including pre-trial proceedings, indictment, arraignment, trial, sentence and judgment, and post-trial remedies and procedures. Because this chapter provides a context for understanding the effect and importance of compliance with the law of criminal procedure at the very earliest stages of a criminal prosecution, it was moved to the beginning of the book and included in the "framework" of Part I.

To complete the "framework," Chapter 3 provides a discussion of "Basic Underlying Concepts" pervading the entire subject matter of criminal procedure. Included are a detailed discussion of the "exclusionary rule" and introductory materials on the concepts of "privacy" and "probable cause." Because these topics appear in a continuous thread throughout the remainder of the book, they have been included at the beginning to sensitize the reader to their importance.

Criminal Procedure for the Criminal Justice Professional also contains one other entirely new chapter—Chapter 15 on "Electronic Surveillance." This new chapter was included because it illustrates the difficulties courts and legislatures have had in balancing privacy interests against the need to maintain law and order in an increasingly complex and technical modern society. The chapter also raises many difficult questions which cut across many of the topics and issues discussed throughout the book and which challenge the efficacy of existing legal theories.

The remainder of the book consists primarily of an update and complete revision of the chapters in *Criminal Procedure for the Law Enforcement Officer* dealing with arrest, search and seizure, admissions and confessions, and pre-trial identification procedures. The updating includes all important developments in the law through September 30, 1984. Emphasis has been placed on United States Supreme Court decisions, but important cases from lower federal and state courts are also included. As stated earlier, the revision attempts to go beyond practical guidelines and to discuss the "reasons behind the rules." In keeping with this goal, the revised chapters contain more discussion of and quotations from United States Supreme Court decisions explaining the rationale of those decisions.

Another new feature of *Criminal Procedure for the Criminal Justice Professional* is the provision of review and discussion questions at the end of each chapter. The questions are designed to encourage the reader to think about the implications and applications of the material presented in the text and do not merely call for a recital of memorized material. In developing the questions, an effort was made to stimulate the reader to apply his or her knowledge to fact situations other than those presented in the text and to consider the interrelationships of different topics in the criminal procedure area.

In the process of revision, three chapters in *Criminal Procedure for the Law Enforcement Officer* were eliminated—Chapter 12, "Investigation of Crime"; Chapter 14, "Evidence"; and Chapter 15, "Testifying in Court." The subject matter of those chapters is more appropriately suited for a book dealing comprehensively with criminal investigation or evidence.

In closing, I would like to repeat two paragraphs from the preface to the first edition of *Criminal Procedure for the Law Enforcement Officer,* because I believe they continue to express the purpose and spirit behind the writing of this book.

"The law of criminal procedure is not only complex, but is constantly changing. The law enforcement officer is expected to understand these complexities and keep abreast of the changes. More importantly, he is required to apply the law to diverse situations which do not always neatly conform to the principles set out to guide him. To compound the law enforcement officer's problem, most court opinions on criminal procedure are written in a rambling, legalistic style that even lawyers and judges have trouble understanding. The result is a gap of communication and understanding between those who make the rules (judges) and those who must enforce them (law enforcement officers). Violation of rights of citizens by officers who are unaware or ignorant of court-imposed limitations on their activities is one of the main causes of the failure of many prosecutions and the reversal of many convictions.

"This book is an attempt to bridge the gap of communication and understanding between judges and law enforcement officers. I believe that law enforcement officers need understandable guidelines for conducting arrests, searches and seizures, interrogations, and lineups. I also believe that law enforcement officers should be familiar with the language and reasoning of the courts in these areas. Officers, however, should not be expected to read through long involved opinions of every state and federal case that affects them and to extract principles of law to guide them in the execution of their duties. They already carry a heavy enough burden. Reading and interpreting the law is the job of an attorney. Therefore, I have tried in this book to reduce the complexity of the law of criminal procedure into simple straight-forward advice illustrated with examples of actual cases. I have also used quotations from cases, when I believed they were written in clear, understandable language."

I hope that *Criminal Procedure for the Criminal Justice Professional* fulfills the purpose of bridging the gap between judges and law enforcement officers and that it proves to be a valuable and informative resource for students and other professionals in the criminal justice system. I welcome any comments and suggestions for the improvement of future editions.

Finally, I would like to thank the staff of the Maine State Law Library in Augusta for their able and friendly assistance throughout the preparation of the manuscript of this book. And I would like to acknowledge everyone at West Publishing Company who participated in the publication and promotion of the book for their competence and their congenial professionalism.

John N. Ferdico

Summary of Contents

PART FOUR

ADMISSIONS AND CONFESSIONS, PRE–TRIAL IDENTIFICATION, AND ELECTRONIC SURVEILLANCE

Table of Contents

PART TWO

ARREST, SEARCH WARRANTS, AND PROBABLE CAUSE

Chapter 4. Arrest—Continued   Page

PART THREE

**EXCEPTIONS TO THE SEARCH WARRANT
REQUIREMENT**

PART FOUR

ADMISSIONS AND CONFESSIONS, PRE-TRIAL IDENTIFICATION, AND ELECTRONIC SURVEILLANCE

Chapter 13. Admissions and Confessions—Continued   **Page**

CRIMINAL PROCEDURE FOR THE CRIMINAL JUSTICE PROFESSIONAL

THIRD EDITION

PART ONE

A Framework for the Study of Criminal Procedure

1

2

3

1

Individual Rights under the United States Constitution

INTRODUCTION

The law of criminal procedure can be described as the rules governing the balancing of the conflicting governmental functions of maintaining law and order and protecting the rights of citizens. These functions, common to every government that is not totally authoritarian or anarchistic, are necessarily conflicting because an increased emphasis on maintaining law and order will necessarily involve increased intrusions on individual rights. And, conversely, an increased emphasis on protecting individual rights will necessarily hamper the efficient maintenance of law and order. For example, an overprotective policy toward preserving individual rights is likely to result in an atmosphere conducive to increased violation of and disrespect for the law. Potential criminals will perceive that restrictions on police authority to arrest, detain, search, and question will decrease the likelihood of their getting caught and that complex and technical procedural safeguards designed to insure the fairness of court proceedings will enable them to avoid punishment if they do get caught. The ultimate result, it is argued, is a society in which people do not feel secure in their homes or communities, and in which illegal activity abounds in government, business, and other aspects of daily life, to the detriment of everyone.

On the other hand, enforcement of the criminal laws would be much easier if persons suspected of crime were presumed guilty, if they had no privilege against self-incrimination, if their bodies, vehicles, and homes could be searched at will, and if they could be detained for long periods of time without a hearing. Life in many totalitarian countries today is characterized by such governmental abuses and the citizenry of these countries lives in daily fear of official intrusion into the home, the disappearance of a loved one, or tighter restrictions on movement, speech, or association.

Because the United States was founded as a direct response to British abuses against the early colonists, although certainly not as severe as those under present-day dictatorships, our form of government has, from the beginning, reflected a strong commitment to the protection of individual rights from governmental abuse. This commitment was embodied in the original Constitution of 1788 and in the Bill of Rights, which was adopted shortly thereafter. We begin our discussion of individual rights with a brief history of events leading to the adoption of the Constitution.

HISTORY

On September 17, 1787, a convention of delegates from all the original thirteen states except Rhode Island proposed a new Constitution to the Continental Congress and the States for ratification. The rights expressed and protected by this Constitution, and by the amendments adopted four years later, were not new. Some had roots in the societies of ancient Rome and Greece, and all were nurtured during almost six hundred years of English history since the signing of the Magna Carta.

As colonists under English rule, Americans before the Revolution were familiar with the ideas that government should be limited in power, and that the law was superior to any government, even the King. As the Declaration of Independence shows, the colonists rebelled because the English King and Parliament refused to allow them their historic rights as free English citizens. In September, 1774, delegates from twelve colonies met in the First Continental Congress to petition England for their rights "to life, liberty, and property" to trial by jury, "a right peaceably to assemble, consideration of their grievances, and petition the King," and other rights that they had been denied. The petition was ignored, and soon afterward fighting broke out at Lexington and Concord. Meanwhile, citizens in Mecklenburg County, North Carolina, declared the laws of Parliament to be null and void and instituted their own form of local government with the adoption of the Mecklenburg Resolves in May 1775. In June 1776, a resolution was introduced in the Continental Congress, and a month later, on July 4, 1776, the Thirteen United Colonies declared themselves free and independent. Their announcement was truly revolutionary. They listed a long number of abuses they had suffered, and justified their independence in the historic words: "We hold these truths to be self-evident, that all men are created equal, that they are endowed by their Creator with certain Inalienable Rights, that among these are Life, Liberty and the pursuit of Happiness."

Two years later, in July 1778, the newly independent States joined in a united government under the Articles of Confederation, which was our nation's first Constitution. But it soon became clear that the Articles of Confederation did not adequately provide for a working, efficient government. Among other weaknesses of the Articles, they gave Congress no authority to levy taxes or to regulate foreign or interstate commerce. In May 1787, a convention of delegates, meeting in Philadelphia with the approval of Congress, began to consider amendments to the Articles. But the delegates realized that a new system of government was necessary. After much debate, and several heated arguments, a compromise Constitution was agreed upon.

Although we now honor the wisdom of the delegates, they themselves had a different opinion of their work. Many were dissatisfied, and a few even thought a new Constitution should be written. No delegate from Rhode Island attended the convention nor signed the document on September 17, 1787, when the proposed Constitution was announced. Delaware was the first state to accept it, on December 7, 1787, and by a unanimous vote. Not all states were as pleased, and for a while it was not certain that a sufficient number of states would ratify. In some states the vote was extremely close. A major argument against ratification was the absence of a Bill of Rights. Only after it became generally agreed that the first order of business of the new government would be to propose amendments for a Bill of Rights was acceptance of the Constitution obtained by a sufficient number of states. On June 21, 1788, New Hampshire became the ninth state, and ratification of the new Constitution was completed. By the end of July, the important states of Virginia and New York had joined.

On September 25, 1789, Congress proposed the first ten amendments to the new Constitution—the Bill of Rights. With the proposal of these guarantees, the states of North Carolina and Rhode Island, the last of the Thirteen Original Colonies, ratified the Constitution. Ratification of the Bill of Rights was completed on December 15, 1791. Since that date, it has served as the testimony of our nation to its belief in the basic and inalienable rights of the people, and in the limitations on the power of government. Together with provisions of the original Constitution, they protect that great body of liberties that belong to every citizen.

For ease of discussion, the remainder of this chapter will treat the original Constitution separately from the Bill of Rights and later amendments.

THE ORIGINAL CONSTITUTION

The Constitution of 1789 has served as the fundamental instrument of our government for almost all of our country's history as an independent nation. Drawn at a time when there were only thirteen original states, dotted with small towns, small farms, and small industry, the Constitution has proved a durable and viable instrument of government despite enormous changes in the political, social, and economic environment. From a weak country on the Atlantic seaboard to a continental nation of fifty states with over 230 million people producing goods and services at a rate thousands of times faster than in 1789, the framework for democratic government set out in the Constitution has remained workable and progressive.

Similarly, the individual rights listed in the Constitution and its twenty-six amendments have also retained an extraordinary vitality despite their being applied to problems and fact situations that could not have been envisioned by the Founding Fathers. Freedom of the press, for example, could only have been understood in the context of the small, still primitive printing presses of the day. Yet today that freedom applies not only to modern presses but to radio, television, and motion pictures—all products of the twentieth century. It is the purpose of this chapter to explain how these basic rights have been applied and to develop a sensitivity to them as a prelude to the study of criminal procedure, in which these rights will confront the countervailing demands of society for the enforcement of the law and the detection and prevention of crime.

Each branch of the government—Legislative, Judicial, and Executive—is charged by the Constitution with the protection of individual liberties, although the Judicial Branch has, within this framework, assumed perhaps the largest role. Chief Justice John Marshall, speaking for the Supreme Court in the early case of Marbury v. Madison, 5 U.S. (1 Cranch) 137, 2 L.Ed. 60 (1803), declared that it was the duty of the judiciary to say what the law is, and that included expounding and interpreting that law. The law contained in the Constitution, he declared, was paramount and other laws that were repugnant to its provisions must fall. It was the province of the courts, he concluded, to decide when other law was in violation of the basic law of the Constitution and, where this was found to occur, to declare those laws null and void. This is the doctrine known as "judicial review," which became the basis for the application of constitutional guarantees by courts in cases brought before them.

The Congress also has played an important role in the protection of constitutional rights by enacting legislation designed to guarantee and apply these rights in specific contexts. Laws that guarantee the rights of Indians, afford due process to military service personnel, and give effective right to counsel to poor defendants are examples of the legislative role.

Finally, the Executive Branch, which is charged with implementing the laws enacted by Congress, also contributes to the protection of individual rights by devising its own regulations and procedures for administering the law without intruding upon constitutional guarantees.

To properly understand the scope of constitutional rights, one must realize that, because of our federal system, Americans live under two governments rather than one—that of the federal government and that of the government of the state in which a person lives. The authority of the federal government is limited by the Constitution to those powers specified in it; the remainder of governmental powers is reserved to the states. The federal government is authorized, for example, to settle disputes between states, to conduct relations with foreign governments, and to act in certain matters of common national concern. States, on the other hand, retain the remainder of governmental power to be exercised within their respective boundaries.

THE BILL OF RIGHTS

Only a few individual rights were specified in the Constitution when it was adopted in 1788. Shortly after its adoption, however, ten amendments—called the Bill of Rights—were added to the Constitution to guarantee basic individual liberties. These liberties include freedom of speech, freedom of the press, freedom of religion, and freedom to assemble and petition the government.

The guarantees of the Bill of Rights originally applied only to actions of the federal government and did not prevent state and local governments from taking action that might threaten civil liberty. As a practical matter, states had their own constitutions, some containing their own bills of rights that guaranteed the same or similar rights as are guaranteed by the Bill of Rights against federal intrusion. These rights, however, were not guaranteed by all the states; if they did exist, they were subject to varying interpretations. In short, citizens were protected only to the extent that the states themselves recognized their basic rights.

In 1868, the Fourteenth Amendment was added to the Constitution. In part it provides that no state shall "deprive any person of life, liberty, or property without due process of law." Not until 1925, in the case of Gitlow v. New York, 268 U.S. 652, 45 S.Ct. 625, 69 L.Ed. 1138, did the Supreme Court interpret the phrase "due process of law" to mean in effect "without abridgement of certain of the rights guaranteed by the Bill of Rights." Since that decision, the Supreme Court has ruled that a denial by a state of certain of the rights contained in the Bill of Rights represents a denial of due process of law. The Court has not ruled that all rights in the Bill of Rights are contained in the notion of "due process," nor is that notion limited only to such rights as are enumerated in the Bill of Rights. It has simply found that there are concepts in the Bill of Rights so fundamental to the American scheme of justice that they must be recognized as part of "due process of law" and made applicable to the states as well as to the federal government.

At present, the following guarantees of the Bill of Rights have been applied to the states under the terms of the Fourteenth Amendment: Amendments I, IV, and VI; the self-incrimination, double jeopardy, and just compensation clauses of Amendment V; and the guarantee against cruel and unusual punishment of Amendment VIII. Only the right to indictment by grand jury in Amendment V, the right to jury trial in a civil suit in Amendment VII, and the prohibition against excessive bail or fines in Amendment VIII have not been applied to the states.

To place these rights in a broader perspective, one should realize that they make up only the core of what are considered to be civil rights—those privileges and freedoms that are accorded all Americans by virtue of their citizenship. There are many other "civil" rights that are not specifically mentioned in the Constitution but that nonetheless have been recognized by the courts, have often been guaranteed by statute, and are embedded in our democratic traditions. The right to buy, sell, own, and bequeath property; the right to enter into contracts; the right to marry and have children; the right to live and work where one desires; and the right to participate in the political, social, and cultural processes of the society in which one lives are a few of the rights that must be considered as fundamental to a democratic society as those specified by the Constitution.

Despite the inherent nature of the rights of American citizenship, it deserves to be emphasized that the rights guaranteed by the Constitution or otherwise are not absolute rights in the sense that they entitle citizens to act in any way they please. Rather, people must exercise their rights in such a way that the rights of others are not denied in order to gain the protections of the law. Thus, as Mr. Justice Holmes has pointed out, "Protection of free speech would not protect a man falsely shouting 'Fire' in a theater and causing a panic." Nor does freedom of speech and press sanction the publication of libel and obscenity. Similarly, the right of free speech and free assembly do not permit one knowingly to engage in conspiracies to overthrow by force the government of the United States. Civil liberties thus carry with them an obligation on the part of all Americans to exercise their rights within a framework of law and mutual respect for the rights of one's fellow citizens.

This obligation implies not only a restraint on the part of those exercising these rights but a tolerance on the part of those who are affected. Thus, citizens may on occasion be subjected to annoying political tirades, or disagreeable entertainment, or noisy demonstrations of protest. They may feel annoyed when a defendant refuses to testify, or when they see a seemingly guilty defendant go free because certain evidence was not admissible in court. But these annoyances or inconveniences are a small price to pay for the freedom one enjoys. If the rights of one are suppressed, it is, in the final analysis, the freedom of all that is jeopardized. Ultimately, a free society is a dynamic society, where thoughts and ideas are forever challenging and being challenged. It is not without the risk that the wrong voice will be listened to or the wrong plan pursued. But a free society is one that learns by its mistakes and can freely pursue the happiness of its citizens.

INDIVIDUAL RIGHTS IN THE ORIGINAL CONSTITUTION

Article I, Section 9, Clause 2

The Privilege of the Writ of Habeas Corpus shall not be suspended, unless when in Cases of Rebellion or Invasion the public Safety may require it.

This guarantee enables a person whose freedom has been restrained in some way to petition a federal court for a writ of habeas corpus, to test whether the restraint was imposed in violation of the Constitution or laws of the United States. This right under the Constitution applies to all cases in which a person is confined by government authority. It can be suspended only when the President, pursuant to congressional authorization, declares that a national emergency requires it and probably only when the courts are physically unable to function because of war, invasion, or rebellion. Habeas corpus is an important safeguard to prevent unlawful imprisonment and is discussed in further detail in Chapter 2.

Article I, Section 9, Clause 3

No Bill of Attainder . . . shall be passed [by the federal government].

Article I, Section 10, Clause 1

No State shall . . . pass any Bill of Attainder . . . .

A bill of attainder historically is a special act of a legislature that declares that a person or group of persons has committed a crime and that imposes punishment without a trial by court. Under our system of separation of powers, only courts may try a person for a crime or impose punishment for violation of the law.

Section 9 restrains Congress from passing bills of attainder, and section 10 restrains the states.

Article I, Section 9, Clause 3

No . . . ex post facto Law shall be passed [by the federal government].

Article I, Section 10, Clause 1

No state shall . . . pass any . . . ex post facto Law . . . .

These two clauses prohibit the states and the federal government from enacting any criminal or penal law that makes unlawful any act that was not a crime when it was committed. They also prevent the imposition of a greater penalty for a crime than that in effect when the crime was committed. However, laws that retroactively determine how a person is to be tried for a crime may be changed so long as the substantial rights of the accused are not curtailed. Laws are not ex post facto if they make punishment less severe than it was when the crime was committed.

Article III, Sections 1 and 2

(Article III, Sections 1 and 2, of the Constitution deal with the judicial system of the United States and for purposes of this book are too long to be reproduced.)

Article III, Section 1, of the Constitution outlines the structure and power of our federal court system and establishes a federal judiciary that helps maintain the rights of American citizens. Article III, Section 2, also contains a guarantee that the trial of all federal crimes, except that of impeachment, shall be by jury. The Supreme Court has interpreted this guarantee as containing exceptions for "trials of petty offenses," cases rightfully tried before court-martial or other military tribunal, and some cases in which the defendant has voluntarily relinquished the right to jury.

Section 2 also requires that a federal criminal trial be held in a federal court sitting in the state where the crime was committed. Thus, a person is given protection against being tried without his or her consent in some part of the United States far distant from the place where the alleged violation of federal laws occurred.

Article III, Section 3

Treason against the United States, shall consist only in levying War against them, or in adhering to their Enemies, giving them Aid and Comfort.

No Person shall be convicted of Treason unless on the Testimony of two Witnesses to the same overt Act, or on Confession in open Court.

The Congress shall have power to declare the Punishment of Treason, but no Attainder of Treason shall work Corruption of Blood, or Forfeiture except during the Life of the Person attainted.

Treason is the only crime defined by the Constitution. The precise description of this offense reflects an awareness by our forefathers of the danger that unpopular views might be branded as traitorous. Recent experience in other countries with prosecutions for conduct loosely labeled "treason" confirms the wisdom of the authors of the Constitution in expressly stating what constitutes this crime and how it shall be proved.

Article VI, Clause 3

[N]o religious Test shall ever be required as a Qualification to any Office or public Trust under the United States.

Together with the First Amendment, this guarantee expresses the principle that church and government are to remain separate, and that religious beliefs are no indication of patriotism, ability, or the right to serve this country. Thus, a citizen need not fear that religious affiliations or convictions may legally bar him or her from holding office in our country.

INDIVIDUAL RIGHTS IN THE BILL OF RIGHTS

Amendment 1

Congress shall make no law respecting an establishment of religion, or prohibiting the free exercise thereof; or abridging the freedom of speech, or of the press; or the right of the people peaceably to assemble, and to petition the Government for a redress of grievances.

Religion

Two express guarantees are given to the individual citizen with respect to his religious freedom. First, neither Congress—nor a state legislature because of the Fourteenth Amendment—may "make any law respecting an establishment of religion." This means no law may be passed that establishes an official church that all Americans must accept and support or to whose tenets all must subscribe or that favors one church over another. Secondly, no law is constitutional if it "prohibits the free exercise" of religion. Citizens are guaranteed the freedom to worship in the way they choose.

The Supreme Court described the establishment clause as providing a "wall of separation between church and state." Everson v. Board of Education, 330 U.S. 1, 16, 67 S.Ct. 504, 512, 91 L.Ed. 711, 723 (1947). Governmental activity that leads to "excessive entanglement" with the church or its related institutions and practices has been ruled unconstitutional. Thus, the Court held that a state may not require prayer in the public schools nor may it supplement or reimburse parochial schools for teachers' salaries and textbooks. To permit or authorize such activities would constitute governmental support of the religious organization affected. On the other hand, the Court held that it is permissible for public schools to release students, at their own request, from an hour of classwork in order that they may attend their own churches for religious instruction; or for a state to provide free bus transportation to children attending church or parochial schools if transportation was also furnished to children in the public schools. Furthermore, the Court upheld the tax-exempt status of church property used exclusively for worship purposes, and has sanctioned federal aid programs for new construction at church-related universities. It also held that the establishment clause does not prevent a state from designating Sunday as a day of rest.

Freedom to worship, as interpreted by the Supreme Court, must not conflict with otherwise valid government enactments. For example, a man may not have two wives and escape conviction for bigamy by attributing his conduct to his religious beliefs. Nor could a person commit an indecent act or engage in immoral conduct and then validly justify the actions on grounds of religious freedom. The Supreme Court also declared that it is an unconstitutional invasion of religious freedom to exclude children from public schools who, because of their religious beliefs, refuse to salute the American flag. The Court further ruled that requiring attendance of children of the Amish religious sect in public schools beyond the eighth grade was an impairment of the free-exercise clause since it prevented education in the traditional Amish framework.

Speech

As a general rule, citizens may freely speak out on any subject they choose. In addition, they may join organizations, wear buttons, buy books, and carry signs that represent their views. And they may take their case to court when they feel they have been wronged.

The Supreme Court ruled, however, that the protections afforded by the First Amendment do not extend to all forms of expression. Highly inflammatory remarks spoken to a crowd that advocate violence and clearly threaten the peace and safety of the community, or present a "clear and present danger" to the continued existence of the government, are not protected. Obscenity, too, has been judged unprotected by the First Amendment, although the Court has held that the mere possession of obscene materials in the home may not be punished.

Courts have also recognized that "symbolic speech," which involves more tangible forms of expression, falls within the protection of the First Amendment. Wearing buttons, or clothing with political slogans, or displaying a sign or a flag, are examples of symbolic speech. The wearing of black armbands by secondary school students in protest against the Vietnam war has been ruled protected by the First

Amendment, so long as the activity was not disruptive or injurious to the rights of other students. Display of a black flag in protest to organized government has also been protected. On the other hand, burning draft cards in protest against the Vietnam war has not been protected, since it could be shown to disrupt or undermine the operation of the Selective Service System. Courts have also been reluctant to overturn hair and dress codes of public schools when the schools could show that the codes were designed to prevent disruption or distraction of classes.

Finally, censorship by requirement of official approval or a license in advance for speaking has been condemned frequently by the courts. Nevertheless, although a citizen is free to make speeches on the public streets, he or she may be prevented from doing so when using a loud and raucous amplifier in a hospital zone or when the location chosen for the address is such that it is likely to interfere with the movement of traffic.

Press

Freedom of the press is a further guarantee of the right to express oneself, in this case by writing or publishing one's views on a particular subject. The Founding Fathers recognized the importance of a free interplay of ideas in a democratic society and sought to guarantee the right of all citizens to speak or publish their views, even if they were contrary to those of the government or the society as a whole. Accordingly, the First Amendment generally forbids censorship or other restraint upon speech or the printed word. Thus, a school board's dismissal of a teacher who had protested school board activities in a letter to the editor of the local newspaper was held to infringe upon his First Amendment rights. And a state court order, issued in anticipation of the trial of an accused mass murderer, restraining the press and broadcasting media from reporting any confessions or incriminating statements made by the defendant or from reporting other facts "strongly implica-tive" of the defendant, was similarly struck down.

As with speech, however, freedom to write or publish is not an absolute right of expression. The sale of obscene materials is not protected nor are printed materials that are libelous. The Supreme Court ruled, however, that public figures cannot sue for defamation unless the alleged libelous remarks were printed with knowledge of their falsity or with a reckless disregard for the truth.

The Court also ruled that the publication of a secret study into the origins of the United States' involvement in the Vietnam war could not be prevented due to the First Amendment guarantee. The Court indicated, however, that freedom of the press may not extend to other similar matters that could be shown to have a more direct and substantial bearing on national security.

Finally, broadcasting, including radio, television, and motion pictures, receives the protections of the free press guarantee, and is subject to its limitations.

Assembly and Petition

American citizens, whether they are meeting for political activity, religious services, or for other purposes, have the right to assemble peaceably. Public authorities cannot impose unreasonable restrictions on such assemblies, but they can impose limitations reasonably designed to prevent fire, hazard to health, or a traffic obstruction. The Supreme Court emphasized that freedom of assembly is just as fundamental as freedom of speech and press. Thus, while no law may legitimately prohibit demonstrations, there may be laws or other governmental actions that legitimately restrict demonstrations to certain areas or prohibit the obstruction and occupation of public buildings.

Picketing is also protected under the free speech guarantee. It may, however, be reasonably regulated to prevent pickets from obstructing movement onto and from the property involved. Picketing on private property has been upheld but only where the property is open to the public and the picketing relates to the business being conducted on the property. Thus, the distribution of antiwar handbills on the premises of a privately-owned shopping center has been held to be unprotected.

The right of petition is designed to enable citizens to communicate with their government without obstruction. When citizens exercise their First Amendment freedom to write or speak to their Senator or member of Congress, they partake of "the healthy essence of the democratic process."

Amendment II

A well regulated Militia, being necessary to the security of a free State, the right of the people to keep and bear Arms, shall not be infringed.

The Second Amendment provides for the freedom of citizens to protect themselves against both disorder in the community and attack from foreign enemies. This right to bear arms has become much less important in recent decades as well-trained military and police forces have been developed to protect the citizenry. No longer do people need to place reliance on having their own weapons available. Furthermore, the Supreme Court held that the state and federal governments may pass laws prohibiting the carrying of concealed weapons, requiring the registration of firearms, and limiting the sale of firearms for other than military uses.

Amendment III

No Soldier shall, in time of peace be quartered in any house, without the consent of the Owner, nor in time of war, but in a manner to be prescribed by law.

Prior to the Revolution, American colonists had frequently been required to provide lodging and food for British soldiers against their will. The Third Amendment prohibited the continuation of this practice.

Amendment IV

The right of the people to be secure in their persons, houses, papers, and effects, against unreasonable searches and seizures, shall not be violated, and no Warrants shall issue, but upon probable cause, supported by Oath or affirmation, and particularly describing the place to be searched, and the persons or things to be seized.

In some countries, even today, police officers may invade a citizen's home, seize his property, or arrest him whenever they see fit. In the United States, on the other hand, the Fourth Amendment protects the individual and his property from unreasonable search and seizure by officers of the law. In general, although there are many exceptions to the rule, a police officer may not search the home of a private citizen, seize any of his property, or arrest him without first obtaining a court order called a warrant. Before the warrant will be issued, the police officer must convince a magistrate that there is "probable cause"—good reason—to believe either that the person involved has committed a crime or that the person has in his possession evidence related to a crime.

Since the major portion of this book deals with the topics of arrest, search and seizure, and probable cause, further discussion of the Fourth Amendment will take place in the chapters dealing with those topics.

Amendment V

No person shall be held to answer for a capital, or otherwise infamous crime, unless on a presentment or indictment of a Grand Jury, except in cases arising in the land or naval forces, or in the Militia, when in actual service in time of War or public danger; nor shall any person be subject for the same offense to be twice put in jeopardy of life or limb; nor shall be compelled in any criminal case to be a witness against himself, nor be deprived of life, liberty, or property, without due process of law; nor shall private property be taken for public use, without just compensation.

Grand Jury

The Fifth Amendment requires that before a person is tried in federal court for an "infamous" crime, he or she must first be indicted by a grand jury. The grand jury's duty is to make sure that there is probable cause to believe that the accused person is guilty. This prevents a person from being subjected to a trial when there is not enough proof that he or she has committed a crime.

An infamous crime is a felony (a crime for which a sentence of more than one year's imprisonment can be given) or a lesser offense that can be punished by confinement in a penitentiary or at hard labor. An indictment is not required for a trial by court-martial or by other military tribunal. Also, the constitutional require-ment of grand jury indictment does not apply to trials in state courts. However, where states do use grand juries in their criminal proceedings, the Supreme Court ruled that the grand juries must be free of racial bias.

Double Jeopardy

The Fifth Amendment also guarantees the individual that he or she will not be placed in double jeopardy, that is, will not be tried before a federal or state court more than once for the same crime. The Supreme Court held that, under the due process safeguard of the Fourteenth Amendment, state courts may not harass defendants by successive prosecutions for the same act of misconduct.

A defendant is considered to be in jeopardy at a criminal trial when the jury is empaneled and sworn. Double jeopardy occurs when the second trial is for the same offense as the first. A second trial can occur, however, when the first trial results in a "mistrial," for instance, when the jury cannot agree on a verdict, or when a second trial is ordered by an appellate court.

Double jeopardy does not arise when a single act violates both federal and state laws and the defendant is exposed to prosecution in both federal and state courts. Nor does a criminal prosecution in either a state or federal court exempt the defendant from being sued for damages by anyone who is harmed by his criminal act. Furthermore, a defendant may be prosecuted more than once for the same conduct if it involved the commission of more than one crime. For instance, a person who kills three victims at the same time and place can be tried separately for each slaying.

Self-incrimination

The right of every person not to be compelled in any criminal case to be a witness against himself applies to federal proceedings and to state proceedings through the Fourteenth Amendment, and signifies that no one is obliged to provide answers to questions tending to convict him of a crime. Questions directed toward eliciting incriminating information may be asked at the very earliest stages of the investiga-tion of a crime and, thus, the Supreme Court ruled that when an individual is interrogated while in the "custody" of the police, or while deprived of his freedom of action in any significant way, the guarantees of the Fifth Amendment apply.

To ensure that the right against self-incrimination is protected, the Court ruled, in the case of Miranda v. Arizona, 384 U.S. 436, 86 S.Ct. 1602, 16 L.Ed.2d 694 (1966), that citizens must be warned prior to custodial interrogation of their right to remain silent, that what they say may be used against them in court, and that they have a right to counsel, which will be furnished them free of charge if they are unable to afford counsel. Failure to give these warnings results in any statements obtained by the questioning being inadmissible in later criminal proceedings.

Although Fifth Amendment rights may be waived, the accused must do so knowingly and voluntarily. Any confession obtained by use of force, threat, or other form of coercion will be excluded from the evidence presented at the trial, whether or not the *Miranda* warnings have been given. The entire subject of admissions and confessions, *Miranda* warnings, and voluntariness will be discussed in detail later in this book.

Courts have ruled that the guarantee against self-incrimination applies only to "testimonial" actions. Thus, it has been held that handwriting samples, blood tests, and confrontations with witnesses for identification purposes do not violate the Fifth Amendment.

Courts have also ruled that the Fifth Amendment prohibits both federal and state prosecutors and judges from commenting on the refusal of a defendant to take the witness stand in his own defense. The refusal of witnesses to testify to matters that could subject them to criminal prosecutions at a later date has also been upheld. The courts recognize, however, a limited right of the government to question employees about the performance of official duties and have upheld the dismissals of such employees for their refusal to answer the questions.

Government regulations that required registration of items such as highly dangerous weapons or narcotics that were a crime to possess have also been invalidated on the grounds that they require information that may be used in a criminal prosecution against the person who registers.

Due Process

The words "due process of law" express the fundamental ideas of American justice. A due process clause is found in both the Fifth and Fourteenth Amendments as a restraint upon both the federal and state governments. The due process clause affords protection against arbitrary and unfair procedures in judicial or administrative proceedings that could affect the personal and property rights of a citizen. Notice of a hearing or trial that is timely and adequately informs the accused of the charges against him or her is a basic concept included in "due process." The opportunity to present evidence in one's own behalf before an impartial judge or jury, to be presumed innocent until proven guilty by legally obtained evidence, and to have the verdict supported by the evidence presented are other rights repeatedly recognized within the protection of the due process clause.

The due process clauses of the Fifth and Fourteenth Amendments also provide other basic protections whereby the state and federal governments are prevented from adopting arbitrary and unreasonable legislation or other measures that would violate individual rights. Thus, constitutional limitations are imposed on governmental interference with important individual liberties—such as the freedom to enter into contracts, to engage in a lawful occupation, to marry, and to move without unnecessary restraints. Governmental restrictions placed on one's liberties must be reasonable and consistent with due process in order to be valid.

Just Compensation

The Fifth Amendment requires that whenever the government takes a person's property the property acquired must be taken for public use, and its full value must be paid to the owner. Thus, property cannot be taken by the federal government from one person simply to give it to another. However, the Supreme Court has held that it is permissible to take private property for such purposes as urban renewal, even though ultimately the property taken will be returned to private ownership, since the taking is really for the benefit of the community as a whole. The property does not have to be physically taken from the owner. If governmental action leads to a lower value of private property, that may also constitute a "taking" and therefore require payment of compensation. Thus, the Supreme Court held that the disturbance of the egg-laying habits of chickens on a man's poultry farm, caused by the noise of low-level flights by military aircraft from a nearby airbase, lessened the value of that farm and that, accordingly, the landowner was entitled to receive compensation equal to his loss.

Amendment VI

In all criminal prosecutions, the accused shall enjoy the right to a speedy and public trial, by an impartial jury of the State and district wherein the crime shall have been committed, which district shall have been previously ascertained by law, and to be informed of the nature and cause of the accusation; to be confronted with the witnesses against him; to have compulsory process for obtaining witnesses in his favor, and to have the Assistance of Counsel for his defence.

This amendment sets forth specific rights guaranteed to persons facing criminal prosecution. Its guarantees apply to both the federal courts and the state courts by virtue of the Fourteenth Amendment.

The right to speedy and public trial requires that the accused be brought to trial without unnecessary delay, and that the trial be open to the public. Intentional or negligent delay by the prosecution that prejudices the defendant's right to defend himself has been held grounds for dismissal of the charges. The Supreme Court ruled that delay in prosecution was not justified by the defendant's confinement on an earlier conviction because he should have been temporarily released for purposes of trial on the later charge.

Trial by an impartial jury supplements the earlier guarantee contained in Article III of the Constitution. The requirements that the jury have twelve members and that these must reach a unanimous verdict were derived from the common law and are not specifically accorded by the Constitution. The Supreme Court ruled, however, that state juries need not necessarily be composed of twelve members and actually has approved a state statutory scheme providing for only six. Moreover the Court has ruled that jury verdicts in state courts need not necessarily be unanimous. The right to jury trial does not apply to trials for petty offenses, which the Supreme Court has suggested as those punishable by six months' confinement or less. In all trials in which a jury is used it must be impartially selected, and no one can be excluded from jury service merely because of race, class, or sex.

The Sixth Amendment requirement that a person "be informed of the nature and cause of the accusation" means that an accused person must be given notice in what respects it is claimed he or she has broken the law in order to provide the person an opportunity to prepare a defense. This also means that the crime must be established by statute beforehand so that all persons are aware of what is illegal before they act. The statute must not be so vague or unclear that it does not inform people of the exact nature of the crime. Generally, the accused is entitled to have all witnesses against him or her present their evidence orally in court; subject to certain exceptions, hearsay evidence cannot be used in federal criminal trials. Moreover, the accused is entitled to the aid of the court in having compulsory process issued—usually a subpoena—which will order into court as witnesses those persons whose testimony is desired at the trial.

Finally, the Sixth Amendment provides a right to be represented by counsel. For many years, this was interpreted to mean only that the defendants had a right to be represented by a lawyer if they could afford one. The Supreme Court held, however, in the case of Gideon v. Wainwright, 372 U.S. 335, 83 S.Ct. 792, 9 L.Ed. 2d 799 (1963), that the Amendment imposed an affirmative obligation on the part of the federal and state governments to provide at public expense legal counsel for those who could not afford it, in order that their cases could be adequately represented to the court. The Supreme Court held that this right extends even to cases involving "petty offenses" if there is a chance that a jail sentence might result. The indigent are entitled to counsel at any "critical stage of the adjudicatory process." Thus, courts have accorded this right at custodial interrogations, at police lineups conducted at or after the initiation of adversary judicial proceedings, and at all stages of the trial process. In addition, indigents were given the right to a free copy of their trial transcript for purposes of appeal of their conviction. Congress enacted the Criminal Justice Acts of 1964 and 1970 to implement this right to counsel by establishing a federal defender system to represent those defendants who could not afford legal counsel. Most state legislatures have enacted similar measures.

Amendment VII

In suits at common law, where the value in controversy shall exceed twenty dollars, the right of trial by jury shall be preserved, and no fact tried by a jury, shall be otherwise re-examined in any Court of the United States, than according to the rules of the common law.

The Seventh Amendment applies only to federal civil trials and not to civil suits in state courts. Except as provided by local federal court rules, if a case is brought in a federal court and a money judgment is sought that exceeds twenty dollars, the party bringing the suit and the defendant are entitled to have the controversy decided by the unanimous verdict of a jury of twelve people.

Amendment VIII

Excessive bail shall not be required, nor excessive fines imposed, nor cruel and unusual punishments inflicted.

Bail

Bail has traditionally meant payment by the accused of an amount specified by the court to ensure the presence of the accused at trial. Accused persons who are released from custody and subsequently fail to appear for trial forfeit their bail to the court.

The Eighth Amendment does not specifically provide that all citizens have a "right" to bail, but only that bail will not be excessive. A right to bail has, however, been recognized in common law and in statute since 1791. In 1966 Congress enacted the Bail Reform Act to provide for pretrial release of persons accused of noncapital crimes. Congress thus sought to end pretrial imprisonment of indigent defendants who could not afford to post money bail and who were, in effect, confined only because of their poverty. The Act also discouraged the traditional use of money bail by requiring the judge to seek other means as likely to ensure that the defendant would appear when the trial was held.

The lack of a specific constitutional guarantee has, nonetheless, indirectly contributed to legislative enactments that have modified the availability of bail. In 1970, Congress provided for a system of pretrial detention in the District of Columbia for those defendants considered to be dangerous and likely to commit additional crimes if released prior to trial. The law was highly controversial and is considered by many to be a violation of the right to bail implied in the Eighth Amendment.

Whether bail, where it is available, is excessive or not will depend upon the facts of each particular case. Bail is "excessive" in violation of the Eighth Amendment when it is set at a figure higher than an amount reasonably calculated to ensure that the accused will stand trial and submit to sentence if found guilty. In a few instances, as when a capital offense such as murder is charged, bail may be denied altogether.

Cruel and Unusual Punishment

Whether fines or periods of confinement are "cruel and unusual" must be determined on the facts of each particular case. Clearly excessive practices, such as torture, would be invalid. The Supreme Court has found that the penalty of death for deliberate murder is not per se cruel and unusual, but that mandatory death statutes leaving the jury or trial judge no discretion to consider the individual defendant and his or her crime are cruel and unusual, and that standards and procedures may be established for the imposition of death that would remove or mitigate the arbitrariness and irrationality characteristic of many death penalty laws.

In addition to excessive forms of punishment, the clause has also been applied to imposition of punishment for a condition that the "criminal" had no power to change. Thus, a law making the status of narcotics addiction illegal was struck down by the Supreme Court as cruel and unusual since it punished a condition beyond the control of the accused. Some courts have held that laws punishing public drunkenness were "cruel and unusual" when applied to homeless alcoholics since it was impossible for them to avoid public places.

Amendment IX

The enumeration in the Constitution, of certain rights, shall not be construed to deny or disparage others retained by the people.

The Ninth Amendment emphasizes the view of the Founding Fathers that powers of government are limited by the rights of the people, and that it was not intended, by expressly guaranteeing in the Constitution certain rights of the people, to recognize that government had unlimited power to invade other rights of the people.

The Supreme Court has on at least one occasion suggested that this Amendment is a justification for recognizing certain rights not specifically mentioned in the Constitution, or for broadly interpreting those that are. The case involving the Ninth Amendment was Griswold v. Connecticut, 381 U.S. 479, 85 S.Ct. 1678, 14 L.Ed.2d 510 (1965). At issue was whether the right to privacy was a constitutional right and, if so, whether the right was one reserved to the people under the Ninth Amendment or was only derived from other rights specifically mentioned in the Constitution.

Courts have long recognized particular rights to privacy that are part of the First and Fourth Amendments. As the Court in *Griswold* said, "the specific guarantees in the Bill of Rights have penumbras, formed by emanations from those guarantees that help give them life and substance." 381 U.S. at 484, 85 S.Ct. at 1681, 14 L.Ed. 2d at 514. Thus, freedom of expression guarantees freedom of association and the related right to be silent and free from official inquiry into such associations. It also includes the right not to be intimidated by government for the expression of one's views. The Fourth Amendment's guarantee against unreasonable search and seizure confers a right to privacy because its safeguards prohibit unauthorized entry onto one's property and tampering with one's person, property, or possessions.

The court in *Griswold* ruled that the Third and Fifth Amendments, in addition to the First and Fourth, created "zones of privacy" safe from governmental intrusion and, without resting its decision upon any one of these or on the Ninth Amendment itself, simply held that the right of privacy was guaranteed by the Constitution.

Amendment X

The powers not delegated to the United States by the Constitution, nor prohibited by it to the States, are reserved to the States respectively, or to the people.

The Tenth Amendment embodies the principle of federalism, which reserves for the states the residue of powers not granted to the federal government or withheld from the states.

LATER AMENDMENTS DEALING WITH INDIVIDUAL RIGHTS

Amendment XIII

Section 1. Neither slavery nor involuntary servitude, except as a punishment for crime whereof the party shall have been duly convicted, shall exist within the United States, or any place subject to their jurisdiction.

Section 2. Congress shall have power to enforce this article by appropriate legislation.

This Amendment prohibits slavery in the United States. It has been held that certain state laws were in violation of this Amendment because they had the effect of jailing a debtor who did not perform his financial obligations. The Supreme Court has ruled that selective service laws, which authorize the draft for military duty, are not prohibited by this Amendment.

The courts have also justified certain civil rights legislation that condemned purely private acts of discrimination but that did not constitute "state action," on the basis of the authority granted in Section 2 of this Amendment and Section 5 of the Fourteenth Amendment, which is similar. An example is the civil rights legislation of 1866 and 1964 designed to end discrimination in the sale or rental of real or personal property. Such discriminatory practices were seen as "badges of servitude," which the Thirteenth Amendment was intended to abolish.

Amendment XIV

Section 1. All persons born or naturalized in the United States, and subject to the jurisdiction thereof, are citizens of the United States and of the State wherein they reside. No State shall make or enforce any law which shall abridge the privileges or immunities of citizens of the United States; nor shall any State deprive any person of life, liberty, or property, without due process of law; nor deny to any person within its jurisdiction the equal protection of the laws.

* * *

Section 5. The Congress shall have power to enforce, by appropriate legislation, the provisions of this article.

Due Process

The Fourteenth Amendment limits the states from infringing upon the rights of individuals. The Bill of Rights—the first ten amendments—does not specifically refer to actions by the states, but applies only to actions by the federal government. Through judicial interpretation of the term "due process of law" in the Fourteenth

Amendment, many of the Bill of Rights guarantees have been made applicable to actions by state governments and their subdivisions, such as counties, municipalities, and cities. Under this principle, certain rights and freedoms are deemed so basic to the people in a free and democratic society that state governments may not violate them, even though they are not specifically barred from doing so by the Constitution.

The Fifth Amendment, as already seen, also contains a "due process" clause that applies to actions of the federal government.

Equal Protection

In addition to the "due process" clause, the Fourteenth Amendment also prohibits denial of the "equal protection of the laws." This requirement prevents the state from making unreasonable, arbitrary distinctions between different persons as to their rights and privileges. Since "all people are created equal" no law could deny red-haired men the right to drive an automobile, although it can deny minors the right to drive. The state, therefore, remains free to make reasonable classifications. There are some classifications, however, that have been held to be patently unreasonable such as classifications based on race, religion, and national origin, for example. Thus, racial segregation in public schools and other public places, laws that prohibit sale or use of property to certain races or minority groups, and laws that prohibit interracial marriage have been struck down. Furthermore, the Supreme Court held that purely private acts of discrimination can be in violation of the equal protection clause if they are customarily enforced throughout the state, whether or not there is a specific law or other explicit manifestation of action by the state.

In another vein, the equal protection clause has been interpreted to mean that a citizen may not arbitrarily be deprived of the right to vote and that every citizen's vote must be given equal weight to the extent possible. Thus, the Supreme Court held that state legislatures and local governments must be apportioned strictly in terms of their populations in such a way as to accord one person one vote.

It should be noted that Section 5 of this Amendment provided the authority for much of the civil rights legislation passed by Congress in the 1960s.

Amendment XV

Section 1. The right of citizens of the United States to vote shall not be denied or abridged by the United States or by any State on account of race, color, or previous condition of servitude.

Section 2. The Congress shall have power to enforce this article by appropriate legislation.

Amendment XIX

Section 1. The right of citizens of the United States to vote shall not be denied or abridged by the United States or by any State on account of sex.

Section 2. Congress shall have power to enforce this article by appropriate legislation.

Amendment XXVI

Section 1. The right of citizens of the United States, who are eighteen years or older, to vote shall not be denied or abridged by the United States or any State on account of age.

Section 2. The Congress shall have power to enforce this article by appropriate legislation.

The intent and purpose of these three amendments are clear. The right to vote, which is the keystone of our democratic society, may not be denied any citizen over the age of eighteen because of race, color, previous condition of servitude, or sex. The Twenty-sixth Amendment, which lowered the voting age for all elections from twenty-one to eighteen years of age, became law on July 1, 1971. These amendments, together with the Fifth and Fourteenth, prohibit any arbitrary attempt to disenfranchise any American citizen.

Amendment XXIV

Section 1. The right of citizens of the United States to vote in any primary or other election for President or Vice President, for electors for President or Vice President, or for Senator or Representative in Congress, shall not be denied or abridged by the United States or any State by reason of failure to pay any poll tax or other tax.

Section 2. The Congress shall have power to enforce this article by appropriate legislation.

The Twenty-fourth Amendment prohibits denial of the right to vote for federal officials because a person has not paid a tax. This Amendment was designed to abolish the requirement of a poll tax which, at the time of its ratification, five states imposed as a condition to voting.

The Supreme Court subsequently held that poll taxes were unconstitutional under the equal protection clause of the Fourteenth Amendment on the basis that the right to vote should not be conditioned on one's ability to pay a tax. Accordingly, poll taxes in any election, state or federal, have been prohibited.

CONCLUSION

In addition to the specific constitutional rights outlined in this chapter, certain safeguards for the individual are inherent in the structure of American government. The separation of powers between legislative, executive, and judicial branches of government is the basis for a system of "checks and balances," which prevents excessive concentration of power—with the inevitable threat to individual liberties that accompanies such concentration. With respect to the legislative power itself, the existence of two Houses of Congress—each chosen by a different process—is itself a protection against ill-advised laws that might threaten constitutional rights. Similarly, our federal system, which divides authority between the national government and the governments of the various states, has provided a fertile soil for the nourishment of constitutional rights.

No matter how well a constitution may be written, the rights it guarantees have little meaning unless there is popular support for those rights and for that constitution. Fortunately, in the United States that support has existed. Indeed, in this country the most fundamental protection of personal liberty rests in the well-established American traditions of constitutional government, obedience to the rule of law, and respect for the individual. These traditions provide the groundwork for the entire body of law dealing with criminal procedure and should be foremost in the minds of students of and participants in our criminal justice system. The remainder of this book will show how the criminal justice system operates to achieve a balance between the protection of individual rights guaranteed by the Constitution and the maintenance of the rule of law and public order in our society.

REVIEW AND DISCUSSION QUESTIONS

1. How has the Constitution been able to remain a durable and viable instrument of government despite the enormous changes that have occurred in our society since its adoption? Discuss in terms of specific changes.

2. Discuss generally the most important roles and functions under the Constitution of each of the following: the three branches of the federal government; the state governments; the average citizen; the law enforcement officer. Explain some of the interrelationships among those roles and functions.

3. The Constitution speaks predominantly in terms of the protection of individual rights from governmental abuse or abridgment. What corresponding obligations and burdens must each citizen undertake or bear to ensure that everyone remains free to exercise these rights to their full extent?

4. Name three constitutional sources for the protection of the right to privacy and explain how they differ.

5. If a state legislature passed a law requiring that all book stores which, in the last six months, had sold or advertised for sale pictures of the Pope were to be immediately closed down and their owners immediately arrested and jailed, what provisions of the Constitution might be violated?

6. If a terminally ill cancer patient wishes to refuse medical treatment and die a "natural" death because of his or her religious beliefs, can the person be required under state law to undergo treatment? What if the person's wish to die is not based on a religious belief, but the person is a minor or is mentally incompetent? What if the person's cancer was caused by exposure to radiation and the person wishes his or her death to be a political statement on the dangers of nuclear power and nuclear war?

7. Discuss the constitutional issues involved in compelling a newsperson to reveal a confidential source of information when it would be useful to the government in a criminal investigation or helpful to a criminal defendant at trial. Should the government be able to obtain a search warrant to look into files, audit tapes, or view films in the possession of the news media to find evidence of crime?

8. Should members of the news media have greater access than members of the general public to court proceedings and court records? What about greater access to prisons to interview prisoners? What about greater access to police investigative files?

9. Would the Fifth Amendment privilege against self-incrimination prohibit any of the following: requiring all participants in a lineup to speak certain words; requiring a person to produce income tax records; threatening a person with a reduction in pay in his government job if he does not make testimonial incriminating admissions about a non-job-related matter?

10. What does "checks and balances" mean? What aspects of the Constitution other than separation of powers help fulfill the purposes of checks and balances?

2

An Overview of the Criminal Court System

The majority of the law enforcement officer's daily law-related duties involve the enforcement of the laws, the keeping of the public peace, and the investigation and prevention of crime. In order to properly perform these duties, officers must be sensitive to the constitutional rights of all persons, as discussed in Chapter 1, must be familiar with the criminal laws of their states, and must understand the law dealing with arrest, search and seizure, confessions, and pre-trial identifications, with which most of the remainder of this book is concerned.

Most law enforcement officers, however, are not as familiar with the rules and procedures that govern the course of a prosecution beyond the investigatory stage. Law enforcement officers play an important role in this process, often as chief witnesses for the prosecution in their cases. Nevertheless, outside their roles as witnesses, officers are often ignored as their cases move through pleadings, motions, jury selection, trial, and appeal. To many officers, the entire process may look like a complex legal jumble involving the prosecuting attorney, the defense attorney, and the judge. Since law enforcement officers are an integral part of the criminal justice system, and since their actions early on in a case vitally affect the outcome of the case at nearly all stages of the prosecution, they should have a basic understanding of what happens to their case when it reaches the prosecutor and the courts and why.

Criminal court procedure in most states is governed by court rules and statutes designed for use by judges and attorneys to ensure the just and efficient processing of criminal offenders. Many of the rules and statutes are quite complex and do not directly concern the law enforcement officer. Therefore, this chapter will highlight pertinent court procedures and legal terms in order to provide a comprehensive view of how the system works, without dwelling too heavily on details that are of little direct concern to the law enforcement officer.

So far as possible, this chapter will present the different stages of criminal court procedure in chronological order, following a criminal case from beginning to end. The discussion will be limited to court procedures for serious offenses and will not discuss procedures for traffic offenses and other petty misdemeanors. Wherever certain aspects of criminal court procedure might be covered in another chapter, reference will be made to that chapter. Because the information in this chapter is general, and because criminal court procedure differs by state, officers should not take the information presented here as the authority for their state, but should consult their state's pertinent statutes or rules.

STRUCTURE OF THE COURT SYSTEM

Before discussing the preliminary proceedings in a criminal case, it is helpful to first briefly outline the basic structure of the federal court system and of a typical state court system, and to briefly describe the criminal trial jurisdiction of the different courts. "Jurisdiction," as used here, simply means the authority of a court to deal with a particular case.

The federal court system is larger and more complex than any state court system, but the basic structures of the two court systems are similar. Both the federal system and the state system consist of courts that have original jurisdiction over criminal matters and courts that have appellate jurisdiction. "Original jurisdiction" means the authority to deal with a case from the beginning, to try it, and to pass judgment upon the facts and the law. "Appellate jurisdiction" means the authority to deal with a case, not in its initial stages, but only after it has been finally decided by an inferior court, and then only to revise or correct the proceedings in the inferior court.

The federal court system is divided into eighty-eight judicial districts, each served by a United States District Court. Each state has at least one district within it. The District Courts have original jurisdiction over criminal cases, and the great majority of federal criminal cases begin in the District Courts.

The U.S. Court of Appeals and the U.S. Supreme Court both have appellate jurisdiction in criminal matters. The Court of Appeals is an intermediate appellate court because its decision can be further appealed to the U.S. Supreme Court. There are eleven divisions or Circuits of the U.S. Court of Appeals throughout the country. The U.S. Supreme Court is the appellate court of last resort, meaning that it is a court from which there is no appeal.

The U.S. Supreme Court has original jurisdiction in certain limited areas, but its greatest workload is to review the decisions of the lower federal courts and the highest state courts. The most common way in which the Supreme Court exercises its appellate jurisdiction is through the granting of a "writ of certiorari." The granting of a writ of certiorari means that the Supreme Court, upon petition of a party, agrees to review a case decided by one of the Circuit Courts of Appeals or by the highest court of a state. Certiorari is granted at the Court's discretion when a case presents questions whose resolution will have an immediate impact and import beyond the particular facts of the case. Some cases may also reach the U.S. Supreme Court by direct appeal, e.g., when a state court declares a statute unconstitutional or a federal court finds that the provisions of a state statute are contrary to the treaties, laws, or Constitution of the United States. Also, a few cases may reach the U.S. Supreme Court upon a certification from a United States Court of Appeals requesting instructions on procedure with respect to a particular point of law.

Besides the courts mentioned, the federal court system also includes a number of specialized courts that have been established to hear particular classes of cases. Examples are the U.S. Court of Claims, the U.S. Court of Customs and Patent Appeals, the U.S. Customs Court, and the U.S. Tax Court. In addition, there are quasi-judicial boards or commissions, which have special and limited jurisdiction under specific federal statutes.

A typical state court system has the same basic structure as the federal system. Courts of original jurisdiction are usually divided into (1) courts that try only misdemeanor cases and (2) higher courts that try both misdemeanors and felonies. The courts that try only misdemeanor cases are usually established on a local level and may be called municipal courts, traffic courts, minor criminal courts, district courts, or something similar. For purposes of this chapter, these courts will be called local courts. The courts with original jurisdiction over both misdemeanors and felonies are usually established on a county or regional level and may be called county courts, district courts, superior courts, or something similar. Generally the more serious criminal cases will be instituted in these courts. In some states these courts may also exercise a limited appellate jurisdiction over certain cases appealed from the local courts. For purposes of this chapter these county, regional, or district courts will be called county courts.

From the county court level, a case may proceed through one or more intermediate appellate courts until it reaches the highest court (or the court of last resort) of the state, usually called the state supreme court. If a case involves important constitutional issues, it may finally reach the U.S. Supreme Court for review. Generally the state supreme court also has the power to prescribe rules of pleading, practice, and procedure before itself and the other lower courts of the state.

PRELIMINARY PROCEEDINGS

The Complaint

Criminal process against a defendant formally begins with the complaint. The reason the word "formally" is used here is that persons can be arrested for an offense before a complaint is filed or a warrant is issued. Such an arrest would be considered the beginning of the criminal process. However, since the arrest without a warrant is considered an exception to the basic warrant requirement, the complaint is still considered the formal beginning of proceedings.

The complaint can serve a dual purpose in a criminal proceeding. If the defendant has been arrested without a warrant, the complaint is prepared, signed, and filed at the defendant's initial appearance before the magistrate. The complaint serves as the charging document upon which the preliminary examination will be held. If the defendant has not been arrested, and is not before the court, the complaint serves as the basis for determining whether there is probable cause to justify the issuance of a warrant for his arrest.

The complaint must be made on oath or affirmation, must state the essential facts of the offense being charged, must be in writing, and must be made before a judicial officer authorized to issue process in criminal cases. This officer is usually called a magistrate. The information in the complaint does not have to be derived from personal observation or experience, but may be based upon information from others or upon circumstantial evidence. Nevertheless the evidence put forth in the complaint must be strong enough to convince the magistrate that there is probable cause to believe that an offense has been committed and that the defendant committed it. A complete discussion of probable cause appears in Chapter 6.

Affidavits

Information that is not contained in the complaint or that comes from witnesses other than the complainant may be brought to the court's attention in the form of an affidavit. An *affidavit* is a sworn written statement of the facts relied upon in seeking the issuance of a warrant. It need not be prepared with any particular formality. It is filed with the complaint and together they can provide a sufficient written record for a reviewing court to examine in determining whether probable cause existed for the issuance of a warrant.

Warrant or Summons Issued on the Complaint

Once the magistrate has determined from the complaint and accompanying affidavits that there is probable cause to believe that an offense has been committed and that the defendant committed it, the magistrate then will issue either a summons or a warrant for the defendant's arrest. Of course, if the defendant is already before the court, no summons or warrant is necessary.

Once the summons or warrant is issued, the law enforcement officer must serve the summons or execute the warrant by arresting and bringing the defendant before a judicial officer as commanded in the warrant. A detailed discussion of arrest warrant procedure appears in Chapter 4.

Proceedings Before the Magistrate

Once a person has been arrested either with or without a warrant, he or she is required by statute to be brought before a magistrate "without unnecessary delay," or "forthwith," depending upon statutory language. The details of this procedure are also discussed in Chapter 4.

The purpose of bringing an arrested person before a magistrate without unnecessary delay is to inform the person of the following:

1. The charge;

2. Their right to retain counsel; and

3. The right to have a preliminary examination.

Under some statutes, defendants must be informed that they are not required to make a statement, and that any statement made by them may be used against them. Also, a few statutes require that a defendant be informed of the right to request the assistance of free counsel in case of indigency. The defendant is then given reasonable time and opportunity to consult an attorney and is admitted to bail where appropriate.

Preliminary Examination

At the preliminary examination (also called the preliminary hearing), the magistrate must determine whether there is probable cause to believe that an offense was committed and that the defendant committed it. The purpose of the preliminary examination is to provide another judicial determination of the existence of probable cause and to protect the defendant from a totally baseless prosecution. Nevertheless, many defendants waive the preliminary examination, allowing their cases to go directly to the grand jury.

The preliminary examination consists mainly of the presentation of evidence against the defendant by the prosecuting attorney. The defense attorney may cross-examine witnesses against the defendant as well as introduce evidence in the defendant's behalf. If probable cause to believe that the defendant committed the offense is found, the defendant will be held to answer to the grand jury in the county where the trial is to be held. This is often called binding the defendant over to the grand jury. The magistrate may admit the defendant to bail at the preliminary examination or may continue, increase, or decrease the original bail. If no probable cause is found, the magistrate will dismiss the complaint and discharge the defendant.

INDICTMENT AND INFORMATION

The indictment and the information are the documents that charge the defendant with an offense and upon which the defendant is brought to trial. The indictment and the information are very similar in nature and content. Each is a concise and definite written statement of the essential facts constituting the offense charged. The main difference between the indictment and the information is that the indictment is issued by a grand jury and signed by the foreman of the grand jury. The information is signed and sworn to by the prosecuting attorney without the approval or intervention of the grand jury. The laws governing when the indictment or the information is used differ from state to state.

A variety of somewhat technical state statutes and rules deal with drafting, amending, and joining indictments or informations and with joining offenses or defendants for trial together. These provisions are of direct concern only to judges and attorneys and will not be discussed here.

An example of a typical indictment appears on page 33.

Grand Jury

The grand jury usually consists of from twelve to twenty-three jurors, selected from their communities according to law to serve during the criminal term of the appropriate court. The duty of the grand jury is to receive complaints in criminal cases, hear the evidence put forth by the state, and find an indictment when they are satisfied that there is probable cause that the defendant has committed an offense. The concurrence of a specified number of grand jurors is required in order to find an indictment.

Grand jury proceedings are traditionally kept secret. During deliberations or voting, no one other than the jurors is allowed to be present. When the grand jury is taking evidence, however, the attorneys for the state, the witnesses under examination, and an official court reporter may be present. Matters occurring before the grand jury, other than the deliberations or the votes of any juror, may be disclosed to the prosecuting attorney for use in performing his or her duties. Otherwise, these matters are to be kept secret, unless the court orders that they be disclosed.

The reasons for keeping grand jury proceedings secret can be summarized as follows:

1. To prevent the escape from the jurisdiction of someone who is not yet in custody but whose indictment may be contemplated;

2. To provide the utmost freedom for the grand jury in its deliberations and to protect them from outside influences;

3. To prevent tampering with witnesses who may testify before the grand jury and later appear at the trial of those indicted;

4. To encourage the free and unrestrained disclosure of information by persons who have information on the commission of crimes; and

5. To protect innocent persons who are exonerated of charges from disclosure of the fact that they were under grand jury investigation.

Waiver of Indictment

In some states a defendant who does not wish to be prosecuted by indictment may waive the indictment and be prosecuted by information. The waiver of an indictment procedure is of great advantage to a defendant who wishes to plead guilty or *nolo contendere*. (These pleas will be discussed in further detail in this chapter.) In effect, the waiver of indictment procedure enables a defendant to begin serving a sentence immediately instead of having to wait for a grand jury, which sits

STATE OF MAINE

Superior Court
Knox_____, ss

SUPERIOR COURT
CR- 120-79_____

STATE OF MAINE

Vs.

INDICTMENT FOR VIOLATION
17-A OF M.R.S.A. SECTION 353

_____Moe Torboat, Jr._____

(__THEFT Class B_____)

THE GRAND JURY CHARGES:

that Moe Torboat, Jr. of Camden, in the County of Knox and State
of Maine, on the second day of February, 1978, in the Town of
Warren, County of Knox and State of Maine, did commit theft
by obtaining or exercising control over the property of Otto
Mabeel, to wit, one Realistic stereo receiver of the value of
fifty dollars; one Winchester single shot, .22 rifle of the
value of fifty dollars; one Zenith 19-inch color TV of the value
of three hundred dollars; one table lamp of the value of
fifteen dollars; one CB radio converter of the value of
thirty dollars; and one buzzay of the value of five dollars,
all of the aggregate value of four hundred and fifty dollars,
with intent to deprive said Otto Mabeel thereof.

A True Bill.

Date: __July 5, 1979_____   _____Clay Potts_____
                                                 Foreman

CR-18

only during the criminal term of court. The defendant can thereby secure release from custody at an earlier date than by going through the indictment procedure.

Warrant or Summons Issued on the Indictment

An indictment may sometimes be found against a defendant before the defendant has been taken into custody and brought before the court. In these cases, upon the request of the attorney for the state, or by direction of the court, the clerk shall issue a summons or a warrant for the arrest of each defendant named in the indictment. This indicates no change of procedure for law enforcement officers. They are required to execute the warrant or serve the summons in the same way as they would any other warrant or summons. Procedures for executing an arrest warrant or serving a summons appear in Chapter 4.

ARRAIGNMENT AND PREPARATION FOR TRIAL

The next step in the criminal proceeding, after an indictment or information is found, is the arraignment. The term "arraignment" is often confused with the initial appearance before a magistrate by a defendant who has been arrested. Part of the reason for the confusion is that in misdemeanor proceedings in many local courts, the two procedures are combined. The essence of the arraignment is that the defendant is *called upon to plead* to the charge after the magistrate reads the substance of the charge. In local court misdemeanor proceedings, if there is no requirement of prosecution by indictment or information, the *complaint* is read to the defendant and the plea is made to the complaint. However, in courts in which prosecution must be by indictment or information, the *indictment* or *information* is read to the defendant and the plea is made to the indictment or information. Therefore, in courts which require prosecution by indictment or information, the arraignment proceeding must be separate from the initial appearance before the magistrate.

Pleas

As mentioned above, the distinctive feature of arraignment is that the defendant is called upon to plead to the charge. Although the pleas available to the defendant differ from state to state, three of the most common pleas are:

1. Not guilty;
2. Guilty; and
3. *Nolo contendere* (no contest).

Each of these merits some explanation.

A plea of not guilty puts in issue all the material facts alleged in the indictment, information, or complaint. A defendant has a right to refuse to plead at all in which case the court must enter a plea of not guilty.

In order to plead guilty or *nolo contendere,* the defendant must obtain the consent of the court. Both these pleas have the same effect on the defendant with one exception. They simply mean that the defendant does not wish to contest the charge but will submit to the judgment of the court. The exception is that a guilty plea may constitute an admission of guilt by the defendant and may be used against him in a *civil* action based on the same facts. A plea of *nolo contendere* is not an admission and cannot be used against the defendant in a civil action. The court may not accept a plea of guilty or *nolo contendere* in a felony proceeding unless the court is satisfied, after inquiry, that the defendant committed the crime charged, and that the plea is made voluntarily with an understanding of the nature of the charge.

In some states, a plea of not guilty by reason of insanity may be entered. This plea is required if the defendant intends to raise the defense of insanity. A defendant may plead not guilty and not guilty by reason of insanity to the same charge. When a plea of not guilty by reason of insanity is entered, the court may, on petition, order the defendant committed to an appropriate institution for the mentally ill for examination. The insanity plea is rarely raised in a misdemeanor proceeding.

Motions

Before trial, there are many contentions and requests that the defendant may put forth by way of motions. These motions are heard by the court and may result in various forms of relief ranging from amending or curing a defect in the complaint, indictment, or information to discharging the defendant. Because most motions are primarily of concern to judges and attorneys, they will not be discussed in detail here. There are two pretrial motions, however, that are of direct concern to the law enforcement officer: (1) the motion to suppress evidence and (2) the motion to suppress a confession. These motions are made by defendants who believe they are aggrieved by either an unlawful search and seizure or an unlawfully obtained admission or confession. Some states do not allow one or both of these motions to be made before trial.

The purpose of a motion to suppress is twofold:

1. To enable the defendant to invoke the exclusionary rule and prevent the use of illegally obtained evidence at trial; and

2. To enable the court to resolve the issue of the legality of a search and seizure or confession without interrupting the trial.

The motion to suppress is important to the law enforcement officer because the hearing on the motion is often the point in the proceedings at which an officer's performance in a case is carefully scrutinized by the court. If the defendant is able to prove that evidence was illegally obtained by an officer and if the evidence is essential to the prosecution's case, suppression of the evidence is likely to result in a dismissal of charges or the granting of a motion for judgment of acquittal. It is important, therefore, for law enforcement officers to know the law not only at the time they conduct a search and seizure or obtain a confession, but also later when they may be called upon to justify their actions at a hearing on a motion to suppress.

Depositions

When a witness is unable to attend a criminal trial, and it is shown that the witness's testimony is material to a just determination of the case, the court may order that a deposition of the witness be taken at any time after the filing of an indictment or information. A deposition involves taking the testimony of a witness out of court and preserving that testimony in writing for later use in court. It is used only in exceptional circumstances and not for the mere convenience of a witness or party. It may be requested by either the state or the defendant, and the opposing party may attend the taking of the deposition.

A deposition, or a part of a deposition, may be used at a trial or hearing if it appears that any of the following circumstances exist:

1. The witness who gave the deposition is dead;

2. The witness is out of the state (unless, of course, the party offering the deposition caused the witness's absence);

3. The witness is unable to attend or testify because of sickness or infirmity; or

4. The party offering the deposition is unable to procure the attendance of the witness by subpoena.

Furthermore, depositions may be used even if the witness does testify at the trial, but only for the purposes of contradicting or impeaching the witness's testimony.

Discovery

Discovery is a procedure whereby the defendant or the prosecution is enabled to inspect, examine, copy, or photograph items in the possession of the other party. Among the items subject to discovery are tangible objects, tape recordings, books, and papers, including written or recorded statements made by the defendants or witnesses, and the results or reports of physical examinations and scientific tests, experiments, and comparisons. The general purpose of discovery is to make the criminal trial a fairer search for the truth.

Ordinarily, to obtain the right to discovery, a party must make a motion before the court and must show that the specific items sought may be material to the preparation of its case and that its request is reasonable. Nevertheless, states differ considerably with respect to the conditions under which discovery is allowed and the items that are subject to discovery. Some states do not allow discovery at all. Other states allow discovery only for the defendant, in an effort to correct the imbalance between the investigative resources of the state and the defendant, thereby enabling the defendant to more adequately prepare a defense. A recent development is automatic informal discovery for certain types of evidence, without the necessity for motions and court orders. The state of the law governing discovery is constantly changing, but the trend appears to be in favor of broadening the right of discovery for both the defense and the prosecution.

Subpoena

The term "subpoena" describes the process used to secure the attendance of witnesses or the production of books, papers, documents, or other objects at a criminal proceeding. The subpoena is issued by a judicial officer and it commands the person to whom it is directed to attend a trial, hearing, or deposition for the purpose of testifying at the proceeding or bringing a named document or object. A subpoena can be served by a law enforcement officer or any other adult person who is not a party to the proceedings.

VENUE

One final pretrial matter to be considered is "venue." Venue is often confused with jurisdiction. Jurisdiction refers to the authority of the court to deal with a particular case. For instance, a municipal court may have *jurisdiction* over misdemeanor offenses. Venue, on the other hand, merely refers to the *place* at which the authority of the court should be exercised. For example, some statutes require that the trial of certain types of cases be held in the geographic division of the court in which the offense was committed.

Most states have special rules relating to the proper venue for an offense that is committed on a boundary of two counties or an offense part of which is committed in one county and another part in another county. These technicalities will not be discussed here.

Change of Venue

Sometimes, because of heavy publicity or intense community feeling, a defendant may wish to have his or her case tried in a different place than the one authorized by statute. A procedure is therefore provided for a defendant to make a motion for a change of venue. The motion usually must be made before the jury is impaneled or, in cases in which there is no jury, before any evidence is received. Defendant must, of course, give adequate reasons in support of the motion. Typical grounds for granting a motion for change of venue are:

1. There is such prejudice in the county where the case is to be tried that defendant cannot obtain a fair and impartial trial there; or

2. Another location is much more convenient for the parties and witnesses than the intended place of trial, and the interests of justice require a transfer of location.

THE TRIAL

The United States Constitution and most state constitutions guarantee a defendant in a criminal prosecution a speedy, public, and impartial trial by jury. This guarantee means that a defendant must be provided a jury trial in all criminal prosecutions except those for petty offenses. Defendants who do not wish to be tried by a jury may, however, with the approval of the court, waive in writing their right to a jury trial.

Trial Without a Jury

When a case is tried without a jury, the judge must perform the jury's function of weighing the evidence, determining the credibility of witnesses, and finding the facts, in addition to the regular duties as judge. The judge must also make a finding as to the guilt or innocence of the defendant based upon the evidence presented. Outside the performance of these jury functions in a non-jury trial, the judge's other regular duties are essentially the same in either a jury or a non-jury trial. Therefore, the remainder of this chapter will be concerned primarily with jury trials.

Selection of Jurors

Once it has been determined that the trial will be by jury, the next step in the criminal proceeding is the selection of the jurors. This step is very important because the jurors will be performing the crucial tasks of finding the facts, determining the credibility of witnesses, weighing the evidence, and ultimately issuing a verdict of guilty or not guilty. Because of the importance of the jury's function, there are detailed rules governing the selection of jurors. These rules are designed to protect the state or the defendant from a person who is prejudiced against its cause sitting as a member of the jury during the trial of the case.

The selection of the jury is accomplished by the court through an examination of prospective jurors on the jury panel or venire. The *jury panel* is a list of members of the community considered fit for jury service. The list is compiled by local officials, often according to statute. It must be indiscriminately drawn and must not *systematically* exclude any class of persons.

The examination of prospective jurors on the panel is commonly referred to as *voir dire*. The usual method of examination is to question the prospective jurors with regard to their feelings and views on various matters. The parties or their attorneys may conduct the examination unless the court elects to conduct the initial examination itself. If the court conducts the initial examination, the court must allow the parties or their attorneys to address additional questions to the prospective jurors on any subject that has not been fully covered and that is relevant to the juror's qualifications.

The purpose of the examination or *voir dire* is to determine whether any prospective juror is prejudiced about the case in any way. Typical questions asked relate to whether prospective jurors know the defendant, the attorneys, or any of the witnesses; whether they have read about the case in the newspapers; and whether they have formed any opinions on the case.

If either attorney wishes to have a prospective juror dismissed on the basis of these questions or for any other reason, the attorney may issue a challenge to that juror. Two types of challenges are available. One is a *challenge for cause* and is directed toward the qualifications of a juror.   Most states have statutes setting out the permissible grounds for a challenge for cause.   Typical grounds are:

1. The juror is related to one of the parties;

2. The juror has given or formed an opinion in the case; or

3. The juror has a bias, prejudice, or particular interest in the case.

Each party has an unlimited number of challenges for cause available to it, assuming that the grounds for such a challenge can be established to the satisfaction of the judge.

The other form of challenge is known as the *peremptory challenge*.   Peremptory challenges are available to each party as a means for dismissing prospective jurors who may be qualified, but who for some other reason are felt to be undesirable by one party's attorney.   No reason need be given for a peremptory challenge.   Peremptory challenges have to be exercised with great care.   It is often difficult to determine from a few questions whether a prospective juror will be receptive or antagonistic to a party's position.   Furthermore, the number of peremptory challenges available to each side is limited in number.

Once all the challenges available to both the prosecution and defense are exercised, a jury of twelve is chosen and is sworn in by the judge to try the case.   In some cases, additional jurors are selected as alternates, who sit in on the case but who do not enter deliberations unless one of the regular twelve jurors becomes ill or dies, or is unable to serve for some other reason.   It should be noted that the parties may agree, with the approval of the court, to a jury of less than twelve.   This is rarely done, however, except in cases in which a juror dies during trial and there is no alternate available.   After administering an oath to the jurors, the judge admonishes the jurors to discuss the case with no one until the jury goes into deliberations to decide the case after hearing all the evidence.

Presentation of Evidence

Once the jury has been impaneled, the presentation of evidence begins with the opening statement of the prosecuting attorney.   The prosecuting attorney gives an outline of what the state intends to prove by the evidence to be presented.   Following this, the defense counsel makes an opening statement to the jury outlining what the defense intends to prove.   Sometimes, however, the defense counsel will wait until the prosecutor has presented the state's evidence before giving an opening statement, thereby concealing the course of the defense until the government has disclosed its proof.

In either case, after the opening statement or statements are given, the prosecutor begins the introduction of the state's proof.   The state is entitled to present its evidence first in a criminal case because it is the plaintiff and therefore has the burden of proof.   The burden of proof means the duty to establish the truth of facts alleged in support of every element of the offense charged against the defendant.   The burden of proof is upon the prosecution from the beginning to the end of the trial because of the presumption that the accused is innocent.   Furthermore, the prosecution is required to prove the defendant's guilt *beyond a reasonable doubt*. Reasonable doubt is a term requiring little interpretation although various courts have attempted to formulate somewhat involved definitions that add little beyond its plain meaning. Suffice it to say that proof beyond a reasonable doubt requires that the guilt of the defendant be established to a reasonable, but not absolute or mathematical, certainty. Probability of guilt is not sufficient.

Rules of Evidence

The rules of evidence govern which evidence will be admissible in court and which will be excluded. These rules are designed to ensure that only trustworthy, competent, and relevant information is presented to the jury. A discussion of the rules of evidence is beyond the scope of this book.

Order of Presentation of Evidence

The order of presentation of evidence begins with the *direct examination* or *examination in chief* of the prosecution's first witness. This witness will be someone whom the prosecution has called. This person will be expected to give evidence favorable to the state's position. The examination of the witness is designed to produce evidence that will prove the state's case against the defendant. A law enforcement officer is usually involved as a witness for the prosecution, sometimes as its only witness.

When the prosecutor is through questioning the prosecution's witness, the defense counsel has a right to question the same witness. This is known as *cross-examination*. Its purpose is either to discredit information given by the witness or to impeach the person's credibility as a witness. In some states, the defense attorney on cross-examination is limited to questioning the witness on matters raised by the prosecutor during direct examination. In other states, the defense attorney is not so limited, and the witness may be cross-examined concerning any matter that is relevant and material to an issue in question. The judge determines what is relevant and material.

After cross-examination, the prosecutor may wish to re-examine the prosecution's witness in order to rehabilitate him or her in the eyes of the jury. This is called *redirect* examination. Unlike cross-examination, the scope of redirect examination is limited to those matters brought out in the previous examination by the adverse party. This same rule applies if the defense counsel wishes to conduct a recross-examination. This order of presenting evidence by direct examination, cross-examination, redirect, and recross is followed for all the prosecutor's witnesses until all the state's evidence has been presented.

Motion for Acquittal

After the prosecutor has presented the state's evidence, the defense counsel may move for a judgment of acquittal. A judgment of acquittal will be granted in cases in which the evidence is insufficient to sustain a conviction on the offense or offenses charged. This will usually mean that the judge has decided that reasonable persons could not conclude that guilt has been proven beyond a reasonable doubt. If the motion is not granted at the close of the state's evidence, the defense may then offer its evidence. The motion for acquittal may be renewed at the close of all the evidence or, at the judge's discretion, it may be renewed after the jury returns a verdict or is discharged without having returned a verdict.

The Defendant's Evidence

Assuming that the court does not grant a motion for judgment of acquittal at the close of the prosecution's evidence, the defense counsel then has an opportunity to present evidence. The defense may put forth one or more of several possible defenses to refute the proof offered by the state. Among the defenses available to the defendant are alibi, insanity, self-defense, and entrapment. In presenting any of these defenses, the defense counsel may call witnesses on direct examination. The prosecutor has a right to cross-examine each of the defense witnesses, just as the defense counsel had a right to cross-examine the state's witnesses.

Defendants may or may not choose to testify in their own behalf. There is an absolute constitutional right *not* to testify. Defendants who do testify, are treated much like any other witness. If a defendant does not choose to testify, the prosecuting attorney is not permitted to comment upon the failure to testify to the jury. The basis for this principle is the constitutional privilege that protects a person from self-incrimination.

Rebuttal by the Prosecution

Assuming that a motion for judgment of acquittal is not granted at the close of defendant's evidence, the prosecution is entitled to present rebuttal proof at this time. Rebuttal proof is designed to controvert evidence presented by the defense and to rebut any special defenses raised. Rebuttal proof is limited to new matter brought out in the defendant's presentation of evidence. Law enforcement officers may be called as witnesses again at this stage of the prosecution to correct any errors or misleading impressions that might be left after the defendant's presentation of evidence.

Closing Arguments

After all the evidence has been presented, both the prosecutor and the defense attorney are allotted certain amounts of time, usually specified by statute or rule, for final argument. In the final argument, attorneys for each side attempt to convince the jury (in non-jury cases, the judge) of the correctness of their positions. The prosecutor presents the state's argument first and is followed by the attorney for the defense. The prosecutor is then allowed to present a short rebuttal. Much leeway is given for the attorneys for both sides to use their wit and imagination to win the jury over to their respective positions. However, they are required to confine themselves to a discussion of the evidence presented and reasonable inferences to be derived from that evidence.

Instructions to the Jury

After the final arguments and before the jury retires for deliberations, the judge must give instructions to the jury regarding the law of the case. Attorneys for both sides are given an opportunity to submit written requests to the judge for particular instructions that they wish to be given. In a typical case, the instructions will cover such matters as the respective responsibilities of the court and the jury, the presumption of innocence and the burden of proof, various evidentiary problems, a definition of the offense or offenses charged, additional clarification of the critical elements of these offenses, any defenses that are properly in the case, and the procedures to be followed in the jury room. The exact content of the instructions is a matter for the judge's discretion but the attorneys are given an opportunity to object to any portion of the charge or any omission therefrom.

The judge may summarize the evidence for the jury, help them recall details, and attempt to resolve the complicated evidence into its simplest elements. However, the judge may not express any opinion on any issue of fact in the case nor favor either side in summarizing the evidence.

Verdict

After receiving instructions, the jury retires to the jury room to begin deliberations on a verdict. The *verdict* is the decision of the jury as to the defendant's guilt or innocence and it must be unanimous. If the jurors are unable to agree on a verdict, a hung jury results. The jurors are then dismissed and the case must be either retried or dropped. If, however, an agreement is reached, the jurors return to the courtroom and the verdict is read in open court by the jury foreman. Any party, or the court itself, may then request a *poll* of the jury. This simply involves asking each individual juror if he or she concurs in the verdict. The purpose of polling the jury is to make sure that the verdict was not reached as a result of the coercion or domination of one juror by others or as a result of sheer mental or physical exhaustion of a juror. If, during the poll, it is found any juror did not concur in the verdict, the whole jury may be directed to retire for further deliberations or they may be discharged by the judge.

SENTENCE AND JUDGMENT

After the defendant's guilt or innocence has been determined, either by verdict of the jury or by a judge without a jury, the judge must enter a judgment in the case. The judgment is merely the written evidence of the final disposition of the case by the court. If the defendant is found not guilty or for some other reason is entitled to be discharged, the judgment is entered accordingly, and the defendant is free forever from any further prosecution for the crime for which he or she was tried.

However, if the defendant is found guilty, the judge must pass sentence on the defendant before entering judgment.

The determination of the sentence is perhaps the most sensitive and difficult decision the judge has to make because of the effect it will have on the defendant's life. For this reason, most states have laws directing and guiding the judge in this determination. A typical provision requires the judge to impose sentence without unreasonable delay. This protects the defendant from a prolonged period of uncertainty about the future. Also, before imposing sentence, the judge is usually required to address the defendant personally and ask if the defendant desires to be heard prior to the imposition of sentence. The defendant may be heard personally or by counsel or both. The purpose of this provision is to enable the defendant to present any information that may be of assistance to the court in determining punishment.

Another typical statutory provision that is designed to assist the court in fixing sentence allows the court, in its discretion, to direct the state probation and parole board to make a pre-sentence investigation and report to the court before the imposition of sentence. This report will contain any prior criminal record of the defendant and such other information on personal characteristics, financial condition, and the circumstances affecting the defendant's behavior as may be helpful to the court in reaching its decision.

The court has a number of alternatives open to it with respect to sentencing, depending largely on individual state criminal statutes. Some criminal statutes have mandatory sentences, some have fixed maximum and/or minimum sentences, and others leave the matter of sentencing to the judge. Therefore, depending upon the offense for which the defendant has been convicted, the court may have very broad discretion in fixing sentence, or no discretion whatsoever. It should be noted that, in a few states, the jury has power to fix the sentence as well as to determine guilt or innocence.

Probation

The court also has the power to place a defendant on probation provided the conviction was not for an offense punishable by life imprisonment. Probation is usually controlled by statute. It is a procedure by which a person found guilty of an offense is released by the court, subject to conditions imposed by the court, without being committed to a state penal or correctional institution. Probation of a defendant is usually effected in one of two ways. The court may sentence the defendant, suspend the execution of the sentence, and place the defendant on probation; or the court may continue the matter for sentencing for a period of not more than two years and during that period place the defendant on probation. A defendant placed on probation is under the control and supervision of the state probation and parole board, although still under the jurisdiction of the court.

In some states, a different type of probation may be imposed by the court for those cases that involve the violation of any statutes concerning controlled or illegal drugs or narcotics. In these cases, the court may impose sentence, place the defendant on probation, and require as a condition of probation that the defendant participate in programs at an approved drug treatment facility.

POST-TRIAL MOTIONS

After judgment has been entered, there are still several motions available to the defendant to challenge the decision of the court. One of these is the motion for judgment of acquittal, sometimes called a motion for "judgment notwithstanding the verdict." The statutes or rules in some states provide that this motion can be made after the jury has been discharged as long as it is made within a specified time after the discharge. Courts will usually not grant such a motion unless:

1. The state's evidence was insufficient or nonexistent on a vital element of the offense charged; or

2. The indictment or information did not state a criminal offense under state law.

Another motion open to the defendant is the motion for a new trial. This motion may be made in addition to a motion for acquittal. When it is made alone, it is sometimes deemed to include a motion for judgment or acquittal. In the latter case, if the defendant moves for a new trial, the court in granting it may either enter a final judgment of acquittal or grant a new trial. A new trial may be granted by the court if it is required in the interest of justice. The usual ground for granting a new trial is the insufficiency of the evidence to support the verdict. Some courts have also considered errors of law and improper conduct of trial participants during the trial under the motion.

Another ground for granting a motion for a new trial, which carries with it a difference in procedure, is the discovery of new evidence. The procedural difference is an extended time period during which a motion for a new trial based on the ground of newly discovered evidence may be made. The time period varies from state to state but is usually longer than the period for a motion based on any other ground. The reason for this is to allow a reasonable amount of time for the discovery of new evidence. In order to justify the granting of a motion for a new trial on the ground of newly discovered evidence, it must be shown that the new evidence will probably change the result of the trial, that it could not have been discovered before the trial by the exercise of due diligence, that it is material to the issue, and that it is not merely cumulative or impeaching.

Either by motion of the defendant or by motion of the court, the defendant may obtain a revision or correction of sentence. The power to revise a sentence is granted to enable the trial court to change a sentence that is inappropriate in a particular case, even though the sentence may be legal and was imposed in a legal manner. This power to revise a sentence includes the power to increase as well as to reduce the sentence.

In contrast with the power to revise, the power to correct a sentence is granted to enable the court to change a sentence because the sentence was either illegal or it was imposed in an illegal manner. An illegal sentence might be one that was in excess of the statutory maximum. An illegally *imposed* sentence might be one in which the defendant was not personally addressed by the judge and given an opportunity to be heard before sentencing, where such a procedure is required by statute. The court must exercise both its power to revise and its power to correct a sentence within specific time periods or the powers are lost.

REMEDIES AFTER CONVICTION

There are two major forms of relief for a defendant after being convicted of a crime—*appeal* and *habeas corpus.* Each will be discussed separately here.

Appeal

A defendant has a right to appeal after being convicted of a crime and after all post-trial motions have been denied by the trial judge. The appeal procedure varies from state to state and will not be detailed here. It involves among other things the filing of a notice of appeal, the designation of the parts of the trial record to be considered on appeal, the filing of a statement of points on appeal, the filing of briefs, and the arguing of the briefs before the appellate court. If a defendant is unable to afford a lawyer to handle the appeal, provision is made by state statute or state court rule for a lawyer to be appointed by the court free of charge.

In some states, by statute, the prosecution is also given a right to appeal adverse decisions of the trial court. The prosecution's right to appeal, however, is usually much more limited than the defendant's right. Typical state statutes allow appeal by the prosecution of adverse rulings made *before* the jury hears the case or in cases in which the defendant has appealed. The procedure for appeal by the prosecution is essentially the same as it is for the defendant.

The important thing to remember about the appeal procedure is that it is *not* a retrial of the case, nor is it ordinarily a reexamination of factual issues. The determination of factual issues is the function of the jury or, in a non-jury case, of the lower court judge. The function of the appellate court in an appeal is primarily to review the *legal* issues involved in the case. A simple example will illustrate this point.

Suppose a law enforcement officer has obtained a confession from a defendant but has forgotten to give the *Miranda* warnings prior to a custodial interrogation. During the trial of the case, the trial judge erroneously permitted the officer who obtained the confession to read it to the jury over the objection of the defense. The jury convicted the defendant. On appeal, the defendant argues that the trial judge committed an error of law in allowing the jury to hear the confession.

The appellate court would very likely reverse the conviction on the basis of the error of law made by the trial judge. Along with reversal, the usual procedure is to remand or send the case to the trial court for a new trial with instructions to exclude the confession from the jury in the new trial. A different jury would then hear the evidence in the case, without the illegally obtained confession, and render another verdict. Therefore, even though a conviction is reversed on appeal, it does not necessarily mean that the defendant is acquitted and can go free. It usually means simply that the defendant has won the right to be tried again.

If the appellate court finds that the trial court committed no errors of law, it will affirm the defendant's conviction. The defendant, however, may still have a chance for further appeal. If the appeal was heard in an intermediate appellate court, there is the possibility of an additional appeal to the highest appellate court in the state. If the defendant's appeal was heard in the highest appellate court in the state, an appeal may be made to the U.S. Supreme Court. It should be noted that the U.S. Supreme Court and the highest appellate courts of some states have discretionary jurisdiction and may select the cases that they will hear. Defendants have no right to insist upon having their appeal heard by such a court.

Appeals may only be taken from cases that have come to a final judgment. This means that an appellate court will not decide any legal issues nor will it review the denial of any motions until the case has been finally disposed of by the trial court. The reason for this rule is to prevent unnecessary delays in the conduct of trials that would result if the parties could appeal issues during the course of a trial. There are some minor exceptions to the final judgment rule, but they will not be discussed here.

When an appellate court decides a case, it delivers a written opinion to explain and justify its decision. In this way the higher court explains the trial judge's errors and also informs the party losing the appeal that it has lost, and why. The decisions of the appellate courts are compiled and published in books of reported court decisions, which can be found in law libraries. These reported decisions are used by attorneys and judges as authorities for arguing and deciding future cases that raise issues similar to those already decided.

Habeas Corpus

Federal Habeas Corpus for State Prisoners   State prisoners may challenge their state convictions on constitutional grounds by means of a petition for a writ of habeas corpus in federal court. The federal statute governing the remedy is 28 U.S.C. 2254. Initially, the constitutional grounds for which habeas corpus relief could be granted were limited to those relating to the jurisdiction of the state court, but the U.S. Supreme Court extended the scope of the writ to all constitutional challenges by its decision in Fay v. Noia, 372 U.S. 391, 83 S.Ct. 822, 9 L.Ed.2d 837 (1963).

Recently, the U.S. Supreme Court again limited federal habeas corpus review of state prisoners' claims of violations of federal constitutional rights, holding that "where the State has provided an opportunity for full and fair litigation of a Fourth Amendment claim, a state prisoner may not be granted federal habeas corpus relief on the ground that evidence obtained in an unconstitutional search or seizure was introduced at his trial." Stone v. Powell, 428 U.S. 465, 494, 96 S.Ct. 3037, 3052, 49 L.Ed.2d 1067, 1088 (1976). With that limitation, however, other constitutional claims of state prisoners may be heard in a federal habeas corpus proceeding even though the claims have been fully adjudicated by a state court. Townsend v. Sain, 372 U.S. 293, 83 S.Ct. 745, 9 L.Ed.2d 770 (1963). Also, constitutional claims that were not adjudicated in a state court because the prisoner forfeited the remedy by failing to observe state procedural rules may nevertheless still be considered on habeas corpus by a federal court.

Defendants may forfeit their right to federal habeas corpus review of a constitutional claim if they *deliberately* fail to comply with valid state procedural requirements for enforcing that claim. Fay v. Noia, supra. Federal habeas corpus review may likewise be barred if a defendant is unable to show cause for noncompliance with a state procedural rule and show some actual prejudice resulting from the alleged constitutional violation. Wainwright v. Sykes, 433 U.S. 72, 97 S.Ct. 2497, 53 L.Ed.2d 594 (1977).

Prisoners must exhaust available state remedies before a federal court will consider their claim on habeas corpus. This means that, if an appeal or other procedure to hear a claim is still available by right in the state court system, the prisoner must pursue that procedure before a federal habeas corpus application will be considered.

Post-Conviction Relief for Federal Prisoners   In 1948, Congress enacted a statute (28 U.S.C. § 2255) that was designed to serve as a substitute for habeas corpus for federal prisoners. The primary purpose of the statute was to shift the jurisdictions of the courts hearing habeas corpus applications. The basic scope of the remedy that had been available to federal prisoners by habeas corpus was not changed by the statute.

Section 2255 provides in part:

> A prisoner in custody under sentence of a court established by Act of Congress claiming the right to be released upon the ground that the sentence was imposed in violation of the Constitution or laws of the United States, or that the court was without jurisdiction to impose such sentence, or that the sentence was in excess of the maximum authorized by law, or is otherwise subject to collateral attack, may move the court which imposed the sentence to vacate, set aside or correct the sentence.

* * *

> An application for a writ of habeas corpus in behalf of a prisoner who is authorized to apply for relief by motion pursuant to this section, shall not be entertained if it appears that the applicant has failed to apply for relief, by motion, to the court which sentenced him, or that such court has denied him relief, unless it also appears that the remedy by motion is inadequate or ineffective to test the legality of his detention.

The section 2255 remedy is similar to the habeas corpus remedy for state prisoners, discussed earlier. Although there are some significant distinctions between the two remedies, they are beyond the scope of this book and will not be discussed here.

State Post-Conviction Relief   Almost all states have post-conviction procedures permitting prisoners to challenge constitutional violations. These procedures may derive from statutes, court rules, or the common law. Many of these state remedies are as extensive in scope as federal habeas corpus for state prisoners. Other states provide much narrower remedies. The differences in post-conviction remedies among the states are also beyond the scope of this book and will not be discussed further here.

SUMMARY

This concludes our discussion of criminal court procedure. The purpose of this chapter has been to provide law enforcement officers with a better understanding of some of the legal terms and procedures involved in a criminal case from the initial report of a crime through an appeal to the U.S. Supreme Court. Although much of the information does not bear directly on law enforcement officers' daily duties, the chapter will have served its purpose if it has helped them to better perceive their role in the entire criminal justice system and the importance of the proper performance of that role to the effective and just operation of the system.

REVIEW AND DISCUSSION QUESTIONS

1. Draw a diagram of the hierarchy of federal and state courts with criminal jurisdiction in your state. Indicate whether each court has original or appellate criminal jurisdiction, and explain any peculiarities in the jurisdiction of each court (e.g., whether it handles only misdemeanors, or whether it has a limited appellate jurisdiction).

2. Draw a diagram of the progress of a state felony case from warrantless arrest through appeal to the U.S. Supreme Court. Assume that, at each stage of the proceedings, the decision is adverse to the defendant who then seeks relief at the next highest tribunal.

3. Discuss the differences and similarities among a complaint, an affidavit, an indictment, and an information.

4. Why is the arraignment sometimes confused with the initial appearance before the magistrate?

5. What is the grand jury and what is its function?

6. What pleas are available to a person charged with a crime and what is the effect of each?

7. What is the difference between "jurisdiction" and "venue" and between a "challenge for cause" and a "peremptory challenge?"

8. Why is a motion to suppress important to a law enforcement officer?

9. Explain the meaning of "burden of proof" in a criminal case. In your explanation, discuss the standard of proof in a criminal case.

10. Name and briefly describe three ways in which a defendant can obtain relief from the courts after a verdict of guilty.

3

Basic Underlying Concepts

Before discussing in detail the law of arrest, search and seizure, admissions and confessions, and pre-trial identification, it is helpful to lay some further groundwork by presenting three basic concepts that underlie much of what is to follow. The concepts to be discussed are the exclusionary rule, privacy, and probable cause. Later in the book these concepts will be developed in greater detail and will be clarified by examples. Nevertheless, because they are so pervasive and so essential to an understanding of criminal procedure, treating them at the outset should make the later chapters more meaningful.

EXCLUSIONARY RULE

The exclusionary rule, simply stated, requires that any evidence obtained by police using methods that violate a person's constitutional rights be excluded from being used in a criminal prosecution against that person. Historically, the rule is of rather recent vintage in the development of our legal system. Under the common law, the seizure of evidence by illegal means did not affect its admissibility in court. Any evidence, however obtained, was allowed as long as it satisfied other criteria for admissibility, such as relevance and trustworthiness. The exclusionary rule was first developed in 1914 in the case of Weeks v. United States, 232 U.S. 383, 34 S.Ct. 341, 58 L.Ed. 652, and was limited to a prohibition on the use of evidence illegally obtained by federal law enforcement officers. Not until 1949, in the case of Wolf v. Colorado, 338 U.S. 25, 27–28, 69 S.Ct. 1359, 1361, 93 L.Ed. 1782, 1785, did the United States Supreme Court rule that the Fourth Amendment was applicable to the states through the due process clause of the Fourteenth Amendment:

> The security of one's privacy against arbitrary intrusion by the police—which is
> at the core of the Fourth Amendment—is basic to a free society. It is therefore

implicit in the "concept of ordered liberty" and as such enforceable against the States through the Due Process Clause.

The Court, however, did not go so far as to require that the Fourth Amendment be enforced against state law enforcement officials by excluding illegally seized evidence in court. That decision did not come until 1961, in the landmark decision of Mapp v. Ohio, 367 U.S. 643, 655, 81 S.Ct. 1684, 1691, 6 L.Ed.2d 1081, 1090 in which the Court said:

> Since the Fourth Amendment's right of privacy has been declared enforceable against the States through the Due Process Clause of the Fourteenth, it is enforceable against them by the same sanction of exclusion as is used against the Federal Government. Were it otherwise then just as without the Weeks rule the assurance against unreasonable federal searches and seizures would be "a form of words," valueless and undeserving of mention in a perpetual charter of inestimable human liberties, so too, without that rule the freedom from state invasions of privacy would be so ephemeral and so neatly severed from its conceptual nexus with the freedom from all brutish means of coercing evidence as not to merit this Court's high regard as a freedom "implicit in 'the concept of ordered liberty.' "

The *Mapp* decision reflects the Court's belief that alternative measures, such as the prosecution of law enforcement officers, administrative disciplining of officers, or the bringing of civil actions against them, were not sufficiently effective methods of enforcing the Fourth Amendment and that the exclusionary rule was the only effective method.

The U.S. Supreme Court has made other constitutional amendments in the Bill of Rights applicable to the states through the Due Process Clause of the Fourteenth Amendment. For example, the Fifth Amendment privilege against self-incrimination was made applicable to the states in Malloy v. Hogan, 378 U.S. 1, 84 S.Ct. 1489, 12 L.Ed.2d 653 (1964). Likewise, the Sixth Amendment right to counsel was made applicable to the states in Gideon v. Wainwright, 372 U.S. 335, 83 S.Ct. 792, 9 L.Ed.2d 799 (1963). The manner in which the exclusionary rule is used to enforce the rights guaranteed in these amendments and others is discussed in detail in later chapters of this book.

It should be noted that the U.S. Supreme Court has also invoked the exclusionary rule to protect certain "due process of law" rights that are not specifically contained in the Constitution or its amendments. For example, a confession that has been coerced and is therefore involuntary will be excluded from evidence, not because of the privilege against self-incrimination, but because a coerced confession is a violation of due process of law. Similarly, pre-trial identification procedures that are not fairly administered may be violations of due process of law.

Since the purpose of the exclusionary rule is to prevent law enforcement officials from violating the rights of individuals when the officials are enforcing the law, it follows that evidence illegally obtained by persons other than law enforcement officials will not be rendered inadmissible in court. In Burdeau v. McDowell, 256 U.S. 465, 41 S.Ct. 574, 65 L.Ed. 1048 (1921), a private citizen illegally seized certain papers from another private citizen and turned them over to the government. The Court said:

> The papers having come into the possession of the government without a violation of petitioner's right by governmental authority, we see no reason why the

fact that individuals, unconnected with the government, may have wrongfully taken them, should prevent them from being held for use in prosecuting an offense where the documents are of an incriminatory character. 256 U.S. at 476, 41 S.Ct. at 576, 65 L.Ed. at 1051.

Of course, if a private citizen is working with or at the direction of a law enforcement official, that person becomes an agent of the official and the citizen's actions are subject to the exclusionary rule in the same way as those of the official.

The exclusionary rule does not affect the jurisdiction of any court to try a person for a crime; the rule applies only to evidence. In Frisbie v. Collins, 342 U.S. 519, 72 S.Ct. 509, 96 L.Ed. 541 (1952), a Michigan law enforcement officer forcefully abducted a person in Illinois and brought him back to Michigan for prosecution. The Court said:

> [T]he power of a court to try a person for crime is not impaired by the fact that he had been brought within the court's jurisdiction by reason of a "forcible abduction."
> . . . [D]ue process of law is satisfied when one present in court is convicted of crime after having been fairly apprised of the charges against him and after a fair trial in accordance with constitutional procedural safeguards. There is nothing in the Constitution that requires a court to permit a guilty person rightfully convicted to escape justice because he was brought to trial against his will. 342 U.S. at 522, 72 S.Ct. at 511–12, 96 L.Ed. at 545–46.

Federal-State Conflict

Mapp v. Ohio did not require the states to follow all interpretations of federal courts in the area of criminal procedure, but only those interpretations dealing with constitutional guarantees. Some of the rulings handed down by the U.S. Supreme Court are based on the Court's statutory authority to promulgate rules for the supervision of federal law enforcement. These rulings apply only in federal courts. The Court explicitly stated in Ker v. California, 374 U.S. 23, 83 S.Ct. 1623, 10 L.Ed. 2d 726 (1963), that *Mapp* established no assumption by the Supreme Court of supervisory authority over state courts, and therefore implied no total obliteration of state laws relating to arrests and searches in favor of federal law. The Court went on to say:

> The States are not thereby precluded from developing workable rules governing arrests, searches and seizures to meet "the practical demands of effective criminal investigation and law enforcement" in the States, provided that those rules do not violate the constitutional proscription of unreasonable searches and seizures and the concomitant command that evidence so seized is inadmissible against one who has standing to complain. 374 U.S. at 34, 83 S.Ct. at 1630, 10 L.Ed.2d at 738.

State courts, therefore, may use their constitutions, statutes, or their constitutional power to establish rules of evidence for their own court systems to provide more rights for their citizens than are provided by the United States Constitution as interpreted by the U.S. Supreme Court. State courts must, however, enforce the United States Constitution in strict compliance with the interpretations of the U.S. Supreme Court. If a state court interprets the U.S. Constitution as giving more or fewer rights than the Supreme Court, the state court is subject to being overruled by the Supreme Court.

Most reversals of state court decisions by the Supreme Court are the result of the state court holding that the Constitution gave less protection to individual rights than that determined by the Supreme Court. Nevertheless, in South Dakota v. Opperman, 428 U.S. 364, 96 S.Ct. 3092, 49 L.Ed.2d 1000 (1976), the South Dakota Supreme Court ruled that an automobile inventory conducted by South Dakota law enforcement officers violated the Fourth Amendment, but the U.S. Supreme Court reversed the decision, holding that the police conduct was reasonable. Then, interestingly, on remand, the South Dakota Supreme Court, in State v. Opperman, 247 N.W.2d 673 (S.D.1976), decided that the police inventory procedure violated the South Dakota Constitution and held that the evidence seized was inadmissible. This South Dakota decision is noteworthy because the search and seizure provision of the South Dakota Constitution is essentially similar to the Fourth Amendment of the U.S. Constitution and because neither the prosecution nor the defense in the case had raised the issue of the state constitution.

The practice of state courts affording the accused greater protection under state law than that required by the federal Constitution has become an emerging trend in response to the decisions of the Burger Court. Several states, rather than follow the Burger Court's reluctant and sparing approach to protecting the rights of the accused, have attempted to keep alive the Warren Court's active commitment to the protection of these constitutional rights. Examples of this trend will be presented in later chapters dealing with the particular areas of conflict.

Criticism of the Exclusionary Rule

The exclusionary rule has, throughout its existence, been the object of criticism and attempted reform. In recent years, no less a public authority than the Chief Justice of the U.S. Supreme Court has complained of the ineffectiveness of the exclusionary rule to achieve its purpose—the deterrence of police misconduct. In his dissent in the case of Bivens v. Six Unknown Named Agents of the Federal Bureau of Narcotics, 403 U.S. 388, 416–18, 91 S.Ct. 1999, 2015, 29 L.Ed.2d 619, 638–39 (1971), Chief Justice Burger said:

> The rule does not apply any direct sanction to the individual official whose illegal conduct results in the exclusion of evidence in a criminal trial. . . . The immediate sanction triggered by application of the rule is visited upon the prosecutor whose case against a criminal is either weakened or destroyed. The doctrine deprives the police in no real sense; except that apprehending wrongdoers is their business, police have no more stake in successful prosecutions than prosecutors or the public. The suppression doctrine vaguely assumes that law enforcement is a monolithic governmental enterprise. . . . But the prosecutor who loses his case because of police misconduct is not an official in the police department; he can rarely set in motion any corrective action or administrative penalties. Moreover, he does not have control or direction over police procedures or police actions that lead to the exclusion of evidence. It is the rare exception when a prosecutor takes part in arrests, searches, or seizures so that he can guide police action. Whatever educational effect the rule conceivably might have in theory is greatly diminished in fact by the realities of law enforcement work. Policemen do not have the time, inclination, or training to read and grasp the nuances of the appellate opinions that ultimately define the standards of conduct they are to follow. . . . Nor can judges, in all candor, forget that opinions sometimes lack helpful clarity. The presumed educational effect of judicial opinions is also reduced by the long time

lapse—often several years—between the original police action and its final judicial evaluation. Given a policeman's pressing responsibilities, it would be surprising if he ever becomes aware of the final result after such a delay. Finally, the exclusionary rule's deterrent impact is diluted by the fact that there are large areas of police activity that do not result in criminal prosecutions—hence the rule has virtually no applicability and no effect in such situations.

The criticism and attempts at reform of the exclusionary rule have resulted in limitations on the application of the rule and refusals to extend the application of the rule further. For example, in United States v. Calandra, 414 U.S. 338, 94 S.Ct. 613, 38 L.Ed.2d 561 (1974), the Supreme Court held that the Fourth Amendment did not prevent the use of illegally obtained evidence by a grand jury. In United States v. Janis, 428 U.S. 433, 96 S.Ct. 3021, 49 L.Ed.2d 1046 (1976), the Court held that illegally obtained evidence need not be suppressed at trial in a civil case brought by the United States. And in Stone v. Powell, 428 U.S. 465, 494, 96 S.Ct. 3037, 3052, 49 L.Ed.2d 1067, 1088 (1976), the Court held that "where the State has provided an opportunity for full and fair litigation of a Fourth Amendment claim, a state prisoner may not be granted federal habeas corpus relief on the ground that evidence obtained in an unconstitutional search or seizure was introduced at his trial." The *Stone v. Powell* decision is noteworthy not only because it limited the application of the exclusionary rule, but also because it strengthened the authority of state courts in interpreting the Fourth Amendment.

Despite the Burger Court's cutting back on certain applications of the exclusionary rule, the basic holding of *Mapp v. Ohio* remains good law and the basic tenets of the exclusionary rule remain valid legal doctrine. Any further limitations or changes in the exclusionary rule will depend largely on the makeup of the Supreme Court and the opportunities presented to the Court in the cases brought before it.

Fruit of the Poisonous Tree

The exclusionary rule is not limited to evidence that is the direct product of illegal police behavior, such as a coerced confession or the items seized as the result of an illegal search. The rule also requires exclusion of evidence that is obtained indirectly as a result of a violation of one's constitutional rights. This type of evidence is sometimes called "derivative" or "secondary" evidence. In Silverthorne Lumber Co. v. United States, 251 U.S. 385, 392, 40 S.Ct. 182, 183, 64 L.Ed. 319 321 (1920), the Court invalidated a subpoena that had been issued on the basis of information obtained through an illegal search. The Court said:

> The essence of a provision forbidding the acquisition of evidence in a certain way is that not merely evidence so acquired shall not be used before the Court but that it shall not be used at all. Of course this does not mean that the facts thus obtained become sacred and inaccessible. If knowledge of them is gained from an independent source they may be proved like any others, but the knowledge gained by the Government's own wrong cannot be used by it in the way proposed.

Thus, the prosecution may not use in court evidence obtained directly or indirectly from an unconstitutional search. The prohibition against using this "derivative" or "secondary" evidence is often called the rule against admission of "fruit of the poisonous tree," the tree being the illegal search and the fruit being the evidence obtained as an indirect result of that search. The fruit, or the evidence indirectly obtained, is sometimes referred to as "tainted" evidence.

It should be noted that, although the rule against admission of "fruit of the poisonous tree" was originally developed in applying the exclusionary rule to unconstitutional searches, it has been applied equally to evidence obtained as the indirect result of other violations of individual rights. Thus, evidence is inadmissible if it is acquired indirectly as a result of an illegal arrest, an illegal identification procedure, an involuntary confession, or a *Miranda* violation. A more detailed treatment of the "fruit of the poisonous tree" doctrine in these situations and in other situations appears in the chapters of this book dealing with the specific subject matter.

There are several recognized exceptions to the "fruit of the poisonous tree" doctrine, allowing the admission of "tainted" evidence under certain conditions. One of these exceptions, already referred to, is the "independent source" exception. This exception allows the admission of "tainted" evidence if that evidence was in fact also obtained through a source wholly independent of the primary constitutional violation. The independent source exception is compatible with the underlying rationale of the exclusionary rule—the deterrence of police misconduct. As stated by the U.S. Supreme Court:

> The independent source doctrine teaches us that the interest of society in deterring unlawful police conduct and the public interest in having juries receive all probative evidence of a crime are properly balanced by putting the police in the same, not a *worse*, position than they would have been in if no police error or misconduct had occurred. Nix v. Williams, ___ U.S. ___, ___, 104 S.Ct. 2501, 2509, 81 L.Ed.2d 377, 387 (1984).

Another exception, first established in Nardone v. United States, 308 U.S. 338, 60 S.Ct. 266, 84 L.Ed. 307 (1939), is referred to as the "attenuation doctrine." This doctrine states that, even where the tainted evidence would not have been discovered except through the constitutional violation, there being no "independent source," the evidence may still be admissible if the means of obtaining the evidence were sufficiently remote from and distinguishable from the primary illegality. The key question, as posed in Wong Sun v. United States, 371 U.S. 471, 488, 83 S.Ct. 407, 417, 9 L.Ed.2d 441, 455 (1963), is "whether, granting establishment of the primary illegality, the evidence to which instant objection is made has been come at by exploitation of that illegality or instead by means sufficiently distinguishable to be purged of the primary taint." If the tainted evidence is obtained by means sufficiently distinguishable from the primary illegality, the causal connection between the primary illegality and the evidence indirectly derived from it is said to be "attenuated," and the evidence is admissible even though tainted. The *Wong Sun* case provides a good example of the "attenuation doctrine."

In the *Wong Sun* case, narcotics agents illegally broke into Toy's laundry and followed Mr. Toy into his living quarters where he was arrested and handcuffed. Almost immediately thereafter, Toy told the agents that Yee had been selling narcotics. The agents subsequently seized heroin from Yee, who told them that it had been brought to him by Toy and Wong Sun. Wong Sun was illegally arrested, arraigned, and released on his own recognizance. Several days later, Wong Sun returned voluntarily and made an oral confession to a narcotics agent.

Toy argued that his statement and the heroin later seized from Yee were fruit of the illegal entry into his dwelling and his illegal arrest. The Court agreed and held both inadmissible. Wong Sun claimed that his statement was the fruit of his illegal arrest. The Court disagreed:

> We have no occasion to disagree with the finding of the Court of Appeals that his arrest, also, was without probable cause or reasonable grounds. At all events no evidentiary consequences turn upon that question. For Wong Sun's unsigned confession was not the fruit of that arrest, and was therefore properly admitted at trial. On the evidence that Wong Sun had been released on his own recognizance after a lawful arraignment, and had returned voluntarily several days later to make the statement, we hold that the connection between the arrest and the statement has "become so attenuated as to dissipate the taint." 371 U.S. at 491, 83 S.Ct. at 419, 9 L.Ed.2d at 457.

In determining whether the connection between the primary illegality and the resulting evidence has sufficiently attenuated, courts look for an intervening independent act between the two, such as Wong Sun's voluntary return to make a statement. In the words of the Supreme Court of California:

> That degree of "attenuation" which suffices to remove the taint from evidence obtained directly as a result of unlawful police conduct requires at least an intervening independent act by the defendant or a third party which breaks the causal chain linking the illegality and evidence in such a way that the evidence is not in fact obtained "by exploitation of that illegality." People v. Superior Court (Casebeer) 71 Cal.2d 265, 271–72, 78 Cal.Rptr. 210, 215, 455 P.2d 146, 151 (1969).

It should be noted that courts applying the attenuation doctrine make a distinction between physical and verbal evidence. In United States v. Ceccolini, 435 U.S. 268, 98 S.Ct. 1054, 55 L.Ed.2d 268 (1978), the Supreme Court held that because of the cost to the truth-finding process of disqualifying knowledgeable witnesses, the exclusionary rule should be invoked with much greater reluctance when the fruit of the poisonous tree is the testimony of a live witness rather than an inanimate object. Therefore, courts will not exclude the testimony of a witness discovered as the result of a constitutional violation, unless the court finds a more direct link between the discovery and the violation than is required to exclude physical evidence. Also, the court must find that the Fourth Amendment violation is the kind that will be deterred by application of the exclusionary rule.

Another exception to the "fruit of the poisonous tree" doctrine is the so-called "inevitable discovery" doctrine. This doctrine is actually a variation of the "independent source" exception. Whereas the independent source exception allows the admission of tainted evidence if the tainted evidence was, in fact, also obtained from an independent source, the inevitable discovery doctrine allows admission of the evidence if it would have inevitably been discovered in the normal course of events. Under this exception, the prosecution must establish by a preponderance of the evidence that, even though the evidence was actually discovered as the indirect result of a constitutional violation, the evidence ultimately or inevitably would have been discovered by lawful means. For example, the evidence would have been discovered as the result of the predictable and routine behavior of a law enforcement agency, some other agency, or a private person.

The U.S. Supreme Court specifically adopted the "inevitable discovery" exception in Nix v. Williams. In that case, police had initiated a search for a 10-year-old girl who had disappeared. While the search was going on, the defendant was arrested and, in response to illegal questioning, the defendant led police to the girl's body. The search was called off, but the girl's body was found in a place which was essentially within the area to be searched. Although the defendant's illegally obtained statements, leading to the discovery of the body, rendered evidence relating to the body inadmissible, the Court allowed the admission of the evidence under the inevitable discovery doctrine. The Court found that the volunteer search parties were approaching the actual location of the body, that they would have resumed the search had the defendant not earlier led the police to the body, and that the body inevitably would have been found.

The Court justified its adoption of the inevitable discovery doctrine using the rationale underlying the independent source exception. The Court said:

> [I]f the government can prove that the evidence would have been obtained inevitably and, therefore, would have been admitted regardless of any overreaching by the police, there is no rational basis to keep that evidence from the jury in order to ensure the fairness of the trial proceedings. In that situation, the State has gained no advantage at trial and the defendant has suffered no prejudice. Indeed, suppression of the evidence would operate to undermine the adversary system by putting the State in a *worse* position than it would have occupied without any police misconduct. ___ U.S. at ___, 104 S.Ct. at 2511, 81 L.Ed.2d at 389.

Furthermore, in response to the defendant's contention that the prosecution must prove the absence of bad faith on the part of the police, the Court said that such a requirement:

> [W]ould place courts in the position of withholding from juries relevant and undoubted truth that would have been available to police absent any unlawful police activity. Of course, that view would put the police in a *worse* position than they would have been in if no unlawful conduct had transpired. And, of equal importance, it wholly fails to take into account the enormous societal cost of excluding truth in the search for truth in the administration of justice. ___ U.S. at ___, 104 S.Ct. at 2510, 81 L.Ed.2d at 388.

Finally, the Court dismissed arguments that the inevitable discovery exception will promote police misconduct. A police officer who is faced with an opportunity to obtain evidence illegally will rarely, if ever, be in a position to calculate whether the evidence sought would inevitably be discovered. Even when an officer is aware that evidence will inevitably be discovered, there will be little to gain from taking dubious "shortcuts" to obtain the evidence. Other significant disincentives to obtaining evidence illegally include the possibility of departmental discipline and civil liability.

"Good Faith" Exception

In United States v. Leon, ___ U.S. ___, 104 S.Ct. 3405, 82 L.Ed.2d 677 (1984) the U.S. Supreme Court adopted another exception to the exclusionary rule—the "good faith" exception for searches conducted pursuant to a warrant. Under this exception, whenever a law enforcement officer acting with objective good faith has obtained a search warrant from a detached and neutral judge or magistrate and acted within its scope, evidence seized pursuant to the warrant will not be excluded, even though the warrant is later determined to be invalid. The Court reasoned that excluding such evidence would not further the purposes of the exclusionary rule—deterrence of police misconduct—since the officer is acting as a reasonable officer would and should act under the circumstances. In determining what is good faith on the part of an officer, the Court said:

> [O]ur good-faith inquiry is confined to the objectively ascertainable question whether a reasonably well-trained officer would have known that the search was illegal despite the magistrate's authorization. In making this determination, all of the circumstances—including whether the warrant application has previously been rejected by a different magistrate—may be considered. ___ U.S. at ___, n. 23, 104 S.Ct. at 3421, n. 23, 82 L.Ed.2d at 698, n. 23.

The following are several circumstances under which an officer would *not* have reasonable grounds for believing that a warrant was properly issued:

■ The magistrate or judge in issuing the warrant was misled by information in an affidavit that the affiant knew was false or would have known was false except for a reckless disregard of the truth;

■ The issuing magistrate wholly abandoned a neutral and detached judicial role and acted, in effect, as an arm of the prosecution;

■ The warrant was based on an affidavit so lacking in indicia of probable cause as to render official belief in its existence entirely unreasonable;

■ The warrant was so facially deficient—i.e., in failing to particularize the place to be searched or the things to be seized—that the executing officers could not reasonably presume it to be valid.

Under such circumstances, not only would the warrant be declared invalid, but any evidence seized pursuant to the warrant would be ruled inadmissible. Officers are encouraged, therefore, to exercise good faith and professional judgment both in applying for and in executing search warrants.

The discussion of the exceptions to the exclusionary rule serves to highlight an important feature of the rule—it does not necessarily bar or stop a prosecution. At most, the rule will cause the suppression of evidence obtained as the direct or indirect result of a constitutional violation. If that evidence is essential to the prosecution's case against a defendant, the prosecution may decide that it is futile to go on with the prosecution. If, however, the prosecution has sufficient other evidence, either legally obtained or falling within one of the exceptions to the exclusionary rule, the prosecution may go forward despite the illegal police conduct.

PRIVACY

In a criminal case, in order for the Fourth Amendment to be applicable to a particular fact situation, there must be a "search" and a "seizure" accompanied by an attempt by the prosecution to introduce what was seized as evidence in court. Whether there was a search and seizure within the meaning of the Fourth Amendment and, if so, whether the search and seizure violated someone's constitutional rights depends on the nature of the interest that the Fourth Amendment protects. Under the common law, it was clear that the security of one's property was a sacred right and protection of that right was a primary purpose of government. In an early English case, Entick v. Carrington, 19 Howell's State Trials 1029, 1035, 95 Eng.Rep. 807, 817–18 (1765), the court said:

> The great end for which men entered into society was to secure their property. That right is preserved sacred and incommunicable in all instances where it has not been taken away or abridged by some public law for the good of the whole. . . . By the laws of England, every invasion of private property, be it ever so minute, is a trespass. No man can set foot upon my ground without my license but he is liable to an action though the damage be nothing. . . .

The protection of property interests as the basis of the Fourth Amendment was adopted by the U.S. Supreme Court, and until relatively recently, analysis of Fourth Amendment issues centered around whether there was an intrusion into a "constitutionally protected area." Three cases involving electronic surveillance illustrate this approach. In Olmstead v. United States, 277 U.S. 438, 48 S.Ct. 564, 72 L.Ed. 944 (1928), one of the reasons for the Court's holding that wiretapping was not covered by the Fourth Amendment was that there had been no physical invasion of the defendant's premises. The Court said:

> The evidence was secured by the use of the sense of hearing and that only. There was no entry of the houses or offices of the defendants. . . . The intervening wires are not part of his house or office. . . . 277 U.S. at 464–65, 48 S.Ct. at 568, 72 L.Ed. at 950.

In Silverman v. United States, 365 U.S. 505, 81 S.Ct. 679, 5 L.Ed.2d 734 (1961), however, in which a spike mike had been pushed through a party wall until it hit a heating duct, the Court held that the electronic surveillance was an illegal search and seizure. And in Clinton v. Virginia, 377 U.S. 158, 84 S.Ct. 1186, 12 L.Ed.2d 213 (1964), the Court ruled inadmissible evidence obtained by means of a mechanical listening device stuck into the wall of an apartment adjoining the defendant's. The rationale for both of these cases was that the listening device had actually physically invaded the target premises, even though the invasion was slight.

This emphasis on property concepts in interpreting the Fourth Amendment began to lose favor in the 1960s. Justice Douglas, concurring in the *Silverman* case, said that "our sole concern should be with whether the privacy of the home was invaded." 365 U.S. at 513, 81 S.Ct. at 683, 5 L.Ed.2d at 740. In a later case, the Court said:

> The premise that property interests control the right of the Government to search and seize has been discredited. . . . We have recognized that the principal object of the Fourth Amendment is the protection of privacy rather than property, and have increasingly discarded fictional and procedural barriers rested on property concepts. Warden v. Hayden, 387 U.S. 294, 304, 87 S.Ct. 1642, 1648, 18 L.Ed.2d 782, 790 (1967).

Finally, in Katz v. United States, 389 U.S. 347, 88 S.Ct. 507, 19 L.Ed.2d 576 (1967), another electronic surveillance case, the Court finally dispensed with the requirement of an actual physical trespass in applying the Fourth Amendment. The issue in the *Katz* case was the admissibility of telephone conversations overheard by FBI agents who had attached an electronic listening and recording device to the outside of a public telephone booth. The Court said:

> [T]his effort to decide whether or not a given "area," viewed in the abstract, is "constitutionally protected" deflects attention from the problem presented by this case. For the Fourth Amendment protects people, not places. What a person knowingly exposes to the public, even in his own home or office, is not a subject of Fourth Amendment protection. . . . But what he seeks to preserve as private, even in an area accessible to the public may be constitutionally protected. 389 U.S. at 351–52, 88 S.Ct. at 511, 19 L.Ed.2d at 582.

The Court held that the government's activities in electronically listening to and recording the defendant's words violated the privacy upon which he justifiably relied while using the telephone booth and thus constituted a "search and seizure" within the meaning of the Fourth Amendment. The Court added: "The fact that the electronic device employed to achieve that end did not happen to penetrate the wall of the booth can have no constitutional significance." 389 U.S. at 353, 88 S.Ct. at 512, 19 L.Ed.2d at 583.

The *Katz* case signalled a major shift in the interpretation of the Fourth Amendment away from a property approach toward a privacy approach. Court decisions after the *Katz* case no longer focus on whether there has been an intrusion into a constitutionally protected area. Now the formula for analysis of Fourth Amendment problems is that "wherever an individual may harbor a reasonable 'expectation of privacy,' . . . he is entitled to be free from unreasonable governmental intrusion." Terry v. Ohio, 392 U.S. 1, 9, 88 S.Ct. 1868, 1873, 20 L.Ed.2d 889, 899 (1968). It would seem that such a sweeping change in approach in interpreting the Fourth Amendment would result in a large-scale overturning of earlier decisions. Yet, as Justice Harlan noted in his concurring opinion in the *Katz* case, the determination of what protection the Fourth Amendment affords to people requires reference to a "place." Therefore, many of the pre-*Katz* decisions are not necessarily changed or overruled by the *Katz* decision. These cases should, however, be evaluated not only in terms of the reasoning employed in them, but also in terms of the new standard announced in *Katz*. In later chapters of this book discussing the Fourth Amendment, both pre-*Katz* and post-*Katz* cases will be discussed, in order to give the reader as complete an understanding as possible of this continually developing area of the law.

In analyzing Fourth Amendment issues many courts take the approach suggested by Justice Harlan in his concurring opinion in the *Katz* case. He said that "there is a twofold requirement, first that a person have exhibited an actual (subjective) expectation of privacy and, second, that the expectation be one that society is prepared to recognize as 'reasonable.' " 389 U.S. at 361, 88 S.Ct. at 516, 19 L.Ed. 2d at 588. If these requirements are satisfied, any governmental intrusion upon the expectation of privacy is a "search" for purposes of the Fourth Amendment. Reflecting Justice Harlan's approach, the U.S. Supreme Court defined the terms "search" and "seizure" as follows:

> A "search" occurs when an expectation of privacy that society is prepared to consider reasonable is infringed. A "seizure" of property occurs when there is some meaningful interference with an individual's possessory interests in that property.

United States v. Jacobsen, ___ U.S. ___, ___, 104 S.Ct. 1652, 1656, 80 L.Ed.2d 85, 94 (1984).

In order to be legal, the search or seizure must be conducted under authority of a valid warrant, or must fall within one of the recognized exceptions to the warrant requirement. Most of the remainder of this book will deal with the search warrant requirement and its exceptions.

As a final note of caution, the reader should be aware that privacy, as one of the basic rights guaranteed to individuals in our society, encompasses much more than the protections offered by the Fourth Amendment, even as interpreted under the *Katz* formula. This point is perhaps best stated in the *Katz* decision itself:

> [T]he Fourth Amendment cannot be translated into a general constitutional "right to privacy." That Amendment protects individual privacy against certain kinds of governmental intrusion, but its protections go further, and often have nothing to do with privacy at all. Other provisions of the Constitution protect personal privacy from other forms of governmental invasion. But the protection of a person's general right to privacy—his right to be let alone by other people—is, like the protection of his property and of his very life, left largely to the law of individual States. 389 U.S. at 350–51, 88 S.Ct., at 510–11, 19 L.Ed.2d at 581.

PROBABLE CAUSE

The Fourth Amendment to the U.S. Constitution provides an introduction to the important concept of probable cause:

> The right of the people to be secure in their persons, houses, papers, and effects, against unreasonable searches and seizures, shall not be violated, and no Warrants shall issue, but upon probable cause, supported by Oath or affirmation, and particularly describing the place to be searched, and the persons or things to be seized.

From this language, it is apparent that probable cause is necessary for the issuance of an arrest or search warrant. In order to explain what probable cause means, it is helpful to start with the U.S. Supreme Court's often-cited definition of probable cause to arrest set forth in Brinegar v. United States:

> Probable cause exists where "the facts and circumstances within their [the arresting officers'] knowledge and of which they had reasonably trustworthy information [are] sufficient in themselves to warrant a man of reasonable caution in the belief that" an offense has been or is being committed [by the person to be arrested]. 338 U.S. 160, 175–76, 69 S.Ct. 1302, 1310–11, 93 L.Ed. 1879, 1890 (1949).

The Court noted that probable cause has come to mean more than bare suspicion. Other courts have held that absolute certainty or "evidence beyond a reasonable doubt" is not required to establish probable cause. The Wisconsin Supreme Court said, in this regard:

> Probable cause to arrest refers to the quantum of evidence which would lead a reasonable man to believe that the defendant probably committed a crime. While the standard is objective . . . it is not necessary that the evidence be sufficient to prove ultimate guilt beyond a reasonable doubt or even that it be sufficient to prove that guilt is more probable than not. It is only necessary that the information

lead a reasonable officer to believe that guilt is more than a possibility.   Browne v. State, 24 Wis.2d 491, 503–04, 129 N.W.2d 175, 180 (1964).

It is important to note that, although we have been talking about probable cause to arrest, the same quantum of evidence is required to establish probable cause to search.   Probable cause to search, however, requires a belief that certain items are contraband or fruit, instrumentalities, or evidence of crime, and that these items are in a particular place or on a particular person, rather than a belief that a particular person has committed or is committing a crime.   Also, as will be discussed in detail in later chapters, many arrests and searches are conducted without a warrant.   The quantum of evidence required to establish probable cause for a warrantless arrest or search is somewhat greater than that required under authority of a warrant.   The reason why a greater degree of probable cause may be required in the warrantless situation is that the Supreme Court has expressed a strong preference for arrest warrants, Beck v. Ohio, 379 U.S. 89, 85 S.Ct. 223, 13 L.Ed.2d 142 (1964), and for search warrants, United States v. Ventresca, 380 U.S. 102, 85 S.Ct. 741, 13 L.Ed.2d 684 (1965).   This preference is so strong that less persuasive evidence will justify the issuance of a warrant than would justify a warrantless search or warrantless arrest.   In Aguilar v. Texas, the U.S. Supreme Court said:

> [W]hen a search is based upon a magistrate's, rather than a police officer's determination of probable cause, the reviewing courts will accept evidence of a less "judicially competent or persuasive character than would have justified an officer in acting on his own without a warrant,"   . . .   and will sustain the judicial determination so long as "there was a substantial basis for [the magistrate] to conclude that [seizable evidence was] probably present. . . ." 378 U.S. 108, 111, 84 S.Ct. 1509, 1512, 12 L.Ed.2d 723, 726 (1964).

The warrant procedure is preferred because it places responsibility for deciding the delicate question of probable cause with a neutral and detached judicial officer.   Thereby, law enforcement is served, because law enforcement officers are enabled to search certain places and seize certain persons or things, when the officers can show reasonable grounds that the person, place, or thing is significantly connected with criminal activity.   The Fourth Amendment rights of citizens are also served by the warrant procedure, because the decision to allow a search and seizure is removed from the sometimes hurried and overzealous judgment of law enforcement officers engaged in the competitive enterprise of investigating crime.

Whether law enforcement officers are applying for a warrant or are determining their authority to arrest or search without a warrant, they must have sufficient information to establish probable cause.   Probable cause may arise through facts or information that an officer has personally observed or gathered.   It may also be based upon apparently reliable information from third parties such as the victim, other police agencies, witnesses, reporters, informants, or even information from the defendant.   Chapter 6 contains a detailed discussion of what information may and may not be considered in arriving at probable cause in addition to procedures to assist the law enforcement officer in establishing probable cause, both when the information comes from informants and when it does not.

Finally, it is important to note that probable cause is evaluated by examining the collective information in the possession of the police at the time of the arrest or search, and not merely on the personal knowledge of the arresting or searching officer. Therefore, if the knowledge of the police in its totality is sufficient to establish probable cause, a law enforcement officer's actions in making a warrantless arrest or search upon orders to do so will be justified, even though that officer does not personally have all the information upon which probable cause is based. State v. Smith, 277 A.2d 481 (Supreme Judicial Court of Maine, 1971). Even if the collective knowledge of the police is not sufficient to establish probable cause, the officer arresting upon orders will be protected from civil and criminal liability. The arrest or search, however, in these circumstances, would be unlawful, because it was not based upon probable cause. Whiteley v. Warden, 401 U.S. 560, 91 S.Ct. 1031, 28 L.Ed.2d 306 (1971).

SUMMARY

This chapter has been designed to round out the reader's preparation for the detailed study of the law of criminal procedure. In Chapter 1, the reader was introduced to the Constitution, the wellspring from which flow all the rules and principles to follow. Emphasis was placed on the constitutional sources of individual rights, and the necessary conflict between the protection of individual rights and the maintenance of law and order was pointed out. Future chapters will deal with specific instances of this conflict and will show how the delicate balance between these competing interests is maintained.

Chapter 2 presented an overview of the criminal court system, the arena in which the balancing takes place and in which the reasonableness, appropriateness, and thoroughness of the law enforcement officer's activities are ultimately tested. Chapter 2 was designed to give the reader an overall picture of the criminal justice system as a backdrop for a more integrated understanding of the law of criminal procedure.

Finally, this chapter, by introducing the basic concepts of the exclusionary rule, privacy, and probable cause, attempts to impress their importance on the reader at the outset and to alert the reader to their pervasive presence as interrelated threads that wind through the following chapters of this book. The law enforcement officer or other criminal justice professional who knows the potentially devastating effects of the exclusionary rule, who is sensitive to the constitutional rights of all citizens, especially to their reasonable expectation of privacy, and who understands the meaning and importance of probable cause, is well on his or her way to appreciating the constitutional restraints that characterize the operation of our criminal justice system. The remainder of this book provides the details of the law of criminal procedure, the knowledge of which will enable a person to function effectively within that system.

REVIEW AND DISCUSSION QUESTIONS

1. Explain why the application of the exclusionary rule does not necessarily mean that the prosecution is ended and the defendant goes free.

2. Discuss the probable effectiveness in terms of deterring illegal police conduct of the following suggested alternatives to the exclusionary rule: criminal prosecution of law enforcement officers; administrative disciplining of officers; bringing of civil actions for damages against officers.

3. Explain why a state court may refuse to follow certain holdings of the U.S. Supreme Court.

4. Give three reasons in support of the exclusionary rule and three reasons why it should be abolished.

5. Discuss three theories under which evidence may be admissible in court even though it is "fruit of the poisonous tree."

6. What did Justice Harlan mean when he said, in his concurring opinion in *Katz v. United States* that the answer to the question of what protection the Fourth Amendment affords to people requires reference to a "place?"

7. Should a person in a telephone booth be given the same degree of Fourth Amendment protection as a person in his or her bedroom? As a person in his or her garage? As a person in his or her automobile?

8. Although *Katz v. United States* dispensed with the requirement of an actual physical trespass to trigger the Fourth Amendment, is a physical trespass always an intrusion on a person's reasonable expectation of privacy?

9. Compare the standard of probable cause to the following statements of degree of certainty: absolutely positive; pretty sure; good possibility; beyond a reasonable doubt; reasonable suspicion; preponderance of the evidence; reasonable probability; strong belief; convinced.

10. Why do reviewing courts accept evidence of a "less judicially competent or persuasive character" to justify the issuance of a warrant than they would to justify officers acting on their own without a warrant?

PART TWO

Arrest, Search Warrants, and Probable Cause

4

Arrest

5

Search warrants

6

Probable Cause

4

Arrest

The power of arrest is the most important power that law enforcement officers possess. It enables them to deprive a person of the freedom to carry out daily personal and business affairs, and it initiates against a person the processes of criminal justice, which may ultimately result in that person being fined or imprisoned. Since an arrest has a potentially great detrimenal effect upon a person's life, the law provides severe limitations and restrictions on the law enforcement officer's exercise of the power of arrest. It is therefore essential for every law enforcement officer to fully understand the body of law governing arrest.

The law of arrest is based upon guarantees embodied in the United States Constitution. The familiar Fourth Amendment to the U.S. Constitution provides as follows:

> The right of the people to be secure in their *persons,* houses, papers, and effects, against unreasonable searches and seizures, shall not be violated and no Warrants shall issue, but upon probable cause, supported by Oath or affirmation, and particularly describing the place to be searched and the *persons* or things *to be seized.* (emphasis supplied) U.S.C.A.Const.Amend.IV.

There is a common belief among law enforcement personnel that the Fourth Amendment applies only to searches and seizures of material things and not to people. The word "persons" has been emphasized in the above passage to indicate clearly that this amendment is not so restricted, but that it also protects individuals from illegal seizures of their persons, i.e. illegal arrests. The U.S. Supreme Court dispelled any lingering uncertainty as to the status of arrest under the Fourth Amendment in the 1959 case of Henry v. United States:

> [I]t is the command of the Fourth Amendment that no warrants either for searches or *arrests* shall issue except "upon probable cause. . . ." (emphasis supplied) 361 U.S. 98, 100, 80 S.Ct. 168, 170, 4 L.Ed.2d 134, 137 (1959).

Keeping in mind this basic requirement that law enforcement officers must respect the rights guaranteed by the Fourth Amendment in order for an arrest to be valid, we turn now to the task of formulating a precise definition of arrest and discussing authority, execution, and various other aspects of the law of arrest.

DEFINITION OF ARREST

Numerous attempts have been made to frame an all-inclusive definition of arrest that would be applicable in all situations. None of these has been entirely satisfactory because arrest is a term that eludes exact definition. In effect, it is a legal conclusion used to describe a complex series of events that have in fact taken place. Nevertheless, we include here the Maine Supreme Judicial Court's definition of arrest, which is readily understandable and is substantially the same as definitions given by courts in other jurisdictions, both state and federal:

> An arrest in criminal law "signifies the apprehension or detention of the person of another in order that he may be forthcoming to answer for an alleged or supposed crime." State v. MacKenzie, 161 Me. 123, 137, 210 A.2d 24, 32–33 (Supreme Judicial Court of Maine, 1965).

The basic elements necessary to constitute an arrest are:

1. A purpose or intention to effect an arrest under real or pretended authority;

2. An actual or constructive seizure or detention of the person to be arrested by one having the present power to control the person;

3. A communication by the arresting officer to the person to be arrested of the intention or purpose then and there to make the arrest; and

4. An understanding by the person to be arrested that it is the intention of the arresting officer then and there to arrest and detain him or her.

Each of these elements will be discussed separately in some detail.

Intention to Arrest

To satisfy the first requirement listed above, there must be an intention on the part of the law enforcement officer to take a person into the custody of the law, and to deprive that person of liberty and freedom of movement at the time the officer takes action. This intention of the arresting officer to take the person into the custody of the law is the basic element that distinguishes an arrest from lesser forms of detention.

Lesser forms of detention occur in the many and varied situations in which the law enforcement officer does not intend to actually take anyone into the custody of the law but merely stops or detains a person. The following are examples of common situations in which a law enforcement officer may detain a person, but in which technically there is no arrest:

1. Restraining a person who is behaving in a manner that is dangerous either to self or others;

2. Stopping a person to establish identity or to seek information relating to a possible crime;

3. Service of a subpoena or other process such as a summons or notice to appear in court;

4. Asking a suspect or material witness to appear at the station for questioning;

5. Stopping a vehicle to inspect license, equipment, or load.

Although this is not a complete list, it illustrates the type of situation in which there is no intention by the law enforcement officer to take the person into the custody of the law. Without further intrusion on the person's freedom of action by the officer, there is ordinarily no arrest. As will be shown later in this chapter, however, if the officer's encounter with a person would cause a reasonable person to believe that he or she was not free to leave, the encounter would be considered a seizure tantamount to an arrest despite the officer's lack of intention to arrest.

There is one further detention situation that deserves mention in this context. This is the situation in which a police officer stops a person under suspicious circumstances and conducts a brief, general on-the-scene investigation about the possible commission of a crime. If, accompanying this brief detention of the person, there is a limited search of the person for possible weapons, this situation would be commonly referred to as "stop and frisk." There has been much discussion and several court decisions in this area in recent years. Because of its importance, stop and frisk will be discussed separately in Chapter 12. For purposes of this chapter, it is important to note that the ordinary stop and frisk situation does not involve an intention to arrest and therefore does not constitute an arrest.

Another requirement of arrest is that the intention to arrest be under real or pretended authority. Real authority is simply the legal right to make an arrest either with or without a warrant. That right may derive from the warrant itself or from the officer's having probable cause to believe that a particular person committed a particular crime. An example of pretended authority would be an officer making an arrest without the legal right to do so, but erroneously assuming to have that right. It is still technically an arrest despite the officer's error. This requirement distinguishes arrest from the situation in which a person is seized and detained without any type of authority being apparent or claimed. An example would be a kidnapping, when a person is seized but no one claims any kind of authority to arrest.

Seizure or Detention

To technically constitute an arrest, the arrested person must come within the actual custody and control of the law enforcement officer. There are two kinds of seizure or detention that will satisfy this requirement—actual and constructive.

An actual seizure or detention is the taking into custody of a person with the use of hands or with force, including the use of weapons. The ordinary situation would include the grabbing, holding, or handcuffing of a person to restrain freedom of action. However, the mere touching of the person of the accused is also considered to be an actual seizure and may constitute an arrest if the other elements of arrest are present. Childress v. State, 227 Md. 41, 175 A.2d 18 (Maryland Supreme Court, 1961).

A constructive seizure may be accomplished when the person being arrested submits to the control of the law enforcement officer without any touching or physical force whatsoever being applied. This peaceable submission eliminates the need for physical action and it satisfies the requirement of seizure or detention.

Merely telling a person "You are under arrest," without anything else, will not be sufficient to satisfy the seizure or detention element of arrest. There must be, in addition, an actual physical restraint or seizure of the person or a submission by the person to the officer's will and control. Furthermore, the seizure need be only momentary and if the other necessary elements of arrest are present, the arrest is completed, even if it is followed by an immediate escape. The person does not have to be permanently confined in order to satisfy the seizure or detention requirement.

Communication and Understanding

The final two elements of arrest can be considered together because they are two aspects of the same issue. Briefly stated, the law enforcement officer's actions in making an arrest must result in the arrested person's understanding that an arrest is being made. This understanding is ordinarily shown by the officer's notifying the person of the arrest. Surrounding circumstances, however, such as handcuffing or other physical restraint or confinement, may make the fact of arrest obvious to the arrested person. The officer may never say a word but the circumstances convey the idea.

There is one exception to the rule that understanding is an essential element of arrest. Despite the fact that an arrested person is unconscious or so drunk as to be incapable of understanding anything, the person may still be placed technically under arrest by a physical seizure or restraint, even though the person's understanding is delayed until consciousness or sobriety returns. State v. Cram, 176 Or. 577, 160 P.2d 283 (Oregon Supreme Court, 1945).

The issues of communication and understanding have been the subject of several court decisions in recent years. The problem, simply stated, is that sometimes an encounter between the police and a person does not fit within the description of a technical arrest, discussed above, but the intrusion on the person's freedom of action is significantly greater than the ordinary brief investigative detention or other minimal street encounter. The next section discusses these seizures, which, although not technical arrests, may be tantamount to an arrest for purposes of the Fourth Amendment.

SEIZURES OF THE PERSON TANTAMOUNT TO AN ARREST

The law enforcement officer investigating crime or otherwise enforcing the laws or keeping the public peace will have contact with members of the public in degrees of intensity varying from the briefest observation or questioning to a full-fledged arrest with the use of force. With respect to the most minimal of these police contacts with members of the public, the U.S. Supreme Court stated:

> [L]aw enforcement officers do not violate the Fourth Amendment by merely approaching an individual on the street or in another public place, by asking him if he is willing to answer some questions, by putting questions to him if the person is willing to listen, or by offering in evidence in a criminal prosecution his voluntary answers to such questions. . . . Nor would the fact that the officer identifies himself as a police officer, without more, convert the encounter into a seizure requiring some level of objective justifications. . . . The person approached, however, need not answer any question put to him; indeed, he may decline to listen to the questions at all and may go on his way. . . . He may not be detained even momentarily without reasonable, objective grounds for doing so; and his refusal to listen or answer does not, without more, furnish those grounds. . . . If there is no detention—no seizure within the meaning of the Fourth Amendment— then no constitutional rights have been infringed. Florida v. Royer, — U.S. at — 103 S.Ct. at 1324, 75 L.Ed.2d at 236 (1983).

Some encounters with members of the public, however, are more intense than those described in the previous paragraph and involved greater intrusions on a person's freedom of movement and privacy. An example is a so-called *Terry*-type investigative stop and frisk, which is a brief detention of a person for investigative purposes accompanied by a limited search. Officers may "stop" a person only if they have a reasonable suspicion that criminal activity is afoot. Officers may "frisk" a person only if they have reason to believe that they are dealing with an armed and dangerous individual. Both the stop and the frisk must be reasonable under the circumstances. "Stop and frisk" will be discussed later in this book, after the discussions of arrest and search and seizure, because "stop and frisk" involves elements of both.

At a still higher level of intensity are police contacts with members of the public involving a detention or temporary seizure of a person that is more intrusive on a person's freedom of action than a brief investigatory "stop," but that does not satisfy the four elements of a technical arrest, discussed earlier. In such instances, courts often hold that, despite the lack of a technical arrest, the seizure is so similar to an arrest in important respects that it should be allowed only if supported by probable cause to believe a crime has been or is being committed. The leading case on this subject is the U.S. Supreme Court case of Dunaway v. New York, 442 U.S. 200, 99 S.Ct. 2248, 60 L.Ed.2d 824 (1979).

In the *Dunaway* case, the defendant was picked up at his neighbor's home by the police and taken to the police station for questioning about an attempted robbery and homicide. Although he was not told that he was under arrest, he would have been physically restrained if he had attempted to leave. The police did not have probable cause to arrest the defendant. He was given *Miranda* warnings, waived his right to counsel, was questioned, and eventually made statements and drew sketches incriminating himself. His motions to suppress the statements and sketches were denied and he was convicted.

The U.S. Supreme Court examined the seizure of the defendant and held that the police violated his Fourth and Fourteenth Amendment rights. The seizure was much more intrusive than a traditional "stop and frisk" (see Chapter 12) and could not be justified on the mere grounds of "reasonable suspicion" of criminal activity. Whether or not technically characterized as an arrest, the seizure was in important respects indistinguishable from a traditional arrest. Instead of being questioned briefly where he was found, the defendant was taken from a neighbor's home to a police car, transported to a police station, and placed in an interrogation room. He was never informed that he was free to go and would have been physically restrained if he had refused to accompany the officers or had tried to escape their custody. The mere facts that the defendant was not under arrest, was not "booked," and would not have had an arrest record if the interrogation had proven fruitless did not make his seizure something less than an arrest for purposes of the protections of the Fourth Amendment. The seizure was, therefore, illegal because unsupported by probable cause.

Therefore, even though an officer does not intend to arrest a person in the traditional sense, a court may find that the officer's actions are tantamount to an arrest if they are indistinguishable from an arrest in important respects. If an officer seizes or detains a person significantly, beyond a mere "stop and frisk" or other minor investigatory detention, but does not comply with all the requirements of a technical arrest, the seizure or detention may nevertheless be considered an arrest for purposes of the Fourth Amendment. As such, the seizure or detention will be declared illegal unless it is supported by probable cause.

In United States v. Mendenhall, 446 U.S. 544, 100 S.Ct. 1870, 64 L.Ed.2d 497 (1980), the U.S. Supreme Court further clarified what constitutes a "seizure" for Fourth Amendment purposes. The Court said:

> [A] person has been "seized" within the meaning of the Fourth Amendment only if, in view of all of the circumstances surrounding the incident, a reasonable person would have believed that he was not free to leave. Examples of circumstances that might indicate a seizure, even where the person did not attempt to leave, would be the threatening presence of several officers, the display of a weapon by an officer, some physical touching of the person of the citizen, or the use of language or tone of voice indicating that compliance with the officer's request might be compelled. . . . In the absence of some such evidence, otherwise inoffensive contact between a member of the public and the police cannot, as a matter of law, amount to a seizure of that person. 446 U.S. at 554–55, 100 S.Ct. at 1877, 64 L.Ed.2d at 509.

In the *Mendenhall* case the Court found no seizure where Drug Enforcement Administration (DEA) agents, wearing no uniforms and displaying no weapons, approached the defendant on the public concourse of an airport, identified themselves as federal agents, and asked to see her identification and airline ticket. Furthermore, the defendant's voluntarily accompanying the agents to a DEA office upon their request was not a seizure, there being no threats or show of force. But in Florida v. Royer, 460 U.S. 491, 103 S.Ct. 1319, 75 L.Ed.2d 229 (1983), another case involving the stopping of a defendant on the public concourse of an airport, the U.S. Supreme Court concluded that the detention of the defendant was tantamount to an arrest. In the *Royer* case, narcotics agents had adequate grounds to suspect the defendant of carrying drugs, based on his traveling under an assumed name and his appearance and conduct fitting the "drug courier profile." The agents therefore had the right to temporarily detain the defendant, within the limits of the *Terry* case, in order to confirm or dispel their reasonable suspicions. The agents, however, not only asked the defendant for his identification and to accompany them to another room. They told him they were narcotics agents and had reason to believe he was carrying illegal drugs; they kept his identification and airline ticket; they took him to a small room where he found himself alone with two police officers; they retrieved his checked luggage from the airlines without his consent; they never informed him he was free to board his plane if he so chose; and they would not have allowed him to leave the interrogation room even if he had asked to do so. Under these circumstances, the Court held that the officers' conduct was more intrusive than necessary to effectuate an investigative detention authorized by the *Terry* case. The detention was, therefore, a seizure tantamount to an arrest, and since the officers did not have probable cause to arrest, it was an illegal seizure. The defendant's consent to search his luggage in the interrogation room was tainted by the illegal seizure and, therefore, the search of the luggage was also illegal.

The important point of advice for law enforcement officers is that they have a certain amount of leeway in making contact with citizens for various purposes before Fourth Amendment considerations become operative. As long as the person to whom questions are put remains free to disregard the questions and walk away, there has been no intrusion upon that person's liberty or privacy as would under the constitution require some particularized and objective justification, such as probable cause or reasonable suspicion of criminal activity. Moreover, such questioning of a citizen may include a request to accompany the officer, and a voluntary compliance with the request does not constitute a seizure. If the questioning is prolonged, however, combined with other indications of arrest such as a police station setting, a court may find that a reasonable person would believe that he or she was not free to leave and that an arrest had occurred for Fourth Amendment purposes.

ARREST AUTHORITY UNDER A WARRANT

Despite the fact that the authority of law enforcement officers and private citizens to arrest without a warrant in proper circumstances has been recognized for a long time, arrests made under the authority of a warrant have always been preferred. The reasons for favoring the warrant procedure is that it places the sometimes delicate decision of determining whether there is probable cause to justify an arrest in the hands of an impartial judicial authority. The U.S. Supreme Court said, in this regard, that " 'the informed and deliberate determinations of magistrates empowered to issue warrants . . . are to be preferred over the hurried action of officers.' " Aguilar v. Texas, 378 U.S. 108, 110–111, 84 S.Ct. 1509, 1512, 12 L.Ed. 2d 723, 726 (1964). This preference for warrants attempts to avoid placing responsibility for determining probable cause upon law enforcement officers who, in their eagerness to enforce the law and investigate crime, might be tempted to violate constitutional rights.

Although warrants are often considered a hindrance by law enforcement officers, they protect the officer in an important way. If a warrant is proper on its face and the officer does not abuse authority in executing the arrest, the officer is protected against civil liability for false arrest or false imprisonment, even though it is later determined that the arrest was unjustified. The officer is not so protected when making warrantless arrests.

The Arrest Warrant

The arrest warrant is a written order, issued by a proper judicial authority upon probable cause, directing the arrest of a particular person or persons. A typical form for an arrest warrant appears on page 75. The person issuing the arrest warrant could be a judge, a magistrate, a complaint justice, a justice of the peace, or a clerk of the court. Every jurisdiction authorizes different judicial officers to issue warrants, and law enforcement officers must know who has the authority in their jurisdictions. For the remainder of this chapter, the term magistrate will be used to designate the judicial officer authorized to issue arrest warrants. The warrant is issued on the basis of a sworn statement, called the complaint, charging that a particularly described accused has committed a described offense against the state or the United States. The person swearing out the complaint is often a law enforcement officer.

The Complaint

The complaint must state the essential facts constituting the offense charged, including the time and place of its commission and the name of the accused or a reasonably definite description if the name is not known. It must be sworn to and signed by the person charging the offense (the complainant). A warrant issued upon an unsworn statement is void, and any arrest made under such a warrant is illegal. A typical complaint form appears on page 76.

The complaint is discussed in further detail in Chapter 2.

Probable Cause

Whether or not the complainant has personal knowledge of the facts connected with the offense, probable cause must be established to the magistrate's satisfaction that the offense charged in the complaint was committed and that the accused committed it. Probable cause has been discussed briefly in Chapter 3 and will be discussed in detail in Chapter 6. For purposes of this discussion, suffice it to say that the magistrate must be satisfied that probable cause exists before issuing an arrest warrant.

Because of the probable cause requirement, a separate affidavit or affidavits setting forth in detail the facts and circumstances upon which probable cause is based are often filed with the original complaint. If there is room, these facts may be set forth in the original complaint, however. A separate affidavit need not be prepared with any particular formality and may be merely a sworn recitation of the facts upon which the complainant relies in seeking the issuance of a warrant. The magistrate may require additional affidavits of other persons having pertinent and reliable information bearing upon probable cause. In any case all information upon which probable cause is based should appear either in the original sworn complaint or in additional affidavits. The reason for this is to maintain a record of the

Warrant for Arrest of Defendant (Rev. 7-52)   Cr. Form No. 12

United States District Court
FOR THE

UNITED STATES OF AMERICA

v.   } No.

To

You are hereby commanded to arrest   and bring h

forthwith before the United States District Court for the   District of

in the city of   to answer to an   charging h   with

in violation of

Dated at ....,
                                                                                        Clerk.
on ....19.......
                                                     By ....,
Bail fixed at $..   *Deputy Clerk.*

RETURN

District of   ss

Received the within warrant the   day of   19   and executed same.

....,

By ....,

────────

¹ Insert designation of officer to whom the warrant is issued, e. g., "any United States Marshal or any other authorized officer"; or "United States Marshal for .... District of ...."; or "any United States Marshal"; or "any Special Agent of the Federal Bureau of Investigation"; or "any United States Marshal or any Special Agent of the Federal Bureau of Investigation"; or "any agent of the Alcohol Tax Unit."

Form A.O. 91 (Rev. 12-1-66)   Complaint

United States District Court
FOR THE

_____

United States of America v	Magistrate's Docket No. Case No. COMPLAINT for VIOLATION of U.S.C. Title Section

BEFORE_____,   _____,
            Name of Magistrate   *Address of Magistrate*

The undersigned complainant being duly sworn states:

That on or about   , 19   , at

in the

            District of

(1)

did(2)

And the complainant states that this complaint is based on

And the complainant further states that he believes that

are material witnesses in relation to this charge.

_____,
                                                                      Signature of Complainant.

_____,
                                                                      Official Title.

Sworn to before me, and subscribed in my presence, _____, 19____.

_____,
                                                                      United States Magistrate.

(1) Insert name of accused.
(2) Insert statement of the essential facts constituting the offense charged.

evidence produced before the magistrate issuing the warrant in case the validity of the warrant is called into question at a later date.

Requirements of Arrest Warrant

The arrest warrant, once issued, should conform to certain requirements. Although these requirements may differ from state to state, the following list is representative:

1. The warrant must bear the caption of the court or division of the court from which it issues.

2. The person to be arrested must be named in the warrant if the name is known. If not known, the warrant should contain any name or description by which the person can be identified with reasonable certainty. In other words, the warrant must show on its face that it is directed toward a particular individual.

3. The warrant should describe the offense charged in the complaint. This description should be in the language of the appropriate statute or ordinance. The important consideration, however, is that the description be in words definite enough for the accused to readily understand the charge. Stating that the accused is charged merely with a "a felony" or "a misdemeanor" is insufficient and will invalidate the warrant.

4. The time of issuance of the warrant should be stated.

5. The warrant should be directed to an appropriate officer or officers and should command that the defendant be brought before the proper judicial official.

6. The warrant must be signed by the issuing magistrate and must state the magistrate's official title.

An officer to whom a warrant is directed should read the warrant carefully. If the warrant satisfies the requirements listed above, the officer may execute the warrant without fear of any civil liability arising from a challenge to the validity of the warrant.

Summons

Law enforcement officers should be aware that a magistrate may issue a summons instead of an arrest warrant in certain situations. The requirements for a summons are the same as those for a warrant except that a summons directs the defendant to appear before a court at a stated time and place rather than ordering the defendant's arrest. Court rules and statutes usually provide that if a defendant fails to appear in response to a summons, a warrant shall be issued for his or her arrest. A typical summons form appears on page 78.

The summons is usually used in instances in which the offense charged in the complaint is a violation of a municipal ordinance or some other misdemeanor or petty offense. If the offender is a citizen with "roots firmly established in the soil of the community," and thus can be easily found for service of a warrant if the summons is ignored, the summons procedure is a much easier and better way of inducing the accused to appear in court, rather than arresting and taking the accused into custody.

Form A. O. 83 (Rev. 1970)   Magistrate's Summons

United States District Court
FOR THE

_____

Magistrate's Docket No. _____

Case No. _____

UNITED STATES OF AMERICA

v

SUMMONS

To

Name of Defendant

You are hereby summoned to appear before the undersigned United States Magistrate

, at

place

on   , 19   , at   o'clock   M. to answer to a complaint charging you

time

with

here describe offense charged in complaint

in violation of U.S.C. Title   Section

Date   , 19   _____

United States Magistrate.

This summons was received by me at   on

19

_____

Defendant.

RETURN*

This summons was served by me on   , 19   in the following manner:

_____,

Name.

_____,

Title.

*As to who may serve the summons and the manner of its service see Rule 4 (c) of the Federal Rules of Criminal Procedure and Rule 4 (c) of the Rules of Civil Procedure.

There is some confusion about the meaning of the term summons because it is often used to describe a citation, ticket, or notice to appear issued by a law enforcement officer, especially in traffic cases. Such a notice is *not* a summons in the legal sense because it is not issued by a magistrate on the basis of a complaint. The citation, ticket, or notice to appear merely gives notice to offenders, that they may be arrested if they do not voluntarily appear in court to answer the charges against them.

ARREST AUTHORITY WITHOUT A WARRANT

Law enforcement officers performing their daily duties will often be faced with the decision whether to apply for an arrest warrant or to make an arrest without a warrant. Since officers often have to make an immediate decision in this respect inexperienced or poorly trained officers will run into problems if they do not know their rights and limitations. It is therefore important for officers to have a clear working knowledge of the law governing arrest without a warrant.

In order to determine whether they have the authority to arrest without a warrant, officers must first know the difference between a felony and a misdemeanor because their authority depends upon the distinction between the two. In most state statutes, a felony is defined as any crime which is or may be punished by death or imprisonment in a state prison. Since most states do not provide for imprisonment in the state prison unless the term of the sentence is one year or more, it is generally agreed that an offense is not a felony unless the penalty is at least one year's incarceration. It should be noted that it is the punishment that *may* be imposed that determines whether an offense is a felony or misdemeanor, not the penalty that finally *is* imposed. *Therefore, a felony can be defined as any offense for which the punishment could possibly be imprisonment for a term of one year or more. All offenses that do not amount to a felony are classified as misdemeanors.*

States differ greatly as to which specific offenses are classified as felonies and which are misdemeanors. It is very important for law enforcement officers to familiarize themselves with the classifications of offenses into felonies and misdemeanors in their states.

Misdemeanors

In most states, unless otherwise provided by statute, a law enforcement officer may make an arrest without a warrant for a misdemeanor only when the misdemeanor is "committed in the officer's presence." Ordinarily, this means that the officer personally observes an offense being committed and then makes the arrest. However, it may be dark or the officer's sight may be blocked or restricted for other reasons, and other senses may have to be utilized. Realizing this, courts have held that an offense is committed in the officer's presence if the officer is able to perceive it though any of the five senses—sight, hearing, touch, taste, and smell. People v. Bock Leung Chew, 142 Cal.App.2d 400, 298 P.2d 118 (California Court of Appeals, 1959). Furthermore, officers may use any legal mechanical or electrical means to enhance their senses such as field glasses, hearing aids, etc. People v. Steinberg, 148 Cal.App.2d 855, 307 P.2d 634 (California Court of Appeals, 1957).

Knowledge of the offense may even come to the officer through information received from the suspect through an admission or confession. Cornish v. State, 215 Md. 64, 137 A.2d 170 (Maryland Supreme Court, 1957).

However, the mere fact that a misdemeanor is actually taking place in the officer's presence is not enough in itself to give the officer authority to make an arrest. The officer must *know* that an offense is being committed *before* making the arrest. State v. Pluth, 157 Minn. 145, 195 N.W. 789 (Minnesota Supreme Court, 1923). Therefore if an officer makes an arrest on mere suspicion or chance that an offense is being committed and later proves to be right, the arrest is not justified and is illegal.

An officer who comes upon the scene of a misdemeanor after the offense has been completed may *not* arrest the alleged offender without a warrant. This is true even though the offender is still at the scene, because the offense was not *committed in the officer's presence*. When the misdemeanor offense has terminated before the officer's arrival, two choices are available:

1. Invite the offender to submit voluntarily to custody;
2. Identify the offender and then seek an arrest warrant.

There is *no* authority to arrest for a *past* misdemeanor without a warrant.

Misdemeanor Arrests on Probable Cause In recent years, some state legislatures have enacted laws making exceptions to the general rule that arrest without warrant for a misdemeanor is only authorized for offenses committed in the officer's presence. These enactments have authorized arrests for certain types of misdemeanors, such as fish and game violations or liquor violations, on probable cause alone. Since the laws of each state are different, each law enforcement officer must determine for what misdemeanor offenses, if any, state law allows arrests on probable cause.

Promptness of Arrest Time is a very important factor in making an arrest without a warrant for a misdemeanor committed in the officer's presence. The arrest must be made promptly and without unnecessary delay. The officer must set out to make the arrest at the time the offense is perceived and must continue the effort until the arrest is accomplished or abandoned. As stated by the Supreme Court of Mississippi in a leading case on the subject:

> The arrest for misdemeanors committed or attempted in the presence of officers must be made as quickly after the commission of the offense as the circumstances will permit. After an officer has witnessed a misdemeanor, it is his duty to then and there arrest the offender. Under some circumstances, there may be justification for delay, as for instance, when the interval between the commission of the offense and the actual arrest is spent by the officer in pursuing the offender, or in summoning assistance where such may reasonably appear to be necessary. . . . If, however, the officer witnesses the commission of an offense and does not arrest the offender, but departs on other business, or for other purposes, and afterwards returns, he cannot then arrest the offender without a warrant; for then the reasons for allowing the arrest to be made without a warrant have disappeared. Smith v. State, 228 Miss. 476, 480, 87 So.2d 917, 919 (1956).

Therefore, a reasonable delay in making a warrantless misdemeanor arrest, which is closely connected with the offense itself or with an attempted flight by the offender, will usually not invalidate the arrest. Examples of reasonable delays would be delays to summon assistance in making the arrest, to plan strategy to overcome the resistance to arrest, to pursue a fleeing offender, or to take safety precautions. If the officer delays a warrantless misdemeanor arrest to do something unconnected with the process of arrest, however, the arrest will be unlawful. Such delays require an officer to obtain a warrant and to make the arrest in accordance with the warrant.

Felonies

Law enforcement officers may make a warrantless public arrest for a felony if, at the time of arrest, they have probable cause to believe that a felony has been committed and that the person to be arrested is committing or has committed the felony. In United States v. Watson, 423 U.S. 411, 96 S.Ct. 820, 46 L.Ed.2d 598 (1976), the U.S. Supreme Court said:

> Law enforcement officers may find it wise to seek arrest warrants where practicable to do so, and their judgments about probable cause may be more readily accepted where backed by a warrant issued by a magistrate. . . . But we decline to transform this judicial preference into a constitutional rule when the judgment of the Nation and Congress has for so long been to authorize warrantless public arrests on probable cause rather than to encumber criminal prosecutions with endless litigation with respect to the existence of exigent circumstances, whether it was practicable to get a warrant, whether the suspect was about to flee, and the like. 423 U.S. at 423–24, 96 S.Ct. at 827–28, 46 L.Ed.2d at 608–09.

Some states, however, either by statute or by court interpretation of the state constitution, place greater restrictions on the arrest authority of law enforcement officers. In People v. Hoinville, 191 Colo. 357, 553 P.2d 777 (Colorado Supreme Court, 1976), the court held that a state statute providing that "[a]n arrest warrant should be obtained when practicable," required police officers to obtain a warrant whenever possible. Officers must determine whether their state has similar requirements and, if so, they must obey them.

Assuming that most states allow warrantless felony arrests on probable cause, the key terms law enforcement officers must know to determine their authority are "felony" and "probable cause." "Felony" has already been defined in an earlier section of this chapter as any offense for which the punishment could possibly be imprisonment for a term of one year or more. It should be noted that, in order to apply the definition of felony, the officer must have a thorough knowledge of the definitions and possible range of punishments for all crimes in his state.

"Probable cause" has also been defined earlier in Chapter 3 and is discussed in detail in Chapter 6. For purposes of this discussion, it should be emphasized that a law enforcement officer, before making a warrantless arrest, must have specific facts or information connecting the person to be arrested with a particular felony. If the officer is unable later to justify the arrest by articulating the facts and circumstances supporting probable cause, the arrest is likely to be declared illegal.

If a felony arrest warrant is outstanding against a particular person, an officer may arrest that person even though neither the officer nor the officer's department has the actual warrant in possession. The officer's knowledge of the outstanding warrant provides probable cause sufficient to support the warrantless arrest. Bartlett v. United States, 232 F.2d 135 (5th Circuit Court of Appeals, 1956).

Finally, if an officer making an arrest has probable cause to believe that a felony has been committed and that the defendant is the one who committed it, it makes no difference whether the officer was right or wrong in making the arrest or that the defendant was later acquitted of the crime for which the arrest was made. The officer is still justified in making the arrest and it is a legal arrest. On the other hand, if the officer, on a hunch or intuition, makes a warrantless arrest without probable cause, it makes no difference whether the defendant is guilty or not. The arrest is still illegal. Therefore, probable cause is the main consideration in determining the validity of an arrest.

Promptness of Arrest   Unlike a warrantless arrest for a misdemeanor, which must be made immediately, a warrantless arrest for a felony may be made after some delay. This is true whether or not the felony was committed in the officer's presence. Carlo v. United States, 282 F.2d 841 (2nd Circuit Court of Appeals, 1961). Delay may be justified for a variety of reasons, as long as the delay in not designed to prejudice the offender's constitutional rights. Thus, an officer may postpone making an arrest to complete further undercover work, to avoid alerting other potential offenders, to protect the identity of undercover agents or informers, or for various other lawful reasons. As the U.S. Supreme Court has said:

> The police are not required to guess at their peril the precise moment at which they have probable cause to arrest a suspect, risking a violation of the Fourth Amendment if they act too soon, and a violation of the Sixth Amendment if they wait too long. Law enforcement officers are under no constitutional duty to call a halt to a criminal investigation the moment they have the minimum evidence to establish probable cause, a quantum of evidence which may fall far short of the amount necessary to support a criminal prosecution. Hoffa v. United States, 385 U.S. 293, 310, 87 S.Ct. 408, 417, 17 L.Ed.2d 374, 386 (1966).

Nevertheless, an extended period of delay between the time of the offense and the time of arrest may be so great as to give rise to a presumption that the accused was prejudiced by it. Jackson v. United States, 122 U.S.App.D.C. 124, 351 F.2d 821 (District of Columbia Court of Appeals, 1965). Therefore, unless there is good reason for delaying the arrest, it should be made as soon as possible after the offense.

EFFECTING THE ARREST

As stated earlier, in order to effect an arrest, law enforcement officers must bring accused persons under their power or control, or the accused must submit to the custody of the officer. The arrest may be made by actually laying hands on the accused. If there is such physical contact with the accused, only the slightest amount of touching or force is necessary. There does not have to be use of force on or confinement of a person in order for there to be a legal arrest.

If there is no touching or physical contact with the accused, any action that shows the intention of the officer to take the accused into custody is sufficient to effect an arrest *provided* the accused submits to the direction of the officer. However, if the accused is not restrained of liberty and brought within the power or control of the law, at least momentarily, there is no arrest.

Notice Required by the Officer

When law enforcement officers are making an arrest, they should, whenever possible, give notice of the following things to the person being arrested:

1. They should make known their authority by giving their identity if it is not obvious or already known to the suspect. An officer's uniform or a display of an official badge is a sufficient indication of authority for this purpose. Wilson v. Superior Court, 46 Cal.2d 291, 294 P.2d 36 (Supreme Court of California, 1956).

2. They should announce their intention to take the suspect into custody. This may be done by simply telling the person that he or she is under arrest. State v. Parker, Mo., 378 S.W.2d 274 (Missouri Court of Appeals, 1964).

3. They should announce the correct grounds or reason for making the arrest. This does not need to be in technical language and need not precede the arrest. United States v. Robinson, 325 F.2d 391 (2nd Circuit Court of Appeals, 1963).

Failure to give notice of the grounds of arrest or stating the wrong grounds will not make an arrest illegal. It is therefore not an absolute requirement for a valid arrest. Gearing v. State, Miss., 185 So.2d 652 (Supreme Court of Mississippi, 1966). However, if officers do not announce their authority, and their identity is unknown, the suspect has a right to resist the arrest as an unlawful assault. The suspect has this right whether guilty of an offense or not. Daniel v. State, Fla.App., 132 So.2d 312 (District Court of Appeal of Florida, 1961).

In certain situations it is not practical for officers to give any notice when making an arrest. These situations are:

1. When it would endanger an officer to do so;

2. When it would adversely affect making the arrest:

3. When the person to be arrested is in the act of committing the crime. Squadrito v. Griebsch, 1 N.Y.2d 471, 154 N.Y.S.2d 37, 136 N.E.2d 504 (New York Court of Appeals, 1956);

4. When the person to be arrested is fleeing the scene of the crime.

Time of Arrest

An arrest, whether made with or without a warrant, may be made on any day of the week and at any time of the day or night, unless otherwise provided in the warrant or by statute. However, common sense dictates that, if possible, arrests should not be made at unreasonable hours of the night or early morning or on the Sabbath.

Monitoring the Arrestee's Movements

In Washington v. Chrisman, 455 U.S. 1, 102 S.Ct. 812, 70 L.Ed.2d 778 (1982), the U.S. Supreme Court held:

> [I]t is not "unreasonable" under the Fourth Amendment for a police officer, as a matter of course, to monitor the movements of an arrested person, as his judgment dictates, following the arrest. The officer's need to ensure his own safety—as well as the integrity of the arrest—is compelling. Such surveillance is not an impermissible invasion of the privacy or personal liberty of an individual who has been arrested. 455 U.S. at 7, 102 S.Ct. at 817, 70 L.Ed.2d at 785.

In the *Chrisman* case, the officer had arrested a college student for possession of alcoholic beverages by a person under twenty-one and the student asked permission to go to his room to get his identification. The officer accompanied the student to his room and while in the room, the officer observed marijuana in plain view. The Court held that the officer had a right to remain literally at the student's elbow at all times and that no showing of "exigent circumstances" was necessary to authorize the officer to accompany the student into the room. The Court said:

> Every arrest must be presumed to present a risk of danger to the arresting officer. . . . There is no way for an officer to predict reliably how a particular subject will react to arrest or the degree of potential danger. Moreover, the possibility that an arrested person will attempt to escape if not properly supervised is obvious. 455 U.S. at 7, 102 S.Ct. at 817, 70 L.Ed.2d at 785.

Effecting the Arrest Under a Warrant

There are several additional considerations involved in effecting an arrest when under authority of a warrant. First of all, when officers are directed to serve a warrant of arrest, their belief in the guilt of the defendant or their personal knowledge of facts pertaining to the offense is immaterial. There is no requirement that the offense be committed in their presence or that they have probable cause to believe that the defendant committed the offense. Officers are required to carry out the command as stated in the warrant and the only questions that concern them are (1) whether the person to be arrested is the one for whom the warrant was issued, and (2) whether the warrant is valid on its face.

When the accused is identified in the warrant by name, law enforcement officers are required to exercise reasonable diligence to make sure that they are arresting the person designated in the warrant and no one else. If the person being arrested denies his or her identity and there is a reasonably simple and direct means of checking, officers may incur liability if they fail to check and go ahead with the arrest. Wallner v. Fidelity & Deposit Co. of Maryland, 253 Wis. 66, 33 N.W.2d 215 (Supreme Court of Wisconsin, 1948). The same holds true where the warrant merely describes the person to be arrested without providing a name. The officer must be very careful in determining whether the person arrested is the person identified in the warrant.

The requirement that the warrant be valid on its face is important, because a warrant that is not valid on its face gives officers no protection and no authority to arrest. Therefore, officers are bound to examine the warrant and if it is obviously bad, they act at their peril in carrying it out. While officers need not be concerned with the actual facts of the case, they are bound to know the law.

In order to determine whether a warrant is valid on its face, officers must examine several things. First of all, if the court issuing the warrant clearly has no jurisdiction, the warrant is void on its face. Likewise, the warrant is void if it does not disclose any legal offense charged against the person to be arrested, or if it fails to name or describe any identifiable person. Gattus v. State, 204 Md. 589, 105 A.2d 661 (Court of Appeals of Maryland, 1954). A warrant that is not signed by the issuing magistrate is also void on its face. Officers must also check the warrant to see that they are either specifically named or come within the class of officers designated to serve the warrant. If the warrant is directed to all law enforcement officers in the state, it is permissible for any authorized officer to execute it. If, however, the warrant is directed only to a sheriff of a certain county, for example, only that sheriff or a deputy sheriff can execute it.

Once it has been determined that the warrant is valid on its face, the officer must carry out its commands and serve it on the named individual. The officer no longer has any personal discretion and is merely carrying out an order of the court:

> When the warrant purports to be for a matter within the jurisdiction of the justice (magistrate), the ministerial officer is obliged to execute it, and of course must be justified by it. He cannot inquire upon what evidence the judicial officer proceeded, or whether he committed an error or irregularity in his decision . . ., the constable has nothing to look to but the warrant as his guide . . . . Alexander v. Lindsey, 230 N.C. 663, 667, 55 S.E.2d 470, 473–74 (Supreme Court of North Carolina, 1949).

Most states have statutes allowing arrest warrants for violations of state law to be executed at any place within the boundaries of the state. However, a law enforcement officer of one state may not go into another state to arrest under a warrant except in cases of fresh pursuit, which will be discussed later.

When actually making the arrest under the warrant, officers should give the same notice, discussed earlier, that they would ordinarily give in making any arrest. Also officers should have the warrant in their possession at the time of arrest and they should show the warrant to the person arrested. In some states, however, statutes provide that officers may make a legal arrest pursuant to a warrant even though the warrant is not in their possession. If they do so, however, they must inform the defendant of the offense charged and of the fact that a warrant has been issued. If the defendant requests, officers must produce the warrant as soon as possible.

It should be noted that, like a warrantless arrest for a felony, an arrest made under a warrant (for a felony or misdemeanor) need not be made immediately. Officers have considerable discretion as to the time and place of making an arrest under a warrant. They may have lawful strategic reasons for delay or they may wish to select a time when the arrest can be accomplished with the least difficulty. As one court stated:

> [O]rdinarily there is no legal requirement that a warrant of arrest must be executed immediatley or at the first opportunity. . . . While its execution should not be unreasonably delayed there may be perfectly valid reasons why further investigation

should be made before the drastic step is taken of arresting a citizen on a criminal charge. Certainly there is no constitutional right to be arrested promptly or otherwise. United States v. Joines, 258 F.2d 471, 472–73 (3rd Circuit Court of Appeals, 1958).

In State v. Heyer, 16 Or.App. 22, 517 P.2d 314 (Oregon Court of Appeals, 1973), the court held that a sixteen-month delay before arresting the defendant was reasonable. The justification for the delay was that the informant was a girl in her junior year of high school, and revealing her identity would have made her known to the students whom she had been investigating.

The arrest warrant will usually direct the officer to make a return of the warrant and to explain what has been done in carrying out the command of the warrant. Officers should carefully comply with the instructions in the warrant and with any state statutory provisions dealing with the return of warrants. If neither the warrant nor a statute provides instructions on returning the warrant, officers should still return the warrant to the judicial officer who issued it and explain what they have done with respect to its commands. Unless prescribed by statute, no particular form of return is required. If law enforcement officers fail to make a return after executing a warrant, the arrest made under the warrant may be held invalid. The officers would then be unprotected by the warrant if sued for false arrest, false imprisonment, or some other wrongful act arising out of the arrest.

Service of Summons

As discussed earlier, a magistrate may, under certain circumstances, issue a summons instead of an arrest warrant. A summons is served by delivering a copy to the defendant personally, or by leaving it at the defendant's dwelling house or usual place of abode with some person of suitable age and discretion who resides there. It may also be served by mailing it to the defendant's last known address. As with an arrest warrant, most states provide that a summons for a violation of state law may be served at any place within the state. Also, a summons must be returned by the officer serving it to the proper magistrate before the return date appearing on the summons.

Aid in Making the Arrest

Law enforcement officers may request private citizens to aid them in making an arrest. The laws of some states require that any person called upon by law enforcement officers to assist them in the execution of their official duties, including the arrest of another person, is legally obligated to obey the officers. Refusal or neglect to aid an officer may be punishable under state law. When private citizens act in aid of a known law enforcement officer, they have the same rights and privileges as the officer. While so acting, they have the status of a temporary law enforcement officer, including the right to use force and to enter property. If the person called upon acts in good faith, there is no need to inquire into the authority of the officer making the arrest.   The person is protected from liability even if the officer was acting illegally:

> It would be manifestly unfair to impose civil liability upon a private person for doing that which the law declares it a misdemeanor for him to refuse to do.   Peterson v. Robison, 43 Cal.2d 690, 697, 277 P.2d 19, 24 (Supreme Court of California, 1954).

Using Discretion in Deciding Not to Arrest

There are many situations in which law enforcement officers clearly have the ability and authority to arrest but good police practice indicates that they should not exercise that power.   Although it is beyond the scope of this chapter to give detailed guidelines in this area, a brief discussion is necessary to set out general principles.

Most importantly, law enforcement officers should be guided by the principle that their primary job is to protect the public at large.   Therefore, when an arrest might either cause greater risk of harm to the public or would only cause embarrassment to an individual who poses no real threat to the community, proper police practice may call for a decision not to exercise the full extent of an officer's arrest powers.

For example, when a crowd is present, it is often unwise to arrest a person or persons who are creating a minor disturbance.   There is always the danger of aggravating the disturbance and possibly precipitating a riot or civil disorder.   If there is a less drastic way to handle the matter, it should be explored even though there may be actual legal grounds for an arrest.   The same considerations apply to minor domestic disputes or the handling of intoxicated persons who are creating no danger and may need no more than an assist in getting home.   *It should always be remembered that an arrest is a significant restraint on a person's freedom and should always be justified by circumstances.*

Some local law enforcement agencies have definite policies covering the behavior of officers in this area.   If there are no such policies, individual officers will be called upon to exercise their own common sense and good judgment.   *In any case, officers should realize that not all situations in which they may make an arrest are situations in which they necessarily should make an arrest.*

PLACE OF ARREST

Most states have statutes providing that law enforcement officers, when acting under authority of a warrant, may make an arrest at any place within the state where the defendant may be found.   Similarly, officers may serve a summons at any place within the state.

However, officers generally have no official authority to arrest *without* a warrant outside of the territorial or geographical limits of the county or district for which they have been elected or appointed.   This area is usually referred to as their *bailiwick*.   Thus, sheriffs may not arrest without a warrant beyond the county in which they have been elected, nor may municipal police officers arrest without a warrant beyond the limits of the city in which they have been appointed.   On the other hand, the authority of state law enforcement officers is statewide and their power to arrest without a warrant runs throughout the state.

A law enforcement officer of one state has no authority to arrest in another state except as a private citizen or when in fresh pursuit. Both these exceptions will be discussed in further detail.

Citizen's Arrest Authority

The general rule limiting officers' warrantless arrest powers to their own bailiwick does not completely prevent officers from making an arrest without a warrant outside their bailiwick. As private citizens, officers have the same authority as any other private citizens to make an arrest without a warrant. This authority comes from the common law, which is a body of unwritten law developed in England and based upon court decisions, that receives its binding force from traditional usage, custom, and universal acceptance. Under the common law rule in force in most states, private citizens have the authority to arrest any person whom they have probable cause to believe has committed a felony. However, they can justify the arrest only by further showing that the felony was *actually committed.* The citizen's arrest authority, therefore, differs significantly from the arrest authority of law enforcement officers operating within their bailiwick. Private citizens act at their peril if no felony was actually committed, whereas law enforcement officers are protected if the arrest is based on probable cause.

Private citizens have the further authority under the common law to arrest for felonies and "breach of peace" misdemeanors *committed in their presence.* In the case of a felony, exercise of the authority to arrest is not only a privilege but a duty. There is no clear definition of "breach of the peace" misdemeanors, but practically speaking, the misdemeanor must cause or threaten direct harm to the public. While this does not mean the harm must always be physical, this will usually be the case.

Therefore, law enforcement officers may, in a state where the common law rule on citizen's arrest is followed, arrest without a warrant in the above-described circumstances anywhere in their state without regard to whether or not they are within their bailiwick. Furthermore, unless neighboring states have modified the common law rule regarding citizen's arrest, law enforcement officers have further arrest authority outside the borders of their state as private citizens. It would be wise, however, for all officers to be familiar with the laws of their states and of neighboring states before making a citizen's arrest, because several states have enacted statutes that differ from the common law.

Fresh Pursuit

Under the common law and most statutes, the area within which law enforcement officers may make lawful arrests without a warrant may also be extended beyond the borders of their bailiwick in cases of fresh pursuit. Fresh pursuit refers to the situation in which an officer is attempting to make an arrest for an offense within his or her bailiwick, and the offender flees into another jurisdiction to avoid arrest, with the officer immediately pursuing the offender. The common law allowed warrantless arrests in fresh pursuit only in felony cases, but today most state statutes allow such arrests both for felonies and misdemeanors. In order for the warrantless arrest made in fresh pursuit to be legal, the following conditions must be met:

1. The officer must have had valid authority to arrest for the offense in the first place;

2. The pursuit must be of a fleeing criminal attempting to avoid immediate capture; and

3. The pursuit must have been started promptly and maintained continuously.

The main thing to remember is that the pursuit should be fresh. It must flow out of the act of attempting to make an arrest and be a part of the continuous process of apprehension. This does not mean that the pursuit has to be instantaneous but it does have to be made without unreasonable delay or interruption. There should not be any side trips or diversions even for outside police business. However, the pursuit is not legally broken by unavoidable interruptions connected with the act of apprehension such as eating, sleeping, summoning assistance, or obtaining further information.

Outside State Boundaries Fresh pursuit may sometimes carry law enforcement officers outside the boundaries of their state. Ordinarily, officers have no authority beyond that of private citizens to make arrests in another state. However, many states have adopted the "Uniform Act on Fresh Pursuit" or similar legislation, which permits law enforcement officers from other states, entering their state in fresh pursuit, to make an arrest. The Uniform Fresh Pursuit Law of Iowa is typical:

> Any member of a duly organized state, county, or municipal law enforcement unit of another state of the United States who enters this state in fresh pursuit, and continues within this state in such fresh pursuit, of a person in order to arrest him on the ground that he is believed to have committed a felony in such other state, shall have the same authority to arrest and hold such person in custody, as has any member of any duly organized state, county or municipal law enforcement unit of this state to arrest and hold in custody a person on the ground that he is believed to have committed a felony in this state. Iowa Code Ann. § 756.1.

Since some states extend the privilege to out-of-state officers to make an arrest in fresh pursuit only on a reciprocity basis, it is important for law enforcement officers to be familiar not only with their state's statute, but also with the fresh pursuit statutes of all neighboring states.

A law enforcement officer who makes an arrest in fresh pursuit under such a statute in a neighboring state must take the person arrested before an appropriate court without unreasonable delay. The best procedure is to immediately contact law enforcement personnel in that state for advice and aid in locating the right court. Also, officers of every state that has adopted the Uniform Act or a similar act should be prepared to assist officers from other states who have made arrests in fresh pursuit in their state.

Some states allow an arresting officer from another state to take a person arrested in fresh pursuit back to the officer's home state after the arrested person is brought before an appropriate court. Other states allow removal of a person arrested by an out-of-state officer in fresh pursuit only upon extradition or waiver of extradition. Extradition is a procedure whereby authorities in one state (the demanding state) demand from another state (the asylum state) that a fugitive from justice in the demanding state, who is present in the asylum state, be delivered to the demanding state. Most states have adopted the Uniform Criminal Extradition Act, which provides uniform extradition procedures among the states.

USE OF FORCE

Law enforcement officers making an arrest have the right to use only that amount of force reasonably necessary to effect the arrest and to detain the arrestee. Officers may use reasonable force also to:

1. Overcome the offender's resistance to lawful arrest;

2. Prevent escape;

3. Recapture an offender who has escaped; and

4. Protect themselves from bodily harm.

Of course, reasonable force depends up all the facts and circumstances surrounding the arrest as they appear to the arresting officer, as a prudent and cautious person, before and at the time of making the arrest. Some of the facts and circumstances to be considered are the nature of the offense, the defendant's reputation, the available help, the presence of weapons, and the defendant's words or actions.

Under no circumstances, however, is an officer permitted to use unreasonable force or subject the offender to wanton violence in effecting an arrest. All law enforcement officers should remember that the sole purpose of an arrest is to bring the alleged offender before a court of law and not to give an officer the opportunity of wreaking public or personal vengeance upon the prisoner.

In general, the amount of force that may be used in making an arrest (outside of self defense) depends on whether the offense is a felony or a misdemeanor. The more serious the offense, usually the greater degree of latitude the officer has in using force.

Felonies

Felonies are considered to be serious offenses and therefore the law allows law enforcement officers to use whatever force is reasonably necessary to arrest a felon. Stinnett v. Virginia, 55 F.2d 644 (4th Circuit Court of Appeals, 1932). Under the common law rule, officers need not retreat from their purpose to arrest in order to avoid the necessity of resorting to extreme measures, but they must stand their ground and use all necessary force to bring the offender into custody. However, the use of deadly force is permitted only as a last resort where otherwise an officer would have to give up the attempt to arrest.

In this context, it is important to remember that the officer always has the right to summon aid. As mentioned above, some states require every private citizen by law to assist an officer in making an arrest, if so requested. Therefore, the officer will not be justified in using firearms or other deadly force if the arrest can be accomplished or flight prevented by summoning and using such assistance.

Furthermore, law enforcement officers should have *actual knowledge* both that a felony has been or is being committed and that the person to be arrested committed it before using deadly force in making an arrest or preventing flight. *Although courts have differed in this area, it is clear that officers use deadly force at their own peril if the wrong person is injured or killed or no felony has been committed.* Even though officers are justified in making an *arrest* on probable cause, if they are in fact proven wrong, they may *not* be able to legally justify a *killing or maiming* to effect that arrest.

It is worthy of note that there has been much criticism of the common law rule with regard to the use of deadly force in felony cases. In response to this criticism, the following change in the rule was proposed in Section 3.07(2)(b) of the Model Penal Code:

The use of deadly force is not justifiable under this Section unless:
  (i) the arrest is for a felony; and
  (ii) the person effecting the arrest is authorized to act as a peace officer or is assisting a person whom he believes to be authorized to act as a peace officer; and
  (iii) the actor believes that the force employed creates no substantial risk of injury to innocent persons; and
  (iv) the actor believes that:
    (1) the crime for which the arrest is made involved conduct including the use or threatened use of deadly force; or
    (2) there is substantial risk that the person to be arrested will cause death or serious bodily harm if his apprehension is delayed.

Some states may have adopted this section of the Model Penal Code or variations of it, either by statute or by court decision. Officers should make sure they know the law in their state. Very serious consequences can arise from the unwarranted use of deadly force, such as death or injury to the officer or other persons, or liability of the officer both civilly and criminally.

Misdemeanors

In arresting for a misdemeanor, a law enforcement officer may use whatever physical force is reasonably necessary under the circumstances to make an arrest or prevent flight. However, except in cases of self-defense, the officer is *never* justified in using firearms or other deadly force to effect an arrest for a misdemeanor. *The rule is that it is better that a misdemeanant escape rather than a human life be taken.* The reason for this rule is that usually the security of life and property is not significantly endangered by a misdemeanant being at large, while the safety and security of society usually require the speedy arrest and containment of a felon. Holloway v. Moser, 193 N.C. 185, 136 S.E. 375 (Supreme Court of North Carolina, 1927). The use of deadly force on a misdemeanant is excessive force constituting an assault. An officer who kills the suspect may be guilty of murder or manslaughter.

Self Defense

Whether the offense is a felony or misdemeanor, a law enforcement officer making a lawful arrest may use whatever force is necessary under the circumstances, including deadly force, if the officer reasonably believes that the person to be arrested is about to commit an assault and that the officer will thereby be placed in peril of death or serious injury.   The law enforcement officer's duty is to be the aggressor and to press forward to bring the person under restraint.   This cannot be accomplished by purely defensive action on an officer's part.   Therefore, if officers have lawful authority to make an arrest, they are not required to back down in the face of physical resistance to the arrest.   State v. Williams, 29 N.J. 27, 148 A.2d 22 (New Jersey Supreme Court, 1959).   When officers are faced with the choice of abandoning the arrest or using deadly force in *self defense* they have the right to use deadly force if it becomes necessary to protect themselves.   Again, it is an officer's duty to be the aggressor in effecting the arrest, and if the person being arrested endangers the officer's life or limb, the officer may match force with force, including deadly force, if necessary.

Many law enforcement agencies have departmental policies with reagrd to self defense.   These policies should be studied carefully and followed.

Resistance to Arrest

Resistance to arrest means opposition by direct, forcible means against an officer's person in order to prevent the officer from taking the accused into custody.   Under statutes defining the offense of resisting arrest, indirect interference or hindrance of an officer will usually not support a conviction.   Resistance requires active opposition such a shooting, striking, pushing, or otherwise struggling with the officer.   Therefore, mere flight, concealment, or other avoidance or evasion of arrest will not constitute resistance.   In the language of the Virginia Supreme Court of Appeals:

> The fact that the accused sought to escape the officer by merely running away was not such an obstruction as the law contemplates.   While it is the duty of every citizen to submit to a lawful arrest, yet flight is not such an offense as will make a person amenable to the charge of resisting or obstructing an officer who is attempting to make an arrest, as there is a broad distinction between avoidance and resistance or obstruction.   Jones v. Commonwealth, 141 Va. 471, 478, 126 S.E. 74, 76–77 (1925).

Nor will verbal objections, protests, or threats unaccompanied by force or danger constitute resistance.   (It should be noted, however, that such behavior may constitute a violation of some other statute prohibiting the hindrance, intimidation, or obstruction of a law enforcement officer.)   If, however, a threat is of a serious nature, accompanied by the apparent ability and present intention to execute it, and the officer is prevented from acting because of reasonable fear of serious bodily injury, the threat may constitute resistance to arrest.

Under the common law rule, the offense of resisting arrest requires that the arrest be lawful.   If the arrest is unlawful, the person being arrested has the *right* to resist.   Also, the person being arrested has a right to resist if the person making the arrest is not an officer of the law, or if the officer does not proceed in a lawful manner in making the arrest. Therefore, it is very important for law enforcement officers making an arrest to:

1. Establish their identity, if not already known or obvious, and;

2. Explain their purpose and authority.

According to the common law rule, persons threatened with an illegal arrest may not only resist the arrest, but may use such force as may be reasonably necessary to defend themselves and prevent an impending injury. State v. McGowan, 243 N.C. 431, 90 S.E.2d 703 (Supreme Court of North Carolina, 1956). Since the impending injury resulting from an arrest is ordinarily only a brief unlawful detention, the degree of force a person may use is strictly limited. A person who uses more force than is reasonably necessary for the purpose may be guilty of an assault and battery on the officer. Deadly force is rarely justified to resist an unlawful arrest, except when a person has reasonable grounds to fear death or serious bodily injury at the hands of an officer.

It should be noted that the law on resisting arrest and on other interferences with law enforcement officers is in a state of flux and differs from state to state. For example, some states do not allow a private citizen to use force to resist an arrest made by one who the citizen knows or has good reason to believe is an authorized police officer engaged in the performance of official duties, whether or not the arrest is illegal. If, however, the officer uses excessive and unnecessary force in effecting the arrest, the citizen may respond or counter with reasonable force for self-protection. As stated by the Supreme Court of New Jersey:

> Despite his duty to submit quietly without physical resistance to an arrest made by an officer acting in the course of his duty, even though the arrest is illegal, his right to freedom from unreasonable seizure and confinement can be protected, restored and vindicated through legal processes. However, the rule permitting reasonable resistance to excessive force of the officer, whether the arrest is lawful or unlawful, is designed to protect a person's bodily integrity and health and so permits resort to self-defense. Simply stated, the law recognizes that liberty can be restored through legal processes but life or limb cannot be repaired in a courtroom. And so it holds that the reason for outlawing resistance to an unlawful arrest and requiring disputes over its legality to be resolved in the courts has no controlling application on the right to resist an officer's excessive force. . . .
>
> Two qualifications on the citizen's right to defend against and to repel an officer's excessive force must be noticed. He cannot use greater force in protecting himself against the officer's unlawful force than reasonably appears to be necesssary. If he employs such greater force, then he becomes the aggressor and forfeits the right to claim self-defense to a charge of assault and battery on the officer. . . .
> Furthermore, if he knows that if he desists from his physically defensive measures and submits to arrest the officer's unlawfully excessive force would cease, the arrestee must desist or lose his privilege of self-defense. State v. Mulvihill, 57 N.J. 151, 156–57, 270 A.2d 277, 280 (1970).

As illustrated by the *Mulvihill* case, the modern trend is away from the common law rule allowing resistance to any illegal arrest, because of the dangers inherent in the rule and because the consequences of an illegal arrest are at the most a brief period of detention during which arrested persons can resort to nonviolent legal remedies for regaining their liberty. It is important for all law enforcement officers to determine whether their state operates under the common law rule, some modification of that rule, or some newly created rule.

Entry of Dwellings

Under the common law, the right of law enforcement officers to enter a dwelling to effect an arrest depended upon whether they had legal authority to arrest. If they had the legal authority to arrest, whether with or without a warrant, they also had the authority to enter any dwelling house, forcibly if necessary, and search for the suspect when they had probable cause to believe that the person whom they sought to arrest was in that dwelling house. As stated by the 9th Circuit Court of Appeals:

> An agent must have probable cause to believe that the person he is attempting to arrest, with or without a warrant, is in a particular building at the time in question before that agent can legitimately enter the building by ruse or any other means. To hold otherwise is to grant the agent a license to go from house to house employing ruse entries in violation of the right of privacy of the respective occupants. United States v. Phillips, 497 F.2d 1131, 1136 (1974).

This authority to enter a dwelling house to arrest applied even to misdemeanor cases if an officer had legal authority to make an arrest for a misdemeanor.

The common law rule allowing entry of dwellings whenever officers had authority to arrest a person believed to be inside is no longer valid. In recent years, the U.S. Supreme Court decided several cases dealing with the entry of dwellings to arrest. Now, the general rule is that a law enforcement officer may not enter a dwelling to arrest a person without a warrant, unless there is consent or exigent circumstances. Whether an arrest warrant or search warrant is required for entry depends on whether the dwelling to be entered is the suspect's home or someone else's home.

Entry of Suspect's Home   In Payton v. New York, 445 U.S. 573, 100 S.Ct. 1371, 63 L.Ed.2d 639 (1980), the U.S. Supreme Court held that, absent exigent circumstances or consent, a law enforcement officer may not make a warrantless entry into a suspect's home in order to make a routine felony arrest. The Court said that the physical entry of the home is the chief evil against which the wording of the Fourth Amendment is directed and that the warrant procedure minimizes the danger of needless intrusions of that sort. The Court went on to say that an arrest warrant requirement, although providing less protection than a search warrant requirement, was sufficient to interpose the magistrate's determination of probable cause between the zealous officer and the citizen. The Court concluded that "an arrest warrant founded on probable cause implicitly carries with it the limited authority to enter a dwelling in which the suspect lives when there is reason to believe the suspect is within." 445 U.S. at 603, 100 S.Ct. at 1388, 63 L.Ed.2d at 661. Therefore, absent consent or exigent circumstances, in order to enter a suspect's home to arrest him, a law enforcement officer must have at least an arrest warrant.

The Court in *Payton* did not specify the nature of the exigent circumstances that would justify a warrantless entry of a home to make an arrest. In Welsh v.

Wisconsin, ___ U.S. ___, ___, 104 S.Ct. 2091, 2099, 80 L.Ed.2d 732, 745 (1984), however, the Court held that:

> [A]n important factor to be considered when determining whether any exigency exists is the gravity of the underlying offense for which the arrest is being made. Moreover, although no exigency is created simply because there is probable cause to believe that a serious crime has been committed . . . application of the exigent-circumstances exception in the context of a home entry should rarely be sanctioned when there is probable cause to believe that only a minor offense . . . has been committed.

In the *Welsh* case, the warrantless arrest of the defendant in his home for a noncriminal traffic offense was held illegal.

The *Payton* decision should cause law enforcement officers to apply for more arrest warrants. Unless suspects are apprehended at or near the scene of a crime or shortly after it is committed, it is more likely that they will be found at home than elsewhere.

Entry of a Third Person's Home In Steagald v. United States, 451 U.S. 204, 101 S.Ct. 1642, 68 L.Ed.2d 38 (1981), the U.S. Supreme Court held that an arrest warrant does not authorize law enforcement officers to enter the home of a third person to search for the person to be arrested, in the absence of consent or exigent circumstances. In order to protect the Fourth Amendment privacy interests of persons not named in an arrest warrant, a search warrant must be obtained to justify entry into the home of any person other than the person to be arrested.

This requirement may place a heavy pratical burden on law enforcement officers, causing them to seek both an arrest warrant and a search warrant in many situations. An alternative, suggested by the U.S. Supreme Court, is that in most instances the police may avoid altogether the need to obtain a search warrant simply by waiting for a suspect to leave the third person's home before attempting to arrest the suspect. When the suspect leaves either the home of a third person or the suspect's own home and is in a public place, officers may arrest on probable cause alone. Neither an arrest warrant nor a search warrant is required to support an arrest made in a public place.

Entry of Dwellings in Hot Pursuit When the arrest of a suspect is set in motion in a public place, but the suspect retreats into his or her home, the right of officers to enter the home in hot pursuit is governed by the case of United States v. Santana, 427 U.S. 38, 96 S.Ct. 2406, 49 L.Ed.2d 300 (1976). In that case, police officers drove to the defendant's house after receiving information that the defendant had in her possession marked money used to make a heroin buy arranged by an undercover agent. The defendant was standing in the doorway of her house holding a paper bag as the police pulled up within fifteen feet of her. The officers got out of the car, shouting "Police," and the defendant retreated into the vestibule of her house where they caught her. When she tried to pull away, envelopes containing heroin fell to the floor from the paper bag. Some of the marked money was found on her person.

The Court held that the defendant, while standing in the doorway of her house, was in a "public place" for purposes of the Fourth Amendment. Since she was not in an area where she had any expectation of privacy and she was exposed to public view, speech, hearing, and touch, it was the same as if she had been standing completely outside her house. When police sought to arrest her, they merely intended to make a warrantless arrest in a public place upon probable cause. Under United States v. Watson, 423 U.S. 411, 96 S.Ct. 820, 46 L.Ed.2d 598 (U.S. Supreme Court, 1976), such an arrest would not violate the Fourth Amendment. By retreating into a private place, the defendant could not defeat an otherwise proper arrest that had been set in motion in a public place. Since the officers needed to act quickly to prevent the destruction of evidence, there was a true hot pursuit, even though there was only a very short chase. Thus the warrantless entry to make the arrest was justified, as was the search incident to that arrest.

Forced Entry   Before officers may lawfully force their way into a dwelling to arrest someone inside, they must first knock on the door, announce their authority and purpose, and then demand admittance. If this demand is refused or met with silence, officers may enter forcibly after waiting a reasonable time under the circumstances. Masiello v. United States, 115 U.S.App.D.C. 57, 317 F.2d 121 (District of Columbia Circuit Court of Appeals, 1963). In the words of the United State Supreme Court:

> The requirement of prior notice of authority and purpose before forcing entry into a home is deeply rooted in our heritage, and should not be given grudging applica-tion. . . . Every householder, the good and the bad, the guilty and the innocent, is entitled to the protection designed to secure the common interest against unlawful invasion of the house. The petitioner could not be lawfully arrested in his home by officers breaking in without first giving him notice of their authority and purpose. Because the petitioner did not receive that notice before the officers broke the door to invade his home, the arrest was unlawful, and the evidence seized should have been suppressed. Miller v. United States, 357 U.S. 301, 313–14, 78 S.Ct. 1190, 1198, 2 L.Ed.2d 1332, 1340–41 (1958).

Forcible entry of a dwelling, in this context, does not necessarily mean only the violent breaking down of a door or the smashing of a window. The United States Supreme Court stated that "[a]n unannounced intrusion into a dwelling . . . is no less an unannounced intrusion whether officers break down a door, force open a chain lock on a partially open door, open a locked door by use of a passkey, or . . . open a closed but unlocked door." Sabbath v. United States, 391 U.S. 585, 590, 88 S.Ct. 1755, 1758, 20 L.Ed.2d 828, 834 (1968). Before making any entry of this type to arrest, officers must first knock, announce their authority and purpose, and demand admittance.

In certain situations, however, the failure to knock, announce and demand admittance will be excused. These situations are:

1. When the officer's purpose is already known to the offender or other person upon whom demand for entry is made. As the U.S. Supreme Court stated in the *Miller* case:

> It may be that, without an express announcement of purpose, the facts known to officers would justify them in being virtually certain that the petitioner already knows

their purpose so that an announcement would be a useless gesture. 375 U.S. at 310, 78 S.Ct. at 1196, 2 L.Ed.2d at 1338.

2. When the officer's personal safety might be imperiled by compliance with such requirements. Fairman v. Warden, 83 Nev. 332, 431 P.2d 660 (Supreme Court of Nevada, 1967).

3. When the incidental delay might defeat the arrest by permitting the offender to escape. State v. Fair, 45 N.J. 77, 211 A.2d 359 (Supreme Court of New Jersey, 1965).

4. When the preliminary announcements might permit destruction of important evidence by those inside the house. This situation often comes up in drug cases, in which the evidence is often small and easily destroyed or disposed of. In Ker v. California, 374 U.S. 23, 83 S.Ct. 1623, 10 L.Ed.2d 726 (1963), the U.S. Supreme Court held that the unannounced entry into the defendant's apartment was proper when otherwise evidence of narcotics activity would have been destroyed. However, the holding in the *Ker* case was limited to the particular facts of that case. There, officers not only reasonably believed that the defendant was in possession of narcotics, but defendant's furtive conduct in eluding them shortly before the arrest gave them grounds to believe that he might have been expecting the police. In Meyer v. United States, 386 F.2d 715 (9th Circuit Court of Appeals, 1967), the officers had nothing to justify their unannounced entry into a dwelling except the claim of a general propensity of narcotics violators to destroy evidence. The court held that the entry was unlawful:

> Under the Fourth Amendment, a specific showing must always be made to justify any kind of police action tending to disturb the security of the people in their homes. Unannounced forcible entry is in itself a serious disturbance of that security and cannot be justified on a blanket basis. Otherwise, the constitutional test of reasonableness would turn only on practical expediency, and the amendment's primary safe-guard—the requirement of particularity, would be lost. Just as the police must have sufficient particular reason to enter at all, so must they have some particular reason to enter in the manner chosen. 386 F.2d at 718.

DISPOSITION OF PRISONER

Initial Appearance Before the Magistrate

When law enforcement officers have arrested a person, either with or without a warrant, they must take the prisoner before a magistrate, or deliver the prisoner according to the mandate of the warrant. State statutes require that this duty be done "immediately," "without unnecessary delay," "forthwith," or in some similar language. These state statutes confer a substantial right upon the defendant and create a corresponding duty upon law enforcement officers. An arrested person has a constitutional right to reasonable access to the courts, and any denial or undue restriction of this right constitutes a denial of due process of law under the Fourteenth Amendment. In re Allison, 66 Cal.2d 282, 57 Cal.Rptr. 593, 425 P.2d 193 (Supreme Court of California, 1967).

The reasons behind the rule requiring arrested persons to be brought before a magistrate without unnecessary delay are as follows:

1. To advise arrested persons of the charges being made against them, so that they may prepare their defense;

2. To fully advise arrested persons of their rights, such as their right to a preliminary hearing, right to counsel, and under some statutes, their right to remain silent;

3. To protect arrested persons from being abandoned in jail and forgotten or otherwise cut off from contact with people who can help them;

4. To prevent secret and extended interrogation of arrested persons by law enforcement officers;

5. To give arrested persons an early opportunity to secure their release on bail while awaiting the final outcome of the proceedings against them;

6. To give arrested persons an opportunity, in petty misdemeanor cases, to speedily conclude the matter by pleading guilty to the charge, paying their fine, and going on their way; and

7. In federal courts, and in some state courts, to obtain a prompt, neutral "judicial determination of probable cause as a prerequisite to extended restraint of liberty following arrest." Gerstein v. Pugh, 420 U.S. 103, 114, 95 S.Ct. 854, 863, 43 L.Ed. 2d 54, 65 (1975).

It should be noted that not all states provide for a judicial determination of probable cause at the initial appearance before a magistrate. According to the U.S. Supreme Court:

> There is no single preferred pretrial procedure, and the nature of the probable cause determination usually will be shaped to accord with a State's pretrial procedure viewed as a whole. . . . It may be found desirable, for example, to make the probable cause determination at the suspect's first appearance before a judicial officer, the determination may be incorporated into the procedure for setting bail or fixing other conditions of pretrial release. In some States, existing procedures may satisfy the requirement of the Fourth Amendment. Others may require only minor adjustment, such as acceleration of existing preliminary hearings. Current proposals for criminal procedure reform suggest other ways of testing probable cause for detention. Whatever procedure a State may adopt, it must provide a fair and reliable determination of probable cause as a condition for any significant pretrial restraint on liberty, and this determination must be made by a judicial officer either before or promptly after arrest. 420 U.S. at 123–25, 95 S.Ct. at 868–69, 43 L.Ed. 2d at 71–72.

Courts have been quite flexible in interpreting the meaning of "immediately," "without unnecessary delay," "forthwith," and like phrases in statutes requiring arrested persons to be brought before a magistrate. Courts have realized that a certain amount of delay is necessary for the officer to perform required duties and other unavoidable activities connected with the arrest such as booking the arrested person, routinely questioning and searching the person (if legally allowed), and checking facts. As one court said:

> The duty enjoined upon arresting officers to arraign "without unnecessary delay" indicates that the command does not call for automatic obedience. Circumstances may justify a brief delay between arrest and arraignment, as for instance, where the story volunteered by the accused is susceptible of quick verification through third parties. Williams v. United States, 273 F.2d 781, 797–98 (9th Circuit Court of Appeals, 1959).

Officers may also have to delay in bringing an arrested person before a magistrate because the person is physically or mentally incapacitated by illness or for some other reason. Drunkenness of an arrested person may be a ground for delay, if the person's condition would prevent understanding of the proceedings. Finally, an officer may have to delay because a magistrate is not readily available, either because the courts are closed, or because the distance to be traveled to reach a magistrate is great.

Therefore, "immediately," "without unnecessary delay," "forthwith," or other similar statutory language cannot be defined in terms of minutes and hours but must be interpreted in light of all the circumstances. If officers bring arrested persons before a magistrate as soon as one is available, and do not detain them to coerce a confession from them or otherwise harass them, the requirements of the rule should be satisfied.

Protection and Welfare of the Prisoner

As indicated above, there will be occasions when a magistrate or bail commissioner is not available, thereby delaying the arrested person's appearance. Furthermore, delay may result from officers carrying out necessary duties, may be requested by the prisoner, or may be caused by the prisoner being sick, intoxicated, or otherwise incapacitated. In these situations, it is the duty of the officer to keep arrested persons safely in custody for the necessary period of time until they can be brought before a magistrate. To accomplish this purpose, the officer may exercise such degree of control over prisoners as may be necessary to prevent their escape, although the officer must not subject prisoners to any greater restraint than is reasonably justified to keep them safely in custody. It may be necessary for the law enforcement officer to physically confine prisoners rather than keep them in the officer's personal custody. Ordinarily the place of confinement will be a jail, but the officer may choose any safe, suitable place if a jail is unavailable.

Once officers have a prisoner in their custody, they have certain responsibilities toward the prisoner. They have the responsibility to take care of the life, health, and safety of the prisoner and may be liable in damages if they fail to do so. Therefore, if the prisoner is sick or injured at the time of the arrest or later, the officer must provide adequate medical attention, including taking the prisoner to a hospital, if necessary. The officer, however, is not personally liable for the expenses involved.

Any unnecessary force, violence, or brutality used against a prisoner is unlawful and the officer may be liable for assault and battery. Furthermore, if the prisoner is assaulted or injured by other prisoners or persons, and the officer either negligently or willfully allowed the assault, the officer may be personally liable for the damages.

Handcuffing

One of the ways in which officers may prevent the escape of a prisoner and also protect themselves from harm is to handcuff the prisoner. The law leaves the decision whether or not to use handcuffs largely up to the discretion of individual law enforcement officers. They will be held liable for assault or otherwise only in cases of clear abuse of this discretion.

The right to handcuff is freely recognized in cases involving felony arrests but it is not confined to such cases. Circumstances often justify such precautions in misdemeanor cases also, especially when a breach of the peace is involved. In deciding whether or not to use handcuffs, the officer is entitled to consider a variety of factors—the nature of the person arrested, the person's reputation or record, the time of day or night, the possibility of violence, the number of prisoners involved, and the distance to the court or confinement facility. If an individual department has a policy regarding handcuffing, it should be consulted and followed by the officers of that department.

Property of Prisoner

When a person is arrested and is to be incarcerated, as part of the routine administrative procedure incident to booking and jailing the person, police may search the person and any container or article in his or her possession, in accordance with established inventory procedures. The U.S. Supreme Court, in Illinois v. Lafayette, ___ U.S. ___, 103 S.Ct. 2605, 77 L.Ed.2d 229 (1983), held that the justification for such searches does not rest on probable cause, and thus the absence of a warrant is immaterial to the reasonableness of the search. The Court said that the governmental interests justifying a stationhouse inventory search are different from, and may in some circumstances be even greater than, those supporting a search incident to arrest. Among those interests are prevention of theft of the arrested person's property; deterrence of false claims regarding that property; prevention of injury from belts, drugs, or dangerous instruments such as razor blades, knives, or bombs; and determination or verification of the person's identity. Furthermore, it does not matter that there might be less intrusive means of satisfying those governmental interests. The Court said:

> It is evident that a stationhouse search of every item carried on or by a person who has lawfully been taken into custody by the police will amply serve the important and legitimate governmental interests involved.
>
> Even if less intrusive means existed of protecting some particular types of property, it would be unreasonable to expect police officers in the everyday course of business to make fine and subtle distinctions in deciding which containers or items may be searched and which must be sealed as a unit. ___ U.S. at ___, 103 S.Ct. at 2610, 77 L.Ed.2d at 72.

A preincarceration inventory search need not be conducted immediately upon the prisoner's arrival at the stationhouse. For example, the U.S. Supreme Court held that a seizure of a prisoner's clothing in the morning, several hours after his arrest and incarceration the previous evening, was reasonble. No substitute clothing was available at the time of arrest and, therefore, the normal processes incident to arrest and custody had not been completed. The Court said:

> [O]nce the accused is lawfully arrested and is in custody, the effects in his possession at the place of detention that were subject to search at the time and place of his arrest may lawfully be searched and seized without a warrant even though a substantial period of time has elapsed between the arrest and subsequent administrative processing, on the one hand, and the taking of the property for use as evidence, on the other. United States v. Edwards, 415 U.S. 800, 807, 94 S.Ct. 1234, 1239, 39 L.Ed.2d 771, 778 (1974).

Sometimes, especially when a vehicle is involved, officers may be required to take positive steps to protect the defendant's property or else they may become liable in damages for failure to do so. For example, in an often cited case, a trucker was arrested and taken to jail, leaving his truck standing in a docking area on the waterfront. Over the trucker's protests, the arresting officer and his superior refused to allow him to remove the truck to a place of safety and refused to take any steps themselves to protect it. While the defendant trucker was in jail, his truck was stripped and, in attempting to steal it, the thieves damages the transmission. The officers were held liable for the damages. Whitehead v. Stringer, 106 Wash. 501, 180 P. 486 (Supreme Court of Washington, 1919).

In order to protect themselves from liability of this nature, many law enforcement agencies have a policy of impounding arrested persons' vehicles and making an inventory of their contents. For a further discussion of impoundment and inventory of vehicles, see Chapter 10.

Identification of Prisoner

Pre-trial procedures for identifying persons arrested for a crime take many different forms. One aspect of these identification procedures is the confrontation of the prisoner with victims or witnesses of the crime, sometimes accomplished through the use of a police lineup or showup. The arrestee has no right to object to being viewed by witnesses for identification purposes and also has no right to demand to be placed in a lineup. For a discussion of pre-trial identification techniques and the right to counsel, see Chapter 14.

In addition, law enforcement officers clearly have the right to take fingerprints, footprints, or photographs of the arrested person for purposes of identification or evidence. These may even be taken by force if necessary. Schmerber v. California, 384 U.S. 757, 86 S.Ct. 1826, 16 L.Ed.2d 908 (U.S. Supreme Court, 1966). Photographs may be useful to show that at the time of arrest, the defendant had dyed hair or a beard, or to show bruises or scratches that might be evidence in crimes of violence. Courts have also held that law enforcement officers may obtain voice exemplars or have a dentist examine a defendant's mouth for a missing tooth for identification purposes:

> [T]he Supreme Court held in *Dionisio* [United States v. Dionisio, 410 U.S. 1, 93 S.Ct. 764, 35 L.Ed.2d 67 (1973)] that the Fourth Amendment does not protect

"what a person knowingly exposes to the public even in his home or office. . . . Like a man's facial characteristics, or handwriting, his voice is repeatedly produced for others to hear. No person can have a reasonable expectation that others will not know the sound of his voice, any more than he can reasonably expect that his face will be a mystery to the world." This doctrine is applicable as well to a missing tooth. (material in brackets added) United States v. Holland, 378 F.Supp. 144, 155 (U.S. District Court, Eastern District of Pennsylvania, 1974).

Law enforcement officers also have the authority to make a physical examination of defendants for measurements, scars, bruises, tattoos, etc. To enable this to be done, defendants may be required to disrobe against their will:

> Such procedures and practices and tests may result in freeing an innocent man accused of crime, or may be part of a chain of facts and circumstances which help identify a person accused of a crime or connect a suspect or an accused with the crime of which he has been suspected or has been accused. The law is well settled that such actions, practices, and procedures do not violate any constitutional right. Commonwealth v. Aljoe, 420 Pa. 198, 202, 216 A.2d 50, 52–53 (Pennsylvania Supreme Court, 1966).

Courts have even allowed an examination of an arrested person's bodily cavities as long as the methods used did not amount to excessive force or brutality and did not "shock the conscience" or offend the sense of justice. Blackford v. United States, 247 F.2d 745 (9th Circuit Court of Appeals, 1957). Furthermore, the U.S. Supreme Court has held that there is no denial of due process of law in taking a blood sample from a person who is unconscious and unable to give consent, and no unreasonable search and seizure or violation of the privilege against self-incrimination when such specimen is taken without consent from a person in lawful custody. Schmerber v. California, 384 U.S. 757, 86 S.Ct. 1826, 16 L.Ed.2d 908 (1966). In the *Schmerber* case, the blood sample was taken in a hospital by a physician following accepted medical procedures. Also, there was a need for immediate action because the alcoholic content in the blood would quickly dissipate. The Court said:

> [W]e reach this judgment only on the facts in the present record. The integrity of an individual's person is a cherished value of our society. That we today hold that the Constitution does not forbid the State's minor intrusions into an individual's body under stringently limited conditions in no way indicates that it permits more substantial intrusions or intrusions under other conditions. 384 U.S. at 772, 86 S.Ct. at 1836, 16 L.Ed.2d at 920.

Courts have generally refused requests by the prosecution to allow surgery to remove a bullet from a person when the operation would pose a substantial risk to the person. Some courts, however, have allowed minor surgery to remove a bullet from a person when the surgical procedure posed no threat of serious bodily injury and the evidence was critical to the prosecution's case. Creamer v. State, 229 Ga. 511, 192 S.E.2d 350 (Supreme Court of Georgia, 1972).

Law enforcement officers should not attempt to arrange for the removal by surgery of bullets or other objects without first contacting a prosecuting attorney. Also, unless there is an emergency, a search warrant or court order must be obtained before such surgery will be allowed.

Release of Prisoner Prior to Appearance Before a Magistrate

After an arrest *without* a warrant has been made, further investigation sometimes indicates to the arresting officer that no offense actually has been committed, that the person arrested is innocent, or that the evidence is insufficient to justify making a formal charge. In these circumstances, law enforcement officers in some jurisdictions will use their own judgment in releasing arrested persons. There is little reason or justice in requiring that persons now believed innocent be held in custody until they can be taken before a magistrate.

Nevertheless, despite the obvious injustice of prolonging the detention of such persons, some courts have been slow to depart from the rule laid down in early cases, that arresting officers have no right to dispose of their prisoners other than by taking them before the nearest magistrate without unnecessary delay. Therefore, in order to protect themselves from liability, the wisest course for officers to follow when they believe a prisoner should be released is to obtain a written waiver from the prisoner. Since arrested persons have the right to go before a magistrate on the offense, they can waive that right, consent to their release, and the arresting officer is protected from any claim of damages for false arrest. It must be re-emphasized, however, that it is the arrested person's *right* to be taken before a magistrate and the officer may not release a person who insists upon being taken to court to remove any possible stigma or suspicion connected with the arrest.

EFFECT OF ILLEGAL ARREST

Although a detailed discussion is beyond the scope of this chapter, law enforcement officers should be made aware of some of the possible consequences of an illegal arrest, both to themselves and to the prosecution of the person arrested.

First, it is an almost universal rule that jurisdiction to try a person actually before the court is in no way affected by the manner in which the person was brought before the court. Therefore, the fact that one is illegally arrested is not grounds for quashing the indictment, information, or complaint brought against the person and does not preclude a trial on the charges, or affect the validity of the proceedings in any way. State v. Boynton, 143 Me. 313, 62 A.2d 182 (Supreme Judicial Court of Maine, 1948).

However, while an illegal arrest does not deprive the court of jurisdiction to try an offender, the exclusionary rule may be applicable and may affect the trial adversely. The exclusionary rule, as it relates to arrest, states that any evidence obtained by exploitation of an unlawful arrest will be inadmissible in court in a prosecution against the person arrested. Therefore, if the only evidence that the state has against an armed robbery suspect is a gun, stocking, and large roll of bills taken from the suspect's person during a search incident to an unlawful arrest, the offender will very likely go free because these items will be inadmissible in court. The exclusionary rule is discussed in detail in Chapter 3.

A confession obtained by exploitation of an illegal arrest will also be inadmissible in court. Officers cannot avoid the effect of the illegal arrest by simply giving the arrested person the *Miranda* warnings.   Other factors indicating that the confession was sufficiently an act of free will be must present.

> The *Miranda* warnings are an important factor, to be sure, in determining whether the confession is obtained by exploitation of illegal arrest.   But they are not the only factor to be considered.   The temporal proximity of the arrest and the confession, the presence of intervening circumstances,   .   .   .   and, particularly, the purpose and flagrancy of the official misconduct are all relevant.   Brown v. Illinois, 422 U.S. 590, 603–04, 95 S.Ct. 2254, 2261–62, 45 L.Ed.2d 416, 427 (U.S. Supreme Court, 1975).

The prosecution has a difficult burden in curing the effect of an illegal arrest on a subsequent confession.   In Taylor v. Alabama, 457 U.S. 687, 102 S.Ct. 2664, 73 L.Ed.2d 314 (1982), police had made an investigatory arrest without probable cause, based on an uncorroborated informant's tip, and had transported the defendant against his will to the station for interrogation in the hope that something would turn up.   The Court held that there was no meaningful intervening event to break the causal connection between the arrest and the confession, even though six hours elapsed between the arrest and the confession, the confession may have been voluntary for purposes of the Fifth Amendment in the sense that *Miranda* warnings were given and understood, the defendant was permitted a short visit with his girlfriend, and the police did not physically abuse the defendant.   Officers should always do everything possible to ensure that a confession is the product of the suspect's free will, especially when there is doubt about the legality of the arrest.

A consent search following an illegal arrest may also be declared invalid.   The Supreme Court of California stated that, " '[a] search and seizure made pursuant to consent secured immediately following an illegal entry or arrest   .   .   .   is inextricably bound up with the illegal conduct and cannot be separated therefrom.' "   People v. Johnson, 68 Cal.2d 629, 632, 68 Cal.Rptr. 441, 443, 440 P.2d 921, 923 (1968).   An identification of a defendant by a witness may be declared inadmissible in court if it is caused by or is the result of an illegal arrest.   State v. Brown, 50 Wis.2d 565, 185 N.W.2d 323 (Supreme Court of Wisconsin, 1971).   In fact, it is safe to assume that any evidence-gathering activity that follows closely upon and is closely related to an illegal arrest will result in any evidence obtained being declared inadmissible.

Another possible consequence of an unlawful arrest, mentioned throughout this chapter, is that the arresting officer can be sued for false arrest or false imprisonment.   All that is necessary to make out a case for false arrest or false imprisonment is that a person be intentionally confined or restrained of liberty or freedom of movement without legal justification.   There does not have to be any malice or bad motive on the part of the arresting officer.   As a practical matter, however, a person is more likely to go to the trouble of suing an officer who displayed ill feeling or who verbally or physically mistreated the person at the time of the illegal arrest.   Furthermore, depending upon the circumstances and the degree of force used, officers' actions in making an *unlawful* arrest may give rise to a civil suit for damages or a criminal prosecution against them for anything from assault and battery to murder, the same as any other aggressor.   In such cases, officers are not entitled to the full right of self-defense if their acts are illegal.   It should again be noted in this context that officers can be civilly and criminally liable even if the arrest is *lawful*, if they use excessive and unreasonable force in making the arrest.

SUMMARY

An arrest is the apprehension or detention of a person so that the person may be held to answer for an alleged crime. The basic elements constituting a technical arrest are (1) an intention to arrest, under real or pretended authority; (2) an actual or constructive seizure of the person to be arrested; (3) a communication by the officer of the intention to arrest; and (4) an understanding of the officer's intention by the person to be arrested. Sometimes, even though these basic elements are not all present, courts will find that an encounter between a law enforcement officer and a person entails such a significant intrusion on the person's freedom of action that it is in important respects indistinguishable from an arrest. Such an encounter, sometimes called a "seizure tantamount to arrest," must be supported by probable cause or it is illegal. The test to determine whether a seizure is tantamount to arrest is whether, in view of all the circumstances surrounding the encounter, a reasonable person would have believed that he or she was not free to leave.

Although warrantless arrests on probable cause are permitted in certain circumstances, courts always prefer arrests made under authority of an arrest warrant. An arrest warrant is a written judicial order directing a law enforcement officer to arrest a particular person. The warrant is issued by a magistrate on the basis of a complaint stating the essential facts constituting the offense charged, if the magistrate is satisfied that the offense was committed and that the person to be arrested committed it. The magistrate may also issue a summons that merely directs the defendant to appear rather than ordering an arrest.

Law enforcement officers may make a warrantless public arrest for a felony if they have probable cause to believe that a felony has been or is being committed and that the person to be arrested has committed or is committing the felony. Officers may make a warrantless public arrest for a misdemeanor, however, only if the misdemeanor was committed in their presence. A warrantless misdemeanor arrest must be made immediately, but a warrantless felony arrest may be delayed for various reasons, so long as the defendant's rights are not prejudiced by the delay.

When law enforcement officers make an arrest, they should notify the person arrested of (1) their authority; (2) their intention to arrest; and (3) the grounds for the arrest. If the arrest is made under authority of a warrant, officers should examine the warrant to make sure it is valid on its face before carrying out the commands of the warrant. When the arrest warrant is executed, officers should return the warrant as directed and explain what they have done in carrying out its commands.

Officers have no official authority to arrest without a warrant outside their bailiwick—the geographical area for which they were elected or appointed. Nevertheless, even though outside their bailiwick, they have the authority of any private citizen to arrest for "breach of the peace" misdemeanors committed in their presence and for felonies on probable cause. They may also arrest outside their bailiwick in fresh pursuit of a criminal who has fled their bailiwick, if the pursuit is begun promptly inside the bailiwick and maintained continuously.

Officers may use only the amount of force reasonably necessary under the circumstances to effect an arrest. Deadly force may be used only as a last resort and then only in specifically limited circumstances. Deadly force may never be used to accomplish an arrest for a misdemeanor. But officers may use deadly force in self defense to protect themselves from death or serious bodily injury, and officers need not abandon an attempt to arrest in the face of physical resistance to the arrest.

Officers may not enter a dwelling to arrest a person without a warrant unless there is consent or exigent circumstances. An arrest warrant is required to enter a suspect's home to arrest the suspect. A search warrant is required to enter the home of a third person to arrest a suspect. But if the arrest is begun in a public place, officers may enter a dwelling without a warrant in hot pursuit, in order to complete the arrest. Before officers may lawfully enter a dwelling forcibly to arrest a person, they must be refused admittance after knocking, announcing their authority and purpose, and demanding admittance. Failure to knock and announce is excused if an officer's purpose is already known or if knocking and announcing would cause danger to the officer, cause the escape of the suspect, or result in the loss or destruction of evidence.

Duties of the officer after the arrest is effected include the following: bringing the arrested person before a magistrate without unnecessary delay; ensuring the health and safety of the prisoner while in the officer's custody; conducting a pre-incarceration inventory search of the prisoner, which may include the search and seizure of any container or object in the prisoner's possession; and conducting identification procedures, including fingerprinting, photographing, physical examinations, and lineups.

Although an illegal arrest will not affect the jurisdiction of the court to try a person, any evidence obtained by exploitation of an illegal arrest will be inadmissible in a criminal proceeding against the defendant. Also, the law enforcement officer may be liable both civilly and criminally for making an illegal arrest or for using excessive force.

REVIEW AND DISCUSSION QUESTIONS

1. Is it possible to technically arrest an insane or extremely mentally retarded person? Explain.

2. Name several ways in which a law enforcement officer or officers can prevent a routine encounter with a person on the street from being considered a seizure tantamount to arrest.

3. Give three practical reasons why a law enforcement officer should obtain an arrest warrant if possible.

4. How is the law enforcement officer's authority to arrest affected by time?

5. Is it valid to say that if an officer has strong probable cause to arrest someone, the officer may arrest the person anywhere in the country? Explain.

6. Under what circumstances may a law enforcement officer use deadly force, and what are the potential consequences of an illegal use of deadly force? Name several circumstances under which little or no force should be used to make an arrest.

7. Do law enforcement officers have a broader right of self-defense when they are assaulted while making an arrest than when they are assaulted while simply walking or cruising their beat?

8. Assume that a law enforcement officer has probable cause to arrest the defendant for armed assault and probable cause to believe that the person is hiding in a third person's garage, which is attached to the house. What warrants, if any, does the officer need to enter the garage to arrest the defendant? What if the officer was in "hot pursuit" of the defendant? What if the defendant is known to be injured and unarmed?

9. Give reasons to support an argument that a law enforcement officer should never have to knock and announce before entering a dwelling to arrest a dangerous felon or a drug offender.

10. If a law enforcement officer has probable cause to arrest, does the officer have to make an arrest? If not, what alternatives to arrest are available and under what circumstances should they be used?

5

Search Warrants

Like the law of arrest, the law governing search warrants is based upon guarantees embodied in the United States Constitution. As a point of departure for the discussion of search warrants, the Fourth Amendment to the Constitution will be quoted again in full:

> The right of the people to be secure in their persons, houses, papers and effects, against unreasonable searches and seizures, shall not be violated, and no Warrants shall issue, but upon probable cause, supported by Oath or affirmation, and particularly describing the place to be searched and the persons or things to be seized.

Whereas, in the foregoing chapter on arrest, the main concern was the *seizure* of the *person,* the discussion of search warrants will be concerned with a broader array of matters including the search of persons *and* places and the seizure of a variety of things. The U.S. Supreme Court definitions of "search" and "seizure," set out in Chapter 3, will be repeated here for emphasis.

> A "search" occurs when an expectation of privacy that society is prepared to consider reasonable is infringed. A "seizure" of property occurs when there is some meaningful interference with an individual's possessory interests in that property. United States v. Jacobsen, ___ U.S. ___, ___, 104 S.Ct. 1652, 1656, 80 L.Ed.2d 85, 94 (1984).

Probable cause, which is a common aspect of both arrest and search and seizure law, will be discussed in detail in Chapter 6.

HISTORY

The Fourth Amendment to the United States Constitution was adopted in response to abuses of governmental search and seizure authority originating in England in the seventeenth and eighteenth centuries. The early development of legally authorized searches and seizures under English common law is somewhat obscure. It appears that search warrants were first used in cases involving stolen property. Their use to recapture stolen goods became widespread and increasing violative of citizens' privacy. Eventually, warrants were extended to the enforcement of other laws. For example, in the eighteenth century the government issued general warrants to enforce the strict libel laws. A general warrant is one which fails to specify the person or place to be searched or the person or item to be seized, and which leaves the time and manner of the search to the discretion of the searching officer. These general warrants were abused by law enforcement officers and soon no person or property was free from unlimited search conducted at the whim of an officer on the mere suspicion that the person possessed literature critical of the king or of others in high places.

Despite their unpopularity with the citizenry, these abusive practices were transplanted to the American colonies. In mid-eighteenth century, Parliament enacted legislation authorizing general searches, called writs of assistance, to be conducted against the colonists to enforce the Trade Acts. Writs of assistance authorized royal customs officers to search houses and ships at will in order to discover and seize smuggled goods or goods on which the required duties had not been paid. The reaction of the colonists against the writs of assistance was strong and was one of the major causes of the American Revolution. As stated in the 1886 United States Supreme Court case of Boyd v. U.S.:

> The practice had obtained in the colonies of issuing writs of assistance to the revenue officers, empowering them, in their discretion, to search suspected places for smuggled goods, which James Otis pronounced "the worst instrument of arbitrary power, the most destructive of English liberty and the fundamental principles of law, that ever was found in an English law book;" since they placed "the liberty of every man in the hands of every petty officer." This was in February, 1761, in Boston, and the famous debate in which it occurred was perhaps the most prominent event which inaugurated the resistance of the colonies to the oppressions of the mother country. "Then and there," said John Adams, "then and there was the first scene of the first act of opposition to the arbitrary claims of Great Britain. Then and there the child of Independence was born." 116 U.S. 616, 625, 6 S.Ct. 524, 528–29, 29 L.Ed. 746, 749.

The experiences of our founding fathers with general warrants and writs of assistance caused them to insist upon including in the basic charters of the states and of the nation suitable guarantees against unreasonable searches and seizures. A prohibition against searches conducted at the whim of a law enforcement officer without any restrictions on the person or place to be searched or the person or item to be seized was first embodied in the Virginia Bill of Rights adopted in 1776. By the close of the Revolutionary War, most of the states had adopted similar provisions. The present Fourth Amendment to the United States Constitution, with its emphasis on the protection of warrants issued upon probable cause, was included in the Bill of Rights in 1791. Today, the constitution of every state in the Union contains a similar provision.

DEFINITION

The discussion of search warrants begins with a clear definition. A search warrant is (1) an order in writing; (2) issued by a proper judicial authority; (3) in the name of the people; (4) directed to a law enforcement officer; (5) commanding the officer to search for certain personal property; and (6) bring it before the judicial authority named in the warrant. In many of its aspects, the search warrant is substantially the same as an arrest warrant, which, in effect, is an order to take a *person* into custody and bring the person before the proper judicial authority. Throughout the course of this discussion, the terms of the above definition will be clarified and important relationships between search warrants and arrest warrants will be highlighted.

OBTAINING A SEARCH WARRANT

Law enforcement officers wishing to obtain a search warrant must follow proper procedures in applying for the warrant. If they do not, the warrant may not be issued or, if issued, may later be declared invalid, resulting in lost evidence and very likely a lost case. Search warrant procedures differ from state to state and are found in various statutes, rules, and court decisions. The procedures common to most states will be summarized and discussed in this chapter.

Who May Issue Search Warrants

The only persons who may issue search warrants are those judicial officers who have been specifically authorized to do so. Most states have laws that give this authority to such officers as clerks of court, magistrates, complaint justices, justices of the peace, and judges. All law enforcement officers should know which judicial officers are authorized to issue search warrants in their state. These judicial officers may not be the same as those authorized to issue arrest warrants. A search warrant issued by an officer without authority is of no legal effect, and a search made pursuant to such a warrant is unlawful. For convenience, the term "magistrate" will be used throughout the rest of this chapter to designate an official authorized to issue search warrants.

Grounds for Issuance

Before issuing a search warrant, the magistrate must have probable cause to believe that items subject to seizure are in a particular place or on a particular person at the time of the issuance of the warrant. It is the duty of law enforcement officers to provide the magistrate with the information upon which probable cause is to be based. Officers do this in their application for a search warrant by means of an affidavit, which must be supported by oath or affirmation. An affidavit is merely a written declaration or statement of facts sworn to before the magistrate. An example of a typical affidavit form appears on page 112.

Officers should note that if they knowingly and intentionally, or with reckless disregard for the truth, make false statements in an affidavit supporting a request for a search warrant, the warrant may not issue or evidence seized pursuant to the

Form A. O. 106 (Rev. Apr. 1973)

Affidavit for
Search Warrant

United States District Court

FOR THE

_____

UNITED STATES OF AMERICA

vs.

Docket No._____

Case No._____

AFFIDAVIT FOR
SEARCH WARRANT

BEFORE

Name of Judge¹ or Federal Magistrate

Address of Judge¹ or Federal Magistrate

The undersigned being duly sworn deposes and says:

That he has reason to believe that (on the person of)
(on the premises known as)

in the   District of

there is now being concealed certain property, namely

here describe property

which are

here give alleged grounds for search and seizure²

And that the facts tending to establish the foregoing grounds for issuance of a Search Warrant are as follows:³

- ,
Signature of Affiant.

- ,
Official Title, if any.

Sworn to before me, and subscribed in my presence,   , 19

- ,
Judge¹ or Federal Magistrate.

¹United States Judge or Judge of a State Court of Record.
²If a search is to be authorized "at any time in the day or night" pursuant to Rule 41(c), show reasonable cause therefor.
³If the warrant is to authorize execution pursuant to 21 U.S.C. § 879 without prior notice of authority or purpose, indicate the circumstances creating the need for such a warrant.

FPI LC 12-10-73 120M 7858

warrant may be suppressed.   In Franks v. Delaware, 438 U.S. 154, 98 S.Ct. 2674, 57 L.Ed.2d 667 (1978), the United States Supreme Court held that a defendant may challenge the veracity of an affidavit used by the police to procure a search warrant.   The Court said:

> [W]here the defendant makes a substantial preliminary showing that a false state-ment knowingly and intentionally, or with reckless disregard for the truth, was included by the affiant in the warrant affidavit, and if the allegedly false statement is necessary to the finding of probable cause, the Fourth Amendment requires that a hearing be held at the defendant's request.   In the event that at the hearing the allegation of perjury or reckless disregard is established by the defendant by a preponderance of the evidence, and, with the affidavit's false material set to one side, the affidavit's remaining content is insufficient to establish probable cause, the search warrant must be voided and the fruits of the search excluded to the same extent as if probable cause was lacking on the face of the affidavit.   438 U.S. at 155–56, 98 S.Ct. at 2676–77, 57 L.Ed.2d at 672.

The following discussion will cover in detail the information that must be presented to enable the magistrate to issue a search warrant.

Probable Cause   Some states require that the sworn affidavit contain *all* the information upon which the magistrate is to base a finding of probable cause to issue a search warrant.   State v. Case, 363 So.2d 486 (Louisiana Supreme Court, 1978).   Other states allow supplementation of a defective affidavit by sworn oral testimony given before the magistrate.   State v. Hendricks, 328 N.E.2d 822 (Ohio Supreme Court, 1974).   A small minority of states permit issuance of search warrants over the telephone.   These states require that the information telephoned by the affiant to the magistrate be taken under oath and be recorded.   Regardless of state law, it is strongly suggested that, when possible, officers include *all* the information upon which probable cause is to be based in the affidavit.   Writing the information down forces the officer to think carefully about the case.   Often, officers may realize that their information is too weak to support a finding of probable cause, and they may save themselves and the magistrate a great deal of time and trouble by not presenting the information.   On the other hand, officers may discover leads on how to further develop weak evidence until it is sufficient to support a finding of probable cause.   Also, when all the information upon which probable cause is based is contained in the affidavit, a complete record is made available later to a court reviewing the decision of the magistrate, upon a motion to suppress evidence or on an appeal.   For these reasons, and for ease of presentation, the remainder of this chapter will speak of the affidavit as the only vehicle for presenting information to the magistrate to obtain a search warrant.

The affidavit should indicate to the magistrate (1) that a criminal offense has been or is being committed and (2) that seizable evidence relating to that offense is in a particular place at a particular time.   The amount of proof required to convince the magistrate to issue the search warrant is essentially the same as that required for the issuance of an arrest warrant or that which is required before an officer may arrest without a warrant for a felony.   The constitutional term used to describe this amount of proof is "probable cause."   Probable cause has been discussed in Chapter 3 and will be discussed in further detail in Chapter 6.   For purposes of this chapter, officers applying for a search warrant should remember that they must state in the affidavit the underlying facts and circumstances upon which probable cause is based. An officer's mere conclusions, beliefs, or opinions will not suffice to establish probable cause.

It is useful, at this point, to point out two important differences between arrest and search with respect to probable cause. First, probable cause to search and probable cause to arrest will usually arise out of different sets of facts. In order to find probable cause to arrest, the magistrate must find sufficient facts to show that an offense was committed and that a particular suspect committed it. Probable cause to search, on the other hand, turns on facts tending to show that particular items are connected with criminal activity and that they will be found in a particular place. Therefore, the same set of facts and circumstances might provide probable cause to arrest, but not probable cause to search, and vice versa.

Another difference between probable cause to arrest and probable cause to search is that time is a very important factor in determining probable cause to search. The items to be seized must be in the place or on the person to be searched at the time the application for a search warrant is made or, in the case of a warrantless search, at the time the search is executed. If too long a time passes between the time when the information upon which probable cause is based is gathered and execution of the search, there may no longer be good reason to believe that the property is still at the same location. Probable cause is said to be "stale" in such situations.

The length of time that an item of property is likely to remain at a given location depends upon the nature of the property, the nature of the criminal activity, the duration of the criminal activity, the criminal suspects, and many other factors. For example, in State v. Willey, Me., 363 A.2d 739 (Supreme Judicial Court of Maine, 1976), the court held that the fact that the informant had made three purchases of marijuana in one week from the defendant was insufficient to justify the conclusion that thirty-one days after the last purchase, marijuana was still at defendant's premises. In cases involving evidence that is likely to disappear or be moved, therefore, officers should apply for a warrant or conduct a warrantless search (in the proper circumstances) as soon as possible. If the items sought are not likely to disappear or be moved, like business records of an illegal real estate scheme, for example, the records will probably remain at their location for an extended period of time after the business transactions have taken place. The U.S. Supreme Court said:

> The business records sought were prepared in the ordinary course of petitioner's business in his law office or that of his real estate corporation. It is eminently reasonable to expect that such records would be maintained in those offices for a period of time and surely as long as the three months required for the investigation of a complex real estate scheme. Andresen v. Maryland, 427 U.S. 463, 479, n. 9, 96 S.Ct. 2737, 2747, n. 9, 49 L.Ed.2d 627, 641, n. 9 (1976).

Another court held that an affidavit stating that hand grenades had been observed at the defendant's residence within the past thirty days was not insufficient because of stale probable cause. The court said that "[u]nlike many other items of contraband, hand grenades are not, to the best of our knowledge, in great demand even by the criminal element in our society; and they do not lend themselves to rapid disposition in the marketplace." U.S. v. Dauphinee, 538 F.2d 1 (1st Circuit Court of Appeals, 1976).

Items Subject to Seizure   Most states have laws stating that a warrant may be issued to search for and seize certain types of property. Although these laws differ in many respects, the following list is typical of the types of property allowed to be seized:

1. Property stolen or embezzled; or

2. Property designed or intended for use or which is or has been used as a means of committing a criminal offense (instrumentalities); or

3. Property, the possession of which is unlawful (contraband); or

4. Property consisting of nontestimonial evidence that will aid in a particular apprehension or conviction.

The first three listed types of property should be self-explanatory. The fourth may need some discussion. This fourth type of property is sometimes called "mere evidence." Examples of mere evidence might be items of clothing, shoes, or business records. "Mere evidence" was added to the list by many states in accordance with the U.S. Supreme Court decision in 1967 in the case of Warden v. Hayden, 387 U.S. 294, 87 S.Ct. 1642, 18 L.Ed.2d 782 (1967). That decision did away with the previous proposition that search warrants could not be used as a means of gaining access to a person's house or office and papers solely for the purpose of making search to secure mere evidence to be used against the person in a criminal proceeding. Nevertheless, even though mere evidence may now be seized, certain limitations are placed on its seizure.

One of these limitations is that the evidence to be seized must be nontestimonial. This requirement protects individuals from being compelled to be witnesses against themselves in violation of their Fifth Amendment rights. It was widely thought that private personal papers and business records could not be seized under this limitation because of their testimonial nature. The U.S. Supreme Court held, however, that a seizure of personal papers or business records from persons under a search warrant does not necessarily compel those persons to be witnesses against themselves. Andresen v. Maryland, 427 U.S. 463, 96 S.Ct. 2737, 49 L.Ed.2d 627 (1976). In the *Andresen* case, the Court quoted an earlier case stating that " 'a party is privileged from producing the evidence, but not from its production.' " 427 U.S. at 473, 96 S.Ct. at 2745, 49 L.Ed.2d at 638. The Court held that the defendant in the *Andresen* case was not compelled to be a witness against himself because he was not required to say or to do anything during the search. If law enforcement authorities had attempted to subpoena the records, however, the defendant could have refused to give up the records by exercising his Fifth Amendment rights. The Court said:

> [A]lthough the Fifth Amendment may protect an individual from complying with a subpoena for the production of his personal records in his possession because the very act of production may constitute a compulsory authentication of

incriminating information, . . . a seizure of the same materials by law enforcement officers differs in a crucial respect—the individual against whom the search is directed is not required to aid in the discovery, production, or authentication of incriminating evidence. 427 U.S. at 473–74, 96 S.Ct. at 2745, 49 L.Ed.2d at 638.

Individuals have even less protection against production of their bank records. The U.S. Supreme Court, in United States v. Miller, 425 U.S. 435, 96 S.Ct. 1619, 48 L.Ed.2d 71 (1976), held that a person's bank records are not private papers of the kind protected against compulsory production by the Fifth Amendment. By choosing to deal with a bank, people lose their expectation of Fourth Amendment protection against government investigation:

> "The checks are not confidential communications but negotiable instruments to be used in commercial transactions. All of the documents obtained, including financial statements and deposit slips, contain only information voluntarily conveyed to the banks and exposed to their employees in the ordinary course of business. 425 U.S. at 442, 96 S.Ct. at 1624, 48 L.Ed.2d at 79.

Although the *Miller* case concerned a subpoena, either a search warrant or subpoena could be used to obtain a person's bank records without violating the person's Fifth Amendment right against compulsory self-incrimination.

Both the *Andresen* and *Miller* cases serve to highlight a basic principle regarding the obtaining of papers as evidence in criminal cases: "There is no special sanctity in papers, as distinguished from other forms of property, to render them immune from search and seizure, if only they fall within the scope of the principles of the cases in which other property may be seized, and if they be adequately described in the affidavit and warrant." Gouled v. United States, 255 U.S. 298, 309, 41 S.Ct. 261, 265, 65 L.Ed. 647, 652 (1921). Nevertheless, officers seizing items such as business records or personal papers under a warrant should refrain from requiring the defendant to assist them in any way. Otherwise the evidence may be suppressed in court because it was seized in violation of the defendant's Fifth Amendment rights.

The other limitation on the seizure of mere evidence is that the evidence to be seized must aid in a particular apprehension or conviction. The reason for this second requirement was stated by the United States Supreme Court:

> The requirements of the Fourth Amendment can secure the same protection of privacy whether the search is for "mere evidence" or for fruits, instrumentalities or contraband. There must of course be a nexus—automatically provided in the case of fruits, instrumentalities or contraband—between the item to be seized and criminal behavior. Thus in the case of "mere evidence," probable cause must be examined in terms of cause to believe that the evidence sought will aid in a particular apprehension or conviction. In doing so, consideration of police purposes will be served. Warden v. Hayden, 387 U.S. 294, 306–07, 87 S.Ct. 1642, 1650, 18 L.Ed.2d 782, 792 (1967).

Law enforcement officers should indicate in every affidavit for a search warrant that the property they wish to seize falls within one of the types of property listed above or listed in their particular state's law defining items subject to seizure. It is good practice to describe the property in the terms of the particular state law.

Particular Description of Place or Person   The affidavit for a search warrant for a place must contain a description of the premises to be searched that points directly to a definitely ascertainable place to the exclusion of all others. The U.S. Supreme Court stated that "[i]t is enough if the description is such that the officer with a search warrant can with reasonable effort ascertain and identify the place intended." Steele v. United States, 267 U.S. 498, 503, 45 S.Ct. 414, 416, 69 L.Ed. 757, 760 (1925).

A street address is usually sufficient to identify premises in an urban area. In State v. Brochu, 237 A.2d 418 (Supreme Judicial Court of Maine, 1967), the property to be searched was described as "the premises known as the dwelling of Armand A. Brochu located at 20 Forest Street, in the City/Town of Biddeford, County of York and State of Maine, said premises being owned/occupied by Armand A. Brochu." The court held that no one could have been misled by the description of the premises in the warrant. Furthermore the description was held to cover not only the dwelling house but also the garage and any other buildings generally associated with and included within a house or home.

It is more difficult to particularly describe the location of rural property, but there is also less chance that an error will be made in locating a particular piece of rural property. Therefore, a description of a farm or other rural property by the name of the owner and general directions will usually suffice. Gatlin v. State, 262 Ark. 485, 559 S.W.2d 12 (Supreme Court of Arkansas, 1977).

When the place to be searched is a multiple-occupancy dwelling such as an apartment house, hotel, or rooming house, the affidavit must go beyond merely stating the location of the premises. In an illustrative case, the affidavit upon which the warrant was based read as follows: "Place to be searched: 313 West 27th Street, a dwelling. The apartment of Melvin Lloyd Manley." The defendant objected to the search on the ground that the apartment to be searched was not sufficiently described in the affidavit and warrant.

The court held that the defendant's apartment was sufficiently described for the searching officers to locate it with very little effort:

> It has been generally held that a search warrant directed against a multiple-occupancy structure is invalid if it fails to describe the particular sub-unit to be searched with sufficient definiteness to preclude search of other units located in the larger structure and occupied by innocent persons. But there are exceptions to the general rule. Even though a search warrant against a multiple-occupancy structure fails to describe the particular sub-unit to be searched, it will ordinarily not be held invalid where it adequately specifies the name of the occupant of the sub-unit against which it is directed and provides the searching officers with sufficient information to identify, without confusion or excessive effort, such apartment unit. Manley v. Commonwealth, 211 Va. 146, 151–52, 176 S.E.2d 309, 314 (Supreme Court of Virginia, 1970).

Whenever possible, however, information like room number, apartment number, or floor should be included in the affidavit. If necessary, a diagram showing the location should be made and attached to the affidavit.

The above cases serve to emphasize the importance of including in the affidavit the *name* of the person who owns or occupies the premises to be searched. In some states, if the owner or occupant of the premises is known to the officer applying for a search warrant, it *must* be included in the description of premises in the affidavit.

In another case involving a multiple-occupancy dwelling, the description in the warrant of the place to be searched (a four-building apartment complex) gave a wrong street address but correctly stated the apartment number. Since there was only one apartment with that number in the entire complex, the court held that the description was sufficient:

> [T]he determining factor as to whether a search warrant describes the premises to be searched with sufficient particularity is not whether the description is technically accurate in every detail but rather whether the description is sufficient to enable the executing officer to locate and identify the premises with reasonable effort, and whether there is any reasonable probability that another premises might be mistakenly searched which is not the one intended to be searched under the search warrant. United States v. Darensbourg, 520 F.2d 985, 987 (5th Circuit Court of Appeals, 1975).

A search warrant may also issue for the search of a person. Again, the standard for determining the validity of a warrant to search an individual's person is whether it describes the individual to be searched with sufficient particularity to enable identification with reasonable certainty. Courts have held that even though a person's name is unknown or incorrectly stated, the warrant may still be valid if a description of the person is included. United States v. Ferrone, 438 F.2d 381 (3rd Circuit Court of Appeals, 1971). Therefore, it is advisable for the law enforcement officer, when applying for a warrant for the search of a person, to state not only the person's name, if known, but also a complete description including weight, height, age, race, clothing, address, and any aliases. State v. Tramantano, 28 Conn.Supp. 325, 260 A.2d 128 (Superior Court of Connecticut, 1969). That way, if the name in the affidavit is incorrect, there is still backup information to enable the person to be identified.

When the search of a person for evidence requires surgery (such as a search for a bullet embedded in the skin) officers may be required to provide additional information in the affidavit to justify the issuance of a warrant. Officers should present medical opinions of more than one doctor that the removal of the evidence will constitute substantially no risk to the patient. Officers should also provide information in the affidavit that the offense is serious, such as murder or armed robbery; that the evidence sought is relevant and material; that there is probable cause that the surgery will produce the evidence; and that the evidence can be obtained in no other way. Some courts require, in addition to the information in the affidavit, an adversary hearing, at which the defendant is represented by counsel, and an opportunity for the defendant to appeal the order directing the surgery. United States v. Crowder, 177 U.S.App.D.C. 165, 543 F.2d 312 (District of Columbia Circuit Court of Appeals, 1976).

Although the U.S. Supreme Court has established exceptions to the warrant requirement allowing warrantless searches of motor vehicles under certain circumstances, the basic rule remains that a warrant is required for the search of a motor vehicle. Since vehicles are considered *places* for search and seizure purposes, the affidavit is required to contain a description of the vehicle to be searched sufficiently particular so that it can be located with reasonable certainty. Some courts have held that only the license place number is necessary to sufficiently describe a motor vehicle for purposes of issuance of a warrant. Bowling v. State, 219 Tenn. 224, 408 S.W.2d 660 (Supreme Court of Tennessee, 1966). License plates, however, can be easily removed or replaced. Therefore, when other information about the vehicle is known, it should be included in the affidavit. Such other information, for instance, would be the make, body style, color, year, location, and owner or operator of the vehicle.

Mail may also be considered a *place* for search and seizure purposes. Courts have ruled that first class domestic mail may not be lawfully opened without a warrant. (Domestic mail is any letter or package traveling wholly within the United States.) Law enforcement officers, therefore, must follow the same procedures to obtain a warrant to search first class mail as to search places, persons, and vehicles.

A problem arises in describing the place to be searched when a search warrant is sought to install a beeper, because the location of the place is precisely what is sought to be discovered through the search. The U.S. Supreme Court responded to this issue as follows:

> [I]t will still be possible to describe the object into which the beeper is to be placed, the circumstances that led agents to wish to install the beeper, and the length of time for which beeper surveillance is requested. In our view, this information will suffice to permit issuance of a warrant authorizing beeper installation and surveillance. United States v. Karo, ___ U.S. ___, ___, 104 S.Ct. 3296, 3305, 82 L.Ed.2d 530, 543 (1984).

Particular Description of Things   Besides a particular description of the place to be searched, the affidavit for a search warrant must contain a particular description of the items to be seized. In general, the items to be seized must be described with sufficient particularity so that the officer executing the warrant (1) can identify the items with reasonable certainty, and (2) is left with no discretion as to which property is to be taken.

Therefore, a description of items merely as "stolen goods," "obscene materials," or "other articles of merchandise too numerous to mention," for instance, would be inadequate. Marcus v. Search Warrant, 367 U.S. 717, 81 S.Ct. 1708, 6 L.Ed.2d 1127 (U.S. Supreme Court, 1961). When an item can be described in detail, all available information about it should be included in the affidavit. For example, number, size, color, weight, condition, brand name, and other distinguishing features of items to be seized should be a part of the description where applicable. Also, as mentioned earlier, officers should indicate why the item of property is subject to seizure.

Often, the nature of the property will give some indication as to how detailed a description is necessary. For example, a court upheld the sufficiency of a warrant which authorized a search for:

> "certain items of property, to-wit:
> "Various instruments and tools used in performing abortion, which were instrumentalities of such offense . . . ."

The court reasoned that because of the unusual nature of the items to be seized, they were described with reasonable particularity in the warrant. A technical identification or description would have required the experience of a trained surgeon. State v. Brown, 205 Kan. 457, 462–63, 470 P.2d 815, 819–20 (Supreme Court of Kansas, 1970).

If it is impossible to describe the items to be seized in detail in the affidavit because of the common nature and nonuniqueness of the items, a general description may suffice. A general description should be accompanied, however, by strong evidence that the items to be seized at a particular place are the actual items that offend against the law, and by evidence that the seizable items cannot be differentiated from similar innocent items. For example, in United States v. Scharfman, 448 F.2d 1352 (2d Circuit Court of Appeals, 1971), a shipment containing hundreds of furs had been hijacked. The F.B.I. applied for a warrant to search the defendant's fur store for "fur coats, stoles, jackets and other finished fur products . . . ." 448 F.2d at 1353 n. 1. The court upheld the general description in the warrant because the affidavit stated that an informant experienced in the fur trade and an employee of the fur shipment's owner had informed the F.B.I. that furs from the shipment were in the defendant's store. The court concluded from these facts that there was a reasonable likelihood that a large collection of similar stolen furs was in the defendant's store.

The primary concern of courts in evaluating descriptions of property in affidavits is to ensure that a person will not be deprived of lawfully possessed property by a seizure made in pursuance of an imprecise search warrant. Even though there is reason to believe that a large collection of similar seizable items are located in a particular place, it may be possible to distinguish the seizable items from similar non-seizable items. An officer applying for a search warrant in this situation must explain in the affidavit the method by which the seizable property can be differentiated from similar innocent property when the warrant is executed. United States v. Klein, 565 F.2d 183 (1st Circuit Court of Appeals, 1977). Otherwise, either the warrant will not issue, or it will be declared invalid on appeal.

In a case involving several different items of property, the items to be seized were described in the warrant as follows:

> one electric heater, one orange colored ice jug, 16 gauge shotgun shells, 22 shells, and so forth . . .

The court held that this language was specific enough:

> We think, as did the trial judge, that these items were about as particularly described as such commodities can be. Such merchandise is difficult to describe. It may be said that the heater should be described as a "G.E." or a "Westinghouse", it could also be argued there are thousands of Westinghouse heaters. Shotgun shells might be described as Remington, Western, or Winchester or by the name of the manufacturers, still it could be argued there are untold numbers of Winchester, Remington, or "Peters" shotgun shells 12's, 16's and 20's. Poole v. State, 4 Tenn. Cr.App. 41, 54, 467 S.W.2d 826, 832 (Court of Criminal Appeals of Tennessee, 1971).

The description in the above case is probably about as general as it could be without being declared insufficient. If the officer knows the brand names and any other pertinent information, they should be included in the affidavit just to be safe.

Courts will generally allow greater leeway in descriptions of contraband material. Thus, a description merely of "paraphernalia for making coins," "heroin," or "narcotics drugs" will be adequate. The reason for this is that the purpose of the warrant is not to seize specified property but only property of a specified character that by reason of its character is contraband. People v. Schmidt, 172 Colo. 285, 473 P.2d 698 (Colorado Supreme Court, 1970).

This relaxation of the requirement of particularity does not apply, however, if the items to be searched for or seized are books, films, recordings, or other materials that have not yet been adjudged obscene. Since these materials are presumed protected by the First Amendment, a very high degree of particularity is required in both the affidavit and the warrant. As the U.S. Supreme Court stated: "[T]he constitutional requirement that warrants must particularly describe the 'things to be seized' is to be accorded the most scrupulous exactitude when the 'things' are books, and the basis for their seizure is the ideas which they contain." Stanford v. Texas, 379 U.S. 476, 485, 85 S.Ct. 506, 511–12, 13 L.Ed.2d 431, 437 (1965). Therefore, in a case in which a magistrate viewed two films from the defendant's "adult" book store, concluded they were obscene, and issued a warrant authorizing the seizure of all other obscene materials, the U.S. Supreme Court held that the warrant was a prohibited general warrant:

> "[T]he search left it entirely to the discretion of the officials conducting the search to decide what items were likely obscene and to accomplish their seizure . . . .
> Nor does the Fourth Amendment countenance open-ended warrants, to be completed while a seizure is being conducted and items seized or after the seizure has been carried out. Lo-Ji Sales, Inc. v. New York, 442 U.S. 319, 325, 99 S.Ct. 2319, 2324, 60 L.Ed.2d 920, 927–28 (1979).

An officer presented with such an open-ended warrant should consult with a local prosecuting attorney before executing the warrant.

Multiple Affidavits Often a law enforcement officer applying for a search warrant will submit more than one affidavit to the magistrate. The additional or supplemental affidavits may be prepared by the officer or by someone else. The Maine Supreme Judicial Court said:

> Since the object of the proceedings before the magistrate is to establish probable cause to justify issuance of a search warrant, law enforcement officers should not be hindered in their efforts to describe the basis for probable cause in supporting affidavits. So long as these affidavits are satisfactorily incorporated to all related documents necessary to the application for the warrant . . . the reviewing court will be assured of the simultaneous presence of these documents before the magistrate, and the search may be subjected to authoritative judicial review. State v. Gamage, 340 A.2d 1, 7 (1975).

The main concern of the officer applying for a search warrant by means of more than one affidavit is to ensure that all "affidavits are satisfactorily incorporated to all related documents necessary to the application for the warrant." The following procedure is suggested to ensure proper incorporation:

1. Entitle the first or primary affidavit AFFIDAVIT AND REQUEST FOR SEARCH WARRANT.

2. Entitle all additional affidavits SUPPLEMENTAL AFFIDAVIT 1, SUPPLEMEN-TAL AFFIDAVIT 2, and so forth.

3. Include the following statement in the first or primary affidavit: "This request is also based upon the information in the sworn statements in SUPPLEMENTAL AFFIDAVIT 1, SUPPLEMENTAL AFFIDAVIT 2, . . . which are attached." (The law requires that clear reference be made to all supplemental affidavits.)

4. Securely attach all supplemental affidavits to the primary affidavit. Use a stapler or other semipermanent method of binding. A paper clip would be unsatisfactory because of its tendency to slip off. By following these simple steps, the officer ensures that the magistrate will be simultaneously presented with all the information upon which probable cause is to be based and that the appellate court will be able to effectively review the magistrate's decision.

Securing of Dwelling While Warrant Is Being Sought

When officers have probable cause to believe that evidence of criminal activity is in a dwelling, the temporary securing of the dwelling to prevent removal or destruction of evidence while a search warrant is being sought is not an unreasonable seizure of either the dwelling or its contents. The U.S. Supreme Court said:

> [T]he home is sacred in Fourth Amendment terms not primarily because of the occupants' *possessory* interests in the premises, but because of their *privacy* interests in the activities that take place within. .   .   .   [A] seizure affects only possessory interests, not privacy interests. Therefore, the heightened protection we accord privacy interests is simply not implicated where a *seizure* of premises, not a search, is at issue. Segura v. United States, ___ U.S. ___, ___, 104 S.Ct. 3380, 3389, 82 L.Ed.2d 599, 612 (1984).

Furthermore, the Court, in the *Segura* case said that insofar as the *seizure* of the premises is concerned, it made no difference whether the premises were secured by stationing officers within the premises or by establishing a perimeter "stakeout" after a security check of the premises revealed that no one was inside. And even if the initial entry into the premises were illegal, that illegality would not affect the reasonableness of the *seizure* of the premises and would not render a subsequently obtained warrant invalid, so long as there was a source of probable cause independent of the illegal entry to support the warrant. (See Chapter 3 for a discussion of the "independent source" exception to the exclusionary rule.) In other words, the initial entry—legal or not—does not affect the reasonableness of the seizure of the premises. Under either method—entry and securing from within or a perimeter stakeout—officers control the premises pending arrival of the warrant. Both an internal securing and a perimeter stakeout interfere to the same extent with the possessory interests of the owners.

Anticipatory Search Warrants

An "anticipatory" search warrant, also called a "prospective" search warrant, is a search warrant issued to search a particular place, container, or person for a particular seizable item that has not yet arrived at the place where the search is to be executed.   In recent years law enforcement officers have applied for anticipatory search warrants in increasing numbers, especially in cases involving contraband in the mails and in cases involving informants or undercover officers.   A leading case in this area is People v. Glen, 30 N.Y.2d 252, 331 N.Y.S.2d 656, 282 N.E.2d 614 (Court of Appeals of New York, 1972).   In that case law enforcement officers applied for a warrant to search a package allegedly containing narcotics.   The affidavit stated that the package was consigned to the defendant, a known drug user, and that it was due to arrive at a Greyhound Bus Depot.   The affidavit added that the defendant had called for the package earlier that morning, but it had not yet arrived.   The information in the affidavit was based on a tip from an informant whose reliability was adequately demonstrated.   The warrant issued and shortly thereafter the officers were advised by a Greyhound clerk that the package had arrived.   When the package went uncalled for that day, the officers removed it and examined it, finding marijuana.   They returned the package to the depot the next morning.   Later that day the defendant accepted delivery of the package and was arrested while leaving the depot.

The defendant contended on appeal that the warrant was invalid because no crime had been committed prior to its issuance and because there was no present and continuing possession of the contraband at the time of issuance.   The court said:

> The ultimate answer to the problem is that as long as the evidence creates substantial probability that the seizable property will be on the premises when searched, the warrant should be sustained.   To be sure, where there is no present possession the supporting evidence for the prospective warrant must be strong that the particular possession of particular property will occur and that the elements to bring about that possession are in process and will result in the possession at the time and place specified.   Otherwise, the hated general writs of assistance of pre-Revolutionary times would be revived, in effect, despite the constitutional limitations.   Moreover, the issuing Judge should be satisfied that there is no likelihood that the warrant will be executed prematurely.   30 N.Y.2d at 259, 331 N.Y.S.2d at 661, 282 N.E.2d at 617.

Law enforcement officers applying for anticipatory search warrants should take special care to satisfy the requirement that the elements to bring about the possession or presence of particular property at a particular time and place are in process, and they should state these elements in detail in the affidavit.   A search warrant was held invalid in State v. Vitale, 23 Ariz.App. 37, 530 P.2d 394 (Court of Appeals in Arizona, 1975), because of failure to satisfy that requirement.   In that case, a warrant to search the defendant's pawn shop was issued on the basis that a reliable informant had agreed to sell a stolen television set to the defendant at the pawn shop.   The police had the television in their possession at the time they applied for the warrant.   After the sale, the warrant was executed and the television was seized.

The defendant contended that the search warrant was invalid. The court agreed, stating that there was no probable cause that a crime had been committed at the time the warrant was issued. The court said:

> The informant had not yet approached appellant regarding the television set at the time the . . . search warrant was issued; also there had not been any recent dealings between the informant and appellant.
>
> * * *
>
> In the instant case, no crime was in progress and it was a matter of speculation whether one would be committed in the future. The course of events strongly suggests that the duty to determine probable cause was improperly shifted from the magistrate to the police. 23 Ariz.App. at 40–41, 530 P.2d at 397–98.

The quoted material suggests that, if there had been some deal or arrangement between the informant and the defendant before the police applied for the warrant, the court might have found the warrant valid on the ground that a crime was in progress or at least was very likely to occur.

In order to ensure that the magistrate is provided with sufficient information to justify the issuance of an anticipatory search warrant, law enforcement officers should present strong evidence in the affidavit that the continuation of a process *already initiated* will result in seizable items arriving at a particular place at a particular time. The affidavit should carefully specify the time when the item to be seized will arrive at the place where the search is to occur and the time thereafter when the execution of the warrant is planned to occur. This information will heip satisfy the magistrate that the warrant will not be executed prematurely.

CONTENTS OF THE WARRANT

A magistrate who is satisfied from the information in the affidavit that there is probable cause to search will issue the warrant. Although search warrants differ from state to state, the following characteristics are common to most search warrants, and law enforcement officers should be familiar with them.

1. The warrant must be directed to an officer or class of officers authorized to enforce the laws of the state.

2. The warrant must particularly identify the property to be searched for. The description of the property must set forth meaningful limits for the officer executing the warrant. If the description is either too vague or too broad, the warrant may be declared invalid.

3. The warrant must particularly describe the person or place to be searched. The description of the person or place to be searched must also set meaningful limits for the officer executing the warrant and must not be too vague or too broad.

4. Some states require that the warrant state the grounds of probable cause for its issuance and the names of the persons whose affidavits have been taken in support of it. Usually, the grounds of probable cause do not appear in the body of the warrant itself, but may appear in attached affidavits. The Supreme Judicial Court of Maine has said:

> A basic reason for requiring the grounds of probable cause to appear on the face of the warrant is to provide a reviewing court with a complete record. Clear reference to an attached affidavit setting forth a basis of probable cause serves the same purpose. State v. Hollander, Me., 289 A.2d 419, 421 (Supreme Judicial Court of Maine, 1972).

5. The warrant must command the designated officer to search the person or place named for the property specified.

6. The warrant may specifically direct that it be served only in the daytime, or it may specifically allow a nighttime search, depending on the laws of the particular state.

7. The warrant must designate the judge to whom it shall be returned.

8. The warrant must state the date and time of its issuance.

9. The warrant must be signed by the issuing magistrate.

On page 126 is a form for a typical search warrant, containing spaces for all the elements listed above. It should be noted that the above characteristics need not appear in any particular order.

EXECUTION OF THE WARRANT

The execution of a search warrant is essentialy the carrying out of the command or commands appearing on the face of the warrant itself. Officers can therefore determine much of their behavior from simply reading the warrant. However, many of the commands of a search warrant need further clarification and other limitations and duties are imposed by various statutes and court decisions. The entire subject of execution of search warrants, therefore, will be covered in detail.

Who May Execute

The only person who may execute a search warrant is an officer who is authorized to enforce or assist in enforcing the laws of the state. The warrant will be directed to a particular officer or class of officers. Only the named officer or a member of the named class of officers is authorized to execute the warrant. Of course, if a warrant is directed to a particular officer such as a sheriff, a deputy may execute the warrant and the sheriff need not be present. Also, private persons may be enlisted to help in the execution of a warrant, but an officer to whom the warrant is directed must be personally present at the search scene.

Time Considerations

There are three aspects of time that affect a law enforcement officer in the execution of a search warrant. The first of these is the allowable time that an officer may delay between the issuance of the warrant and its execution. In states that have no time limit fixed by statute, court rule, or judicial decision, the law presumes that a

Form A. O. 93 (Rev. Apr. 1973)   Search Warrant
_____

United States District Court
FOR THE

_____

UNITED STATES OF AMERICA   Docket No.

VS.   Case No.

                                                SEARCH WARRANT

To

   Affidavit(s) having been made before me by

that he has reason to believe that { on the person of
                                     on the premises known as }

                    in the   District of

there is now being concealed certain property, namely

                                        here describe property

and as I am satisfied that there is probable cause to believe that the property so described is being concealed on the person or premises above described and that grounds for application for issuance of the search warrant exist as stated in the supporting affidavit(s).

   You are hereby commanded to search within a period of _____
(not to exceed 10 days) the person or place named for the property specified, serving this warrant and making the search { in the daytime (6:00 a.m. to 10:00 p.m.) at any time in the day or night* } and if the property be found there to seize it, leaving a copy of this warrant and receipt for the property taken, and prepare a written inventory of the property seized and promptly return this warrant and bring the property before _____ as required by law.
   Federal judge or magistrate

         Dated this   day of   , 19

         _____
                    Judge (Federal or State Court of Record) or Federal Magistrate.

*The Federal Rules of Criminal Procedure provide: "The warrant shall be served in the daytime, unless the issuing authority, by appropriate provision in the warrant, and for reasonable cause shown, authorizes its execution at times other than daytime." (Rule 41(c)). A statement of grounds for reasonable cause should be made in the affidavit(s) if a search is to be authorized "at any time day or night" pursuant to Rule 41(c).

reasonable time will be allowed for the warrant to be executed. What is a reasonable time will depend on the facts and circumstances of each case. Several states have statutes that set the outer time limit for the execution of a search warrant. Most require that it be executed and returned within ten days after its date of issuance. Many of these statutes *also* require that the warrant be executed "forthwith." In order to resolve this apparent ambiguity, federal and state courts interpreting these statutes have required that the warrant be executed within a reasonable time after issuance, so long as it is within the statutory period. United States v. Harper, 450 F.2d 1032 (5th Circuit Court of Appeals, 1971). *Therefore, even though an officer executes the warrant within the statutory ten (10) day period, the search could still be held unlawful.* The search would be unlawful if there were:

1. *Unnecessary delay* in executing the warrant; and

2. Such delay resulted in some *legal prejudice* to the defendant.

What is an unnecessary delay is determined by the circumstances of each case. One of the chief concerns of courts is that probable cause, existing at the time of issuance of the warrant, continues until the time of its execution. In a case interpreting a statute with both a "ten day" and a "forthwith" provision, a warrant for the seizure of equipment used to manufacture LSD was executed six days after its issuance. The court held that the execution was timely, as the premises were under daily surveillance, and no activity was noted until after the first five days. The court said:

> While it is desirable that police be given reasonable latitude to determine when a warrant should be executed, it is also necessary that search warrants be executed with some promptness in order to lessen the possibility that the facts upon which probable cause was initially based do not become dissipated.
> We adopt the reasoning of the Second Circuit in *Dunnings* to the effect that "forthwith" means any time within 10 days after the warrant is issued, provided that the probable cause recited in the affidavit continues until the time of execution, giving consideration to the intervening knowledge of the officers and the passage of time. U.S. v. Nepstead, 424 F.2d 269, 271 (9th Circuit Court of Appeals, 1970).

There are several reasons why an officer would be justified in delaying the execution of a search warrant. For example, weather conditions, long travel distances, traffic problems, and similar obstacles may prevent the prompt execution of the warrant. Delays may be necessary to gather sufficient human resources for the search or to protect the safety of the searching officers. Other reasons accepted by the courts for delaying the execution of a search warrant are prevention of destruction of evidence and prevention of the flight of a suspect. When the warrant is for the search of both a person and premises, the officers may delay the search until the person is present on the premises. People v. Stansberry, 47 Ill.2d 541, 268 N.E.2d 431 (Illinois Supreme Court, 1971). It is suggested that officers always be prepared to give convincing reasons for any delay in executing a warrant.

The second aspect of time that relates to the execution of a search warrant is the time of day during which it may be executed. Some state laws require that search warrants be executed in the daytime, and the warrants in those states will usually direct the law enforcement officer accordingly. Some of these states may also allow nighttime searches upon a showing of special circumstances by the officer applying for the warrant. Officers, therefore, should take great care in determining when the warrant can be executed. They should not only read the search warrant carefully, but should know their state law regarding the time of day when warrants can be executed.

Courts have differed in their interpretations of when "daytime" and "nighttime" begin and end. This chapter will not go into a discussion of those differences. Probably the safest standard for a law enforcement officer to adopt is that it is "daytime" when there is sufficient natural light to recognize a person's features. Otherwise, it is "nighttime." Even if nighttime searches are prohibited, the execution of a search warrant, begun in the daytime, may be continued into the nighttime as long as it is a reasonable continuation of the search begun earlier. An officer is not required to cut short the reasonable execution of a daytime search warrant just because it becomes dark outside. United States v. Joseph, 278 F.2d 504 (3d Circuit Court of Appeals, 1959).

The third aspect of time, as it relates to the execution of a search warrant, is the amount of time allowed for the law enforcement officer to perform the search *once it is initiated.* Since the warrant is a mandate of the court, the officer should be allowed to take as much time as necessary to carry out its purposes. This is particularly so when the items specified are small and easily concealed. State v. Gray, 152 Mont. 145, 447 P.2d 475 (Supreme Court of Montana, 1968). However, if the officer searches a place or person beyond a reasonable time, for purposes of harassment or intimidation, it is likely that the search will be declared unlawful.

Gaining Entry

The manner of entry into premises to execute a search warrant must meet constitutional standards of "reasonableness." If the officer does not meet these standards, any subsequent search and seizure may be held illegal and the evidence obtained as a result may therefore be inadmissible in a criminal prosecution.

Statutes ordinarily provide that in order to lawfully gain entry to premises to execute a search warrant, law enforcement officers must:

1. Knock on the door;
2. Announce their identity as law enforcement officers;
3. Indicate that they possess a search warrant; and
4. Announce that it is their purpose to execute the warrant.

If they are then refused entry, they may break open any outer or inner door, any window, or any other part of the house to carry out the command of the warrant.

There are, however, recognized exceptions to this rule requiring that officers first be refused admittance after an announcement of purpose before they are allowed to break in. One exception is for cases involving possible concealment or destruction of evidence or escape of a person to be searched. These situations arise frequently and often involve officers knocking on a door and announcing their identity, but before they can complete their announcement of authority and purpose, they hear footsteps running from the door, whispers, flushing toilets, or other suspicious sounds. This most often occurs in drug, gambling, and illicit liquor cases. In these cases, where officers have reason to believe that evidence will be concealed or destroyed, or that a person to be searched will escape, they may enter by force without completing their announcement of authority or purpose and without waiting for a specific refusal of admittance. *The important thing to remember, however, is that officers must have specific substantial reasons for believing that evidence would be lost or that a person would escape if they did not act immediately. A forced entry wthout announcement of purpose will not be justified simply by the fact that a case involves narcotics, gambling, liquor, or anything else.* As the Supreme Court of California said:

> Under the Fourth Amendment, a specific showing must always be made to justify any kind of police action tending to disturb the security of the people in their homes. Unannounced forcible entry is in itself a serious disturbance of that security and cannot be justified on a blanket basis. Otherwise, the constitutional test of reasonableness would turn only on practical expediency, and the amendment's primary safeguard—the requirement of particularity—would be lost. Just as the police must have sufficiently particular reason to enter at all, so must they have some particular reason to enter in the manner chosen. People v. Gastelo, 67 Cal.2d 586, 588–89, 63 Cal.Rptr. 10, 12, 432 P.2d 706, 708 (1967).

It is therefore strongly urged that officers keep a careful record of all the facts and circumstances that led them to believe that there was an immediate danger of loss of evidence or escape. Otherwise, if the officers cannot specifically justify their actions, any evidence they seize after an unannounced forcible entry may not be admissible in court.

Another exception to the rule requiring announcement of authority and purpose before entry to search is that the announcement is not necessary if the occupants of the premises to be searched already know of an officer's authority and purpose before any announcement. In an illustrative case, officers with a search warrant knocked on the defendant's apartment door and it swung open partially so the officer and occupants were clearly visible to each other. One of the officers was known to the occupants as a narcotics officer. The officers made no announcement of purpose, but waited about twenty seconds and then entered the apartment to conduct the search.

The court held that the unannounced police intrusion here was reasonable. Because the defendant recognized the officers through the partially open door and knew one to be a narcotics officer, the court found that the defendant was reasonably certain of the police purpose before the officers entered his apartment. A formal announcement of authority and purpose in this case would have been a useless gesture. United States ex rel. Dyton v. Ellingsworth, 306 F.Supp. 231 (U.S. District Court, D. Delaware 1969).

Again it is strongly urged that officers keep a careful record of the facts and circumstances that gave them reason to believe that the defendant already knew their authority and purpose, making a formal announcement unnecessary. Also, it is a good idea for officers to announce that they possess a warrant, even though they do not announce anything else. This fact may not be as obvious to the occupant of the premises as an officers' authority and purpose may be.

A third exception exists when officers are justified in a belief that there would be a danger to the life or limb of an officer or someone within the premises if an announcement of authority and purpose were given. In a case illustrating this exception, FBI agents believed that a suspect who was a prison escapee with a reputation for always being armed and who was also wanted for murder of a policeman and armed bank robbery was within an apartment. They entered the apartment quietly without making any announcement of their authority or purpose. The court found that the entry to arrest the defendant was lawful on the theory that an announcement would have increased the peril of the agents. Gilbert v. United States, 366 F.2d 923 (9th Circuit Court of Appeals, 1966). Although this case involved an entry to arrest, the principle applies equally to an entry to search.

Entry When No Response or No One Home

The requirement that officers must be refused admittance after their announcement of authority and purpose before they may break into premises does not necessarily mean that the refusal must be actually stated. If an occupant of the premises is silent, and fails to call out or open the door after a reasonable opportunity to do so, this may be considered the equivalent of a refusal to admit an officer and the officer may then break in. United States v. Poppitt, 227 F.Supp. 73 (U.S. District Court, D. Delaware, 1964). What constitutes a reasonable opportunity to respond depends on the circumstances of each case. It has been held that an officer who yelled "Police Officer" and simultaneously kicked down the door did not comply with standards of reasonableness. People v. Benjamin, 71 Cal.2d 296, 78 Cal.Rptr. 510, 455 P.2d 438 (Supreme Court of California, 1969).

A like rule applies if the residents of the premises are absent. There is no prohibition against executing a search warrant when premises are unoccupied. In fact, if an officer reasonably believes from the circumstances that no one is in the house, no announcement need be made. As one court stated:

> In this case it would have been an empty gesture for the officers to have announced to an empty house that they were officers and that they were present for the purpose of executing a search warrant. United States v. Hawkins, 243 F.Supp. 429 (U.S. District Court, E.D.Tennessee, 1965).

Search and Detention of Persons on the Premises

When a search warrant is issued for the search of a named person or a named person *and* premises, there is no question that officers executing the warrant can detain and search the person named. However, often a person not named in the warrant is on the premises to be searched and the question arises whether that person may be detained or searched. *The general rule is that the search warrant gives a law enforcement officer no authority to search a person who merely happens to be on the premises.* In Ybarra v. Illinois, 444 U.S. 85, 100 S.Ct. 338, 62 L.Ed.2d 238 (1979), the defendant was a mere patron in a bar and the police had a warrant to search the bar and the bartender. The U.S. Supreme Court held that the search of the defendant was illegal because the police did not have probable cause particularized with respect to the defendant. The Court said that a warrant to search a place cannot normally be construed to authorize a search of each individual in that place. Therefore, if an officer wishes to search a place and also wishes to search specific persons expected to be at that place, the officer should obtain a search warrant to search the place and each specific individual. In order to obtain such a warrant, the officer will be required to establish in the affidavit probable cause to search the place and each specific individual. A search warrant for the place only will not justify a search of persons who happen to be there.

Detention of persons present on premises to be searched under a warrant may be allowed in certain circumstances, however. In Michigan v. Summers, 452 U.S. 692, 101 S.Ct. 2587, 69 L.Ed.2d 340 (1981), the U.S. Supreme Court held that officers executing a valid search warrant for contraband may detain the occupants of the premises while the search is being conducted. The Court said that "[i]f the evidence that a citizen's residence is harboring contraband is sufficient to persuade a judicial officer that an invasion of the citizen's privacy is justified, it is constitutionally reasonable to require that citizen to remain while officers of the law execute a valid warrant to search his home." 452 U.S. at 704–05, 101 S.Ct. at 2595, 69 L.Ed.2d at 351. In further explaining the justification for the detention, the Court emphasized the limited additional intrusion represented by the detention once a search of the home had been authorized by a warrant. The Court also pointed out that when a search warrant for contraband is involved law enforcement officers have a legitimate interest in preventing flight if incriminating evidence is found and in minimizing the risk of harm to themselves, since the execution of a search warrant for contraband, especially narcotics, "is the kind of transaction that may give rise to sudden violence or frantic efforts to conceal or destroy evidence." 452 U.S. at 702, 101 S.Ct. at 2549, 69 L.Ed.2d at 349–50.

The possibility of danger at the search scene gives an officer the additional authority to conduct a limited pat-down search or "frisk" for weapons of any person who the officer reasonably believes is dangerous. The officer must be able to point to specific facts and circumstances to support the belief that a particular person was dangerous. A mere blanket statement that the officer believed that a person was dangerous will not justify a protective frisk. (See Chapter 12 for details on conducting protective searches.)

Of course, if an officer, while on the search scene, obtains information constituting probable cause to make a felony arrest, or if an offense is being committed in the officer's presence, the officer may arrest the offender. The officer may then conduct a search incident to the arrest. (See Chapter 7 for details on conducting searches incident to arrest.)

Intensity of the Search

A search conducted under authority of a search warrant may extend to the entire premises described in the warrant. For example, an individual's dwelling place will include the house, garage, and other buildings generally associated with and included within a house or home. State v. Brochu, Me., 237 A.2d 418 (Supreme Judicial Court of Maine, 1967). It does not follow, however, that officers executing the warrant may look everywhere within the described premises. They may look only where the items described in the warrant might be concealed. For example, a search warrant for stolen tires would not authorize officers to rummage through desk drawers and other places too small to hold tires. Yet, officers would have authority to search drawers and small places if the items described in the warrant were coins or pills. Officers should be prepared to justify their looking into any enclosed areas such as drawers and containers by the nature and size of the items they are looking for.

Officers executing a search warrant must use only reasonable force in conducting the search. An otherwise reasonable search may become unreasonable due to the manner in which it is conducted. A search warrant gives officers authority to break into a house or other objects of search if they are denied access to them. Nevertheless, they must exercise a high degree of care to avoid unnecessary damage to the premises or objects. They must conduct the search in a manner designed to do the least damage possible, while still making a thorough examination of the premises. They should carefully replace articles that were necessarily disturbed during the search. Finally, they should avoid any unnecessary injury to the feelings of those present. As the Supreme Judicial Court of Maine said in an early case:

> Officers must not allow their zeal and beliefs to blind them to the rights of the owners, and occupants of the dwelling house they search. Those rights, as well as the interests of the prosecutor, are to be regarded and protected by officers. . . . However confident the officers were of the guilt of the occupant, the house and its owner were not thereby outlawed. Buckley v. Beaulieu, 104 Me. 56, 61, 71 A. 70, 72 (1908).

Seizure of Items Not Named in the Warrant

Is it proper for a law enforcement officer to seize items *not* named in the warrant when found during the lawful execution of a warrant? By lawful execution of a warrant is meant a search (1) limited in area to the place named in the warrant and (2) limited in the sense that the police were only looking in places where the items named in the warrant might be concealed. There has been a great deal of differing opinion on this question in the past. Some courts have held that the only items that may be seized pursuant to a search warrant are those named in the warrant, leaving nothing to the discretion of the law enforcement officer. State v. Brochu, Me., 237 A.2d 418 (Supreme Judicial Court of Maine, 1967). Other courts have allowed a seizure of *contraband,* not named in the warrant, that was found in *plain view* during a lawful execution. United States v. Zeidman, 444 F.2d 1051 (7th Circuit Court of Appeals, 1971). Still other courts have allowed the seizure of any unlisted evidentiary material observed in plain view as long as the search was not "exploratory," there was probable cause to seize the material, and the material seized had a direct relation to the primary purpose of the search. State v. Quigg, 155 Mont. 119, 467 P.2d 692 (Supreme Court of Montana, 1970).

The U.S. Supreme Court dealt with the question of the seizure of items unlisted in the warrant during the execution of a warrant in the case of Cady v. Dombrowksi, 413 U.S. 433, 93 S.Ct. 2523, 37 L.Ed.2d 706 (1973). In that case, the police were investigating a possible homicide. The defendant informed them that he believed there was a body lying near his brother's farm. The police found the body and they also found defendant's car at the farm. Through the window of the car, the police observed a pillow case, a backseat, and a briefcase covered with blood. Police then obtained a warrant to search the car. While executing the warrant, police discovered, in "plain view" in the car, a blood-covered sock and a blood-covered floormat. The defendant claimed that the sock and the floormat taken from his car were illegally seized since they were not specifically listed on the application for the search warrant.

The Court held that the seizure of the items were constitutional. Since the warrant was validly issued, and the car was the item designated to be searched, the police were authorized to search the car. Although the sock and floormat were not listed in the warrant, the officers discovered these items in plain view in the car while executing the warrant and therefore could constitutionally seize them without a warrant.

Although the U.S. Supreme Court did not elaborate on its decision, the Cady v. Dombrowski case would appear to authorize seizures of *any item of evidence subject to seizure* that is found in plain view during the execution of a valid search warrant. The officer is cautioned, however, that such a seizure will probably be held illegal if:

1. The seizure was the product of an "exploratory" search; or

2. The items seized had no direct relation to the primary purpose of the search; or

3. The officer did not have probable cause to believe that the items fell within one of the categories of items subject to seizure.

The seizure will also be held illegal if the officer did not meet all the requirements of the plain view doctrine.

The plain view doctrine is discussed in detail in Chapter 9. One of the requirements of the doctrine deserves mention here, however. In the 1971 case of Coolidge v. New Hampshire, the U.S. Supreme Court required that absent exigent circumstances, the discovery of evidence in plain view must be *inadvertent*. This means that if officers are in a position or place where they have a lawful right to be (e.g., in someone's home for purposes of executing a search warrant), they may not seize evidence in plain view *if they knew before they entered the premises that the evidence would be there*. When officers know in advance the location of evidence and they intend to seize it, they must obtain a search warrant, or the seizure will be unlawful and the evidence will be inadmissible in court. Coolidge v. New Hampshire, 403 U.S. 443, 470, 91 S.Ct. 2022, 2040, 29 L.Ed.2d 564, 585 (U.S. Supreme Court, 1971). The safest procedure for law enforcement officers applying for a search warrant, then, is to list in the affidavit all items to be seized, and not to rely on discovering evidence in plain view during the execution of the warrant.

Duties After Search is Completed

As discussed earlier, a search warrant must be executed and returned either within a reasonable time or within a set time period, usually ten days after its date of issuance. Proper execution of a warrant requires more than merely conducting a search and seizing items described in the warrant. Most state laws require that an officer who takes property under a warrant must give to the person from whom or from whose premises the property is taken a copy of the warrant and a receipt for the property taken. If the person is unavailable, the officer must leave a copy of the warrant and a receipt at the place from which the property was taken.

The officer is also required to return the warrant to the judicial officer designated in the warrant promptly after its execution. The warrant must be accompanied by a written inventory or list of all property taken whether the items were described in the warrant or not. A form for making the return and inventory usually appears on the back of the search warrant form. A typical example of a return and inventory form appears on page 135. Some states further require that the inventory be made in the presence of the applicant for the warrant and the person from whose possession or premises the property was taken, if they were present. If they were not present, the inventory must be made in the presence of at least one other credible person. Courts have held that despite statutory provisions regulating the execution and return of search warrants, the giving of a receipt for property taken and the return of the warrant with inventory are ministerial acts. A ministerial act is one that is performed in obedience to the command of a legal authority and that requires no exercise of judgment or discretion by the person performing it. Failure to perform acts of this nature will not void a search warrant or the search conducted under the warrant. People v. Hawthorne, 45 Ill.2d 176, 258 N.E.2d 319 (Supreme Court of Illinois, 1970).

Although the performance of ministerial duties after the search is completed does not affect the validity of the warrant, officers should not take these duties lightly. In the words of the Supreme Judicial Court of Maine:

> Official dereliction in the punctilious observance of Rule 41(d) which has the force of law respecting the steps to be taken in the execution of search warrants cannot be overlooked and imposes upon us the instant duty of forewarning all enforcement authorities that we expect full compliance in the future. We are inclined to believe that there exists no such general practice justifying at this time the adoption of an exclusionary rule to compel obedience. State v. Martelle, Me., 252 A.2d 316, 321 (1969).

It is strongly urged, therefore, that officers take pains to carefully comply with the requirements of statutes governing the execution and return of search warrants. Otherwise, the courts may take stronger steps to ensure strict compliance.

ADMINISTRATIVE SEARCH WARRANTS

An administrative search is a routine inspection of a home or business to determine compliance with various statutes and regulations. An administrative search seeks to enforce fire, health, and housing codes, licensing provisions, and the like. It differs from a criminal search in that a criminal search focuses on gathering evidence in order to convict a person of a crime. An administrative search ordinarily does not result in a criminal prosecution.

Before 1967, courts consistently held that administrative searches were not subject to the restrictions of the Fourth Amendment and that a search warrant was not needed to inspect residential or commercial premises for violations of regulatory and licensing provisions. In 1967, in the cases of Camara v. Municipal Court, 387

RETURN

I received the attached search warrant   19   , and have executed it as follows:

On   , 19   at   o'clock   **M,** I searched the person or premises de-scribed in the warrant and

I left a copy of the warrant with _____
                                                    name of person searched or owner or "at the place of search"
together with a receipt for the items seized.

The following is an inventory of property taken pursuant to the warrant:

This inventory was made in the presence of

and

I swear that this Inventory is a true and detailed account of all the property taken by me on the warrant.

_____

Subscribed and sworn to and returned before me this   day of   , 19

_____
                                                    Federal Magistrate

FPI LC 12-10-73 100M 7851

U.S. 523, 87 S.Ct. 1727, 18 L.Ed.2d 930, and See v. City of Seattle, 387 U.S. 541, 87 S.Ct. 1737, 18 L.Ed.2d 943, the U.S. Supreme Court reversed earlier decisions and held that such administrative inspections were subject to the warrant requirement of the Fourth Amendment. The basis for both the *Camara* and *See* decisions was the Court's belief that a person's right of privacy should not be determined by the nature of the search. In *Camara,* the Court said, "It is surely anomalous to say that the individual and his private property are fully protected by the Fourth Amendment only when the individual is suspected of criminal behavior." 387 U.S. at 530, 87 S.Ct. at 1732, 18 L.Ed.2d at 936. Nevertheless, the Court held that, because administrative searches differ in nature and purpose from criminal searches, the probable cause standard for administrative searches differs in nature and is less stringent than the standard for criminal searches. The Court said:

> The warrant procedure is designed to guarantee that a decision to search private property is justified by a reasonable governmental interest. But reasonableness is still the ultimate standard. If a valid public interest justifies the intrusion contemplated, then there is probable cause to issue a suitably restricted search warrant. 387 U.S. at 539, 87 S.Ct. at 1736, 18 L.Ed.2d at 941.

Despite the less stringent probable cause standard, the U.S. Supreme Court and other courts have carved out various exceptions to the warrant requirement for administative searches. There are exceptions based on emergency, consent, plain view, and open fields. These exceptions are similar to the exceptions to the warrant requirement for criminal searches discussed in Part Three of this book, but the standards are generally less stringent than those required for criminal searches. Another exception, allowing warrantless inspection of certain *licensed and closely regulated enterprises,* has been recognized by the U.S. Supreme Court. In United States v. Biswell, 406 U.S. 311, 92 S.Ct. 1593, 32 L.Ed.2d 87 (1972), the Court upheld a warrantless search of a storeroom of a gun dealer licensed under the Gun Control Act of 1968. The Court said:

> [I]f inspection is to be effective and serve as a credible deterrent, unannounced, even frequent, inspections are essential. In this context, the prerequisite of a warrant could easily frustrate inspections; and if the necessary flexibility as to time, scope and frequency is to be preserved, the protections afforded by a warrant would be negligible.
> It is also plain that inspections for compliance with the Gun Control Act pose only limited threats to the dealer's justifiable expectations of privacy. When a dealer chooses to engage in this pervasively regulated business and to accept a federal license, he does so with the knowledge that his business records, firearms, and ammunition will be subject to effective inspection. 406 U.S. at 316, 92 S.Ct. at 1596, 32 L.Ed.2d at 92–93.

This exception to the warrant requirement for inspections of licensed and closely regulated businesses has been applied by state and federal courts to a great variety of businesses since the *Biswell* decision.

Administrative searches will not be discussed in further detail because they are seldom conducted by law enforcement officers. Nevertheless, officers should be aware that the line between an administrative and a criminal search can sometimes become blurred. When an administrative search begins to take on the characteristics of a criminal search, the stricter standards applicable to criminal searches come into play. If these stricter standards are not followed, any evidence obtained will be held inadmissible in a criminal prosecution.

The line between administrative and criminal searches often becomes blurred in fire investigation cases, because there are several different purposes which may be served by a fire investigation and fire scenes present varying degrees of emergency. Also, reasonable privacy expectations may remain in fire-damaged premises, thereby affecting the necessity to obtain a warrant.

> Privacy expectations will vary with the type of property, the amount of fire damage, the prior and continued use of the premises, and in some cases the owner's efforts to secure it against intruders. Some fires may be so devastating that no reasonable privacy interests remain in the ash and ruins, regardless of the owner's subjective expectations. The test essentially is an objective one: whether "the expectation [is] one that society is prepared to recognize as 'reasonable.'" . . . If reasonable privacy interests remain in the fire-damaged property, the warrant requirement applies, and any official entry must be made pursuant to a warrant in the absence of consent or exigent circumstances. Michigan v. Clifford, ___ U.S. ___, ___, 104 S.Ct. 641, 646, 78 L.Ed.2d 477, 483 (1984).

If a warrant is necessary, the purpose of the search determines the type of warrant required. If the primary purpose is to determine the cause and origin of a recent fire, only an administrative warrant is needed. To obtain an administrative warrant, fire officials need show only that "a fire of undetermined origin has occurred on the premises, that the scope of the proposed search is reasonable and will not intrude unnecessarily on the fire victim's privacy, and that the search will be executed at a reasonable and convenient time." Michigan v. Clifford, ___ U.S. ___, ___, 104 S.Ct. 641, 647, 78 L.Ed.2d 477, 484 (1984). If the primary purpose of the search is to gather evidence of criminal activity, a criminal search warrant may be obtained only on a showing of probable cause to believe that relevant evidence will be found in the place to be searched.

If evidence of criminal activity is discovered during the course of a valid administrative search, it may be seized under the "plain view" doctrine and used to establish probable cause to obtain a criminal search warrant. Fire officials may not, however, rely on this evidence to expand the scope of their administrative search without first satisfying an independent judicial officer that probable cause exists.

It should be noted that the purpose of the search is important even if exigent circumstances exist.

> Circumstances that justify a warrantless search for the cause of a fire may not justify a search to gather evidence of criminal activity once that cause has been determined. If, for example, the administrative search is justified by the immediate need to ensure against rekindling, the scope of the search may be no broader than reasonably necessary to achieve its end. A search to gather evidence of criminal activity not in plain view must be made pursuant to a criminal warrant upon a traditional showing of probable cause. Michigan v. Clifford, ___ U.S. ___, ___, 104 S.Ct. 641, 647, 78 L.Ed.2d 477, 484–85 (1984).

An example of an administrative search that took on the characteristics of a criminal search is the case of Michigan v. Tyler, 436 U.S. 499, 98 S.Ct. 1942, 56

L.Ed.2d 486 (U.S. Supreme Court, 1978).   That case involved a late night fire in a furniture store leased by the defendant.   When the fire was reduced to smoldering embers, the fire chief, while investigating the cause of the fire, discovered two plastic containers of flammable liquid.   The chief summoned a police detective to investigate possible arson.   The detective took several pictures but, because visibility was hindered by darkness, steam, and smoke, the investigators departed the scene at 4 A.M. and returned shortly after daylight to continue the investigation.   More evidence of arson was found and seized at this time.   About a month later, a state police arson investigator made several visits to the fire scene and obtained evidence that was used at trial in convicting the defendant.   At no time was any warrant or consent to search obtained.

The Court held that the investigative activity on the date of the fire was legal, but that the evidence-gathering activity a month after the fire was an illegal search and seizure.

> [W]e hold that an entry to fight a fire requires no warrant, and that once in the building, officials may remain there for a reasonable time to investigate the cause of the blaze.   Thereafter, additional entries to investigate the cause of the fire must be made pursuant to the warrant procedures governing administrative searches. . . .
> Evidence of arson discovered in the course of such investigations is admissible at trial, but if the investigating officials find probable cause to believe that arson has occurred and require further access to gather evidence for a possible prosecution, they may obtain a warrant only upon a traditional showing of probable cause applicable to searches for evidence of crime.   436 U.S. at 511–12, 98 S.Ct. at 1951, 56 L.Ed.2d at 500.

The important thing for the law enforcement officer to remember is that once a search is directed toward gathering evidence for a criminal prosecution, the officer must obtain a criminal search warrant as described in this chapter.   The officer cannot avoid this requirement by using other governmental officials to conduct searches under the guise of an administrative or regulatory inspection.

EFFECT OF ILLEGAL SEARCH AND SEIZURE

The most important effect of an illegal search or seizure is the exclusion of the evidence obtained from being used in court against the person whose rights were violated by the search.   This so-called exclusionary rule has been discussed in detail in Chapter 3.   Suffice it to repeat at this point that application of the exclusionary rule in a particular case will usually result in a lost case for the prosecution and the release of the person charged with crime.   From the law enforcement officer's standpoint, the suppression of crucial evidence may represent a total waste of weeks or months of investigation, evidence-gathering, and case evaluation.   It should be clear, then, that strict compliance with all statutes, court rules, and court decisions dealing with search and seizure procedures is of the utmost importance from the first report of a possible crime through the ultimate disposition of the case. Anything less unjustifiably risks both the efficiency and the fairness and justness of our system of criminal justice.

Other possible effects of an illegal search and seizure are civil and criminal liability of the officer conducting the search and seizure. As with an illegal arrest, the consequences for the officer depend upon the circumstances of each case including the officer's good faith, the degree of care used, the degree of force used, and the seriousness of the situation.

It should be obvious that the effects of an illegal search and seizure are far-reaching and potentially devastating to the prosecution of a criminal case or to the furtherance of the law enforcement officer's career. It is vitally important for law enforcement officers not only to learn and apply the information in this chapter and in Part Three, but to keep abreast of continually changing developments in the law of search and seizure.

SUMMARY

The general rule is that all searches and seizures conducted without a warrant are unreasonable and in violation of the Fourth Amendment to the U.S. Constitution. Although there are many well-defined exceptions to this rule, searches made under the authority of a warrant are not only greatly preferred by the courts, but also give the law enforcement officer greater protection from liability.

A search warrant is a written order issued by a proper judicial authority (the magistrate) commanding a law enforcement officer to search for certain personal property and bring it before the judicial authority named in the warrant. An officer may obtain a search warrant by submitting a written application in the form of a sworn affidavit to a magistrate. The affidavit must state underlying facts and circumstances supporting probable cause to believe that particularly described items are located in a particularly described place or on a particularly described person. Items that may be seized are those connected with criminal activity, such as stolen property, contraband, and instrumentalities and evidence of crime.

If the magistrate finds probable cause to search, he or she will issue a search warrant directing an officer or class of officers to execute the warrant. Officers must conduct the search within a reasonable time after the warrant's issuance and within any time period specified by state law or court rule. Before entering premises by force to execute the warrant, officers must knock and announce their authority and purpose, unless this notice will result in the loss or destruction of evidence, the escape of a suspect, or a danger to officer or others. Persons on the premises may not be searched, unless the search warrant authorizes the search of a particular person. If officers are executing a warrant to search for contraband, persons on the premises may be detained during the course of the search. Any person on the premises whom officers reasonably believe to be dangerous may be frisked for weapons.

A search under authority of a search warrant may extend to the entire premises described in the warrant, but only to those areas of the premises where the items to be seized might be concealed. The search must be conducted in a manner to avoid unnecessary damage to the premises or objects. Items not named in the warrant may be seized if all elements of the "plain view doctrine" are satisfied. After the search is completed, the officer must leave a copy of the warrant and a receipt for property taken at the searched premises. The officer must return the warrant along with a written inventory of property seized to the judicial officer designated in the warrant.

An administrative search is a routine inspection of a home or business to determine compliance with codes and licensing provisions dealing with fire safety, health, housing, etc. Although administrative searches are not directed toward convicting a person of a crime, they are still subject to the warrant requirement of the Fourth Amendment. The probable cause standard for administrative searches is less stringent than the standard for criminal searches. If, however, an administrative search takes on the characteristics of a criminal search, the traditional probable cause standard applies.

An illegal search and seizure, whether caused by a failure to comply with warrant procedures or failure to satisfy one of the exceptions to the warrant requirement will result in application of the exclusionary rule. This means that evidence seized during the search will be inadmissible in court and will very likely mean termination of the prosecution and release of the person charged. Furthermore, officers conducting an illegal search may be civilly or criminally liable for their actions. Because of these serious potential ramifications, officers should be thoroughly familiar with search and seizure law and should implement this knowledge in their daily operations.

REVIEW AND DISCUSSION QUESTIONS

1. Why is time a more important factor in determining probable cause to search than it is in determining probable cause to arrest?

2. Formulate a set of circumstances in which there is probable cause to search but not probable cause to arrest. In which there is probable cause to arrest but not probable cause to search. In which there is probable cause both to arrest and search.

3. Name three kinds of property that are *unlikely* to remain in a particular place for longer than a week. Name three kinds of property that are *likely* to remain in a particular place for longer than a week.

4. Why should law enforcement officers executing a search warrant refrain from asking the person against whom the search is directed to assist them in any way?

5. Assume that you are a law enforcement officer attempting to obtain a search warrant for urban premises, rural premises, a multiple unit dwelling, and a motor vehicle. Describe, as you would in the affidavit, one of each of the above places that is familiar to you. (For example, describe for purposes of a search warrant application a friend's farm in the country.)

6. Discuss three ways in which a search warrant and an arrest warrant are affected by time differently.

7. Law enforcement officers have a search warrant to search a house for heroin and to search the person of the house owners' 18-year-old daughter. When the officers arrive to execute the warrant, the following persons are present at the house:

    a. The owners;

    b. The 18-year-old daughter;

    c. Her 15-year-old brother, who appears extremely nervous;

    d. Her boyfriend, whom the officers recognize as a local gang member who is known to carry a knife;

    e. An unidentified elderly couple.

To what extent may the officers search or detain each of the persons present?

8. A law enforcement officer has a search warrant to search the defendant's house for cameras stolen from a particular department store. May the officer:

    a. Look in desk drawers?

    b. Search the defendant's body?

    c. Seize a brown paper bag containing a white powder resembling heroin, found in a desk drawer?

    d. Search the defendant's garage?

    e. Look in the defendant's wife's jewelry box?

    f. Break open a locked wall safe?

    g. Seize a portable radio found on a table with a tag from the department store attached to it?

9. Are the following descriptions in a search warrant of items to be seized sufficiently particular:

    a. An unknown make .38 caliber, blue steel with wood grips, revolver? See United States v. Wolfenbarger, 696 F.2d 750 (10th Circuit Court of Appeals, 1982).

    b. Video tape and equipment used in a copyright infringement? See United States v. Smith, 686 F.2d 234 (5th Circuit Court of Appeals, 1982).

    c. All doctor's files concerning an accident patient? See United States v. Hershenow, 680 F.2d 847 (1st Circuit Court of Appeals, 1982).

    d. Plaques, mirrors, and other items? See United States v. Apker, 705 F.2d 293 (8th Circuit Court of Appeals, 1983).

    e. Items related to the smuggling, packing, distribution, and use of controlled substances? See United States v. Ladd, 704 F.2d 134 (4th Circuit Court of Appeals, 1983).

    f. Business papers that are evidence and instrumentalities of a violation of general tax fraud statute? See United States v. Cardwell, 680 F.2d 75 (9th Circuit Court of Appeals, 1982).

10. Does a warrant to search a house authorize a search of a vehicle parked on the premises near the house? Does a warrant authorizing the seizure of stolen typewriters authorize the seizure of non-stolen typewriters commingled with them? Is the seizure of an entire book of accounts permissible when only two or three pages of the book are relevant to the specifications of the search warrant?

6

Probable Cause

Probable cause has already been discussed to a limited extent in Chapter 3. Every law enforcement officer, therefore, should be generally familiar with the term. Nevertheless, because probable cause is so basic to criminal procedure, it is important that all officers have as complete an understanding of it as possible. This chapter will attempt to explain in detail all aspects of probable cause as it concerns the law enforcement officer. The material presented here should not be read in isolation but is designed to be read in conjunction with the previous chapters.

DEFINITION

The discussion of probable cause begins with a definition. Two different but similar definitions of probable cause will be quoted, one for search and one for arrest, because different types of information are required to establish probable cause in each instance. The most quoted definition of probable cause to *search* is that found in Carroll v. United States, 267 U.S. 132, 45 S.Ct. 280, 69 L.Ed. 543 (U.S. Supreme Court, 1925). In that case, the Court said that probable cause exists when:

> [T]he facts and circumstances within their (the officers') knowledge and of which they had reasonably trustworthy information (are) sufficient in themselves to warrant a man of reasonable caution in the belief that (seizable property would be found in a particular place or on a particular person). (parenthetical material supplied) 267 U.S. at 162, 45 S.Ct. at 288, 69 L.Ed. at 555.

Paraphrasing the *Carroll* case, the U.S. Supreme Court defined probable cause to arrest in Brinegar v. United States, 338 U.S. 160, 175–76, 69 S.Ct. 1302, 1310–11, 93 L.Ed. 1879, 1890 (1949):

> Probable cause exists where "the facts and circumstances within their [the arresting officers'] knowledge and of which they had reasonably trustworthy information [are]

sufficient in themselves to warrant a man of reasonable caution in the belief that" an offense has been or is being committed [by the person to be arrested].

These definitions differ only in that the facts and circumstances that would justify an arrest may be different from those that would justify a search. This chapter will be concerned with that part of the definition of probable cause that is common to both arrests and searches, namely, the nature, quality, and amount of information necessary to establish probable cause. We will concentrate on facts and circumstances that law enforcement officers must have within their knowledge before they can arrest or search, with or without a warrant. Of course, it is impossible to say exactly what combination of facts will provide probable cause in any given situation, because every situation is different in some way. Nevertheless, an attempt will be made to indicate the types of information that a judge or magistrate will consider in deciding whether probable cause exists, whether in an application for an arrest or search warrant, at a motion to suppress hearing, or at a trial.

Sources of Information

Information about possible criminal activity can come to the attention of a law enforcement officer in two possible ways: (1) the officer may perceive the activity; or (2) someone else may perceive the activity and relay the information to the officer. These two types of information sources are treated differently by the courts in determining whether there is probable cause for a warrantless arrest or search or for the issuance of an arrest or search warrant. Because of these differences in treatment, the two types of information sources will be discussed separately.

INFORMATION OBTAINED THROUGH THE OFFICER'S OWN SENSES

When applying for an arrest or search warrant, law enforcement officers should state, *in writing,* in the complaint or affidavit the underlying facts upon which probable cause for the issuance of the warrant is to be based. The laws of some states allow law enforcement officers to supplement their affidavits for warrants with oral testimony. Nevertheless, as stated in Chapter 5, the better and safer practice for all officers is to include *all* the information from which probable cause is to be determined in the affidavit itself. Then, if the validity of the warrant is later challenged, the court hearing the challenge would have a complete record before it. Officers need not state all they know about a particular case as long as they state sufficient facts to support a finding of probable cause. However, because judges and magistrates differ, and because probable cause is such an elusive concept, officers take a chance if they do not state all the facts within their knowledge in the complaint or affidavit.

Most warrantless arrests and searches must also be based on probable cause. Even though the officers do not have to write down the facts to support a finding of probable cause in warrantless situations, they must be prepared to justify their arrest or search if it is later challenged at trial or at a motion to suppress hearing.

Therefore, whether they seek a warrant or not, officers must have sufficient information for probable cause in their minds *before* conducting an arrest or search.

One type of information that officers will use to support their finding of probable cause is information that comes to them through their own senses. This would include not only what officers might have seen, but also what they might have heard, smelled, touched, or tasted. Furthermore, an officer's perceptions may be given additional weight because of personal experience or expertise in a particular area. As one court said:

> Among the pertinent circumstances to be considered is the qualification and function of the person making the arrest. An officer of a narcotics detail may find probable cause in activities of a suspect and in the appearance of paraphernalia or physical characteristics which to the eye of a layman could be without significance. His action should not, therefore, be measured by what might not be probable cause to an untrained civilian passerby, but by a standard appropriate for a reasonable, cautious, and prudent narcotics officer under the circumstances of the moment. State v. Poe, 74 Wash.2d 425, 428–29, 445 P.2d 196, 199 (Supreme Court of Washington, 1968).

Indications of Criminal Activity That May Contribute to Probable Cause

When criminal activity is committed in an officer's presence, and is perceived by the officer through one or more of his or her senses, these perceptions are clearly information that would be sufficient for probable cause to support either the issuance of a warrant or, in the proper circumstances, an arrest or search without a warrant. Most information that comes to the attention of law enforcement officers, however, is seldom so complete as an offense being committed in their presence. Usually officers have to develop probable cause from a series of facts that do not add up to an obvious crime being committed in their presence. The following is a list of the types of facts and circumstances that may be used by law enforcement officers in developing probable cause along with a discussion of the relative importance each is likely to be accorded by a judge or magistrate.

Flight   The flight of a suspect when approached by a law enforcement officer is one factor to be considered in determining probable cause. An example is a case in which officers in a patrol car had received information by radio about illegal activities involving non-tax-paid whiskey. They had been given a description of a car and of its occupants who were said to be involved in this illegal activity. When the officers spotted the car, they pulled up to it and called out the nickname of the defendant, whom they recognized. Defendant then threw his car into reverse and sped away. The officers overtook him after a short chase and approached his car. As they approached, they smelled the odor of moonshine whiskey and observed tin cans and plastic jugs in the back seat of the vehicle. They then arrested the defendant.

The court held that the arrest was valid and supported by probable cause. For purposes of this discussion, it is important that the court specifically held that the flight of the defendant was one factor *among others* to be considered in determining whether there was probable cause.   United States v. Brock, 408 F.2d 322 (5th Circuit Court of Appeals, 1969).

Flight by itself, however, will not support a finding of probable cause, as exemplified by the U.S. Supreme Court case of Wong Sun v. United States, 371 U.S. 471, 83 S.Ct. 407, 9 L.Ed.2d 441 (1963).   In that case, federal officers arrested a man named Hom Way at two o'clock in the morning and found narcotics in his possession.   Hom Way told the officers that he had purchased an ounce of heroin from a person named "Blackie Toy."   At six o'clock that same morning, the officers went to a laundry operated by James Wah Toy.   When Toy answered the door, one officer identified himself, whereupon Toy slammed the door and ran to his living quarters at the rear of the building.   The officers broke in, following Toy to his bedroom, and arrested him there.

The U.S. Supreme Court held that the arrest was made without probable cause. First, the officers had no basis in experience for confidence in the reliability of Hom Way's information.   (More will be said about reliability of informants later.)   Second, the mere fact of Toy's flight did not provide a justification for a warrantless arrest without further information.   On this point, the Court said:

> Toy's refusal to admit the officers and his flight down the hallway thus signified a guilty knowledge no more clearly than it did a natural desire to repel an apparently unauthorized intrusion.   .   .   .
> A contrary holding here would mean that a vague suspicion could be transformed into probable cause for arrest by reason of ambiguous conduct which the arresting officers themselves have provoked.   371 U.S. at 483–84, 83 S.Ct. at 415, 9 L.Ed.2d at 452–53.

Real or Physical Evidence   Another way in which officers may establish probable cause is by the observation and evaluation of real or physical evidence.   A good example is a case in which officers were summoned at 2:00 A.M. to a store that had been recently burglarized.   The officers discovered two sets of footprints in fresh-fallen snow leading from the store to the tire tracks of an automobile.   Two persons apparently had entered the automobile.   Since the automobile tire tracks were identifible by a distinctive tread the officers followed them.   After a short distance, the officers met another officer who had found a checkbook belonging to the store owner in the road.   Further down the road the officers found a bag containing electrical parts.   They then came upon a car parked in the middle of the road with its lights off.   The only other vehicle the officers had seen since leaving the scene of the crime was driven by a person known to the officers.   As the patrol car approached the parked car, the parked car turned on its lights and drove off.   The officers stopped the car, arrested its two occupants for breaking and entering, and searched them incident to the arrest.

The court found that the items of real evidence found and the reasonable inferences drawn from the evidence, together with the highly suspicious circumstances, provided probable cause to arrest the defendants.   The court added:

> Although the possibility of mistake existed, as it invariably does in a probable cause situation, they would have been remiss in their duty if they had not arrested the defendants promptly.   State v. Heald, Me., 314 A.2d 820, 825 (Supreme Judicial Court of Maine, 1973).

Furtive Conduct   Law enforcement officers are frequently confronted with suspicious circumstances, secretive movements, or other furtive conduct, that give them reason to believe either that criminal activity is afoot or that the person or persons observed are attempting to hide contraband, instrumentalities, or other evidence of crime. Usually, such circumstances or conduct will at least justify an officer's further investigation to determine whether a crime is being or is about to be committed. (See Chapter 12 on Stop and Frisk.)

Furtive conduct by itself, however, will usually be insufficient to establish probable cause to arrest or search because a person may be making a totally innocent gesture, asserting a constitutional right, or reacting in fear to an officer's approach. Also, a person's nervousness in the presence of a law enforcement officer will not alone amount to probable cause. The Supreme Court of Colorado stated that "[i]t is normal for law-abiding persons, as well as persons guilty of criminal activity, to be nervous when stopped by a policeman for a traffic offense." People v. Goessl, 186 Colo. 208, 211, 526 P.2d 664, 665 (1974). These innocent actions may often be mistaken for guilty behavior by a law enforcement officer investigating a possible crime. An individual should not be subject to arrest or search on such uncertain information.

A typical case illustrating this point involved a police officer who had spotted a car parked illegally with the defendant sitting in it. The officer pulled up next to the vehicle in order to advise the defendant it was illegally parked. As the officer approached, he noticed the defendant lean forward in the driver's seat. The officer directed the defendant to get out of the car, patted him down, and searched under the seat of the car. Marijuana was found and seized.

The court held the search and seizure illegal. In order to constitute probable cause for a search, there must be something more than a furtive gesture such as a motorist bending over in the front seat. The gesture must have some guilty significance arising either from specific information known to the officer or from additional suspicious circumstances observed by the officer. In this case, there were no such additional factors, and the search was not justified. Gallik v. People, 5 Cal. 3d 855, 97 Cal.Rptr. 693, 489 P.2d 573 (Supreme Court of California, 1971).

When there are additional circumstances, however, furtive action may provide one of the factors upon which probable cause may be based. In one such case, officers entered the home of one Bracamonte to execute a search warrant. As they entered, they spotted the defendant standing in the living room. The officers recognized the defendant because they had been told by informants that he was a narcotics dealer, and they had observed him in the company of narcotics suppliers on several occasions. The officers noticed that the defendant's right hand was clenched in a fist behind his right leg and they asked him what he was concealing. He made a further gesture to conceal his hand from view and then raised it in an upward motion toward his mouth. One officer grabbed his hand and opened his fist finding a balloon that contained what was later determined to be heroin. The defendant was placed under arrest.

The court held that the officers had probable cause to arrest the defendant and to search him incident to the arrest. The court said that the defendant's presence in a place suspected of narcotics activity, his past dealings in narcotics, combined with his furtive movements supplied the necessary probable cause. With respect to furtive movements, the court said:

> [T]o add to the highly suspicious circumstances, appellant not only attempted to hide something behind his leg in a clenched fist, but when the officer inquired as to what he was hiding, appellant moved his clenched fist rapidly toward his mouth. Swallowing narcotics is a popular method of avoiding detection, and movements of the hand toward the mouth have consistently been held to be the type of furtive movement that may be assessed in the probable cause equation. People v. Rodriquez, 274 Cal.App.2d 770, 775, 79 Cal.Rptr. 240, 243–44 (California Court of Appeal, 1969).

Perceptions of Narcotics Usage An officer's perceptions of narcotics usage may be considered in determining the existence of probable cause. This is similar to perceptions of furtive conduct except that furtive conduct is usually voluntary whereas indications of narcotics usage are usually involuntary. The indications of narcotics usage that are considered by courts in determining whether there is probable cause are abnormal contraction of pupils, discolored tissue on arms, fresh needle marks on arms, slurred speech, difficulty in balancing, nervousness, sweating, and heavy eyelids. Observation of one or two of these factors, standing alone, is probably not sufficient information to establish probable cause. When many such factors are present, however, or when there are other suspicious circumstances, chances are greater that the information available will support a finding of probable cause.

An example of perceptions of narcotics use providing probable cause is a case in which officers were investigating a report of suspicious activity of a person who had boarded a bus. The officers checked the bus and asked the suspicious person to dismount. While talking to him, they noticed that he was extremely nervous, sweating profusely, and the pupils of his eyes were extremely constricted despite poor lighting. The officers shined a flashlight in his eyes and noticed no apparent reaction to the light. Questions had to be repeated to him as though he were in a daze. The officers, being experienced narcotics officers, formed the opinion that the defendant was under the influence of a narcotic and arrested him. The court held that the observations of the officers were sufficient to establish probable cause to arrest. People v. Gregg, 267 Cal.App.2d 567, 73 Cal.Rptr. 362 (Court of Appeal of California, 1968).

Admissions A defendant's admission of criminal conduct to a law enforcement officer can often provide probable cause for an arrest. In fact, this is often all that is needed because an admission provides such direct evidence of the defendant's guilt that the officer need look no further. An example is a case in which officers observed a vehicle driven by the defendant fail to stop for a traffic light, and they followed it into a gas station. The officers intended only to issue a traffic citation. As the vehicle stopped, the defendant and two passengers stepped from the vehicle and advanced toward the officers. The officers patted them down to protect themselves and one officer thought he felt capsules in the defendant's pocket. He asked him if he had any pills in his pocket and the defendant responded, "They're reds. They belong to my mother." The officer then asked the defendant to take out the pills. When he did, the officer seized them. Later chemical analysis indicated they were seconal.

The court found that the usage of the term "reds" to describe seconal was so common that they could take judicial notice of it. The admission by the defendant was held to be sufficient in itself to provide probable cause and the arrest and seizure were both upheld. People v. Hubbard, 9 Cal.App.3d 827, 88 Cal.Rptr. 411 (California Court of Appeal, 1970).

It is worthy of note that in the preceding case, the court discussed at length whether the defendant should have been given *Miranda* warnings before the officer asked him about the pills. It was held that defendant was not in custody for purposes of *Miranda* because there was no "compelling atmosphere" and he was only subject to a "transitory" restraint. The important thing for the law enforcement officer to remember, however, is that whenever a defendant's admission or confession becomes part of a case, the requirements of *Miranda* must be satisfied, if they apply. Otherwise the admission or confession itself and any evidence seized as a result of it will be inadmissible in court. Guidelines for the law enforcement officer with respect to *Miranda* can be found in Chapter 13.

Failure to Explain or Evasiveness When a suspect, confronted by a law enforcement officer, fails to explain or provides unsatisfactory explanations for suspicious conduct or presence near the scene of a crime, this uncooperativeness or evasiveness may contribute to probable cause for an arrest. Common examples of this type of behavior are failing to produce identification, giving a false identification or alias, and giving false information about other matters. Usually, failure to explain or evasiveness standing alone will not be enough to provide probable cause.

In one case, state police had been notified that rental trucks were being used to transport stolen goods in a certain area of the state. An officer patrolling in this area stopped a rental truck for a routine check for registration, driver's license, and rental papers. Noticing that the truck was heavily loaded, the officer asked the defendant what he was carrying. The defendant claimed that his truck was empty. A subsequent search revealed a cargo of stolen cigarettes.

The court held that probable cause to search was provided by the officer's knowledge that rental trucks were being used in the area to transport stolen goods combined with the defendant's obvious lie. A search warrant was not needed in this situation because the truck was a movable vehicle and could be searched under the *Carroll* doctrine once there was probable cause to search. United States v. Gomori, 437 F.2d 312 (4th Circuit Court of Appeals, 1971). For a complete discussion of search and seizure of vehicles without a warrant, see Chapter 10.

High Crime Area Another factor that may contribute to a finding of probable cause is a suspect's unusual behavior in or near a high crime area. In a case illustrating this point, officers at 3:30 A.M. spotted a parked car with its headlights on in an area in which drug offenses were frequently committed. They noticed a man in a second car across the street receiving something from a white paper sack held by the driver of the first car. The officers approached the second car and observed a broken left window vent and the defendant in the back seat stuffing something behind the seat cushion. They ordered all four occupants out of the car and, as they emerged, a sack fell to the ground and broke, disgorging numerous pills and capsules resembling dangerous drugs. The occupants of the car were then arrested.

The court held that the combination of circumstances—the high-crime neighborhood, the hour, the apparent transfer of something, the suspicious conduct of some of the men, the broken window vent, and finally the broken bag full of pills and capsules—was sufficient to give the officers probable cause to arrest the occupants of the car. People v. Nieto, 267 Cal.App.2d 1, 72 Cal.Rptr. 764 (Court of Appeal of California, 1968).

It should be noted that the mere observation of a suspect acting in an innocent manner in a high crime area will not be enough for probable cause. There must be other facts indicative of possible criminal activity before there can be justification for an arrest or search.

Presence at the Crime Scene   Closely related to the observation of suspects in a high crime area is the observation of suspects and their conduct near the scene of recent criminal activity. Again, this standing alone will not support probable cause for an arrest or search, but combined with other factors, it may be sufficient.

In a case illustrating the point, an officer received a radio report that a break was in progress at a certain building. When the officer got to the building, he discovered that the rear window had been broken and metal bars over the window spread wide enough to permit the entrance of a person. He observed no suspects at the scene but heard voices coming from the second floor porch of an adjoining building. He entered this building and went up to the roof where he found the defendants, lightly clad on a cold night, attempting to conceal themselves. He arrested them, frisked them for weapons, and found coins that were later admitted into evidence.

The court found that the radio warning that a break was in progress, the observations of the officer at the scene, the presence of the defendants near the scene of the crime, lightly clad on a cold winter night, and their attempt to conceal themselves were sufficient to give the officer probable cause to arrest the defendants. State v. Mimmovich, Me., 284 A.2d 282 (Supreme Judicial Court of Maine, 1971).

Association With Other Known Felons   Association of a suspect with other known felons is considered in much the same way as presence in a high crime area for purposes of determining probable cause. It will not be sufficient alone to provide probable cause to arrest or search, but is one factor to be considered along with other indications of criminality.

In an illustrative case, police had arrested two associates of the defendant and her companion in connection with a bank robbery and had found part of the stolen money on these associates. The police knew that the defendant and her companion and the alleged robbers had been staying at the same motel when the alleged robbers were arrested only two days after the robbery. The police also knew that they had recovered only a portion of the money from the bank. The additional fact that the defendant and her companion had moved from the motel where they were staying immediately after their associates were arrested and registered under an assumed name at another motel convinced the court that officers had probable cause to arrest the defendant. United States v. Whitney, 425 F.2d 169 (8th Circuit Court of Appeals, 1970).

Past Criminal Conduct The mere fact that a suspect has a known criminal record will not alone provide probable cause for an arrest. As the U.S. Supreme Court said in the case of Beck v. Ohio:

> We do not hold that the officer's knowledge of the petitioner's physical appearance and previous record was either inadmissible or entirely irrelevant upon the issue of probable cause. . . . But to hold that knowledge of either or both of these facts constituted probable cause would be to hold that anyone with a previous criminal record could be arrested at will. 379 U.S. 89, 97, 85 S.Ct. 223, 228, 13 L.Ed.2d 142, 148 (1964).

As the court implies, however, the prior criminal activity of the suspect is a factor to be considered among others in the determination of probable cause. In an illustrative case, an officer observed in plain view in the back of a truck coils of copper wire, which were of a type and amount that was not readily available to the ordinary citizen, nor would the ordinary citizen ever have use for that type and amount. The officer knew this because he had considerable experience investigating copper wire thefts. Furthermore, the officer knew the defendant to be a copper wire thief and had arrested him on several felony charges before.

Based on this information the court found probable cause to seize the wire in the truck. The court emphasized, however, that the officer could not have seized the wire unless he had a reasonable foundation for the belief that it was stolen. The large amount and unusual nature of the copper wire observed in the back of the defendant's truck provided this reasonable foundation. These observations plus the knowledge of the defendant's prior criminal activity provided probable cause to seize the wire. The defendant's prior criminal activity alone would not have been enough. State v. Temple, 7 Or. 91, 488 P.2d 1380 (Court of Appeals of Oregon, 1971).

Unusual Hour The time of day can also be a factor in determining whether there is probable cause to arrest or search. Of course, a person will not be subject to search merely as a result of acting in an innocent manner at an early hour of the morning. If other factors are present, however, such as furtive conduct in a high crime area, the hour of the day may be a relevant factor in determining whether an arrest or search is justified. The case of *People v. Nieto* appearing above under "High Crime Area" is a good example of how the time of day enters into the probable cause equation.

Suspect Resembles Description A law enforcement officer may have obtained a physical description of a suspect or seen a mug shot from a police bulletin or wanted poster. If the officer spots someone who closely resembles such a description, an arrest of that person will be valid as based on probable cause. In fact, it has been held that the arrest would be justified even if the person arrested was the wrong person.

An example is a case in which an officer had received a photograph of a murder suspect at an early morning briefing session. He studied the photograph and later, while cruising in his patrol car, observed the defendant, who closely resembled the suspect in the photograph, driving the other way. The officer pulled the defendant's car over, arrested him for murder, and found evidence of another crime as a result of a search incident to arrest. It turned out that the defendant was not the person portrayed in the police photograph.

The court held, however, that the arrest was valid because probable cause could be found where the defendant bore a striking resemblance to a picture of a murder suspect in a police bulletin. And even though the defendant was not the murder suspect, the court said that once the police have reasonable cause to arrest one party, and when they reasonably mistake a second party for the first party, the arrest of the second party is a valid arrest. The evidence seized incident to the arrest was therefore found to be admissible. People v. Prather, 268 Cal.App.2d 748, 74 Cal. Rptr. 82 (California Court of Appeal, 1969).

Facts Arising During Investigation or Temporary Detention   It is very important for the law enforcement officer to realize that probable cause to arrest or search may arise during routine investigation or questioning of a suspect or in the typical "stop and frisk" situation. In these situations, the officer may initially only be seeking information or merely investigating suspicious circumstances. Yet during the course of investigation other facts may come to the officer's attention either from the words or actions of a detained person or from other sources. For example, the person may give evasive answers, attempt to flee, act in a furtive manner, or the officer may perceive any of the other indications of possible criminal activity discussed above. If these facts and circumstances are sufficient to establish probable cause to arrest or search, the officer may act accordingly.

The most important case in this area is the U.S. Supreme Court case of Terry v. Ohio, 392 U.S. 1, 88 S.Ct. 1868, 20 L.Ed.2d 889 (1968). This case and the entire subject of "stop and frisk" are discussed in Chapter 12. Several of the cases summarized in that chapter deal with the manner in which probable cause to arrest or search may arise from the stop and frisk situation. The reader is encouraged to read Chapter 12 and study the examples given.

Summary

Law enforcement officers should look for the types of information discussed above when they are on the beat and should know what relative importance a judge or magistrate is likely to place on each type of information in determining whether there is probable cause. Most importantly, however, officers should make sure that they have sufficient information *before* they act. Thus, if they decide to make an arrest or search without a warrant, they should be prepared *at that time* to justify their actions with specific facts and circumstances sufficient for probable cause. Likewise, if officers decide to apply for a warrant, they should state *in writing,* in the complaint or affidavit, the specific facts and circumstances that they believe give them probable cause to arrest or search. Of course, because probable cause is such an indefinite concept and because some judges and magistrates have stricter standards than others, the court may still find a lack of probable cause despite an officer's painstaking efforts.   Nevertheless, a careful and systematic approach by officers is likely to result in more solidly based cases, less waste of time and effort, and fewer violations of individual rights.

INFORMATION OBTAINED BY THE OFFICER THROUGH INFORMANTS

While a law enforcement officer's perceptions are an important source of information in determining probable cause, it is not possible for a law enforcement officer to be present at the scene to observe every crime that happens.   In fact, the majority of crimes are committed out of the presence of law enforcement officers, and yet there is still an obvious need to make arrests and searches for these crimes.   More importantly, arrests and searches made in connection with crimes committed out of the presence of law enforcement officers must conform to the same constitutional standards as those made in connection with observed crimes.

The difficulty for law enforcement officers lies in obtaining the authority to arrest or search when they have not personally observed any facts or circumstances upon which probable cause may be based.   The only solution, of course, is that their information must come from third persons, or informants, who have themselves personally observed the facts and circumstances.   The difficulty does not stop there, however.   Officers are still faced with the task of convincing a magistrate that the information supplied to them by the informant is reliable and worthy of being acted upon.   The following discussion will be devoted to setting forth the procedures to be followed by law enforcement officers in establishing probable cause to arrest or search, with or without a warrant, when the information comes from persons other than the officers themselves.

For purposes of discussion, we will concentrate on the situation in which the officer is applying for a search warrant based upon information from third persons. We do this to make the presentation more easily understandable and to emphasize again that the officer should *write down,* in the complaint or affidavit, all the information upon which probable cause is to be based.   The same probable cause considerations, however, are involved in arrest warrants and in warrantless arrests and searches, except of course, that the information need not be written down in the warrantless situation.   The term *informant* will be used throughout the discussion to refer to any third person from whom a law enforcement officer obtains information on criminal activity.

The method of establishing probable cause through the use of an informant's information is sometimes referred to as the *hearsay* method of establishing probable cause, as opposed to the direct observation method discussed above.   The hearsay method of establishing probable cause was the subject of a landmark decision by the U.S. Supreme Court in 1983.   That decision, Illinois v. Gates, 462 U.S. 213, 103 S.Ct. 2317, 76 L.Ed.2d 527, abandoned an approach to determining probable cause through the use of informants that had been established by two previous U.S. Supreme Court decisions, Aguilar v. Texas, 378 U.S. 108, 84 S.Ct. 1509, 12 L.Ed.2d 723 (1964) and Spinelli v. United States, 393 U.S. 410, 89 S.Ct. 584, 21 L.Ed.2d

637 (1969).   The *Aguilar* and *Spinelli* decisions had established specific requirements for law enforcement officers to follow in preparing complaints or affidavits
when using information received from informants.   The *Gates* decision abandoned
these specific requirements in favor of a "totality of the circumstances" approach to
determining probable cause.   In order to fully understand the *Gates* decision, and
also because the underlying rationales of *Aguilar, Spinelli,* and cases interpreting
them still retain their vitality, our discussion of the hearsay method of determining
probable cause will begin with a detailed analysis of the *Aguilar-Spinelli* line of
cases.   We will then evaluate the effect of the *Gates* "totality of the circumstances"
approach to the hearsay method of determining probable cause.

The Aguilar Case

Before the *Gates* decision, the leading case setting out the standards for establishing
probable cause under the hearsay method was the U.S. Supreme Court case of
Aguilar v. Texas, 378 U.S. 108, 84 S.Ct. 1509, 12 L.Ed.2d 723 (1964).   The *Aguilar*
case set out a *two-pronged test* for determining probable cause when the information in the affidavit was either entirely or partially obtained from an informant:

1. The affidavit must describe underlying circumstances from which a neutral and
detached magistrate may determine that the informant had a sufficient basis for his
or her knowledge and that the information was not the result of mere rumor or
suspicion.

2. The affidavit must describe underlying circumstances from which the magistrate
may determine that the informant was credible or that the informant's information
was reliable.

Both prongs of the *Aguilar* test had to be satisfied in order to establish probable
cause.   Each prong of the *Aguilar* test will be discussed separately here, emphasizing the duties of the law enforcement officer in each case.

Prong 1: Informant's Basis of Knowledge   The law enforcement officer must
demonstrate to the magistrate in the affidavit underlying circumstances enabling the
magistrate to independently evaluate the accuracy of an informant's conclusion.
This is usually done by showing how the informant knows the supplied information.
To satisfy this requirement, the affidavit must show either:

1. That the informant personally saw or perceived firsthand the information given
to the officer; or

2. That the informant's information came from another source, but there is good
reason to believe it.

Informant's Information is Firsthand   If the informant came upon the information
by personal observation, the law enforcement officer should have few problems in
satisfying the first prong of the *Aguilar* test.   The officer merely has to state, in the

affidavit, *how, when,* and *where* the informant obtained the information furnished to the officer. A good example is a case in which the officer stated in the affidavit:

> For approximately the past two months I have received information from an informant whose information has recently resulted in narcotic arrests and convictions that a Gregory Daniels who resides at 929 Logan N, (down) has been selling marijuana, hashish and heroin. My informant further states that he has seen Daniels sell drugs, namely: heroin and further that he has seen Daniels with heroin on his person. The informant has seen heroin on the premises of 929 Logan N, (down) within the past 48 hours. State v. Daniels, 294 Minn. 323, 325, 200 N.W.2d 403, 404 (Supreme Court of Minnesota, 1972).

The court said, with regard to this affidavit:

> There seems to be no dispute that such personal observation satisfies that part of the *Aguilar* test which requires that the affidavit contain facts to enable the magistrate to judge whether the informant obtained his knowledge in a reliable manner. 294 Minn. at 328–29, 200 N.W.2d at 406.

It is very important that the officer state in the affidavit the *time* when the informant obtained the information. This is especially true in affidavits used to apply for search warrants because probable cause to search can become stale with time. In one case, a law enforcement officer stated in his affidavit that his informant had told him that he had sold certain (stolen) property to the defendant. But the officer did not state when the sale took place. The court said that the affidavit was deficient because it failed to show that the information received from the informant was fresh as opposed to being remote. Windsor v. State, 48 Ala.App. 474, 265 So. 2d 916 (Court of Criminal Appeals of Alabama, 1972).

Sometimes, no matter how carefully an officer establishes an informant's method of obtaining the information, unavoidable errors in that information result in a serious injustice to a defendant. Courts will refuse to find probable cause to support the officer's actions in these situations. An example is a case in which officers picked up the defendant for hitchhiking and sent his name through the computer at the National Crime Information Center (N.C.I.C.), a national clearinghouse for law enforcement agencies administered by the FBI. The computer reported that the defendant was wanted in another city for a parole violation. The officers booked the defendant and subsequently found a gun in his possession. The defendant was eventually charged for the possession of the gun. The N.C.I.C. report was later found to be false. The defendant had satisfied the parole violation five months earlier. The court ordered the suppression of all evidence resulting from the defendant's arrest. The court said:

> [A] computer inaccuracy of this nature and duration, even if unintended, amounted to a capricious disregard for the rights of the defendant as a citizen of the United States. The evidence compels a finding that the government's action was equivalent to an arbitrary arrest, and that an arrest on this basis deprived defendant of his liberty without due process of law. United States v. Mackey, 387 F.Supp. 1121, 1125 (U.S. District Court for Nevada, 1975).

In this case, then, although the officers acted properly in all respects, evidence was ruled inadmissible through no fault of their own. It should be noted that a computer, as an informant, is usually assumed to have accurate information and officers should feel free to act on such information.

Informant's Information is Hearsay   If the informant's information comes from a third person, that person and his or her information must satisfy both prongs of the *Aguilar* test.   The officer preparing the affidavit must, therefore, show how the third person knows the information furnished to the informant, as described in the previous section.   For example, if the third person saw criminal activity taking place, a statement in the affidavit to that effect would be sufficient to satisfy the first prong of the *Aguilar* test.   The officer must also, however, satisfy prong 2 of the *Aguilar* test with respect to *both* the informant *and* the third person.   Prong 2 of *Aguilar* will be discussed later in this chapter.

Detailing Informant's Information   Courts recognize one other method of satisfying the first prong of the *Aguilar* test besides stating how, when, and where the informant came by the information provided.   In the U.S. Supreme Court case of Spinelli v. United States, 393 U.S. 410, 89 S.Ct. 584, 21 L.Ed.2d 637 (1969), the Court said:

> In the absence of a statement detailing the manner in which the information was gathered, it is especially important that the tip describe the accused's criminal activity in sufficient detail that the magistrate may know that he is relying on something more substantial than a casual rumor circulating in the underworld or an accusation based merely on an individual's general reputation.   393 U.S. at 416, 89 S.Ct. at 589, 21 L.Ed.2d at 644.

The *Spinelli* case cited another U.S. Supreme Court case, Draper v. United States, 358 U.S. 307, 79 S.Ct. 329, 3 L.Ed.2d 327 (1954), as an example of sufficient use of detail to satisfy the first prong of the *Aguilar* test.   In the *Draper* case, the informant did not state the way in which he had obtained his information. The informant did, however, report that the defendant had gone to Chicago the day before by train and that he would return to Denver by train with three ounces of heroin on one of two specified mornings.   In addition, the informant went on to describe, with minute particularity, the clothes that the defendant would be wearing and the bag he would be carrying upon his arrival at the Denver station.   The Supreme Court said:

> A magistrate, when confronted with such detail, could reasonably infer that the informant had gained his information in a reliable way.   393 U.S. at 417, 89 S.Ct. at 589, 21 L.Ed.2d at 644.

In Soles v. State, 16 Md.App. 656, 299 A.2d 502 (Maryland Court of Special Appeals, 1973), probable cause to conduct a warrantless search of an automobile was found even though the officer was unable to tell how, when, or where the informant obtained his information.   The court held that the information given by the informant was sufficiently detailed to indicate that he had gained his information in a reliable way.   Relevant parts of the officer's testimony at the motion to suppress hearing are quoted below, because the testimony indicates the type of detail that courts require to show that an informant spoke from personal knowledge:

> The informant described the appellant in the following detail:
>
> "A. The source described Mr. Soles. He gave—told me that the name of the subject was Soles. He didn't know any other name. Just Soles. He described Mr. Soles as being approximately five foot eight inches in height, approximately 160 pounds, as being a Negro male, approximately in his early 30's. I believe one age was 35 years of age. He said he had a receding hairline slightly, a small bush cut. He said his hair wasn't a big bush. He said it was short. He said he had a goatee and he was light skinned."
>
> The informant described the appellant's automobile in the following detail:
>
> "A. It was a late model blue convertible with a white top bearing New York tags, I believe WQ 9579, something like that; WX 9579. My recollection isn't real good on that."
>
> The informant described the operation generally and the cocaine specifically in the following detail:
>
> "THE WITNESS: The source called me at home and related to me that he had information about a male subject from New York who was a major distributor of cocaine to several known narcotics dealers in Washington. He related to me that this source was named Soles. He also indicated to me that he had given the tag number of Soles' car to my partner, Officer Robert Polzin, earlier that week, and in the conversation with this source he related to me that Soles had in excess of an eighth of a kilo of cocaine in his trunk of his car inside a briefcase. He said this cocaine would be inside a glass jar. He stated that Soles had several thousand dollars in cash on him, which were the assets from the sale of part of the cocaine he brought down from New York. He stated he was armed with a pistol, and stated that he would be leaving Washington for New York before three o'clock that evening."
>
> The trial judge, "when confronted with such detail, could reasonably infer that the informant had gained his information in a reliable way," . . . that is, via first-hand observation. Upon our independent review, we draw such an inference. 16 Md.App. at 663–66, 299 A.2d at 507–08.

The important thing for law enforcement officers to remember is that if they do not know the manner in which their informant obtained the information, they can still satisfy the first prong of the *Aguilar* test by obtaining as much detail as possible from the informant and stating *all* of it in the complaint or affidavit.

Prong 2: Informant's Veracity   In addition to demonstrating how the informant obtained the information, the officer must demonstrate to the magistrate in the affidavit underlying circumstances to convince the magistrate of the informant's veracity, i.e., that the informant is credible or that the informant's information is reliable. There are very few cases dealing with the reliability of the informant's information. This aspect of the informant's veracity is only relied upon when it is impossible to establish the informant's credibility. Nevertheless, given this impossibility, one may still ask if the informant's information was furnished under circumstances giving reasonable assurances of trustworthiness. In Thompson v. State, 16 Md.App. 560, 298 A.2d 458 (1973), the court found that information supplied by an unnamed street drug seller to one of his clients about a future drug "drop" was "reliable." The court said:

> Though from the criminal milieu, to be sure, he was not, wittingly at least, working with the police. He was not in the position of "the common informant . . . hidden behind a cloak of immunity from prosecution for his own misdeeds." . . . This street seller was, so far as he knew, engaged in a purely commercial venture for his own profit. He was dealing with a regular and presumably valued customer. Being unable initially to satisfy his customer's demand, it was to his every advantage to assure the prompt return of that customer as soon as fresh merchandise was available for sale. He simply had no purpose in misleading his own clientele. The circumstances in which the seller passed on the information to a customer and confidant are replete, we think, with reasonable assurances of trustworthiness. Upon our constitutionally-mandated independent review, we believe the information furnished by this secondary informant to have been reliable, notwithstanding his utter lack of demonstrated credibility. 16 Md.App. at 565, 298 A.2d at 462.

With this alternative in mind, the remainder of this discussion of the informant's veracity will be devoted to methods for establishing the "credibility" aspect of veracity. The amount and type of information that must be provided depends partially upon whether the informant's identity is disclosed or undisclosed.

Disclosure of Informant's Identity Whether or not the informant's identity is disclosed is an important consideration in establishing the credibility of an inform- ant. If law enforcement officers identify the informant by name in the affidavit, magistrates are more likely to accept the credibility of the informant because they can have the disclosed informant appear before them if they feel further facts are necessary. Therefore, usually, if the informant's name and address are provided in the affidavit, the officer does not need to do anything further to establish the informant's credibility. In People v. Glaubman, 175 Colo. 41, 50–52, 485 P.2d 711, 716–17 (1971), the court said:

> She made her information known to the police, and the police verified the information which was available. She was identified by name and is not on the same footing as the common informant who seeks to remain nameless and hidden and barters and sells information to the police. The nature of informants, which are a necessary part of police work, is such that the common informant is hidden behind a cloak of anonymity. A special privilege has been granted to the police to insure that the identity of the informant is not disclosed, except under circumstances that would promote or cause a failure of justice if identity of the informer was withheld from the defendant. . . . More often than not, the informant is paid or provides information in exchange for immunity from prosecution for his own misdeeds.
> Our view, which is supported by a number of decisions, is that the citizen-informer, adviser, or reporter who acts openly to see that our laws are enforced should be encouraged, and his information should not be subjected to the same tests as are applied to the information of an ordinary informer. . . .
> When citizens are involved, it cannot be expected that they would have had past transactions or dealings with the police. . . .
>
> * * *
>
> We now announce that henceforth, Colorado will follow the citizen-informer rule and will recognize that a citizen who is identified by name and address and was

a witness to criminal activity cannot be considered on the same basis as the ordinary informant. We believe, and hold, that the constitutional safeguards afforded under the Fourth and Fourteenth Amendments to the United States Constitution .   .   . are met when the affidavit supporting an arrest warrant or search warrant contains the name and address of the citizen-informant who was a witness to criminal activity and includes a statement of the underlying circumstances.

When the informant's identity is undisclosed, however, the magistrate needs some information upon which to determine credibility. This information must come from the law enforcement officer's affidavit. The amount and quality of the information that the officer must supply depends upon whether the informant is an ordinary citizen informant or a criminal informant.

Ordinary Citizen Informant Some courts have said that an undisclosed ordinary citizen informant is presumed credible and no further evidence of credibility need be stated in the affidavit beyond the informant's status as a victim of or witness to a crime. One court stated:

> One cannot approach the problem of informants whose information may or may not be sufficient to create "probable cause" as if there was only two classes: reliable informants whose information has previously been tested by the police and "all others." A multitude of cases .   .   . attest to the fact that information from a citizen who purports to be the victim of or to have witnessed a crime may, under certain circumstances, provide a sufficient basis for an arrest. People v. Griffin, 250 Cal.App.2d 545, 550–51, 58 Cal.Rptr. 707, 711 (California Court of Appeals, 1967).

The reason behind this rule has been stated by the Supreme Court of Wisconsin:

> [A]n ordinary citizen who reports a crime which has been committed in his presence, or that a crime is being or will be committed, stands on much different ground than a police informer. He is a witness to criminal activity who acts with an intent to aid the police in law enforcement because of his concern for society or for his own safety. He does not expect any gain or concession for his information. An informer of this type usually would not have more than one opportunity to supply information to the police, thereby precluding proof of his reliability by pointing to previous accurate information which he has supplied. State v. Paszek, 50 Wis.2d 619, 184 N.W.2d 836, 843 (1971).

In addition, the credibility of a citizen informant is accepted because, in contrast to the underworld informant, the citizen informant would be likely to fear the consequences of committing perjury. Also, ordinary citizens would not want to risk a civil suit that might require them to pay damages if they were vindictive in their report. People v. Hicks, 38 N.Y.2d 90, 378 N.Y.S.2d 660, 341 N.E.2d 227 (Court of Appeals of New York, 1975).

Some courts have suggested that more information about an undisclosed ordinary citizen informant is required to establish credibility. The Arkansas Supreme Court held that there was no probable cause to arrest when the only information officers had was an anonymous telephone tip that a certain car was occupied by two armed men. The court said:

> [I]f this arrest must be upheld on the basis of sufficient probable cause, any officer may arrest anyone at any time and justify his action by attributing it to an

anonymous telephone call. The protection of the Bill of Rights is not to be so readily circumvented. Conor v. State, 260 Ark. 172, 175, 538 S.W.2d 304, 305 (1976).

The court indicated that the officers should have either obtained more information about the informant or more facts pointing to the commission of an offense before the court would find probable cause to arrest. The Supreme Court of Virginia, however, found the informant credible in a case in which the affidavit stated that, while the informant had not previously furnished information to the police concerning violations of the narcotics laws, he was steadily employed, was a registered voter, enjoyed a good reputation in his neighborhood, and had expressed concern for young people involved with narcotics. Brown v. Commonwealth, 212 Va. 672, 187 S.E.2d 160 (1972).

In another Virginia case, an officer applying for a search warrant stated in the affidavit that he had known the ordinary citizen informant and his family for many years and that the informant was known to be credible. The court said:

> Although more extensive background information would be highly desirable, "a common sense and realistic" interpretation of the affidavit . . . leads us to the conclusion that it contains information reported by a first time citizen informer whose name was withheld by the affiant.
>
> Public-spirited citizens should be encouraged to furnish to the police information of crimes. Accordingly, we will not apply to citizen informers the same standard of reliability as is applicable when police act on tips from professional informers or those who seek immunity for themselves, whether such citizens are named . . . or, as here, unnamed. Guzewicz v. Commonwealth, 212 Va. 730, 735–36, 187 S.E.2d 144, 148 (Supreme Court of Virginia, 1972).

As these cases illustrate, there is some disagreement on how much backup information needs to be stated in the affidavit to establish the credibility of the undisclosed ordinary citizen informant. Since the issue has not been settled, it is strongly recommended that the law enforcement officer make every effort to provide in the affidavit additional information, if available, relating to the citizen informant's credibility as was done in the two Virginia cases cited above.

Criminal Informant Unlike the ordinary citizen, whose credibility may sometimes be presumed, the criminal informant's credibility must be established by a statement of underlying facts and circumstances establishing credibility. Criminal informants may be professional police informants, persons with a criminal record, accomplices in a crime, or persons seeking immunity for themselves. Usually, criminal informants will not want their identity disclosed in the affidavit. The U.S. Supreme Court held that police officers need not disclose identity of informants if their credibility is otherwise satisfactorily established. In McCray v. Illinois, 386 U.S. 300, 306–07, 87 S.Ct. 1056, 1060, 18 L.Ed.2d 62, 68 (1967), the Court quoted the New Jersey Supreme Court with approval:

> "If a defendant may insist upon disclosure of the informant in order to test the truth of the officer's statement that there is an informant or as to what the informant related or as to the informant's reliability, we can be sure that every defendant will demand disclosure. He has nothing to lose and the prize may be the suppression

of damaging evidence if the State cannot afford to reveal its source, as is so often the case. And since there is no way to test the good faith of a defendant who presses the demand, we must assume the routine demand would have to be routinely granted. The result would be that the State could use the informant's information only as a lead and could search only if it could gather adequate evidence of probable cause apart from the informant's data. Perhaps that approach would sharpen investigatorial techniques, but we doubt that there would be enough talent and time to cope with crime upon that basis. Rather we accept the premise that the informer is a vital part of society's defensive arsenal. The basic rule protecting his identity rests upon that belief."

Whether or not the informant's identity is disclosed in the affidavit, officers should state in the affidavit the reasons why they believe a criminal informant to be a credible person. The following facts will be considered relevant by a magistrate in establishing the credibility of a criminal informant:

1. Informant has given accurate information in the past. The usual method of establishing the credibility of a criminal informant is by showing that the informant has given accurate information in the past that has led to arrests, convictions, recovery of stolen property, or some like accomplishment. This is sometimes referred to as establishing the informant's "track record."

Courts will usually not read affidavits attempting to establish the credibility of informants with undue technicality. United States v. Ventresca, 380 U.S. 102, 85 S.Ct. 741, 13 L.Ed.2d 684 (U.S. Supreme Court, 1965). Nevertheless, a law enforcement officer may not simply state by way of conclusion that the informant is credible because of proven credibility. The officer must give a factual statement citing other cases or incidents in which the informant has given accurate information in the past.

The key factor in establishing the credibility of an informant by this method is the *accuracy* of the information supplied by the informant in the past. In one case, a defendant argued that the credibility of an informant against him had not been established because there was no proof that his prior tips had resulted in convictions. The court found the informant credible despite the failure of any of his tips to result in convictions. The language of the court in emphasizing the importance of the *accuracy* of the tips, rather than their resulting in convictions, is worthy of quotation:

> Convictions, while corroborative of an informer's reliability, are not essential in establishing his reliability. Arrests, standing alone, do not establish reliability, but information that has been proved accurate does. Arrestees may not be prosecuted; if prosecuted they may not be indicted; if indicted they may not be tried; if tried, they may not be convicted. If a case is tried, the informer may never testify; his credibility may never be passed upon in court. The true test of his reliability is the accuracy of his information. People v. Lawrence, 133 Ill.App.2d 542, 544, 273 N.E.2d 637, 639 (Appellate Court of Illinois, 1971).

It is worthwhile to give some examples of the kinds of statements in affidavits that have been found sufficient to establish the credibility of a criminal informant. In one case, the court found sufficient a statement that the informant had "furnished reliable and accurate information on approximately 20 occasions over the past four years."   United States v. Dunnings, 425 F.2d 836, 839 (2nd Circuit Court of Appeals, 1969).   In another case, the court held that the credibility of the informant was sufficiently shown where the affidavit stated that the informant's information "has recently resulted in narcotic arrests and convictions."   State v. Daniels, 294 Minn. 323, 329, 200 N.W.2d 403, 406–07 (Supreme Court of Minnesota, 1972).   A third more detailed affidavit, which was found to be sufficient, specified that on one occasion within the last two weeks a search warrant had been issued pursuant to information from the informant and narcotics were seized, and within the last month the informant introduced the officer to an individual who he said was a dealer and heroin was purchased by the officer from that person.   United States v. Smith, 462 F.2d 456 (8th Circuit Court of Appeals, 1972).

It is strongly suggested that, where possible, the officer follow the example of the third case cited and give as much detail as to the informant's credibility as possible.   In the other two cases, even though the court found the informant credible, the information in the affidavits came very close to being mere conclusions of the affiant, and the affidavits were, therefore, very close to being insufficient. Officers should tell the magistrate in the affidavit when previous information was furnished; whether evidence was found that the informant said would be found; whether an informant's information was the major basis for an arrest or conviction or only a minor factor; whether the informant always provided correct information; and any other information that will help the magistrate make an informed judgment about an anonymous informant's credibility.   In addition, the officer could describe for the magistrate such things as "the informer's general background, employment, personal attributes that enable him to observe and relate accurately, position in the community, reputation with others, personal connection with the suspect, any circumstances which suggest the probable absence of any motivation to falsify, the apparent motivation for supplying the information, the presence or absence of a criminal record or association with known criminals, and the like."   United States v. Harris, 403 U.S. 573, 600, 91 S.Ct. 2075, 2090, 29 L.Ed.2d 723, 743 (U.S. Supreme Court, 1971) (dissenting opinion).   Officers should realize that no special words will automatically convince a magistrate of an informant's credibility.   Therefore, officers should recite in the affidavit all they know about an informant without revealing the informant's identity.

If officers have no *personal* knowledge of circumstances demonstrating that an informant is credible, they may state in the affidavit information about the informant's credibility received from other law enforcement officers.   State v. Lambert, Me., 363 A.2d 707 (Supreme Judicial Court of Maine, 1976).   Officers should state the names of other law enforcement officers and they should state in detail how those officers acquired personal knowledge of the informant's credibility.

A dog trained to react to controlled substances may also be considered an informant.   The dog's credibility can also be established by presenting the "track record" of the dog and its handler.   In United States v. Race, 529 F.2d 12 (1st Circuit Court of Appeals, 1976), a dog reacted positively to two wooden crates in an airline warehouse containing some 300 crates.   The dog's reaction provided the basis for probable cause to arrest the defendant.   The court said:

We do not, of course, suggest that any dog's excited behavior could, by itself, be adequate proof that a controlled substance was present, but here the Government laid a strong foundation of canine reliability and handler expertise. Murphy [the dog's handler] testified that the dog had undergone intensive training in detecting drugs in 1971, that he had at least four hours a week of follow-up training since then, as well as work experience, and that the strong reaction he had to the crates was one that in the past had invariably indicated the presence of marijuana, hashish, heroin or cocaine.   529 F.2d at 14.

2. Informant made admissions or turned over evidence against his or her own penal interest.   The U.S. Supreme Court, in the case of United States v. Harris, 403 U.S. 573, 91 S.Ct. 2075, 29 L.Ed.2d 723 (1971), held that an admission made by an informant against his own penal interest is sufficient information to establish the credibility of the informant.   The informant admitted that over a long period and currently he had been buying illicit liquor at a certain place.   The Court said:

> People do not lightly admit a crime and place critical evidence in the hands of the police in the form of their own admissions.   Admissions of crime, like admissions against proprietary interests, carry their own indicia of credibility—sufficient at least to support a finding of probable cause to search.   That the informant may be paid or promised a "break" does not eliminate the residual risk and opprobrium of having admitted criminal conduct.   403 U.S. at 583–84, 91 S.Ct. at 2082, 29 L.Ed. 2d at 734.

The Supreme Judicial Court of Maine extended the U.S. Supreme Court's decision to include the turning over of self-incriminating evidence as worthy of consideration toward establishing an informant's credibility.   In the case of State v. Appleton, Me., 297 A.2d 363 (1972), an informant had purchased certain drugs at the defendant's apartment and the same day brought those drugs into the police to be tested.   A law enforcement officer applied for a warrant to search the apartment, stating both that the defendant had purchased the drugs and that he had delivered them to the police.

The court held that these actions of the informant justified a belief in the credibility of his story.   The court said that "[a]n informant is not likely to turn over to the police such criminal evidence unless he is certain in his own mind that his story implicating the persons occupying the premises where the sale took place will withstand police scrutiny."   297 A.2d at 369.

3. Informant has served as such over a period of time.   Some courts have held that the credibility of an informant can be established by a law enforcement officer even though the officer does not demonstrate the informant's "track record" or the informant's admission or turning over of evidence against his or her penal interest. In the case of U.S. v. Stallings, 413 F.2d 200 (7th Circuit Court of Appeals, 1969), the officer, applying for a search warrant, merely stated in the affidavit that his informant had been an informant of the local police department and the Federal Bureau of Narcotics during a two-month period, and that the informant had been purchasing unlawful drugs from the defendant during this period.   The court held that the informant's credibility, while not expressly stated, could be inferred from the statement made by the officer.

It should be noted that this method of establishing credibility is only to be used in emergencies or where it is impossible to use other methods. Also, some courts may not accept this method of establishing the credibility of the informant.

4. Informant conducted investigation under supervision of law enforcement officer. The Maine Supreme Judicial Court has approved another method of establishing the credibility of an informant. If an officer can show the magistrate that an informant worked under the close supervision of the officer in gathering evidence of criminal activity, the magistrate can consider such supervision as an indication of the informant's credibility. The Maine court said:

> We think that where an informer works in tandem with a law officer, the law officer continually coaching and observing the informer, the reports of the informer may be deemed credible even where certain material aspects of the informer's activities are without the officer's personal knowledge or observation. We think the law officer's physical proximity and active participation in the informant's intrigue is sufficient corroboration at least to provide, in part, a factual basis for the magistrate's conclusion that the informant is credible or his information reliable. State v. Gamage, Me., 340 A.2d 1, 16 (1975).

The officer preparing the affidavit in support of a request for a search warrant should state the details of observations of and transactions with the informant. A mere statement that the officer supervised the informant will probably not suffice. Officers should note that some courts may not accept this method of establishing the credibility of the informant.

This concludes our discussion of the two-pronged *Aguilar* test for establishing probable cause when the information is obtained by the officer through informants. The law enforcement officer should keep in mind when applying for an arrest or search warrant that his main purpose is to show in the affidavit or complaint that there is a substantial basis for crediting the information supplied. This means that the officer must convince the magistrate that the affidavit is not merely based upon casual rumor overheard at a bar or on the street, nor is it an accusation based merely on an individual's reputation. This is the reason for the requirement of stating underlying facts to establish the informant's basis of knowledge and veracity. If the officer, in the complaint or affidavit, can satisfy both prongs of the test and the informant's information is sufficient to establish probable cause, the magistrate will very likely issue the arrest or search warrant. If, however, the officer is unable to satisfy the second *Aguilar* prong on the informant's veracity *or* if the informant's information is not sufficient to establish probable cause, even though both prongs of *Aguilar* are satisfied, there is still the possibility that the information in the affidavit may be *corroborated* by other information to establish probable cause. We turn now to a discussion of how corroboration may work to cure an otherwise insufficient affidavit.

CORROBORATION

When law enforcement officers attempt to obtain an arrest or search warrant based on information from an informant, they will often be unable to satisfy one or both of the *Aguilar* standards in their complaint or affidavit. They may not have sufficient information to establish the informant's credibility or they may not be able to show how the informant came upon the information or obtain sufficient detail on criminal activity from the informant to convince a magistrate that the information was obtained in a dependable manner. Despite this initial failure to satisfy the *Aguilar* requirements, however, officers still have one method by which they may cure the deficiencies of the affidavit. This is by *corroboration* of the information in the affidavit from independent investigation by themselves or other law enforcement officers. *Corroboration* simply means strengthening or making more certain the information supplied by the informant by stating in the affidavit backup or supporting information obtained by law enforcement officials.

Corroboration is a very useful tool of the law enforcement officer in establishing probable cause. Most cases involve many pieces of information that are neither purely a result of the direct observation of a law enforcement officer nor purely the observations of an informant. There is usually a mixture of these two types of information. For instance, an officer may receive a tip from a third person about criminal activity, and through surveillance or independent investigation, the officer may personally perceive certain indications of criminal activity. By writing this corroborating information in the affidavit in addition to establishing the credibility of the informant and the basis of knowledge of the informant's information, the officer enables the magistrate to consider all facts that may bear upon probable cause, no matter what the source of the information is. Therefore, the magistrate is not limited to considering only the informant's information, but may also consider other information provided by the law enforcement officer in support of the informant's information. This additional information can very often mean the difference between a magistrate's issuing or not issuing a warrant.

Effect of Corroborative Information on Probable Cause

The corroborative information provided by the law enforcement officer in the affidavit may work in three possible ways:

1. The information may result from direct perception of crime or perception of such strong indications of criminal activity that the information may *itself* provide the basis for probable cause to search or arrest, independent of the informant's information. See above under "Indications of Criminal Activity That May Contribute to Probable Cause." Corroborative information of this nature will provide probable cause to search even if neither Prong 1 nor Prong 2 of the *Aguilar* test is met.

2. The officer's information may support or verify the hearsay information provided by the informant. For example, if an officer has not been able to satisfy the requirements of Prong 2 of the *Aguilar* test, the independent supporting information may provide the necessary verification of the informant's report. In other words, if some of the significant details of the informant's information are shown to be true by independent observation of the law enforcement officer, the magistrate is encouraged to believe that all the story is probably true and that the informant is credible.

3. The officer's information may be added to hearsay information that meets *Aguilar* standards. Although neither are sufficient unto themselves to establish probable cause, when combined they may provide enough incriminating information to establish probable cause. It must be strongly emphasized here that the officer's perceptions will serve to corroborate the hearsay information in the affidavit *only* if these perceptions are presented to the magistrate. As stated earlier, the preferred method of presenting information on probable cause to the magistrate is by writing it in the complaint or affidavit. Therefore, officers are strongly advised to *write down* in the affidavit in addition to the information supplied to satisfy the *Aguilar* test: (1) All of *their* perceptions that relate to the criminal activity for which the search warrant is being sought; and (2) All of *their* perceptions relating to the information provided by the informant.

Rather than discuss further the ways in which corroboration works and how the law enforcement officer should use corroborative information to obtain a search warrant, we turn now to a detailed discussion of two cases that illustrate the use of corroboration. The cases have been chosen because their fact situations are similar, their results are different, and they both contain an extensive discussion of corroboration. This method of presentation has been chosen because corroboration does not easily lend itself to a setting out of specific guidelines. More importantly, the law in this area is still somewhat unsettled and any hard and fast rules would not be meaningful.

Spinelli v. U.S.

The first case to be discussed is the U.S. Supreme Court decision in Spinelli v. United States, 393 U.S. 410, 89 S.Ct. 584, 21 L.Ed.2d 637 (1969). This is the leading case on corroboration and should therefore be familiar to all law enforcement officers.

In this case, the defendant was convicted of traveling to St. Louis, Missouri, from a nearby Illinois suburb with the intention of conducting gambling activities prohibited by Missouri law. On appeal, the defendant challenged the validity of a search warrant that was used to obtain incriminating evidence against him. The affidavit in support of the search warrant contained the following allegations:

1. The FBI had kept track of the defendant's movements on five days during August 1965. On four of these occasions, the defendant was seen crossing a bridge from Illinois to St. Louis between 11 A.M. and 12:15 P.M. On four of the five days, the defendant was seen parking his car in a lot used by residents of a certain apartment house between 3:30 P.M. and 4:45 P.M. On one day, the defendant was followed further and seen to enter a particular apartment in the building.

2. An FBI check with the telephone company revealed that this apartment contained two telephones listed under the name of Grace Hagen and carried two different numbers.

3. The defendant was known to the affiant and to federal law enforcement agents and local law enforcement agents as a "bookmaker, an associate of bookmakers, a gambler, and an associate of gamblers." 393 U.S. at 414, 89 S.Ct. at 588, 21 L.Ed. 2d at 642.

4. The FBI had been informed by a confidential reliable informant that the defendant was operating a handbook and accepting wagers and disseminating wagering information by means of telephones assigned the same numbers as the phones in the above-mentioned apartment.

The Court first discussed in detail allegation number 4, the information obtained from the informant. The Court said:

> The informer's report must first be measured against *Aguilar's* standards so that its probative value can be assessed. If the tip is found inadequate under *Aguilar,* the other allegations which corroborate the information contained in the hearsay report should then be considered. 393 U.S. at 415, 89 S.Ct. at 588, 21 L.Ed.2d at 643.

The Court found the informant's tip inadequate under *Aguilar.* Prong 2 was not satisfied because the affiant merely stated that he had been informed by a "confidential reliable informant." This was a mere conclusion or opinion of the officer-affiant because no *underlying circumstances* were stated to show the magistrate that the informant was credible.

For similar reasons, Prong 1 was not satisfied either. The affidavit did not state sufficient *underlying circumstances* from which the informant concluded that the defendant was running a bookmaking operation. There was no statement as to how, when, or where the informant received his information—whether he personally observed the defendant at work or whether he ever placed a bet with him. Furthermore, if the informant came by his information from third persons, there was no explanation why these sources were credible or how they obtained their information.

Finally, the affidavit did not describe the defendant's alleged criminal activity in sufficient detail to convince a magistrate that the information was more than mere rumor or suspicion. The only facts supplied were that the defendant was using two specified telephones and that these phones were being used in gambling operations. As the Court said, this meager report could easily have been obtained from an offhand remark at a neighborhood bar.

The Court then turned to a consideration of the other information supplied in the affidavit—allegations 1 and 2 above—to see if they provided sufficient corroboration of the informant's information or provided probable cause in themselves. The Court found that these two items reflected only innocent-seeming activity and data. Defendant's travels to and from the apartment building and his entry into a particular apartment could not be taken as indicative of gambling activity. And there was certainly nothing unusual about an apartment containing two separate telephones. The Court, therefore, concluded:

> At most, these allegations indicated that Spinelli could have used the telephones specified by the informant for some purpose. This cannot by itself be said to

support both the inference that the informer was generally trustworthy and that he had made his charge against Spinelli on the basis of information obtained in a reliable way. 393 U.S. at 417, 89 S.Ct. at 589, 21 L.Ed.2d at 644.

Finally, the Court considered allegation 3—that defendant was "known" to the FBI and others as a gambler. The Court called this a bald and unilluminating assertion of police suspicion and said that it may not be used to give additional weight to allegations that would otherwise be insufficient.

It is important to note that since the decision in the *Spinelli* case, the U.S. Supreme Court has decided that the alleged criminal reputation of a suspect *may* be considered by a magistrate in evaluating an affidavit for a search warrant. United States v. Harris, 403 U.S. 573, 91 S.Ct. 2075, 29 L.Ed.2d 723 (1971). In the *Harris* case, the Court said that the reason criminal reputation couldn't be used in *Spinelli* was because *Spinelli* contained no factual indication of past criminal activities on the defendant's part to back up the assertion. The affiant officer in the *Harris* case had stated in the affidavit that the defendant had a reputation for four years as a trafficker of non-tax-paid distilled spirits, that the officer had received information from all types of persons as to the defendant's activities, and that during this period a sizeable stash of illicit whiskey had been found in an abandoned house under defendant's control. The Court held that when a criminal reputation is supported by such factual statements indicating prior criminal conduct, the reputation can be considered along with the other allegations. Criminal reputation will be considered again below in the discussion of the case of *Dawson v. State.* The important thing for law enforcement officers to remember is that if they wish to use a suspect's criminal reputation in an affidavit in support of a warrant, they should provide *underlying facts* indicating prior criminal conduct.

The *Spinelli* case is valuable to the law enforcement officer in that it traces through all the *Aguilar* requirements for establishing probable cause using an informant's information and gives reasons why each test was not met by the affidavit in that case. It then considers other information in the affdiavit as corroboration of the informant's information and gives specific reasons why the corroborative information is inadequate. Officers should read the case in its entirety to clear up any questions not answered in this chapter.

We turn now to a consideration of Dawson v. State, 11 Md.App. 694, 276 A.2d 680 (Court of Special Appeals of Maryland, 1971), a case also involving gambling. The case is very similar to the *Spinelli* case, except that the search warrant in *Dawson* was found to be valid. Our discussion will center on the differences between the two cases that caused the court in the *Dawson* case to reach a different conclusion.

Dawson v. State

In the *Dawson* case, the defendant was convicted of unlawfully maintaining premises for the purpose of selling lottery tickets and of unlawfully betting, wagering, or gambling on the results of horse races. He appealed, claiming among other things that the search warrant for his home was illegal because adequate probable cause had not been shown. The affidavit for the warrant contained nine paragraphs. The first paragraph listed the investigative experience of the affiant and ended with his conclusion that gambling activities were at that time being conducted at defendant's premises. The third through ninth paragraphs contained the direct observations of the affiant officer. These paragraphs will be considered later. The second paragraph dealt with hearsay information and is quoted below:

> That on Thursday April 17, 1969 your affiant interviewed a confidential source of information who has given reliable information in the past relating to illegal gambling activities which has resulted in the arrest and conviction of persons arrested for illegal gambling activities and that the source is personally known to your affiant. That this source related that there was illegal gambling activities taking place at 8103 Legation Road, Hyattsville Prince George's County, Maryland by a one Donald Lee Dawson. That the source further related that the source would call telephone #577–5197 and place horse and number bets with Donald Lee Dawson. 11 Md.App. at 704–05, 276 A.2d at 685.

The court analyzed this paragraph in terms of the two-pronged *Aguilar* test. Considering the informant's basis of knowledge first, the court found that *Aguilar* was satisfied. The affidavit stated that the informant had personally called the phone number 577–5197 and had placed horse and number bets with the defendant. This is in contrast with the *Spinelli* case, where nothing was said about how the informant obtained his information.

As to the credibility of the informant, the court felt that the information furnished was close to borderline. In that the affidavit stated that both arrests and convictions had resulted from the informant's information in the past, it was more than a mere conclusion or opinion of the officer-affiant. Also the circumstances stated went further to establish the informant's credibility than those in *Spinelli* where the informant was merely described as a "confidential reliable informant." The court implied that more specific information on the informant's credibility would have been desirable but said:

> It may well be that the facts here recited are enough to establish the credibility of the informant. In view of the strong independent verification hereinafter to be discussed, however, it is unnecessary for the State to rely exclusively on such recitation. 11 Md.App. at 706–07, 276 A.2d at 686.

The court, then, assumed for purposes of discussion that the credibility of the informant had *not* been adequately established and it went on to discuss *corroboration*.

In its discussion of corroboration, the court made a concerted effort to compare the affidavit in this case with that in *Spinelli*. We turn now to a discussion of the information in paragraphs three through nine of the affidavit in *Dawson* to see how it corroborates the informant's information.

In these paragraphs, the affiant stated that a surveillance of the defendant's activities had been conducted over a six-day period in April 1969. The following things were observed or otherwise learned during this period and stated in the affidavit:

■ The defendant was observed to be engaged in no apparent legitimate employment during the period.

■ The defendant had two telephones in his residence with two separate lines, both of which had silent listings.

■ One of the defendant's silent listings had been picked up in the course of a raid on a lottery operation three years earlier in another town.

■ On each day of observation, the defendant was observed to purchase an Armstrong Scratch Sheet, which gives information about horses running at various tracks that day.

■ On each morning of observation, the defendant was observed to leave his house between 9:02 and 10:20 A.M., to return to his house between 11:20 A.M. and 12:06 P.M. and to remain in his house until after 6:00 P.M. The affiant, who was experienced and expert in gambling investigations, stated that the hours between noon and 6:00 P.M. are those when horse and number bets can be placed and when the results of betting become available.

■ On each day of observation, the defendant was observed during his morning rounds to stop at a number of places, including liquor stores and restaurants, for very short periods of time. He never purchased anything from any of the stores nor did he eat or drink at the restaurants. The affiant stated that such brief regular stops are classic characteristics of the pick-up man phase of a gambling operation:

> He picks up the "action" (money and/or list of bets) from the previous day or evening from prearranged locations—"drops." At the same time, he delivers cash to the appropriate locations for the payoff of yesterday's successful players. 11 Md. App. at 711, 276 A.2d at 689.

■ On one of the days, the defendant was observed in close association all day with another person who was known to have been arrested for alleged gambling violations three years before.

■ Finally, it was ascertained that the defendant himself had been arrested and convicted of gambling violations about three years before.

The court considered each one of these allegations in detail. It found that each allegation, taken separately, could admittedly have been consistent with innocent conduct on the defendant's part. The court, however, refused to consider each allegation separately. Instead, the court said:

> [P]robable cause emerges not from any single constituent activity but, rather, from the overall pattern of activities. Each fragment of conduct may communicate nothing of significance, but the broad mosaic portrays a great deal. The whole may, indeed, be greater than the sum of its parts. 11 Md.App. at 707–08, 276 A.2d at 687.

Furthermore, the court placed great weight on the investigating officer's experience in investigating gambling activities and the interpretations he was able to place on the defendant's conduct.

The court, therefore, concluded:

> In reviewing the observations, the ultimate question for the magistrate must be What is revealed by the whole pattern of activity? In the case at bar, the various strands of observation, insubstantial unto themselves, together weave a strong web of probable guilt. 11 Md.App. at 712, 276 A.2d at 689.

The court then went on to compare this case with the *Spinelli* case and to explain why the affidavit here was sufficient to provide probable cause where the one in *Spinelli* was not. The court pointed out several differences between this case and the *Spinelli* case:

■ In *Spinelli*, there were no observations whatsoever of the "pick-up man" type of activity.

■ In *Spinelli*, there was no observed association with a previously arrested gambler.

■ In *Spinelli*, there was no daily purchase of an Armstrong Scratch Sheet to evidence some daily interest in horseraces.

■ In *Spinelli*, neither Spinelli's nor Grace Hagen's phone number had been previously picked up in a raided gambling headquarters.

■ In *Spinelli*, Spinelli was not a convicted gambler.

■ Finally, and perhaps most importantly, the confidential hearsay information in *Spinelli* was so inadequate under *Aguilar* as to lend *no* additional light or interpretation to the direct observations. In contrast, in the *Dawson* case, the confidential hearsay information was very substantial and would significantly enhance the direct observations, if it were so needed. This is important to the law enforcement officer because it emphasizes the point that the courts will look to the totality of the information provided in the affidavit rather than attempt to mechanically determine the existence of probable cause through a rigid formula. As the court in the *Dawson* case stated:

> The hearsay information may, of course, reinforce the direct observation just as the direct observation may reinforce the hearsay information. There is no one-way street from direct observation to hearsay information. Rather, each may simultaneously cross-fertilize and enrich the other. 11 Md.App. at 713, 276 A.2d at 690.

It is therefore again strongly urged that law enforcement officers, when applying for a search warrant, *write down* in the affidavit *all* the information they have relating to a suspect's criminal activity, whether it be direct observation or hearsay. Then, if either the hearsay or direct observation information, taken separately, is insufficient to establish probable cause, the court still has the opportunity to consider the two types of information in corroboration of each other, and perhaps find enough for probable cause in this manner. Note: This is *not* to say that law enforcement officers should just state all their information in a haphazard manner in the affidavit and hope the magistrate can somehow put it all together and find probable cause. Where an informant's information is involved, officers should carefully set out the required information to satisfy both prongs of the *Aguilar* test. They should also, however, state in an *orderly* manner any corroborative information, in order to give the magistrate the chance to consider that information on its own merits and also to consider it in conjunction with the informant's information.

"TOTALITY OF THE CIRCUMSTANCES" TEST

As stated earlier in this chapter, the U.S. Supreme Court decision in *Illinois v. Gates* abandoned the *Aguilar-Spinelli* "two-pronged" test for determining probable cause through the use of informants for a "totality of the circumstances" test. It is perhaps more correct to say that a rigid adherence to the *Aguilar-Spinelli* test was abandoned, because, as the following discussion will reveal, the elements of the *Aguilar-Spinelli* test remain important considerations under the new *Gates* test. To begin the discussion of the *Gates* test, it is necessary to state the facts of the case.

On May 3, 1978, the Bloomingdale, Illinois, Police Department received an anonymous letter that included statements that the defendants, a husband and wife, made their living selling drugs; that the wife would drive their car to Florida on May 3 and leave it to be loaded up with drugs; that the husband would fly down in a few days to drive the car back, loaded with over $100,000 worth of drugs; and that they had over $100,000 worth of drugs in the basement of their home. Acting on the tip, a police officer determined the defendants' address and learned that the husband had made a reservation for a May 5 flight to Florida. The officer then made arrangements with a Drug Enforcement Administration (DEA) agent for surveillance of the May 5 flight. The surveillance revealed that the husband took the flight, stayed overnight in a motel room registered to his wife, and the next morning headed north with an unidentified woman toward Bloomingdale in a car bearing Illinois license plates issued to the husband. A search warrant for the defendants' residence and automobile were obtained, based on the anonymous letter and the facts stated above. When the defendants arrived home, the police were waiting and a search of the car and the residence produced marijuana.

The Illinois Supreme Court found that the *Aguilar-Spinelli* "two-pronged test" had not been satisfied. First, the "veracity" prong was not satisfied because there was no basis for concluding that the anonymous person who wrote the letter to the police department was credible. Second, the "basis of knowledge" prong was not satisfied because the letter gave no information on how its writer knew of the defendants' activities. The court therefore concluded that no showing of probable cause had been made.

The U.S. Supreme Court initially stated:

> We agree with the Illinois Supreme Court that an informant's "veracity," "reliability" and "basis of knowledge" are all highly relevant in determining the value of his report. We do not agree, however, that these elements should be understood as entirely separate and independent requirements to be rigidly exacted in every case, which the opinion of the Supreme Court of Illinois would imply. Rather . . . they should be understood simply as closely intertwined issues that may usefully illuminate the commonsense, practical question whether there is "probable cause" to believe that contraband or evidence is located in a particular place. 462 U.S. at ——, 103 S.Ct. at 2327–28, 76 L.Ed.2d at 543.

The Court was in effect saying that the elements of the *Aguilar-Spinelli* two-pronged test are important considerations in determining the existence of probable cause, but they should be evaluated only as part of the ultimate commonsense determination and not as rigid rules to be applied mechanically. The Court believed that this "totality of the circumstances" approach was more in keeping with the nature of probable cause as a fluid concept, depending on probabilities arising from varying fact situations, and not lending itself to a neat set of legal rules. The Court reiterated the following quotation from Brinegar v. United States, 338 U.S. 160, 175, 69 S.Ct. 1302, 1310, 93 L.Ed. 1879, 1890 (1949):

> In dealing with probable cause, . . . as the very name implies, we deal with probabilities. These are not technical; they are the factual and practical considerations of everyday life on which reasonable and prudent men, not legal technicians, act."

The Court suggested that originally the two prongs of the *Aguilar-Spinelli* test were intended simply as guides to a magistrate's determination of probable cause, not as inflexible, independent requirements applicable in every case. The two prongs should be understood as "relevant considerations in the totality of circumstances analysis that traditionally has guided probable cause determinations: a deficiency in one may be compensated for, in determining the overall reliability of a tip by a strong showing as to the other, or by some other indicia of reliability." 462 U.S. at ——, 103 S.Ct. at 2329, 76 L.Ed.2d at 545. The entire process of determining probable cause could, therefore, be simplified as follows:

> The task of the issuing magistrate is simply to make a practical, common-sense decision whether, given all the circumstances set forth in the affidavit before him, including the "veracity" and "basis of knowledge" of persons supplying hearsay information, there is a fair probability that contraband or evidence of a crime will be found in a particular place. And the duty of a reviewing court is simply to ensure that the magistrate had a "substantial basis for . . . conclud[ing]" that probable cause existed. 462 U.S. at ——, 103 S.Ct. at 2332, 76 L.Ed.2d at 548.

Despite this new simplified approach to the determination of probable cause, it is absolutely essential for law enforcement officers to understand that the quantum of information that they must provide in the affidavit remains the same. They must still provide sufficient information for the magistrate to make an independent determination of probable cause. Mere conclusory statements, without supporting facts and circumstances, will be inadequate under the new test as they were under the old test. Furthermore, the new "totality of the circumstances" test by no means reduces the importance of any of the elements of the *Aguilar-Spinelli* "two-pronged test." In fact, if officers are able to provide information in the affidavit on all aspects of the "two-pronged test," they should do so, because satisfying that test will almost always satisfy the "totality of the circumstances" test.

Nevertheless, as the *Gates* opinion indicated, overly rigid application of the "two-pronged test" tended to overlook useful and valuable information such as anonymous tips, because ordinary citizens generally do not provide extensive recitations of the basis of their everday observations and the veracity of anonymous informants is largely unknown and unknowable. The Court said:

> [A]nonymous tips seldom could survive a rigorous application of either of the . . . prongs. Yet, such tips, particularly when supplemented by independent police investigation, frequently contribute to the solution of otherwise "perfect crimes." While a conscientious assessment of the basis for crediting such tips is required by the Fourth Amendment, a standard that leaves virtually no place for

anonymous citizen informants is not. 462 U.S. at ——, 103 S.Ct. at 2332, 76 L.Ed. 2d at 548.

With respect to the anonymous letter in the *Gates* case, the Court said that the corroboration of the letter's predictions that the defendants' car would be in Florida, that the husband would fly to Florida in a few days, and that he would drive the car back to Illinois indicated that the informant's other assertions also were true. The letter's accurate predictions of the defendants' future actions, especially, made it more likely that the informant also had access to reliable information of the defendants' alleged illegal activities. Although the tip was corroborated only as to the defendants' seemingly innocent behavior, and although it by no means indicated with certainty that illegal drugs would be found, the Court believed that it sufficed "for the practical, common-sense judgment called for in making a probable cause determination. It is enough, for purposes of assessing probable cause, that 'corroboration through other sources of information reduced the chances of a reckless or prevaricating tale,' thus providing 'a substantial basis for crediting the hearsay.'" 462 U.S. at ——, 103 S.Ct. at 2335, 76 L.Ed.2d at 552.

SUMMARY

Probable cause exists when the facts and circumstances within a law enforcement officer's knowledge and of which the officer has reasonably trustworthy information are sufficient in themselves to warrant a person of reasonable caution in the belief either that:

1. A particular person has committed or is committing a crime; or

2. Seizable items are located at a particular place or on a particular person.

Probable cause does not require certainty or proof beyond a reasonable doubt, but something beyond mere suspicion is required. It is a practical, nontechnical, commonsense concept dealing with probabilities arising out of the varying facts and circumstances of everyday life.

Information upon which probable cause is to be based may come to a law enforcement officer's attention in two possible ways:

1. Through the officer's own perceptions; or

2. Through the perceptions of an informant who then relays the information to the officer.

Some of the indications of criminal activity that may contribute to probable cause are:

1. A suspect's flight or furtive conduct;

2. Physical indications of narcotics usage;

3. Incriminating admissions;

4. A suspect's presence at a crime scene or in a high crime area;

5. A suspect's association with other known criminals;

6. Knowledge of a suspect's past criminal conduct; or

7. A suspect's resemblance to a description of a known criminal.

Although standing alone none of these indications of criminal activity may be sufficient to establish probable cause, when combined with other indications each is a relevant factor in determining whether an arrest or a search is justified. Before law enforcement officers act, either to apply for a warrant, or to conduct a warrantless arrest or search (in the proper circumstances), they should make sure that they have sufficient information upon which to base their actions and that they can justify their actions before a magistrate or judge.

When the information about criminal activity comes from an informant, the officer must satisfy the "totality of circumstances" test set out in the case of *Illinois v. Gates.* That test simply requires the officer to provide underlying facts and circumstances indicating a substantial basis for a magistrate to determine that probable cause to arrest or search exists. Highly relevant to this determination are the elements of the *Aguilar-Spinelli* "two-pronged test." According to the guidelines of this test, the officer should provide underlying circumstances indicating the basis of the informant's knowledge about the criminal activity and underlying circumstances from which the officer concluded that the informant was credible or that the information was reliable. These guidelines need not be followed in a rigid, technical manner but, on the other hand, mere conclusions or opinions of the officer will not suffice to establish probable cause. The magistrate must be satisfied that the informant's information is not mere rumor, suspicion, or reckless or malicious fabrication. Corroboration of the details of an informant's tip by independent police work is a valuable means of satisfying the "totality of the circumstances" test for determining probable cause.

Finally, it should be emphasized that officers applying for a warrant should write down in the affidavit, in an orderly manner, all the relevant information in their possession, whether based on their own perceptions or those of an informant. This is the best way to ensure that the magistrate will consider all the available information in determining whether there is probable cause for the issuance of a warrant.

REVIEW AND DISCUSSION QUESTIONS

1. Why is it important for the law enforcement officer to write down in the complaint or affidavit the facts and circumstances upon which probable cause is based?

2. Give an example of a strong indication of probable cause to *arrest* that is arrived at through each of the five senses—sight, hearing, smell, taste, and touch.

3. Give an example of a strong indication of probable cause to *search* that is arrived at through each of the five senses—sight, hearing, smell, taste, and touch.

4. List three possible strong indications of probable cause to *arrest* for each of the following crimes: Theft; Assault; Arson; Breaking and entering; Rape; Driving to endanger.

5. Discuss the significance in the probable cause context of the phrase "conduct innocent in the eyes of the untrained may carry entirely different 'messages' to the experienced or trained . . . observer." Davis v. United States, 409 F.2d 458, 460 (District of Columbia Circuit Court of Appeals, 1969). Discuss specifically in terms of drug offenses and gambling offenses.

6. Must law enforcement officers know exactly the specific crime for which they are arresting or searching in order to have probable cause? See *People v. Georgev*, 38 Ill.2d 165, 230 N.E.2d 851 (1967).

7. What does "corroboration" mean and why is it important to the law enforcement officer in establishing probable cause through the use of informants?

8. How did the U.S. Supreme Court case of *Illinois v. Gates* change the requirements for establishing probable cause through the use of informants? Does the *Gates* decision make the law enforcement officer's task easier or harder?

9. Mr. A walks into a police station, drops three wristwatches on a table, and tells an officer that Mr. B robbed a local jewelry store two weeks ago. Mr. A will not say anything else in response to police questioning. A quick investigation reveals that the three watches were among a number of items stolen in the jewelry store robbery. Do the police have probable cause to:

    a. Arrest Mr. A?
    b. Arrest Mr. B?
    c. Search Mr. A's home?
    d. Search Mr. B's home?

10. If you answered "No" to any of the items in the preceding question, explain why in detail. If you answered "Yes" to any of them, draft the complaint or affidavit for a warrant or explain why a warrant is not needed.

PART THREE

Exceptions to the Search Warrant Requirement

7
Search Incident to Arrest

8
Consent Searches

9
Plain View

10
Search and Seizure of Vehicles and Containers

11
Open Fields and Abandoned Property

12
Stop and Frisk

7

Search Incident to Arrest

The preceding three chapters have concentrated on the procedures and requirements for obtaining and executing arrest and search warrants. The main reason for this early emphasis is to impress upon law enforcement officers the importance of obtaining a warrant whenever possible. From the time of the adoption of the U.S. Constitution, the law has preferred warrants based upon probable cause as the chief means of balancing the need for efficient and effective law enforcement against the need to protect the rights of individual citizens to be secure against unreasonable searches and seizures. In Aguilar v. Texas, 378 U.S. 108, 84 S.Ct. 1509, 12 L.Ed.2d 723 (1964), the U.S. Supreme Court stated that the preference for warrants is so strong that less persuasive evidence will justify the issuance of a warrant than would justify a warrantless search or warrantless arrest. The Court said:

> [W]hen a search is based upon a magistrate's, rather than a police officer's determination of probable cause, the reviewing courts will accept evidence of a less "judicially competent or persuasive character than would have justified an officer in acting on his own without a warrant," . . . and will sustain the judicial determination so long as "there was a substantial basis for [the magistrate] to conclude that [seizable evidence was] probably present . . . .." 378 U.S. at 111, 84 S.Ct. at 1512, 12 L.Ed.2d at 726.

The warrant procedure is preferred because it places responsibility for deciding the delicate question of probable cause with a neutral and detached judicial officer. Law enforcement is thereby served, because law enforcement officers are enabled to search certain persons or places and to seize certain persons or things when the officers can show reasonable grounds that the person, place, or thing is significantly connected with criminal activity. The Fourth Amendment rights of citizens are also served by the warrant procedure, because the decision to allow a search and seizure is removed from the sometimes hurried and overzealous judgment of law enforcement officers engaged in the competitive enterprise of investigating crime.

Nevertheless, in practice, situations often arise in which the time and effort needed to obtain a warrant would unjustifiably frustrate enforcement of the laws. In order to ensure that the delicate balance between individual rights and law enforcement is maintained, courts have carved out various exceptions to the warrant requirement and have allowed warrantless searches in certain situations. One of the most important of these situations is a search made incident to a lawful arrest. We begin our coverage of the exceptions to the search warrant requirement, therefore, with a discussion of Chimel v. California, 395 U.S. 752, 89 S.Ct. 2034, 23 L.Ed.2d 685 (U.S. Supreme Court, 1969), the leading case on search incident to arrest.

CHIMEL v. CALIFORNIA

Since June 23, 1969, the law of search incident to arrest has been controlled by the U.S. Supreme Court case of Chimel v. California. This case, like *Miranda, Wade-Gilbert-Stovell,* and *Terry,* which will be discussed later, is considered a landmark case and should be very familiar to all law enforcement officers.

In the *Chimel* case, law enforcement officers arrived at the defendant's home with a warrant for his arrest for the burglary of a coin shop. The defendant was not at home, but his wife let the officers in to wait for him. When the defendant arrived, the officers handed him the warrant and asked if they could look around. He objected, but the officers searched the entire house anyway on the basis of the lawful arrest. The officers found coins and other items that were later used in court to obtain a conviction against the defendant.

The U.S. Supreme Court found the search of the entire house unreasonable. The following quotation from the case summarizes the court's reasoning:

> When an arrest is made, it is reasonable for the arresting officer to search the person arrested in order to remove any weapons that the latter might seek to use in order to resist arrest or effect his escape. Otherwise, the officer's safety might well be endangered, and the arrest itself frustrated. In addition, it is entirely reasonable for the arresting officer to search for and seize any evidence on the arrestee's person in order to prevent its concealment or destruction. And the area into which an arrestee might reach in order to grab a weapon or evidentiary items must, of course, be governed by a like rule. A gun on a table or in a drawer in front of one who is arrested can be as dangerous to the arresting officer as one concealed in the clothing of the person arrested. There is ample justification, therefore, for a search of the arrestee's person and the area "within his immediate control"—construing that phrase to mean the area from within which he might gain possession of a weapon or destructible evidence. 395 U.S. 752, 762–63, 89 S.Ct. 2034, 2040, 23 L.Ed.2d 685, 694.

This decision drastically changed the allowable area of search incident to arrest from that allowed under previous law. Under pre-*Chimel* law, an officer was allowed to search incident to arrest the area considered to be in the "possession" or under the "control" of the arrested person. These vague standards were interpreted by the courts to include areas that were not necessarily under the defendant's "physical control" but were within his "constructive possession." This interpretation allowed law enforcement officers to search an entire residence incident to an arrest made therein and gave police almost free reign in deciding what would be searched. Furthermore, because neither a written application for a warrant nor proof of probable cause before a magistrate was required, the search incident to arrest was administratively more convenient and was heavily relied on by law enforcement officers.

The *Chimel* case has changed all this. Although a warrant or probable cause is still not needed, *Chimel* has made it much more difficult for officers to obtain admissible evidence as a result of a search incident to arrest. The remainder of this chapter will be devoted to discussing the effect of the *Chimel* case and various other aspects of the law of search incident to arrest.

Allowable Purposes of a Search Incident to Arrest

Under the rule of the *Chimel* case, there are only two legitimate purposes for which a law enforcement officer may search a person incident to an arrest. The officer may:

1. Search for and remove weapons that the arrestee might use to resist arrest or effect an escape; and

2. Search for and seize evidence in order to prevent its concealment or destruction.

Law enforcement officers should always keep these allowable purposes in mind because all the other rules regarding the scope, intensity and allowable objects of a search incident to arrest relate to the purpose for which the search is made. A search incident to arrest made for any reason other than these allowable purposes will be held unreasonable by a court and any evidence seized will be inadmissible in court.

SCOPE OF SEARCH INCIDENT TO ARREST

Types of Evidence That May Be Seized

In general, the types of evidence that a law enforcement officer may search for and seize incident to an arrest are the same as they are for any search and seizure, whether under warrant or not. The range of seizable objects therefore includes:

1. *Weapons* that the prisoner may use to injure the officer or others or effect an escape;

2. *Fruits of the crime* for which the arrest is made;

3. *Instrumentalities* used to commit the crime;

4. *Contraband,* the possession of which constitutes a crime; and

5. *Evidence* of the crime or evidence that the person arrested committed it. People v. Lewis, 26 N.Y.2d 547, 552, 311 N.Y.S.2d 905, 909, 260 N.E.2d 538, 541 (Court of Appeals of N.Y., 1970).

Furthermore, in connection with a search incident to arrest, an officer may seize not only evidence tending to establish the crime for which the arrest is made but also evidence of other crimes. In a case illustrating this point, the defendant was arrested under a warrant for possessing and transporting explosives. During a search incident to the arrest, the arresting officer found a third person's Selective

Service Certificate and Classification Card. Defendant was convicted of knowingly and unlawfully having in his possession a Selective Service Certificate and Classification Card issued to another. The court held that the certificate and card were admissible in court, despite the fact that they did not relate to the offense of possessing explosives:

> The general rule is that incident to a lawful arrest, a search without a warrant may be made of portable personal effects in the immediate possession of the person arrested. The discovery during a search of a totally unrelated object which provides grounds for prosecution of a crime different than that which the accused was arrested for does not render the search invalid. U.S. v. Simpson, 453 F.2d 1028, 1031 (10th Circuit Court of Appeals, 1972).

Relationship Between Scope of Search and Offense Arrested For

Courts differ with regard to whether or not a law enforcement officer may conduct a full-scale search of the person incident to *every* arrest. Prior to 1973, the generally accepted rule was that an officer conducting a search incident to arrest had to have a definite object or class of objects in mind, and the search could not go beyond the reasonable limits within which that object or class of objects was likely to be found. Also, the object searched for had to be related to the offense that prompted the arrest. In 1973, the U.S. Supreme Court decided two cases that greatly expanded the allowable scope of a search incident to arrest—United States v. Robinson, 414 U.S. 218, 94 S.Ct. 467, 38 L.Ed.2d 427 (1973) and Gustafson v. Florida, 414 U.S. 260, 94 S.Ct. 488, 38 L.Ed.2d 456 (1973).

Both the *Robinson* and *Gustafson* cases involved full-scale searches conducted incident to lawful arrests for minor traffic violations, and in both cases the Court found that it was reasonable for the officer to inspect the contents of a cigarette package found on the arrestee's person. (Illegal drugs were found in both cases.)

In the *Robinson* case, the Court said:

> It is the fact of the lawful arrest which establishes the authority to search, and we hold that in the case of a lawful custodial arrest a full search of the person is not only an exception to the warrant requirement of the Fourth Amendment, but is also a "reasonable" search under that Amendment. 414 U.S. at 235, 94 S.Ct. at 477, 38 L.Ed.2d at 441.

This language was quoted with approval in the *Gustafson* decision, 414 U.S. at 263–64, 94 S.Ct. at 491, 38 L.Ed.2d at 460. Therefore, under the *Robinson* and *Gustafson* decisions, whenever officers make a lawful custodial arrest, they are entitled to make a full-scale search of the arrestee's person incident to the arrest.

Certain aspects of these decisions require further clarification. First of all, when conducting a search incident to arrest, the officer need not have a specific object or class of objects in mind. Even if the arrest is for an offense which could produce no evidence, such as loitering or many minor traffic offenses, the officer is still allowed to conduct a full-scale search of the arrestee's person. The fact of the lawful arrest justifies the search.

Also, the court in the *Robinson* and *Gustafson* decisions authorized a full-scale search of the person incident only to a lawful *custodial* arrest. The reason that the word custodial is important is that in many states the term arrest is applied to situations in which an officer stops a person and issues a ticket, citation, or notice to appear in court, instead of taking the person into custody. A full-scale search would not be authorized in situations in which the officer merely issues a ticket, citation, or notice to appear. In other words, the officer must take the arrested person into custody in order to justify a full-scale search.

Finally, officers need not satisfy any standard of probability that weapons or evidence will be found as a result of the search. Whether or not there is any such probability, the custodial arrest alone provides sufficient justification for the search. Officers need not provide any underlying facts and circumstances justifying their need to search.

Some state courts have refused to follow the rule of the *Robinson* and *Gustafson* decisions. These state courts, based on interpretations of their *state* constitutions, have held that a warrantless search of a person incident to a lawful custodial arrest must be limited despite the *Robinson* and *Gustafson* decisions. The Supreme Court of Hawaii, for example, has limited the warrantless search of an arrestee's person incident to a lawful custodial arrest (1) to disarming the arrested person when there is reason to believe from the facts and circumstances that the person may be armed; and (2) to discovering evidence related to the crime *for which the person was arrested.* State v. Kaluna, 55 Hawaii 361, 372, 520 P.2d 51, 60 (Supreme Court of Hawaii, 1974). Under this more restrictive rule, officers may not search for *evidence* incident to offenses that would not produce evidence (such as loitering and minor traffic offenses), and they may not search for weapons unless they can point to specific facts and circumstances indicating the likelihood that the arrested person was armed and dangerous. It is recommended, as the safest procedure, that officers follow this more restrictive rule, unless they are certain that their state courts have adopted the rule of the *Robinson* and *Gustafson* cases or a different rule.

The California Supreme Court also refused to go along with the U.S. Supreme Court's decisions in the *Robinson* and *Gustafson* cases. In California, an officer may not conduct a full body search of an arrested person when the arrest will be disposed of by a mere citation or the arrested person will be transported in a law enforcement vehicle to a police facility where the opportunity to post bond is available. Officers may, however, conduct a pat-down frisk for weapons before placing an arrested person in a law enforcement vehicle for transportation to the station house. The court recognized the increased danger to law enforcement officers in this situation. People v. Longwill, 14 Cal.3d 943, 123 Cal.Rptr. 297, 538 P.2d 753 (1975).

Several other states, including Alaska, Colorado, and Oregon, have placed various limitations on the *Robinson-Gustafson* rule. Because of the lack of uniformity in the law in this area, law enforcement officers should make a special effort to find out what rules apply in their state. Otherwise, the safer procedure would be to follow the more restrictive rule set out in the *Kaluna* case, discussed above.

SEARCH OF ARRESTEE'S BODY

A search incident to arrest of the arrestee's body may include:

1. A search of the arrestee's body and a seizure of items of evidence on or in the arrestee's body. Items seized during such a search might include hair samples, fingernail clippings, blood, and drugs hidden within the body. Of course, officers must use reasonable and painless procedures in obtaining such evidence. An example is the case of Commonwealth v. Tarver, 369 Mass. 302, 345 N.E.2d 671 (Supreme Judicial Court of Massachusetts, 1975), in which the court upheld a seizure of hair samples from the head, chest, and pubic area of a person incident to the arrest of that person for murder and sexual abuse of a child.

2. A seizure of items of evidence or weapons immediately associated with the arrestee's body. Items that might be seized would include clothing, billfolds, jewelry, wristwatches, and weapons strapped or carried on the person. An example is the case of State v. Smith, 295 Minn. 65, 203 N.W.2d 348 (Supreme Court of Minnesota, 1972), in which the court held that the seizure of the defendant's boots at the time of booking was a valid search and seizure incident to arrest.

3. A search of items of evidence or weapons immediately associated with the arrestee's body that have been seized under number 2 above. Such a search would include going through the pockets of clothing, examining clothing for bloodstains, hair, dirt, or other such evidence, and examining weapons for bloodstains, finger-prints, or serial numbers. An example is the case of Parker v. State, Tex.Crim.App., 544 S.W.2d 149 (Court of Criminal Appeals of Texas, 1976), in which officers, while on surveillance, stopped the defendant and another man as they emerged from an apartment that was suspected of containing illegal drugs. While the officers were attempting to obtain information about the apartment, they discovered a weapon on the defendant and a bag containing a white powder nearby. They arrested the defendant, searched him, and seized his billfold. In the billfold were found packets of a white powder that was later determined to be cocaine. The court held that the officers had probable cause to arrest the defendant. The full search of the defendant and the seizure and search of his billfold incident to the lawful custodial arrest were held reasonable under the Fourth Amendment.

4. A seizure of other personal property not immediately associated with the arrestee's body, but which the arrestee is carrying or otherwise has under his immediate control. Property that might be seized would include luggage, attache cases, bundles, or packages. Before 1977, many courts held that law enforcement officers could not only *seize* personal property carried by or under the immediate control of the arrestee, but could also *search* that property for weapons or evidence. For example, in United States v. Mehciz, 437 F.2d 145 (9th Circuit Court of Appeals, 1971), the defendant was lawfully arrested on a drug possession charge while carrying a small overnight suitcase. The arresting officers took the suitcase and handcuffed the defendant so there was no danger he could get to the suitcase. An officer then opened the suitcase and found drugs inside. The court upheld the search of the suitcase as a valid search incident to arrest.

In 1977 the U.S. Supreme Court, in United States v. Chadwick, 433 U.S. 1, 97 S.Ct. 2476, 53 L.Ed.2d 538, severely limited the *search* of luggage and other personal property after it has been seized incident to arrest. In the *Chadwick* case, the defendants arrived in Boston from San Diego by train and loaded a large double-locked footlocker, which they had transported with them, into the trunk of their waiting car. Federal narcotics agents, who had probable cause to arrest and to search the footlocker, but no warrants, arrested the defendants. The agents took exclusive control over the footlocker and took it and the defendants to the federal building in Boston. An hour and a half later, the agents, without the defendants' consent and without a search warrant, opened the footlocker and found large amounts of marijuana.

The U.S. Supreme Court held that the search of the footlocker was illegal and that the seized marijuana was inadmissible evidence. The Court said:

> The potential dangers lurking in all custodial arrests make warrantless searches of items within the "immediate control" area reasonable without requiring the arresting officer to calculate the probability that weapons or destructible evidence may be involved. [citing United States v. Robinson and Terry v. Ohio] However, warrant-less searches of luggage or other property seized at the time of an arrest cannot be justified as incident to that arrest either if the "search is remote in time or place from the arrest," . . . or no exigency exists. Once law enforcement officers have reduced luggage or other personal property not immediately associated with the person of the arrestee to their exclusive control, and there is no longer any danger that the arrestee might gain access to the property to seize a weapon or destroy evidence, a search of that property is no longer an incident of the arrest.
> Here the search was conducted more than an hour after federal agents had gained exclusive control of the footlocker and long after respondents were securely in custody; the search therefore cannot be viewed as incidental to the arrest or as justified by any other exigency. Even though on this record the issuance of a warrant by a judicial officer was reasonably predictable, a line must be drawn. In our view, when no exigency is shown to support the need for an immediate search, the Warrant Clause places the line at the point where the property to be searched comes under the exclusive dominion of police authority. Respondents were therefore entitled to the protection of the Warrant Clause with the evaluation of a neutral magistrate, before their privacy interests in the contents of the footlocker were invaded. 433 U.S. at 15–16, 97 S.Ct. at 2485–86, 53 L.Ed.2d at 550–51.

Footnotes to the *Chadwick* opinion indicate that the Court's decision was based in large part on its belief that the defendants' legitimate privacy interests were violated. In footnote 10 the Court said:

> Unlike searches of the person, United States v. Robinson, 414 U.S. 218 (1973); United States v. Edwards, 415 U.S. 800 (1974), searches of possessions within an arrestee's immediate control cannot be justified by any reduced expectations of privacy caused by the arrest. Respondents' privacy interest in the contents of the footlocker was not eliminated simply because they were under arrest. 433 U.S. at 16 n. 10, 97 S.Ct. at 2486 n. 10, 53 L.Ed.2d at 551 n. 10.

In footnote 8 the Court said:

> Respondents' principal privacy interest in the footlocker was of course not in the container itself, which was exposed to public view, but in its contents. A search of the interior was therefore a far greater intrusion into Fourth Amendment values than the impoundment of the footlocker. Though surely a substantial infringement with respondents' use and possession, the seizure did not diminish respondents'

legitimate expectation that the footlocker's contents would remain private. 433 U.S. at 13–14 n. 8, 97 S.Ct. at 2485 n. 8, 53 L.Ed.2d at 550 n. 8.

In United States v. Berry, 560 F.2d 861, 864 (7th Circuit Court of Appeals, 1977), the court expanded upon the Supreme Court's brief mention of privacy interests:

> The Court appears to be distinguishing—for purposes of whether a warrant is required to search property in police custody that was seized from a suspect at the time of arrest—between searches of an arrestee's clothing, as in *Edwards,* or items that were in his pockets, as in *Robinson,* from searches of other possessions, such as luggage, that were within his immediate control. Warrantless searches of the former items after they come in police custody can be characterized as searches of the arrestee's person because they do not involve any greater reduction in the arrestee's expectations of privacy than that caused by the arrest itself. Warrantless searches of the latter items, however, affect privacy interests other than those reduced by the arrest itself and thus can be conducted only as long as the danger exists that the arrestee might gain access to the property to seize a weapon or destroy evidence.

To summarize, law enforcement officers may *seize* incident to arrest luggage and other personal property not immediately associated with the arrestee's body if it is within the arrestee's immediate control. Once officers have such property under their immediate control and there is no further danger that the arrestee might gain access to the property to seize a weapon or destroy evidence, officers may *not search* the property without a warrant or consent. Of course, if officers believe that the property contains some immediately dangerous instrumentality, such as explosives, they may search the property and disarm the weapon or otherwise end the danger. They may do so even if the property is under their exclusive control.

Use of Force

When making a search of a person incident to arrest, law enforcement officers may use the degree of force necessary to protect themselves, prevent escape, and prevent the destruction or concealment of evidence. Because the courts will review the use of force strictly, officers should use as little force as is necessary to accomplish their legitimate purpose.

Courts have upheld seizures of drugs when the arrested person attempted to swallow them and an officer put a "choke hold" on the defendant, forcing him to spit out the drugs. Salas v. State, 246 So.2d 621 (District Court of Appeal of Florida, 1971). A search incident to arrest to prevent the concealment of evidence may even extend to pumping the stomach or probing body cavities. However, the following conditions should be met before such a search is conducted:

1. There must be good reason to believe that the person's body contains evidence that should be removed. In one case, officers actually observed the defendant thrust drug capsules into his mouth and quickly swallow them. People v. Jones, 20 Cal.App.3d 201, 97 Cal.Rptr. 492 (Court of Appeal of California, 1971).

2. The search must be made by a doctor working under sanitary conditions and in a medically approved way.

3. Force may be used only to the extent necessary to make the person submit to the examination. Blackford v. United States, 247 F.2d 745 (9th Circuit Court of Appeals, 1957).

SEARCH OF AREA WITHIN ARRESTEE'S IMMEDIATE CONTROL

We begin the discussion of search of the area within the arrestee's immediate control by repeating the second part of the quotation from the *Chimel* case that appeared at the beginning of this chapter:

> And the area into which an arrestee might reach in order to grab a weapon or evidentiary items must, of course, be governed by a like rule. A gun on a table or in a drawer in front of one who is arrested can be as dangerous to the arresting officer as one concealed in the clothing of the person arrested. There is ample justification, therefore, for a search of the arrestee's person and the area "within his immediate control"—construing that phrase to mean the area from within which he might gain possession of a weapon or destructible evidence. 395 U.S. at 763, 89 S.Ct. at 2040, 23 L.Ed.2d at 694.

It is difficult to derive from this quotation definite guidelines as to how large an area around an arrestee is "within his immediate control" and is therefore subject to search by an officer. This determination depends on several factors such as the size and shape of the room, the size and agility of the arrestee, whether the arrestee was handcuffed or otherwise subdued, the size and type of evidence being sought, the number of people arrested, and the number of officers present. The following case summaries should give some idea of how courts have recently treated the question of permissible area of search incident to arrest.

In a case dealing with the area within a defendant's reach, officers went to the defendant's trailer home to arrest him as a participant in an armed robbery. They found him lying in bed. One officer immediately searched under the blankets for a gun as other officers attempted to subdue the defendant, who was resisting. Two revolvers were found in a box at the foot of the bed. The court held that this was within the area of defendant's reach and that the revolvers were admissible in evidence. People v. Spencer, 22 Cal.App.3d 786, 99 Cal.Rptr. 681 (Court of Appeal of California, 1972).

If a person is arrested out of doors, a search of that person's home or apartment cannot be justified as incident to the arrest. Thus, in a case in which the defendant was arrested in his back yard and the arresting officers then went up to his apartment and searched it, the evidence found in the apartment was inadmissible. The court held that the search was an unreasonable search incident to arrest because it extended beyond the arrestee's reach. Frazier v. State, 488 P.2d 613 (Court of Criminal Appeals of Oklahoma, 1971).

However, if it is necessary for an arrested person to go into a different area of the premises from that in which he was arrested, the officer, for his own protection, may accompany him and search if necessary. A case illustrating this point involved an arrest under warrant for conspiracy to commit extortion. The arrest took place early in the morning and the arrested person was in his bedclothes. One of the officers suggested that the defendant change into street clothes before leaving for the station. The defendant agreed and went to his bedroom followed by the officers. As the defendant went to a chest of drawers to obtain clothing, one of the officers searched the drawer and found a blackjack and several other weapons. The defendant was convicted of illegal possession of a blackjack.

The court held the search was lawful:

> Certainly, if immediately after a lawful arrest, the arrestee reads the arrest warrant and without coercion consents to go to his bedroom to change into more appropriate clothing, the arresting officers—incident to that arrest—may search the areas upon which the arrestee focuses his attention and are within his reach to gain access to a weapon or to destroy evidence. Giacalone v. Lucas, 445 F.2d 1238, 1247 (6th Circuit Court of Appeals, 1971).

Search of Motor Vehicles

In New York v. Belton, 453 U.S. 454, 460–461, 101 S.Ct. 2860, 2864, 69 L.Ed.2d 768, 775 (1981), the U.S. Supreme Court held:

> [W]hen a policeman has made a lawful custodial arrest of the occupant of an automobile, he may, as a contemporaneous incident of that arrest, search the passenger compartment of that automobile.
>
> It follows from this conclusion that the police may also examine the contents of any containers found within the passenger compartment, for if the passenger compartment is within reach of the arrestee, so also will containers in it be within his reach . . . .   Such a container may, of course, be searched whether it is open or closed, since the justification for the search is not that the arrestee has no privacy interest in the container, but that the lawful custodial arrest justifies the infringement of any privacy interest the arrestee may have.

In a footnote, the Court defined a container as any object capable of holding another object. A container thus includes "closed or open glove compartments, consoles or other receptacles located anywhere within the passenger compartment, as well as luggage, boxes, bags, clothing, and the like." 453 U.S. at 460–61 n. 4, 101 S.Ct. at 2684 n. 4, 69 L.Ed.2d at 775 n. 4. The Court also pointed out that only the interior of the passenger compartment of an automobile may be searched incident to arrest and not the trunk.

It is important to note that the *Belton* case deals only with the search incident to arrest exception to the warrant requirement and has nothing to do with the so-called automobile exception under the *Carroll* doctrine (see Chapter 10). The Court specifically referred to the *Chimel* case, stating that articles inside the relatively narrow compass of the passenger compartment of an automobile are in fact generally, even if not inevitably, within "the area into which an arrestee might reach in order to grab a weapon or evidentiary item." 395 U.S. at 763, 89 S.Ct. at 2040, 23 L.Ed.2d at 694. Therefore, the holding in the *Belton* case does not apply unless there has been a custodial arrest of the occupant of an automobile. And it is the custodial arrest that provides the justification for examining the contents of containers seized from the passenger compartment of the automobile. Moreover, as the above-quoted passage from the *Belton* case indicates, the searching of any containers found in the automobile must be substantially contemporaneous with the arrest of the automobile's occupant. If a container is seized and searched some time later, after it is in the exclusive control of the police, the *Chadwick* case requires that a warrant be obtained.

Search of Persons Other Than the Arrestee

Often, when an arrest is made, there are other persons in the vicinity besides the arrested person. If a potential accomplice of the arrested person is located on the premises where the arrest was made, courts have held that police may search the area within the accomplice's immediate control. In such a case, two defendants were arrested in their apartment. The arresting officers then noticed two men lying on two couches in the living room. A gun and ammunition had already been found on the premises and the officers did not know the identity of the other two men. One officer directed the two men to stand and another officer searched two end tables near the men. The officer found obscene materials.

The court held that the search was reasonable for the protection and safety of the officers. Not only had weapons already been found in the apartment but it was reasonable to assume that the two men were accomplices of the arrested persons:

> Both men had apparently been sleeping in the Portela apartment and were likely relatives or intimate friends of the Portelas. Since they were both in full view of Portela, who had already been placed under arrest, it would be reasonable for the agents to assume that if Portela had signalled the two unidentified men, they would have been able to reach over and draw a weapon out of the end tables. U.S. v. Manarite, 314 F.Supp. 607, 615 (U.S. District Court, Southern District of N.Y., 1970).

In United States v. Vigo, 487 F.2d 295 (2nd Circuit Court of Appeals, 1973), the court upheld the search of the purse of the defendant's female companion incident to the arrest of the defendant. The court said that a woman's purse is a reasonable place to conceal a weapon.

SEARCH OF OTHER AREAS OF THE PREMISES

Under the rule of the *Chimel* case, officers are not allowed to search any other areas of the premises except the limited area within the arrestee's immediate control. There may, however, be circumstances justifying an officer's going into other areas to merely look around. For example, officers, for their own protection, may look into other rooms, to see if other persons are present. Also, they may have to go through other rooms in leaving the premises. These movements of law enforcement officers are not considered searches because the officers are not looking for weapons or incriminating evidence. Nevertheless, an officer who observes a weapon or other seizable item lying open to view may seize it, and it will be admissible in court under the "plain view" doctrine (see chapter 9).

In a bank robbery case, the defendant was arrested in his girl friend's apartment. At the time of his arrest, the apartment was dark and the defendant was nude. One of the officers went to get clothing for the defendant and found two jackets of the type that had been described as having been worn by the bank robbers. On the way out of the apartment, one of the officers turned on the kitchen light so he could see his way. Money taken during the robbery was on the kitchen floor.

The court held that both the jackets and the money were admissible in evidence. Finding no violation of the *Chimel* rule, the court said:

> Since they were bound to find some clothing for Titus rather than take him nude to FBI headquarters on a December night, the fatigue jackets were properly seized under the "plain view" doctrine. Welch was entitled to turn on the kitchen lights, both to assist his own exit and to see whether the other robber might be about; when he saw the stolen money, he was permitted to seize it. Everything the agents took was in their "plain view" while they were where they had a right to be; there was no general rummaging of the apartment .   .   . . U.S. v. Titus, 445 F.2d 577, 579 (2nd Circuit Court of Appeals, 1971).

In another case, officers arrested the defendant in a dentist's office for robbery of a liquor store. They went into other rooms of the dentist's suite to look for possibly dangerous persons and found a stolen bottle of whiskey in plain view in the dentist's laboratory.

The court held that the bottle of whiskey was admissible in evidence. The officers had no way of knowing who else might be on the premises. They were justified in conducting a search of the suite to assure themselves that no hostile and possibly dangerous persons were hiding in other rooms. The bottle of whiskey was in plain view in the dentist's laboratory and there was no evidence that the officers engaged in any general search of the premises beyond that necessary to find other persons who might have been present. United States v. Miller, 145 U.S.App.D.C. 312, 449 F.2d 974 (District of Columbia Court of Appeals, 1971).

OTHER REQUIREMENTS FOR A VALID SEARCH INCIDENT TO ARREST

Arrest Must Be Lawful

In our discussion up to this point, whenever we have spoken of search incident to arrest, it has been assumed that the arrest was a *lawful* arrest. If the arrest is not lawful, the search incident to that arrest will automatically be held unlawful by the court, even if all proper procedures are followed in conducting the search. Therefore, it is very important for the law enforcement officer to both know and carefully comply with the law of arrest. The law of arrest is discussed in detail in Chapter 4.

Search Must be Contemporaneous With Arrest

The general rule is that a search made incident to arrest is not reasonable unless it is made contemporaneously with the arrest. To be contemporaneous, a search must be conducted as close in time to the arrest as is practically possible. In a case illustrating this point, the defendant, a suspected possessor of narcotics, was lawfully arrested on a downtown street corner. The officers then took him to his home some distance away and there conducted an intensive search that yielded narcotics. On the basis of this evidence, defendant was convicted of narcotics possession. The Court held the search of the house was unreasonable:

> In the circumstances of this case, however, the subsequent search of the petitioner's home cannot be regarded as incident to his arrest on a street corner more than two

blocks away. A search "can be incident to an arrest only if it is substantially contemporaneous with the arrest and is confined to the immediate vicinity of the arrest." James v. Louisiana, 382 U.S. 36, 37, 86 S.Ct. 151, 151, 15 L.Ed.2d 30, 31 (U.S. Supreme Court, 1965).

The reason for this rule is that, under the *Chimel* case, officers may search an arrested person only (1) to protect themselves and (2) to prevent the destruction or concealment of evidence. If officers delay a search, it indicates a lack of concern about either of these possibilities and that the search was conducted for another reason, thereby making the search illegal.

Sometimes, however, it is not feasible for an officer to search immediately upon making an arrest. This would be true if the officer intended to make a search of the arrestee's body cavities for drugs, if the arrestee was a person of the opposite sex, or if other circumstances made a search inadvisable. In these situations, the officer should remove the arrested person from the scene and conduct the search as soon as favorable circumstances prevail. For example, in one case, an arrest for an armed bank robbery took place in a crowded hotel lobby, which was lit only by candles because of a power failure. The court held that under these circumstances it was proper for officers to make a cursory search for weapons at the hotel and to make a more thorough search later at the station. United States v. Miles, 413 F.2d 34 (3d Circuit Court of Appeals, 1969).

Sometimes, even though it is feasible to search an arrested person at the time of arrest, under certain circumstances courts will allow a delay between the arrest and search for a good reason. The U.S. Supreme Court made such an exception to the general rule in the case of United States v. Edwards, 415 U.S. 800, 94 S.Ct. 1234, 39 L.Ed.2d 771 (1974). In that case the defendant was arrested shortly after 11 P.M. for attempting to break into a building. The defendant was taken to jail. Law enforcement officials had probable cause to believe that the defendant's clothing contained paint chips from the crime scene. Since the police had no substitute clothing for the defendant, they waited until the next morning to seize his clothing without a warrant. Paint chips matching those at the break scene were found on the clothing.

The Court held that, despite the delay, the clothing was lawfully seized incident to the defendant's arrest. The administrative process and the mechanics of arrest had not yet come to a halt the next morning. The police had custody of the defendant and the clothing and could have seized the clothing at the time of arrest. It was reasonable to delay the seizure until substitute clothing was available. It is worthwhile to repeat here the Court's language that was quoted earlier in Chapter 1 on "Arrest":

> [O]nce the accused is lawfully arrested and is in custody, the effects in his possession at the place of detention that were subject to search at the time and place of his arrest may lawfully be searched and seized without a warrant even though a substantial period of time has elapsed between the arrest and subsequent administrative processing, on the one hand, and the taking of the property for use as evidence on the other. 415 U.S. at 807, 94 S.Ct. at 1239, 39 L.Ed.2d at 778.

Officers should note that the *Edwards* case does *not* say that law enforcement officers may delay a search incident to the arrest of a person for as long as they wish. Nor does the case sanction *all* delays in searching and seizing evidence incident to arrest. Officers must be able to provide good reasons for delaying a search incident to arrest and the duration of the delay must relate to those reasons. Otherwise the search and seizure may be declared illegal.

It should also be noted that the *Edwards* case involved the search of an item closely associated to the arrestee's person, namely his clothing. Under the ruling of United States v. Chadwick (discussed earlier under "Search of Arrestee's Body") officers would not be justified in delaying a search incident to arrest of luggage, briefcases, and other portable effects.

Therefore, officers may delay a search incident to arrest only under the following conditions:

1. There is a good reason for the delay;

2. The duration of the delay is reasonable under the circumstances; and

3. The item or items searched were closely related to the arrestee's person, e.g., clothing and pocket items, when they were seized.

The requirement that the search be substantially contemporaneous with the arrest does not necessarily mean that the arrest must precede the search. Although this will almost always be the case, under certain circumstances the search may precede the arrest and still be a valid search incident to arrest. In order for this to be true, the following requirements must be present:

1. There must be probable cause for arrest before either the search or the arrest is carried out; and

2. Both the arrest and search must be integral parts of a single incident.

An example is a case in which a law enforcement officer had probable cause to arrest the defendant based upon another officer's tip, his own observations, and other information. The officer encountered the defendant outside his house, immediately searched him, finding heroin, and then arrested him. The court upheld the search on the ground that the fruits of the search were in no way necessary to establish probable cause for the arrest that immediately followed. Also, the search was substantially contemporaneous with the arrest and confined to the immediate vicinity of the arrest. United States v. Thomas, 432 F.2d 120 (9th Circuit Court of Appeals, 1970).

Arrest Must Not Be a Pretext to Justify Search

A law enforcement officer may not use an arrest as a pretext to search for evidence. If the arrest, even though technically valid, is actually a mere pretext by which the officer attempts to justify an otherwise illegitimate search, the search will be held unreasonable. The standard by which a law enforcement officer will be judged has been stated in Williams v. U.S., 418 F.2d 159, 161 (9th Circuit Court of Appeals, 1969):

> Whether or not an arrest is a mere pretext to search is a question of the motivation or primary purpose of the arresting officer. Improper motivation has been found where the arrest is for a minor offense which serves as a mere "sham" or "front" for a search for evidence of another unrelated offense for which there is

no probable cause to arrest or search . . .   It has also been found where the arresting officer deliberately delays making the arrest in order to allow the arrestee to enter the premises which the officer desires to search.

Who May Conduct the Search

If practical, the law enforcement officer making the arrest should conduct the search incident to the arrest. As mentioned earlier, this search should be made at substantially the same time as the arrest. If an officer makes an arrest and does not search the arrested person right away, but some time later allows another officer to search the person, the later search may be held unlawful. It would not meet the requirement of spontaneousness nor would it indicate a concern for the protection of the officer or the prevention of the destruction or concealment of evidence.

Nevertheless, if the arresting officer transfers an arrested person to the custody of another officer, the second officer may again search the arrested person. This second search is allowed because the second officer is entitled to take personal safety measures and need not rely on the assumption that the arrestee has been thoroughly searched for weapons by the arresting officer. United States v. Dyson, 277 A.2d 658 (District of Columbia Court of Appeals, 1971).

SEARCH INCIDENT TO DETENTION

The U.S. Supreme Court, in Cupp v. Murphy, 412 U.S. 291, 93 S.Ct. 2000, 36 L.Ed.2d 900 (1973), decided that a law enforcement officer may conduct a limited warrantless search of a person merely *detained* for investigation. The Cupp v. Murphy case does not technically belong in an article on search incident to arrest because there was no arrest in the case. Nevertheless, the Court relied heavily on the *Chimel* case in its opinion, and therefore because of its importance, Cupp v. Murphy will be discussed here separately from the materials on search incident to arrest.

In Cupp v. Murphy, the defendant having been notified of his wife's strangulation, voluntarily came to police headquarters and met his attorney there. Police noticed dark spot on the defendant's finger and asked if they could take a scraping from his fingernails. The defendant refused. Under protest and without a warrant, police proceeded to take the samples, which turned out to include particles of skin and blood of the defendant's wife and fabric from her clothing. The evidence was admitted at trial and the defendant was convicted of second-degree murder.

The Court held that the momentary seizing of the defendant to get the fingernail scrapings constituted a seizure governed by the Fourth Amendment. The Court, citing the *Chimel* case, also recognized that under prescribed conditions warrantless searches incident to an arrest are constitutionally valid. In this case, however, no formal arrest was made, nor was there a search warrant. Without a formal arrest or search warrant, a full *Chimel* search, extending to the defendant's person and the area into which he could have reached, would not have been permissible.

The Court found that *probable cause* to arrest the defendant did exist, however. Furthermore, after the police requested the scrapings, the defendant began rubbing his hands behind his back, perhaps attempting to destroy the evidence. Stressing the limited nature of the search, i.e., only taking fingernail scrapings, and the easily destructible nature of the evidence, the Court allowed the search under a limited application of the *Chimel* case.

Certain aspects of this decision should be emphasized to clear up any possible misunderstanding about the permissible extent of the search of a detained person by law enforcement officers. First of all, the Court clearly held that even though the defendant was not arrested, his detention against his will constituted a seizure of his person and was governed by the Fourth Amendment. Since the police in this case did not have a search warrant, nor could they satisfy any of the exceptions to the warrant requirement, the Supreme Court had to justify the search incident to the detention on the basis of the unique facts of the case. These facts were:

1. The defendant was not arrested but was detained only long enough to take the fingernail scrapings.

2. The search was very limited in extent. (The Court was careful to point out that a full *Chimel* search would not have been justified without an arrest. The officers therefore could not have searched the defendant's entire person and the area into which he could reach.)

3. The evidence—blood on the fingernails—was readily destructible.

4. The defendant made attempts to destroy the evidence.

5. There was probable cause to arrest the defendant, even though he was not actually arrested.

All these considerations were essential to the Court's decision. Therefore, law enforcement officers should make sure all five factors are present when they conduct a warrantless search of a detained person. If they are not all present, officers should take the safer route and apply for a search warrant.

SUMMARY

Search incident to arrest is a recognized exception to the Fourth Amendment requirement of a warrant for all searches and seizures. The U.S. Supreme Court case of *Chimel v. California* permits the search of a lawfully arrested person for the limited purposes of removing weapons and preventing the concealment or destruction of evidence. If the arrest is a custodial arrest, a full-scale search for weapons and seizable evidence is permitted, whether or not there is any likelihood of danger or any reason to believe evidence will be found.

A search incident to arrest must be substantially contemporaneous with the arrest and may extend to the arrestee's body and to the area within his or her immediate control—the area from which the arrestee might gain possession of a weapon or destructible evidence. Any weapon or seizable evidence found within this area may be seized. If, however, the item seized is luggage or other personal property not immediately associated with the person of the arrestee, a delayed search of the property, after it has come within the exclusive control of the police, may not be conducted without a warrant. A search incident to the arrest of an occupant of a motor vehicle may extend to the passenger area of the vehicle and may include a search of containers found in the vehicle, if the search is contemporaneous with the arrest.

Searches of persons in the vicinity of the arrested person and the areas within their immediate control may be conducted incident to the arrestee's arrest, if reasonably necessary to remove weapons and prevent the concealment or destruction of evidence. Searches of areas of the premises beyond the immediate control of the arrestee or companions may not be conducted. Nevertheless, if officers are in a place or position in which they have a right to be, they may seize evidence lying open to view under the plain view doctrine. Searches incident to arrest may be delayed in a variety of circumstances, but there must be a good reason for the delay and the duration of the delay must be reasonable under the circumstances.

The U.S. Supreme Court has approved a limited warrantless search of a person merely detained for investigation. Such a search may be conducted, however, only if there is probable cause to arrest the suspect and if there is an imminent danger that crucial evidence will be destroyed if the search is not made immediately.

REVIEW AND DISCUSSION QUESTIONS

1. Assume that a person is legally arrested while riding in the first-class section of an airplane for transporting illegal drugs. Can the arresting officers immediately conduct any of the following searches incident to the arrest?

a. A search of the person's clothing.
b. A search of the person's suitcase.
c. A search of the entire first-class section of the airplane.
d. A search of the person's body cavities.

If you answered yes to any of the above, consider whether such a search *should* be made and what are the possible alternatives.

2. If the defendant is arrested in an automobile for stealing the automobile, may the arresting officer search other passengers in the automobile incident to the defendant's arrest?

3. In the typical search incident to arrest situation, the arrest is followed by a search and then by a seizure. Would a search followed by a seizure and then by an arrest be valid? Would a seizure followed by an arrest and then by an additional search be valid?

4. What search incident to an arrest problems are presented when the person arrested is a person of the opposite sex?

5. Does the nature of the offense arrested for have any effect on the scope of a search incident to arrest?

6. Assume that the defendant is arrested in the kitchen of his home for the armed robbery of a bank earlier that day. The arresting officers have an arrest warrant but no search warrant. The defendant is one of three persons wanted in the robbery. The defendant's automobile, the suspected getaway car, is parked in his driveway. Indicate the full extent of the arresting officers' authority to search the defendant, his premises, and his automobile.

7. Assume the same facts as in the preceding question except that the defendant is arrested while running from his house to his automobile. Indicate the full extent of the arresting officers' authority to search the defendant, his premises, and his automobile. What if the officers had a search warrant for the defendant's house only, but no arrest warrant? What if it is raining heavily?

8. Is the scope of a search incident to arrest affected by any of the following circumstances?

    a. The defendant is handcuffed and chained to a pole.

    b. The defendant is unconscious.

    c. The defendant is surrounded by a group of friends.

    d. The defendant is arrested on a dark street.

9. Since the search of containers in the passenger compartment of an automobile is now allowed incident to a custodial arrest under the ruling in *New York v. Belton,* should law enforcement officers wait until a defendant is in an automobile before making an arrest, when possible? Should officers make custodial arrests for offenses for which they would ordinarily not make custodial arrests?

10. Discuss the meaning of the statement, "It is not at all clear that the 'grabbing distance' authorized in the *Chimel* case is conditioned upon the arrested person's continued capacity 'to grab.'" People v. Fitzpatrick, 32 N.Y.2d 499, 508, 346 N.Y.S.2d 793, 797, 300 N.E.2d 139, 143 (1973).

8

Consent Searches

Another well-established exception to the search warrant requirement is the "consent search." A consent search occurs when an individual voluntarily allows a law enforcement officer to search his or her person, premises, or belongings. The consenting individual thereby relinquishes any right to object to the search on constitutional grounds, and any evidence seized as a result of the search will be admissible in court despite the fact that there was no warrant and no probable cause to search. A consent search may also provide a benefit to the consenting party who is innocent of any wrongdoing.

> If the search is conducted and proves fruitless, that in itself may convince the police that an arrest with its possible stigma and embarrassment is unnecessary, or that a far more extensive search pursuant to a warrant is not justified. In short, a search pursuant to consent may result in considerably less inconvenience for the subject of the search, and, properly conducted, is a constitutionally permissible and wholly legitimate aspect of effective police activity. Schneckloth v. Bustamonte, 412 U.S. 218, 228, 93 S.Ct. 2041, 2048, 36 L.Ed.2d 854, 863 (U.S. Supreme Court, 1973).

It is not surprising, then, that the consent search is frequently relied upon by law enforcement officers, because it is faster than warrant procedures and it does not require the often difficult determination of whether there is probable cause, either to search or to arrest. However, because of the comparative lack of effort required to obtain a consent to search, there are many opportunities for abuse of an individual's Fourth Amendment rights by law enforcement officers. In order to protect those rights, courts will look closely at the circumstances surrounding every consent search to determine if the consent was truly voluntary. The U.S. Supreme Court said:

> [T]he Fourth and Fourteenth Amendments require that consent not be coerced, by explicit or implicit means, by implied threat or covert force. For, no matter how subtly the coercion were applied, the resulting "consent" would be no more than a

pretext for the unjustified police intrusion against which the Fourth Amendment is directed.   .   .   .

The problem of reconciling the recognized legitimacy of consent searches with the requirement that they be free from any aspect of official coercion cannot be resolved by any infallible touchstone.   To approve such searches without the most careful scrutiny would sanction the possibility of official coercion;   to place artificial restrictions upon such searches would jeopardize their basic validity.   Just as was true with confessions the requirement of "voluntary" consent reflects a fair accommodation of the constitutional requirements involved.   In examining all the surrounding circumstances to determine if in fact the consent to search was coerced, account must be taken of subtly coercive police questions, as well as the possibly vulnerable subjective state of the person who consents.   Those searches that are the product of police coercion can thus be filtered out without undermining the continuing validity of consent searches.   In sum, there is no reason for us to depart in the area of consent searches, from the traditional definition of "voluntariness." Schneckloth v. Bustamonte, 412 U.S. 218, 229, 93 S.Ct. 2041, 2048–49, 36 L.Ed.2d 854, 864 (1973).

When the prosecuting attorney attempts to introduce into court evidence obtained as a result of a consent search, the court will require proof by "clear and convincing evidence" that the consent was in fact voluntarily given, and was not the result of duress or coercion, express or implied.   The prosecutor's proof will consist almost entirely of the law enforcement officer's testimony about the circumstances surrounding the obtaining of the consent and the conducting of the search.   The remainder of this chapter will therefore be devoted to explaining in detail the meaning of the voluntariness requirement and providing guidelines for the law enforcement officer in conducting consent searches.

REQUIREMENT THAT THE CONSENT BE VOLUNTARY

As the U.S. Supreme Court said in *Schneckloth v. Bustamonte,* there are no set rules for determining whether or not a consent to search has been voluntarily and freely given.   Courts will examine all the circumstances surrounding the giving of the consent in making this decision.   The following examples should give helpful guidelines to law enforcement officers in determining what circumstances the courts consider important in deciding the question of voluntariness of consent.

Force or Threat of Force

Courts will always find a lack of voluntariness of consent when law enforcement officers use force or threats of force in obtaining the consent.   Thus, in a case in which the defendant was confronted by police with drawn guns and a riot pistol, and was told they would get a warrant if necessary, the court held that the defendant did not give free and voluntary consent to search when he gave the officers the keys to his car in an atmosphere of "dramatic excitement."   Weed v. United States, 340 F.2d 827 (10th Circuit Court of Appeals, 1965).   Also, in a case in which the defendant permitted entry into his apartment only after officers threatened to kick down his door, the court held that the consent was obviously not free and voluntary. People v. Loria, 10 N.Y.2d 368, 373, 223 N.Y.S.2d 462, 466–67, 179 N.E.2d 478,

482 (Court of Appeals of New York, 1961). Any such blatant display of force will always cause a consent to be held invalid because it was involuntary.

Sometimes, in order to protect themselves and others, officers must use force or the threat of force in their initial confrontation with a suspect. Despite the coercive nature of an initial confrontation, officers may still be able to obtain a valid consent to search. Officers must, however, do everything in their power to ensure that the consent is voluntary. In People v. Parker, 45 Cal.App.3rd 24, 119 Cal.Rptr. 49 (California Court of Appeal, 1975) officers, believing a suspect to be armed, entered his hotel room with guns drawn. After they ascertained that the room's occupant was unarmed, the officers holstered their guns. They then obtained consent to search after indicating to the occupant that he could deny permission to search. The court found that the consent to search was voluntary under the totality of the circumstances.

Submission to Authority

The show of force or coercion by law enforcement officers need not be of such intensity as in the above cases for a court to hold that a consent to search was not voluntary. Even an implied or suggested assertion of authority by law enforcement officers may be enough to cause a resulting consent to search to be considered involuntary. The rationale behind this is that a person's submission to a show of authority may not be an expression of free will but may be nothing more than a show of respect for the supremacy of the law. Therefore, a person's mere acquiescence or submission to an assertion of authority by a law enforcement officer will usually not support a finding of voluntary consent. In the often cited case of *Bumper v. North Carolina,* officers went to the home of a rape suspect to look for evidence. The home was owned and occupied by the defendant's grandmother. The officers told the grandmother that they had a search warrant and she let them in. During the course of their search, a rifle was found.

At the hearing on the motion to suppress the rifle as evidence, the prosecutor did not rely on the warrant to support the legality of the search but relied on the grandmother's consent. (In fact, no warrant was ever returned nor was there any information about the conditions under which it was issued.)

The U.S. Supreme Court held that a search cannot be justified on the basis of consent when that consent has been given only after an announcement by the officers conducting the search that they have a search warrant:

> When a prosecutor seeks to rely upon consent to justify the lawfulness of a search, he has the burden of proving that the consent was, in fact, *freely and voluntarily given.* This burden cannot be discharged by showing no more than acquiescence to a claim of lawful authority. A search conducted in reliance upon a warrant cannot later be justified on the basis of consent if it turns out that the warrant was invalid. The results can be no different when it turns out that the State does not even attempt to rely upon the validity of the warrant, or fails to show that there was, in fact, any warrant at all.
> When a law enforcement officer claims authority to search a home under a warrant, he announces in effect that the occupant has no right to resist the search. The situation is instinct with coercion—albeit colorably lawful coercion. Where

there is coercion there cannot be consent. Bumper v. North Carolina, 391 U.S. 543, 548–50, 88 S.Ct. 1788, 1792, 20 L.Ed.2d 797, 802–03 (1968).

Another example is a case in which officers arrested the defendant for driving the wrong way on a one-way street. As the defendant was standing between his car and the police car, one of the officers went to the passenger side of his car and attempted to open the door in order to look for "anything in violation of the law." Finding it locked, the officer requested that defendant open it, and defendant complied. When the door opened, a shaving kit fell to the ground. The kit was later found to contain marijuana.

The court held that the defendant did not voluntarily consent to the search of his car:

> Mere acquiescence in the orders, suggestions, or requests of the police can never be equated with consent. . . . Thus, a finding of voluntary consent can never rest solely on the fact that an accused did some consensual act or gave permission to the police to search, but is a question of fact which must be decided in light of the circumstances attending the alleged consent. . . .
>
> Among the factors to be considered are the setting in which the consent was obtained; what was said and done by the parties present; the age, intelligence, and educational background of the person consenting. . . . Commonwealth v. Burgos, 223 Pa.Super. 325, 329–30, 299 A.2d 34, 37 (Superior Court of Pennsylvania, 1972).

The court noted that the officer had already attempted to enter the car when he asked defendant to open the door. Consent under such circumstances could hardly be voluntary, because it is unlikely that a suspect would assert opposition to a search that appeared inevitable. Furthermore, the defendant in this case was under arrest and did not speak English very well. It is likely that he understood the request as an order, and thus merely acquiesced rather than voluntarily consented to the request.

Failure to Object to Search

A person's mere failure to object to a search will not in itself constitute the full and unqualified voluntary consent required by the law. In an illustrative case, an officer investigating the ringing of a burglar alarm in an office building saw the defendant in one of the offices. The defendant let the officer into the office and satisfactorily explained his presence as the owner of the office. As the defendant walked away, he picked up a large envelope and placed in in his pocket. The officer then asked him "What did you put in your pocket? Let me see it." The defendant then handed over the package, saying that it contained marijuana and that he had a permit for it. The officer arrested him for felonious possession of a narcotic drug.

The court found that the defendant's handing over of the package at the policeman's direction was the equivalent of a search and seizure:

> This was not a voluntary act, a consent to waive the constitutional right to be free from unreasonable searches and seizures, but rather a submission to authority. No inference of consent may be drawn from the mere failure of a person to argue or object to a demand of an officer. Our courts "indulge every reasonable presump-

tion against waiver" of fundamental constitutional rights. . . . People v. Abramson, 40 Misc. 723, 724, 243 N.Y.S.2d 819, 821 (Supreme Court of New York, 1963).

Nevertheless, although failure to object, by itself, will not establish a valid consent, it is still *some evidence* of consent, and when it is accompanied by other factors such as the defendant's active cooperation with the officers in conducting the search, it may satisfy the requirement of free and voluntary consent on the defendant's part. Thus, there was voluntary consent in a case in which the defendant directed the route to his apartment, pointed out the closet where his clothing was, and made no objection to the examination of bloodstained clothing or the taking and retention of it by the police. It is to be noted that there was nothing in this case to suggest violence, threats of violence, intimidation, or overawing of the defendant by the police. State v. Hannah, 150 Conn. 457, 191 A.2d 124 (Supreme Court of Connecticut, 1963).

Misrepresentation or Deception

The courts look with disfavor upon any consent to search that is obtained by misleading or deceiving the person giving the consent as to the authority of the officer conducting the search. An example is a case in which officers had arrested the defendant for robbery and murder and questioned him at police headquarters. He made no incriminating statements at that time. The next day, officers, without a search warrant, went to the defendant's home to conduct a search. They falsely told the defendant's wife that he had admitted the crime and had sent the police for the "stuff." The frightened and upset wife admitted the officers to the apartment and led them to money evidence from the robbery.

The court held that the consent given by the wife was not voluntary:

> [I]t is well established that the consent may not be gained through stealth, deceit, or misrepresentation, and that if such exists this is tantamount to implied coercion. . . . Commonwealth v. Wright, 411 Pa. 81, 85, 190 A.2d 709, 711 (Supreme Court of Pennsylvania, 1963).

Custody or Arrest

In United States v. Watson, 423 U.S. 411, 96 S.Ct. 820, 46 L.Ed.2d 598 (1976), the U.S. Supreme Court held that a consent to search will not be held involuntary solely because the person giving the consent is under arrest or is otherwise in custody. Nevertheless, the fact that a person is deprived of freedom of action by law enforcement officers or is under arrest is important in determining voluntariness of consent. Courts tend to examine very carefully any consent given under these circumstances. A person who has been taken into custody or arrested is believed to be "more susceptible to duress or coercion from the custodial officers." United States v. Richardson, 388 F.2d 842, 845 (6th Circuit Court of Appeals, 1968). Some courts have gone so far as to require counsel for a person in custody before police may obtain a valid consent to search. The Indiana Supreme Court held that because of the inherently coercive nature of in-custody interrogation, a person in custody of the police is entitled to the presence and advice of counsel prior to deciding whether to give consent to search. Pirtle v. State, 263 Ind. 16, 323 N.E.2d 634 (1975). Therefore, when the validity of the search is tested in court, a heavier burden is placed on the prosecutor to prove the consent was freely and voluntarily given, if the person was in custody when consent was given.

Law enforcement officers must be especially careful in ensuring that consent is voluntary when the person giving the consent is in custody or under arrest. They can do this by carefully noting indications of the person's willingness to allow the search, and by not doing anything themselves that would tend to influence or coerce the person to consent. For example, if a person in custody consents to a search and actively cooperates with the officer, or expresses a belief that no incriminating evidence will be found, courts will usually find these factors indicative of voluntariness. Also, if a person has been informed of the right to refuse to allow the search by the custodial officer, a subsequent consent is usually considered to be voluntarily given.

On the other hand, if the person in custody is subjected to additional coercive action by the law enforcement officer such as handcuffing, display of weapons, or incarceration, courts are likely to consider a subsequent consent to search involuntary. The same would be true if an officer conducted an interrogation of a person in custody without giving *Miranda* warnings, or attempted to deceive or mislead the person. Furthermore, evasive or uncooperative conduct on the part of the person in custody is considered to be an indication that the consent is not voluntary.

It must be reemphasized here that none of the above-mentioned factors will determine by itself whether a consent is voluntary or involuntary. Courts will examine *all* the surrounding facts and circumstances, and it is nearly impossible to predict how a court will decide in any given situation. It is clear, however, that it will be harder to prove a consent was voluntary when the person giving the consent was in custody than if the person was not. Law enforcement officers should be aware of all the variables that the courts consider so they can control the situation as much as possible or at least make a rational decision on whether to conduct a search based on consent or to get a warrant.

Note: The foregoing principles apply when the defendant's arrest or detention is legal. However, when the arrest or detention is illegal, courts will generally hold that any consent given is "fruit of the poisonous tree" and necessarily involuntary. In Florida v. Royer, 460 U.S. 491, 103 S.Ct. 1319, 75 L.Ed.2d 229 (1983), the U.S. Supreme Court, after finding that the defendant was being illegally detained when he consented to the search of his luggage, held that the consent was tainted by the illegality and was ineffective to justify the search.

It is very important, therefore when a consent to search is obtained from a person under arrest that the arrest be carried out in compliance with the requirements set out in Chapter 4. Otherwise, the illegal arrest is likely to render the consent search also illegal. When possible, officers should obtain consent to search from a person before the person is arrested or otherwise restrained. As a general rule, the sooner consent is sought, the fewer factors tending to show involuntariness will be present.

Knowledge of Right to Refuse Consent

Another factor that courts consider in determining the voluntariness of consent is whether or not the consenting person knew of the right to refuse to consent. Prior to the U.S. Supreme Court decision in *Schneckloth v. Bustamonte,* discussed above, some courts ruled that the state had to prove that the person from whom a consent search was sought knew of the right to refuse consent or none of the evidence seized would be admissible in court. Other courts ruled that the knowledge of the right to refuse consent was only one of the factors to be considered in determining voluntariness. The U.S. Supreme Court settled the matter with respect to non-custodial searches in *Schneckloth v. Bustamonte,* agreeing with the latter view:

> Voluntariness is a question of fact to be determined from all the circumstances, and while the subject's knowledge of a right to refuse is a factor to be taken into consideration, the prosecution is not required to demonstrate such knowledge as a prerequisite to establishing a voluntary consent. . . . 412 U.S. at 248–49, 93 S.Ct. at 2059, 36 L.Ed.2d at 875.

Therefore, a law enforcement officer seeking to obtain a valid consent to search from a person not in custody need not give any warnings or otherwise ensure that the person is aware of the right to refuse consent.

Nevertheless, even though formal warnings are not required for non-custodial consent searches, the courts still consider a person's knowledge of the right to refuse consent as *one* of the factors in determining voluntariness. Officers who want to make sure they are obtaining a valid consent to search *may* give a person formal warning of this right. Furthermore, since the courts have not yet decided whether knowledge of the right to refuse consent is necessary for a valid consent when the consenting person is *in custody,* it would be a good idea for officers to give such warnings when a person is under arrest or otherwise in custody. The following suggested simple warnings should adequately inform a person of the right to refuse consent:

> I am a law enforcement officer. I would like to request permission from you to search your premises (person, belongings).
> You have an absolute right to refuse to grant permission for me to search unless I have a search warrant.
> If you do grant permission to search, anything found can be used against you in a court of law. If you refuse, I will not make a search at this time.

A consent to search given by a person after receiving warnings such as these is likely to be considered voluntary by a court, assuming there has been no coercion by the officer.

Of course, if an officer has clear indications that the person consenting already knows of the right to insist on a search warrant, there would be no need for the officer to give any warnings. An example is a case in which the defendant, when asked by an officer to sign a Consent Search form said, "If I don't sign this, you are going to get a search warrant." The court said that this statement demonstrated the defendant's awareness of his right to resist the officer's search in the absence of a warrant. His subsequent signature on the form was therefore a relinquishment of a *known* right. United States v. Curiale, 414 F.2d 744 (2d Circuit Court of Appeals,

1969). It is very important for an officer in situations like the above to make careful notes of any indications that the person knows of the right to refuse consent. Such information can greatly help the court in determining voluntariness of consent.

Some state courts have refused to follow the *Schneckloth v. Bustamonte* "totality of the circumstances" test and have required that consenting persons be aware of their right to refuse consent in addition to their consent being otherwise voluntary. The New Jersey Supreme Court held that the state constitution demands that "the validity of a consent to search, even in a noncustodial situation, must be measured in terms of waiver; i.e., where the state seeks to justify a search on the basis of consent it has the burden of showing that the consent was voluntary, an essential element of which is knowledge of the right to refuse consent." State v. Johnson, 68 N.J. 349, 353–54, 346 A.2d 66, 68 (1975). Likewise, the court in Case v. State, Okl.Cr.App., 519 P.2d 523 (Court of Criminal Appeals of Oklahoma, 1974), held that officers must give *Miranda* warnings prior to obtaining consent. Officers should determine whether courts in their state interpret their state constitution to require that consenting persons be aware of their rights before a consent search is conducted.

Clearness and Explicitness of Consent

Another factor to be considered in determining the voluntariness of consent is whether the expression of consent is clear, explicit, and unequivocal. Hesitation or ambiguity in the expression of consent could be one indication that the consent is not voluntary.

It is immaterial whether a person's verbal consent to search is written or oral. Both are equally effective in waiving the person's right to object later to the search on constitutional grounds. A signed and witnessed writing, however, provides the best proof of a clear, voluntary, waiver of a known right. A suggested form for obtaining a written consent to search appears on page 205.

Consent need not be expressed in words but may be implied from a person's acts or conduct. An example is a case in which police were investigating the death of an infant and went to the home of the defendant. The officers asked the defendant's husband if they could go into the room containing the infant's crib. The husband handed the officers the keys, saying that he did not want to go in there himself. Incriminating evidence against the defendant was found in the room.

The court held that a valid consent to search had been given by the husband although he did not express it orally or in writing. The fact that he handed the officers the keys, knowing their intent to search the room, was a clear and unequivocal expression of his consent. People v. Crews, 38 Ill. 331, 231 N.E.2d 451 (Supreme Court of Illinois, 1967).

Officers should describe in their reports any statements or conduct of the consenting person. Even statements or conduct that seem unimportant at the time of the search may prove meaningful later to a judge or an attorney.

Physical and Mental Condition

Officers should take note of physical or mental deficiencies of persons from whom they obtain consent to search. Persons giving consent may claim later in court that

---

CONSENT TO SEARCH

I, _____ , have been requested to consent to a search of my _____ , located at _____ . I have also been advised of my constitutional rights to refuse consent and to require that a search warrant be obtained prior to any search. I have further been advised that if I do consent to a search, any evidence found as a result of the search can be seized and used against me in any court of law, and that I may withdraw my consent to search at any time prior to the conclusion of the search.

After having been advised of my constitutional rights as stated above, I hereby voluntarily waive those rights and consent to a search and authorize _____ and _____ to conduct a complete search of the above-described _____ .

_____
Signature

_____
Location and Date

WITNESSES:

_____
Signature, Title and Date

_____
Signature, Title and Date

---

they lacked the mental capacity to consent because of insanity, use of alcohol or drugs, or physical disability. Officers can negate such claims by testifying about their observations at the time consent was given. Also, some courts determine the voluntariness of the consent on the basis of facts as they objectively appeared to the officer at the time of consent. People v. Gurley, 23 Cal.App.3d 536, 100 Cal.Rptr. 407 (California Court of Appeal, 1972).

The emotional state of the consenting person may also be important. If an officer can testify that the consenting party was calm and cooperative, a court is more likely to find voluntary consent.

Notification of Counsel

If a defendant has retained counsel in connection with a criminal charge, officers should notify the defendant's counsel before obtaining a consent to search. In

Tidwell v. Superior Court, 17 Cal.App.3d 780, 95 Cal.Rptr. 213 (California Court of Appeal, 1971), a law enforcement officer obtained from the defendant, who was being held in the county jail, consent to search the defendant's automobile. At the time, the defendant was represented by appointed counsel on a separate charge, but the officer did not notify counsel before obtaining consent. The court suppressed the evidence holding that once counsel is appointed the police may not obtain consent to search without notifying counsel.

Experience and Background

The experience and background of a person consenting to a search can be important factors in determining the voluntariness of consent. A person who is knowledgeable about investigative and legal proceedings is less likely to be coerced or intimidated by law enforcement authorities than a person ignorant in these areas. On the other hand, it may be more difficult to establish voluntary consent by an illiterate person or one who cannot speak or understand English. Officers should tell the court what they know about the experience and background of consenting persons to assist the court in determining the voluntariness of consent.

SCOPE OF CONSENT SEARCHES

There are several limitations on the scope or extent to which a law enforcement officer can conduct a search by consent. One of the most obvious of these limitations is that, although there may be a valid consent in all respects to an officer's request, it may not be a consent to *search* at all. The best example of this is the situation in which an officer is permitted to *enter* someone's home in compliance with the officer's request for an interview. This does *not* automatically give the officer a right to search the place. There is a vital distinction between the granting of admission to one's home for the purposes of conversation and the granting of permission to thoroughly search the place.

In a case illustrating this principle, officers investigating a murder knocked on the defendant's hotel room door and were invited in by the defendant. The defendant was not advised that they were police officers nor was any request made by them to search his room. Nevertheless, a search was conducted and incriminating evidence found.

The court held that the invitation to enter his room, extended by the defendant to the person who knocked on the door, did not constitute a consent to search his room. Quoting from another case, the court said:

> "To justify the introduction of evidence seized by a police officer within a private residence on the ground that the officer's entry was made by invitation, permission, or consent, there must be evidence of a statement or some overt act by the occupant of such residence sufficient to indicate his intent to waive his rights to the security and privacy of his home and freedom from unwarranted intrusions therein. An open door is not a waiver of such rights. . . ." Duncan v. State, 278 Ala. 145, 159, 176 So.2d 840, 853 (Supreme Court of Alabama, 1965).

Throughout the rest of this discussion of the scope of consent searches, officers should keep in mind that they must first carefully determine the scope of consent given by the consenting person, and then they must be careful not to exceed those limits. When a consent search is challenged in court or at a hearing on a motion to suppress the prosecution must establish that the scope of the search did not exceed the scope of the consent.

"Plain View" Doctrine

Although an invitation to enter premises is not the equivalent of a consent to search the premises, an officer need not ignore contraband or other criminal evidence lying in plain view. Under the "plain view" doctrine, if officers are in a place or position in which they have a legal right to be as the result of a prior valid intrusion into a constitutionally protected area, they may seize any criminal evidence that is lying open to view. In a case illustrating this point, officers were investigating a robbery, and preliminary information led them to suspect a man named Albert. The officers went to Albert's apartment, knocked on the door, identified themselves, and were invited into the apartment by Albert, who opened the door and walked back into the room. The defendant was present in the apartment as a guest of Albert. While talking to the two men, the officers noticed various objects fitting the description of items stolen in the robbery lying in plain view. They arrested the two men and seized the evidence observed.

The court held that the evidence seized was admissible against the defendant (Albert's guest). Because the officers were rightfully in the room by Albert's invitation, they were also rightfully there with respect to defendant. Seeing what was patently and obviously open to view was therefore not a search, and seizing the evidence was not a violation of the defendant's rights. Robbins v. MacKenzie, 364 F.2d 45 (1st Circuit Court of Appeals, 1966). The plain view doctrine is discussed in detail in Chapter 9.

Area of Search

Assuming that an officer is able to obtain a valid consent not just to *enter* premises, but consent to actually *search* those premises, there may still be limitations on the scope or extent of the search. One such limitation relates to the bounds of the area to be searched. Although it is impossible to give operational guidelines as to how large an area a law enforcement officer may search after obtaining a person's consent, in general it can be said that it depends on the words or actions used by the person giving the consent. It should be noted that the area allowed to be searched is different for consent searches, for searches incident to arrest, and for searches made under warrant.

In a case in which an officer had received permission to "look around" an apartment, the court held that this did not authorize the officer to open and search boxes and suitcases that he had been informed were the property of persons other than the person giving consent. In other words, an officer can search only those parts of premises over which the person giving consent has some possessory right or control, and not personal property that he knows belongs to some other person.

People v. Cruz, 61 Cal.2d 861, 40 Cal.Rptr. 841, 395 P.2d 889 (Supreme Court of California, 1964). In another case, in which a valid consent was given to officers to search the trunk of a car, the court held that this consent did not extend to a search of the passenger area of the car and that evidence found in the passenger area was inadmissible in court. State v. Johnson, 71 Wn.2d 239, 427 P.2d 705 (Supreme Court of Washington, 1967).

Furthermore, the limitation on the area of search allowed by consent applies equally to searches of the person as to searches of premises. For example, in a case in which an individual consented to a search of his person for *weapons*, the court held that this did not constitute a consent to conduct a general exploratory search of his person. Incriminating evidence seized was held inadmissible in court. People v. Rice, 259 Cal.App.2d 399, 66 Cal.Rptr. 246 (Court of Appeal of California, 1968).

In a particularly interesting case involving both a nonverbal consent and a limitation on the area of the person allowed to be searched by consent, a police officer, while questioning the defendant with regard to narcotics, asked him whether he was still using or carrying narcotics. When the defendant replied that he was not, the officer asked him if he minded if he checked him for needle marks. The defendant said nothing but put his arms out sideways. The officer did not check the defendant's arms but instead patted down his coat and found marijuana cigarettes.

The court held that the search went beyond the area to which the defendant had consented to allow a search:

> Bowens' putting out his arms sideways in response to a query whether he minded allowing the officer to check "if he had any marks on him" could hardly be said to be naturally indicative or persuasive of the giving of an intended consent to have the officer switch instead to a general search of his pockets—in which he had two marijuana cigarettes. Oliver v. Bowens, 386 F.2d 688, 691 (9th Circuit Court of Appeals, 1967).

As a general rule, if officers ask for and obtain consent to search a specific area, whether in a place or on a person, they are limited to that specific area. If they search beyond it, any evidence they seize is likely to be held inadmissible in court.

Time

Another limitation on the scope of a search by consent relates to the length of time over which the consent is valid. In a case illustrating this limitation, officers were investigating the death of the defendant's wife and they obtained a valid consent from the defendant to search his home. The officers conducted a search and found nothing. At this point in time, the defendant had not been accused of anything. However, later in the day, police received information giving them probable cause to arrest the defendant for his wife's murder and to obtain a search warrant for his premises. The defendant was arrested that evening but the search warrant could not be executed at that time because it ran only in the daytime. Therefore, officers went back the next day with the search warrant and found certain incriminating evidence.

Since there was some question as to the validity of the warrant, the state attempted to justify this second search on the basis that the defendant's earlier consent continued in effect after his arrest, to the next day. The court rejected this contention with the following reasoning:

> The officers entered the defendant's home on the 5th under the protection of his consent. By nightfall, however, the defendant had ceased to be the husband assisting in the solution of his wife's death and had become the man accused of his wife's murder by poison (and) held under arrest for hearing.
> When the defendant became the accused, the protective cloak of the Constitution became more closely wrapped around him. . . .
> The consent of December 5 in our view should be measured on the morning of the 6th by the status of the defendant as the accused. There is no evidence whatsoever that the consent of the 5th was ever discussed with the defendant at or after his arrest, or that he was informed of the State's intent to enter and search his home on the 6th on the strength of a continuing consent. We conclude, therefore, that consent of the defendant had ended by December 6, and accordingly the officers were not protected thereby on the successful search of the 6th. State v. Brochu, 237 A.2d 418, 421 (Supreme Judicial Court of Maine, 1967).

Once officers conduct a consent search and stop it for whatever reason, if they desire to conduct a search of the same place or person the next day or later the same day, they should obtain a new consent from the person involved. This would be especially true in cases in which intervening events, such as the arrest of the consenting person, suggest that a second consent might not be given so readily as the original consent.

Object of Search

The scope of the search may also be limited by the object for which the consenting person allows the officer to search. In People v. Superior Court (Arketa), 10 Cal. App.3d 122, 89 Cal.Rptr. 316 (California Court of Appeal, 1970), a person gave officers consent to search his premises for a possible suspect of a crime. The officers conducted a thorough search of the house and its closets for a crowbar without advising the person that they wanted to look for a crowbar. The court invalidated the search because it went beyond the scope of the consent granted. Therefore, officers should not look in areas where the object for which they have consent to search could not be located because of its size, shape, or character.

Revocation of Consent

Although there is some disagreement on the question, the prevailing view appears to be that consent, once given, may be revoked or withdrawn at any time after the search has been partially completed. A case illustrating this principle involved a police officer who was investigating the defendant who was parked at a late hour in a high arrest area of town. The defendant consented to let the officer look around inside his vehicle. After doing so, the officer asked to look into the defendant's trunk. The defendant also initially consented to this. However, after the officer had spent some time looking in the trunk, the defendant felt he was being harassed and he told the officer to stop.   The officer did not stop at this time and later found contraband in the trunk.

The court held that the defendant had withdrawn his consent and that the evidence found after the withdrawal was inadmissible in court:

> Neither do we find any reason to hold that a consent, once given, may not be withdrawn. It is true that the contrary view has been expressed. . . . We do not believe that this is the present law, particularly in view of the explicit statement in the *Miranda* case that a defendant consenting to answer police questioning without a lawyer may withdraw such waiver at any time. We see no reason, in this respect, to distinguish between withdrawal of waiver of legal representation during investigation and withdrawal of consent to search once given. People v. Martinez, 259 Cal.App. 2d 943, 945–46, 65 Cal.Rptr. 920, 922 (Appellate Department, California Superior Court, 1968).

WHO MAY GIVE CONSENT

In general, the only person who is able to give a valid consent to a search is the person whose constitutional protection against unreasonable searches and seizures would be invaded by the search if it were conducted without consent. This means, for example, that when the search of an individual's body or clothing is contemplated, the only person who can consent to such a search is the individual involved. The same rule applies to searches of premises except that when several people have varying degrees of interest in the same premises, more than one person may be qualified to give consent to search.

In certain situations, the law recognizes authority in a third person to consent to a search of property even though he or she is not the person against whose interests the search is being conducted. In United States v. Matlock, 415 U.S. 164, 94 S.Ct. 988, 39 L.Ed.2d 242 (1974), the U.S. Supreme Court stated the test for determining whether a third person could consent to a search of premises or effects:

> [W]hen the prosecution seeks to justify a warrantless search by proof of voluntary consent, it is not limited to proof that consent was given by the defendant, but may show that permission to search was obtained from a third party who possessed *common authority over or other sufficient relationship to the premises or effects sought to be inspected.* 415 U.S. at 171, 94 S.Ct. at 993, 39 L.Ed.2d at 249–50 (emphasis supplied).

The Court then defined "common authority":

> Common authority is, of course, not to be implied from the mere interest a third party has in the property. The authority which justifies the third-party consent does not rest upon the law of property, with its attendant historical and legal refinements, . . . but rests rather on mutual use of the property by persons generally having joint access or control for most purposes, so that it is reasonable to recognize that any of the co-inhabitants has the right to permit the inspection in his own right and that the others have assumed the risk that one of their number might permit the common area to be searched. 415 U.S. at 171 n. 7, 94 S.Ct. at 993 n. 7, 39 L.Ed.2d at 250 n. 7.

Since questions of who may give valid consent are often confusing and complicated, and since courts tend to carefully scrutinize any waiver of a person's constitutional rights, it is worthwhile to examine some examples of consent search situations in which the person giving consent is not the person against whose interests the search is being conducted. Officers should keep in mind, throughout the discussion of third-party consent situations, that they must make the necessary inquiries to determine if the party from whom consent is sought is a proper party to authorize the search.

Persons Having Equal Rights or Interests in Property

It is well settled that when two or more persons have substantially equal rights of ownership, occupancy, or other possessory interest in premises to be searched or property to be seized, any one of the persons may legally authorize a search and seizure, and thereby bind the others and waive their right to object. An example is a case in which police obtained a valid consent to search a defendant's apartment from a co-defendant in a case involving a break into a bank. The co-defendant who gave the consent was living with the defendant at the time and evidence showed that he had a right to use and occupy the premises. The police found evidence incriminating the defendant in the apartment.

The court held that the co-defendant, being a joint tenant or resident of the apartment, could consent to the entry and search of the apartment:

> This court and other courts have held that where there are multiple lawful residents of a premises, any one of such persons may give permission to enter and that if incriminating evidence is found, it may be used against all. Wright v. U.S., 389 F.2d 996, 998 (8th Circuit Court of Appeals, 1968).

In determining whether a person is a joint occupant of premises, courts will consider whether the person paid rent, how long the person stayed, whether the person left belongings on the premises, whether the person possessed a key, and whether there was any written or oral agreement among other parties as to the person's right to use and occupy the premises.

Another case that illustrates the same principle, only applied to personal property, is the U.S. Supreme Court case of *Frazier v. Cupp*. In that case, the defendant, at his murder trial, objected to the introduction into evidence of clothing seized from his duffel bag. At the time of the seizure, the duffel bag was being used jointly by the defendant and his cousin and had been left in the cousin's home. When police arrested the cousin, they asked him if they could have his clothing. The cousin directed them to the duffel bag and both the cousin and his mother consented to its search. During the search, the officers came upon the defendant's clothing in the bag and it was seized as well.

The Court upheld the legality of the search over defendant's objections:

> Since Rawls [the cousin] was a joint owner of the bag, he clearly had authority to consent to its search. The officers therefore found evidence against the petitioner while in the course of an otherwise lawful search. *[plain view doctrine]* . . .
> Petitioner argues that Rawls only had actual permission to use one compartment of

the bag and that he had no authority to consent to a search of the other compartments. We will not, however, engage in such metaphysical subtleties in judging the efficacy of Rawls' consent. Petitioner, in allowing Rawls to use the bag and in leaving it in his house, must be taken to have assumed the risk that Rawls would allow someone else to look inside. We find no valid search and seizure claim in this case. Frazier v. Cupp, 394 U.S. 731, 740, 89 S.Ct. 1420, 1425, 22 L.Ed.2d 684, 693–94 (1969).

A third party who has common authority to use the premises may give consent to a search of the premises even if not *actually* using the premises at the time of the search. In United States v. Cook, 530 F.2d 145 (7th Circuit Court of Appeals, 1976), the defendant's landlady consented to a search of a poultry house on her property. The poultry house consisted of a large room in which the landlady had segregated an area with wire fence for her exclusive use. She gave the defendant permission to use the remaining space, but she retained the right to use the space if necessary. The defendant claimed that, since neither the landlady nor her family *actually* used the defendant's area, there was no common authority. The court upheld the search, however, ruling that the defendant had assumed the risk that the landlady would permit others to inspect the premises.

A third party cannot consent to a search of more than that over which he or she has common authority. In United States v. Bussey, 507 F.2d 1096 (9th Circuit Court of Appeals, 1974), the court held that a participant with the defendant in a bank robbery had authority to consent to a search of the motel room which she and the defendant occupied with others. She did not, however, have authority to consent to a search of the defendant's personal luggage.

Landlord—Tenant

A landlord has *no* implied authority to consent to a search of a tenant's premises or a seizure of the tenant's property during the period of the tenancy. This rule holds true even though the landlord has the authority to enter the tenant's premises for the limited purposes of inspection, performance of repairs, or housekeeping services. Chapman v. United States, 365 U.S. 610, 81 S.Ct. 776, 5 L.Ed.2d 828 (U.S. Supreme Court, 1961). However, once the tenancy has terminated, and the landlord has the primary right to occupation and control of the premises, the landlord may consent to a search of the premises. Furthermore, the landlord's consent will be valid after the termination of the tenancy even though the former tenant has left personal belongings on the premises. People v. Urfer, 274 Cal.App. 2d 307, 79 Cal.Rptr. 60 (California Court of Appeal, 1969).

Hotel Employee—Hotel Guest

The U.S. Supreme Court held that the principles governing a landlord's consent to a search of tenant's premises apply with equal force to consent searches of hotel (and motel) rooms allowed by hotel employees. In *Stoner v. California,* police were investigating a robbery and they went to the defendant's hotel. The defendant was not in his room and police obtained permission from the hotel clerk to search the room. Items of evidence incriminating the defendant in the robbery were found in the room.

The Court held that the search was illegal and that the items seized could not be used against the defendant in court. The defendant's constitutional right was at stake here—not the clerk's or the hotel's. Therefore, only the defendant, either directly or through an agent, could waive that right. There was no evidence that the police had any basis whatsoever to believe that the night clerk had been authorized by the defendant to permit the police to search his room:

> It is true . . . that when a person engages a hotel room he undoubtedly gives "implied or express permission" to "such persons as maids, janitors or repairmen" to enter his room "in the performance of their duties." . . . But the conduct of the night clerk and the police in the present case was of an entirely different order. . . .
>
> No less than a tenant of a house . . . a guest in a hotel room is entitled to constitutional protection against unreasonable searches and seizures. . . . That protection would disappear if it were left to depend upon the unfettered discretion of an employee of the hotel. Stoner v. California, 376 U.S. 483, 489–90, 84 S.Ct. 889, 893, 11 L.Ed.2d 356, 361 (1964).

Host—Guest

A different situation is presented when the person against whom a search for evidence is directed is merely a guest on the premises of a host and the host consents to a search of the premises. Here, courts have generally held that the host or primary occupant of the premises may give a valid consent to a search of the premises and any evidence found would be admissible against the guest. An example is a case in which a lady householder had "taken in," without payment of rent, her grandnephew and another young man. While she was tidying up her home, she found a loaded pistol and other items that alarmed her. She called the police and gave them permission to search the premises. The incriminating evidence found by the police as a result of this consent search was held admissible in court over the objections of the guests. Woodard v. United States, 254 F.2d 313 (District of Columbia Court of Appeals, 1958).

However, if the person against whom the search for evidence is directed is a long-term guest and has a section of the premises set aside for exclusive personal use, the consent of the host may not be effective to authorize a search. Reeves v. Warden, 346 F.2d 915 (4th Circuit Court of Appeals, 1965). The question whether a host may consent to a search of the guest's area of the premises turns on considerations such as the length of time of the guest's stay, the exclusiveness of the guest's control of a particular area of the premises, and the guest's reasonable expectation of privacy in that area of the premises.

Employer—Employee

In general, an employer may consent to a search of any part of the employer's premises that is used by an employee. Thus, it has been held that a search of an employee's locker in his employer's plant was legal upon the consent of the employer. The court in that case considered that the employer owned the property and, under the terms of the contract between the employer and the employee's union, the employer retained a master key to all employee lockers. State v. Robinson, 86 N.J.Super. 308, 206 A.2d 779 (Superior Court of New Jersey, 1965).

However, an employer who does not retain such control over the premises may not effectively consent to a search of an area used by an employee. For example, a leading case in this area held that the official superior of a government employee who was assigned a desk for her exclusive use could not validly consent to the search of the employee's desk. The court reasoned:

> In the absence of a valid regulation to the contrary, appellee was entitled to, and did keep private property of a personal sort in her desk. Her superiors could not reasonably search the desk for her purse, her personal letters, or anything else that did not belong to the government and had no connection with the work of the office. Their consent did not make such a search by the police reasonable. U.S. v. Blok, 188 F.2d 1019, 1021 (District of Columbia Circuit Court of Appeals, 1951).

Courts have generally held that the reverse situation—whether an employee can consent to the search of his employer's premises—depends upon the scope of the employee's authority. Generally, the average employee, such as a clerk, janitor, handyman, driver, or other person temporarily in charge, may not give such consent. United States v. Block, 202 F.Supp. 705 (U.S. District Court, Southern District of New York, 1962). However, if the employee is a manager or other person of considerable authority who is left in complete charge for a substantial period of time, then it is likely that the employee would be able to effectively consent to a search of the employer's premises. United States v. Antonelli Fireworks Co., 155 F.2d 631 (2nd Circuit Court of Appeals, 1946). In People v. Litwin, 44 A.D.2d 492, 355 N.Y.S.2d 646 (New York Supreme Court, Appellate Division, 1974), the court held that a babysitter has insufficient interest in the premises of his or her employer to give a valid consent to search the premises.

School Official—Student

Situations often arise in which a high school or college administrative official consents to a search of student lockers or rooms by law enforcement authorities. The high school situation usually involves the search of lockers and the college situation the search of dormitory rooms. Courts have treated these two situations differently.

Courts have held that the search of a high school student's locker, when authorized by a school official, is valid because of the relationship between the school authorities and the students. The school authorities have an obligation to maintain discipline over students and usually they retain partial access to the students' lockers so that neither has an exclusive right to use and possession of the lockers. Thus, in a case in which the locker of a student suspected of burglary was opened by police with the consent of school authorities and incriminating evidence found, the court said:

> Although a student may have control of his school locker as against fellow students, his possession is not exclusive against the school and its officials. A school does not supply its students with lockers for illicit use in harboring pilfered

property or harmful substances. We deem it a proper function of school authorities to inspect the lockers under their control and to prevent their use in illicit ways or for illegal purposes. We believe this right of inspection is inherent in the authority vested in school administrators and that the same must be retained and exercised in the management of our schools if their educational functions are to be maintained and the welfare of the student bodies preserved. State v. Stein, 203 Kan. 638, 640, 456 P.2d 1, 3 (Supreme Court of Kansas, 1969).

The courts have arrived at a different conclusion when college dormitory rooms are the subject of the search. In these cases, the courts have stressed that a search cannot be based on the college's authority to maintain discipline over young students. People v. Cohen, 57 Misc. 366, 292 N.Y.S.2d 706 (District Court of New York, 1968). Also, even though a college may reserve the right to enter the rooms of students for inspection purposes, such a regulation cannot be applied so as to give consent to a search for evidence for the primary purpose of criminal prosecution. Piazzola v. Watkins, 442 F.2d 284 (5th Circuit Court of Appeals, 1971). Therefore, in a case in which police, aided by the Dean of Men, searched the defendant's room at a university and found marijuana, the evidence was held to be inadmissible in court. Even though the university had the right to check the room for damages, wear, and unauthorized appliances, this did *not* mean that the defendant "was not entitled to have a 'reasonable expectation of freedom from governmental intrusion', or that he gave consent to the police search, or gave the University authority to consent to such search." Commonwealth v. McCloskey, 217 Pa.Super. 432, 435–36, 272 A.2d 271, 273 (Superior Court of Pennsylvania, 1970).

Attorney—Client

An attorney may consent to a search of a client's premises if the attorney has been specifically authorized to do so by the client. A search of the defendant's premises and a seizure of his calf and cow were upheld because consent to search had been given by the defendant's attorney after consultation with the defendant. Brown v. State, 81 Nev. 397, 404 P.2d 428 (Supreme Court of Nevada, 1965). Nevertheless, without a specific authorization to give consent to search, the mere existence of an attorney-client relationship gives the attorney no authority to waive a client's personal rights.

Husband—Wife

Although there is some disagreement on the issue, it is generally held that one spouse may consent to a search of family premises on the basis that husband and wife are joint occupants with equal rights in the premises. An example of this is a case in which officers were investigating a murder and questioned the defendant's wife in regard to it. The wife volunteered information that the defendant had fired a pistol into the ceiling of their home some time ago. She later validly consented to officers searching for and seizing the bullet in the ceiling, which was used as evidence in convicting the defendant.

The court sustained the search on the basis that the consent was voluntary, the place of the search was the home of the defendant's wife, and the premises were under the immediate and complete control of the wife at the time of the search. Furthermore, the bullet could not be considered a personal effect of the husband, over which the wife would have no power to consent to search.

It is important to note the underlying rationale of the court's decision that the wife could consent to a search of the family premises:

> It is not a question of agency, for a wife should not be held to have authority to waive her husband's constitutional rights. This is a question of the wife's own rights to authorize entry into premises where she lives and of which she had control. Roberts v. U.S., 332 F.2d 892, 896–97 (8th Circuit Court of Appeals, 1964).

A similar situation was presented in the U.S. Supreme Court case of Coolidge v. New Hampshire, 403 U.S. 443, 91 S.Ct. 2022, 29 L.Ed.2d 564 (1971). In that case, two officers went to the defendant's home, while he was at the police station under investigation for murder, in order to check out his story with his wife. While there, the officers asked the wife if the defendant owned any guns, and she replied, "Yes, I will get them in the bedroom." She then took four guns out of a closet and gave them to the officers. The officers then asked her what her husband had been wearing on the night in question, and she produced several pairs of trousers and a hunting jacket. The police seized all this evidence, and it was used against the defendant in court.

The Court found no objection to the introduction of the above described evidence in court. In fact the Court found that the actions of the police did not even amount to a search and seizure. Because the Court discussed in detail the significance of the actions of the police, and because of the importance of the issue, it is worthwhile to quote the Court's opinion at length:

> [I]t cannot be said that the police should have obtained a warrant for the guns and clothing before they set out to visit Mrs. Coolidge, since they had no intention of rummaging around among Coolidge's effects or of dispossessing him of any of his property. Nor can it be said that they should have obtained Coolidge's permission for a seizure they did not intend to make. There was nothing to compel them to announce to the suspect that they intended to question his wife about his movements on the night of the disappearance or about the theft from his employer. Once Mrs. Coolidge had admitted them, the policemen were surely acting normally and properly when they asked her, as they had asked those questioned earlier in the investigation, including Coolidge himself, about any guns there might be in the house. The question concerning the clothes Coolidge had been wearing on the night of the disappearance was logical and in no way coercive. Indeed, one might doubt the competence of the officers involved had they not asked exactly the questions they did ask. And surely when Mrs. Coolidge of her own accord produced the guns and clothes for inspection, rather than simply describing them, it was not incumbent on the police to stop her or avert their eyes.
>
> *   *   *
>
> In assessing the claim that this course of conduct amounted to a search and seizure, it is well to keep in mind that Mrs. Coolidge described her own motive as that of clearing her husband, and that she believed that she had nothing to hide. She had seen her husband himself produce his guns for two other policemen earlier in the week, and there is nothing to indicate that she realized that he had offered only three of them for inspection on that occasion. The two officers who questioned her behaved, as her own testimony shows, with perfect courtesy. There

is not the slightest implication of an attempt to coerce or dominate her, or for that matter, to direct her actions by the more subtle techniques of suggestion that are available to officials in circumstances like these. To hold that the conduct of the police here was a search and seizure would be to hold, in effect, that a criminal suspect has constitutional protection against the adverse consequences of a spontaneous, good-faith effort by his wife to clear him of suspicion. 403 U.S. at 488–90, 91 S.Ct. at 2049–50, 29 L.Ed.2d at 596.

Parent—Child

A parent's consent to search premises owned by the parent will usually be effective against a child who lives on those premises. As one court said:

> Hardy's father gave his permission to the officers to enter and search the house and the premises *which he owned* and in which his son lived with him. Under the circumstances presented here the voluntary consent of Hardy's father to search *his own* premises is binding on Hardy and precludes his claim of violation of constitutional rights. Commonwealth v. Hardy, 423 Pa. 208, 216, 223 A.2d 719, 723 (Supreme Court of Pennsylvania, 1966).

A parent may not consent to a search of an area of the parent's home occupied by the child, however, if the child uses the room exclusively, has sectioned it off, has furnished it with his own furniture, pays rent, or otherwise establishes an expectation of privacy. State v. Peterson, 525 S.W.2d 599 (Missouri Court of Appeals, 1975). Furthermore, parents may not consent to a search of a child's room in their home if the child has already refused to grant such consent. People v. Mortimer, 46 A.D.2d 275, 361 N.Y.S.2d 955 (New York Supreme Court, Appellate Division, 1974). The court in that case said, "Constitutional rights may not be defeated by the expedient of soliciting several persons successively until the sought-after consent is obtained." 46 A.D.2d at 277, 361 N.Y.S.2d at 958.

As a general rule, minors living in their parents' home do not have sufficient authority to consent to a search of the home in the absence of their parents. May v. State, 199 So.2d 635 (Supreme Court of Mississippi, 1967).

Bailor—Bailee

A bailee of personal property may consent to its search if the bailee has full possession and control of the property. (A bailee is a person in rightful possession of personal property by permission of the owner or bailor). One example of this situation is the case of *Frazier v. Cupp* discussed earlier. Another example involved a defendant who loaned his car to a friend for his personal use. Police, who were investigating a theft, asked the friend for permission to search the trunk of the car. The friend opened the trunk and the police found incriminating evidence against the defendant.

The court held that the search was legal and that the evidence found was admissible against the defendant. The friend had been given rightful possession and control over the automobile and could do with it whatever was reasonable under the circumstances. The defendant had reserved no exclusive right to the trunk when he gave his friend the key. The friend's opening of the trunk for the police, then, was a reasonable exercise of his control over the car for the period during which he was permitted to use it. United States v. Eldridge, 302 F.2d 463 (4th Circuit Court of Appeals, 1962).

However, if the person giving consent has only limited custody over the property, such as for shipment or storage purposes, evidence found by law enforcement officers would not be admissible in court against the owner of the property. Thus an airline could not consent to the search of a package that defendant had wrapped and tied and delivered to the airline solely for transportation purposes. Corngold v. United States, 367 F.2d 1 (9th Circuit Court of Appeals, 1966). Nor could the owner of a boat who had agreed to store certain of the defendant's items on his boat give a valid consent to police to search and seize the items. Commonwealth v. Storck, 442 Pa. 197, 275 A.2d 362 (Supreme Court of Pennsylvania, 1971).

Reasonable Expectation Of Privacy

Since the U.S. Supreme Court decision in Katz v. United States, 389 U.S. 347, 88 S.Ct. 507, 19 L.Ed.2d 576 (1967), courts have considered a person's reasonable expectation of privacy as one factor in determining whether consent to search that person's property could be given by a third person. In U.S. v. Novello, 519 F.2d 1078 (5th Circuit Court of Appeals, 1975), the defendant rented an enclosed storage area and was informed that the area was accessible only to the rental agent and to those working with him. The defendant's truck, which contained marijuana, was stored in the area. Law enforcement officers, acting on an informant's tip, obtained consent to enter the enclosed area from one of the persons having access. The officers discovered marijuana in the truck. The court held that the defendant had no reasonable expectation of privacy in the storage area and upheld the search. The court said, "One who knows that others have of right general and untrammeled access to an area, a right as extensive as his own, can scarcely have much expectation of secrecy in it or confidence about whom they may let inspect it." 519 F.2d at 1080.

The Oregon Court of Appeals relied upon a defendant's reasonable expectation of privacy to invalidate the search of a bedroom in a private residence that the defendant occupied under a rental agreement. A Mr. Larson and his two daughters leased and occupied the residence along with the defendant. The defendant was the only occupant of a private room under an agreement with Larson. One of Larson's daughters gave consent to search defendant's room where incriminating evidence was found. The court held that Larson's daughter could not consent to a search of the defendant's room. The defendant had a reasonable expectation of privacy in the room because he rented the room, was the sole occupant of the room, and had never given anyone permission to enter it. State v. Fitzgerald, 19 Or.App. 860, 530 P.2d 553 (Court of Appeals of Oregon, 1974).

Officers must determine whether a person has exhibited a reasonable expectation of privacy before they may search the person's premises pursuant to consent given by a third person. Officers should find out whether the consenting person had common authority over the premises or the object to be searched. Also, officers should look for indicators that the occupant or owner intended to keep the premises or object private. The indicators might be written or verbal agreements, locks, or partitions. If an officer cannot give good reasons for believing that a consent to search given by a third party does not violate another person's reasonable expectation of privacy, the search is likely to be declared invalid.

SUMMARY

Consent to search may often be obtained by law enforcement officers with little effort. Courts therefore tend to look very closely at the totality of the circumstances surrounding the giving of consent. The courts exercise a strong presumption against consents to search and they place a heavy burden on prosecutors to prove that a consent to search was given voluntarily. Evidence seized as a result of a consent to search that was not voluntary will be inadmissible in court. The following factors are considered in determining voluntariness of consent:

1. Force or threat of force by officers;

2. Indications of consenting person's submission to authority;

3. Indications that a person merely failed to object to a search rather than actively consented;

4. Misrepresentation or deception of officers;

5. Consenting person was under arrest or otherwise in custody;

6. Consenting person's awareness of the right to refuse consent to search; and

7. Clearness and explicitness of the expression of consent.

The scope of a consent search may be limited in area, in time, and by the object for which the search is allowed. These limitations are usually determined by the intent of the consenting person as indicated by that person's words or actions. Officers should carefully determine the extent of their authority to search before beginning. Moreover, consent to search may be revoked by the person giving it at any time.

The constitutional right to refuse to consent to a search is a personal right of the individual against whom the search is directed. A person other than the person against whose interests the search is being conducted cannot effectively consent to a search of property unless (1) the person has been specifically authorized to do so, or (2) the person possesses common authority over or has other sufficient relationship to the premises or effects sought to be inspected. If a person establishes a reasonable expectation of privacy in premises or other property, another person may not consent to a search of the premises or property.

REVIEW AND DISCUSSION QUESTIONS

1. If a person is deprived of freedom of action in a significant way by law enforcement officers, should the person be given warnings of the right to refuse consent before being asked for consent to search?

2. If a law enforcement officer asks a person for consent to search his or her home for stolen jewelry when the officer's real purpose is to look for marked money, is the consent voluntary?

3. Assume that law enforcement officers have obtained a valid consent to search an arrested defendant's automobile for drugs and an initial search proves fruitless. Can the officers search the automobile again two hours later without obtaining a new consent to search? What about two days later? What about two weeks later? What changes in the defendant's status might render the initial consent no longer valid?

4. If a person becomes nervous and revokes or limits the scope of a consent to search, once given, can this reaction be used by the officers as an indication of probable cause to obtain a search warrant?

5. Are third-party consents to search the defendant's premises valid in the following circumstances?

a. A husband, out of anger at his wife, the defendant, invites the police into the house and points out evidence incriminating the wife.

b. The defendant's girlfriend, who lives with him part time, consents to a search of his apartment.

c. A wife disobeys the instructions of her husband, the defendant, not to allow a search of their home. Does it matter if the police know of the instructions or not?

6. Is it proper for a law enforcement officer to deliberately avoid attempting to obtain consent to search from the defendant and instead attempt to obtain consent from someone with equal authority over the defendant's premises? Does it matter whether the law enforcement officer had an opportunity to attempt to obtain consent from the defendant and deliberately failed to take it? What if the defendant was deliberately avoiding the police?

7. Is a consent to search voluntary if it is obtained after a law enforcement officer tells a person that a search warrant will be obtained if consent is refused? What if the officer only says that an attempt will be made to obtain a search warrant? What if the officer explains that it might not be possible to obtain a search warrant?

8. Should a person be able to limit the number of officers conducting a consent search? Should a person be able to choose which officer or officers will conduct the consent search? Should a person be allowed to follow around the officer conducting the search?

9. Can the following persons give a valid consent to search?

a. A highly intoxicated person.

b. A five-year old; a seven-year old; a ten-year old.

c. A mentally retarded or senile person.

d. An emotionally upset person.

e. An uneducated person.

10. Can the driver of a motor vehicle consent to a search of the vehicle even though a passenger objects? Can the owner of a store consent to a search of a store even though an employee objects? Can a parent consent to a search of the home even though a child objects?

9

Plain View

Observation by law enforcement officers of items of evidence lying in plain view has for some time been one of the most important methods of gathering evidence of crime. Mere observation is seldcm thought of as a means of gathering evidence, perhaps because, on the surface, this method is so simple and seemingly self-evident. Also, observations of evidence in plain view usually occur as a byproduct of other activities that a law enforcement officer is performing, and the observations are therefore often unintentional. Nevertheless, the plain view doctrine enables alert and observant law enforcement officers to obtain admissible evidence against offenders of the law who are careless or unwary enough to leave such evidence in open view. Furthermore, the observation and seizure of such evidence may, in most cases, be made without probable cause or the necessity of going through complex warrant procedures. In this sense, the plain view doctrine can be considered another exception to the search warrant requirement.

Of course, the apparent simplicity of the plain view doctrine does not convert it into a license to conduct general exploratory searches anywhere, any time, and in any manner. The doctrine has carefully prescribed limitations that have been set out in court decisions over the years. This chapter will define the plain view doctrine and illustrate its various aspects through the use of recent court decisions from various jurisdictions. Whenever possible, suggested procedures for law enforcement officers will be set out.

DEFINITION

The plain view doctrine was defined simply and concisely in the U.S. Supreme Court decision in *Harris v. United States:*

> It has long been settled that objects falling in the plain view of an officer who has a right to be in a position to have that view may be introduced in evidence. . . .
> 390 U.S. 234, 236, 88 S.Ct. 992, 993, 19 L.Ed.2d 1067, 1069 (1968).

It is worthwhile to note at the outset that the observation by a law enforcement officer of evidence in plain view is *not* considered to be a *search*. A search can be defined as a prying quest for something concealed from observation. If an item is lying in the open, unconcealed, it follows that an officer's merely looking at the item does not constitute a search. Furthermore, because such an observation does not constitute a search, it is not governed by the Fourth Amendment, and the officer, in most cases, need not obtain a warrant to seize the evidence. As one court said:

> Where no search is required, the constitutional guaranty is not applicable. The guaranty applies only in those instances where the seizure is assisted by a necessary search. It does not prohibit a seizure without a warrant where there is no need of a search, and where the contraband subject matter is freely disclosed and open to the eye and hand. . . . State v. Mosher, 270 A.2d 451, 453 (Supreme Judicial Court of Maine, 1970).

ELEMENTS OF THE PLAIN VIEW DOCTRINE

For purposes of discussion, the plain view doctrine can be divided into six separate elements or requirements, all of which must be satisfied by law enforcement officers before a seizure of an item of evidence under the doctrine can be legally justified. These requirements are:

1. The officer, as a result of a prior valid intrusion into a constitutionally protected area, must be in a position in which he or she has a legal right to be;

2. The officer must not unreasonably intrude on any person's reasonable expectation of privacy;

3. The officer must actually observe the item of evidence;

4. The item of evidence must be lying in the open;

5. It must be immediately apparent to the officer that the item observed is evidence "subject to seizure";

6. The discovery of the item of evidence by the officer must be inadvertent.

The remainder of this chapter will be devoted to an elaboration on and explanation of these requirements.

1. The officer, as the result of a prior valid intrusion into a constitutionally protected area, must be in a position in which he or she has a legal right to be.

The first requirement is the most important element of the plain view doctrine and also the one that causes the most problems. It would be impossible to list all the situations in which a law enforcement officer would be in a position in which he or she has a legal right to be as the result of a prior valid intrusion into a constitutionally protected area. The U.S. Supreme Court, however, listed some of these situations in its 1971 decision in *Coolidge v. New Hampshire:*

> What the "plain view" cases have in common is that the police officer in each of them had a prior justification for an intrusion in the course of which he came inadvertently across a piece of evidence incriminating the accused. The doctrine serves to supplement the prior justification—whether it be a warrant for another object, hot pursuit, search incident to lawful arrest, or some other legitimate reason for being present unconnected with a search directed against the accused—and permits the warrantless seizure. . . . 403 U.S. at 466, 91 S.Ct. at 2038, 29 L.Ed. 2d at 583.

The following is a discussion of cases illustrating the first element of the plain view doctrine.

Effecting an Arrest or Search Incident to Arrest   A law enforcement officer may lawfully seize an object that comes into view during a lawfully executed arrest or a search incident to arrest. There is a possibility of confusion here between the plain view doctrine and the law of search incident to arrest. The law of search incident to arrest was discussed in detail in Chapter 7. There it was stated that under the rule of Chimel v. California, 395 U.S. 752, 89 S.Ct. 2034, 23 L.Ed.2d 685 (U.S. Supreme Court, 1969), a law enforcement officer may search an arrested person only for weapons or to prevent the destruction or concealment of evidence. The extent of such a search is limited to the arrestee's person and the area within the arrestee's immediate control, "construing that phrase to mean the area from within which he might gain possession of a weapon or destructible evidence." 395 U.S. at 763, 89 S.Ct. at 2040, 23 L.Ed.2d at 694.

The plain view doctrine does *not* extend the permissible area of search incident to arrest. The Court in the *Chimel* case specifically said:

> There is no comparable justification, however, for routinely searching any room other than that in which an arrest occurs—or for that matter, for searching through all the desk drawers or other closed or concealed areas in that room itself. Such searches, in the absence of well-recognized exceptions, may be made only under the authority of a search warrant. 395 U.S. at 763, 89 S.Ct. at 2040, 23 L.Ed.2d at 694.

Nevertheless, when the arresting officer inadvertently observes a piece of evidence, unconcealed, but outside the area under the immediate control of the arrestee, the officer may seize it, so long as the plain view observation was obtained in the course of a lawful arrest or an appropriately limited search incident to arrest.

Conducting a "Stop and Frisk"   A seizable item observed by an officer during the course of a lawful "stop and frisk" may also be seized without a warrant. (See Chapter 12 for a discussion of "Stop and Frisk.") This authority to seize is not limited to items observed on the person of the detained suspect, but extends to the passenger compartment of an automobile. In the words of the U.S. Supreme Court, "[i]f, while conducting a legitimate *Terry* search of the interior of the automobile, the officer should . . . discover contraband other than weapons, he clearly cannot be required to ignore the contraband, and the Fourth Amendment does not require its suppression in such circumstances." Michigan v. Long, ——— U.S. ———, ———, 103 S.Ct. 3469, 3481, 77 L.Ed.2d 1201, 1220 (1983).

Executing a Search Warrant In the case of Cady v. Dombrowski, 413 U.S. 433, 93 S.Ct. 2523, 37 L.Ed.2d 706 (1973), the U.S. Supreme Court held that an officer executing a valid search warrant could legally seize items of evidence lying in plain view even though they were not particularly described in the warrant. For purposes of this discussion, law enforcement officers executing a valid search warrant are in a position in which they have a legal right to be.

The *Cady v. Dombrowski* case is discussed in detail in Chapter 2. A part of that discussion, however, should be reemphasized here. Although officers executing a search warrant are authorized to seize items not named in the search warrant lying in plain view, their authority is limited. A seizure of unnamed items will probably be held illegal if:

1. The seizure was the product of an "exploratory search"; or

2. The items seized had no direct relation to the primary purpose of the search; or

3. The officer did not have probable cause to believe that the items fell within one of the categories of items subject to seizure.

If any of these conditions exist, the officer should obtain another search warrant for items unnamed in the original warrant.

If an officer does not have a warrant to search premises, he may not enter the premises to secure them while a search warrant is being obtained, unless there are exigent circumstances. It follows that any evidence observed open to view after such an illegal entry will not be admissible under the plain view doctrine, because the officer was not in a position in which he or she had a legal right to be. United States v. Griffin, 502 F.2d 959 (6th Circuit Court of Appeals, 1974).

Controlled Deliveries The U.S. government has the right to inspect all incoming goods from foreign countries at the port of entry. Also, common carriers have a common law right to inspect packages they accept for shipment, based on their duty to refrain from carrying contraband. Although the sheer volume of goods in transit prevents systematic inspection of all or even a large percentage of these goods, common carriers and customs officials do inevitably discover contraband in transit in a variety of circumstances. When such a discovery is made, it is routine procedure for them to notify the appropriate authorities, so that the authorities may identify and prosecute the person or persons responsible for the movement of the contraband. The arrival of law enforcement authorities on the scene to confirm the presence of contraband and to determine what to do with it does not convert the otherwise legal search by the common carrier or customs official into a government search subject to the Fourth Amendment. United States v. Edwards, 602 F.2d 458 (1st Circuit Court of Appeals, 1979).

Law enforcement authorities, rather than simply seizing the contraband and destroying it, will often make a so-called controlled delivery of the container, monitoring the container on its journey to the intended destination. The person dealing in the contraband can then be identified upon taking possession of and asserting control over the container. The typical pattern of a controlled delivery has been described as follows:

> They most ordinarily occur when a carrier, usually an airline, unexpectedly discovers what seems to be contraband while inspecting luggage to learn the identity of its owner, or when the contraband falls out of a broken or damaged piece of luggage, or when the carrier exercises its inspection privilege because some suspicious circumstance has caused it concern that it may unwittingly be transporting contraband. Frequently, after such a discovery, law enforcement agents restore the contraband to its container, then close or reseal the container, and authorize the carrier to deliver the container to its owner. When the owner appears to take delivery he is arrested and the container with the contraband is seized and then searched a second time for the contraband known to be there. United States v. Bulgier, 618 F.2d 472, 476 (7th Circuit Court of Appeals, 1980).

The U.S. Supreme Court, relying on the plain view doctrine, held that no protected privacy interest remains in contraband in a container once government officers lawfully have opened that container and identified its contents as illegal. Furthermore, the simple act of resealing the container to enable the police to make a controlled delivery does not operate to revive or restore the lawfully invaded privacy rights. The Court said:

> The plain view doctrine is grounded on the proposition that once police are lawfully in a position to observe an item first-hand, its owner's privacy interest in that item is lost; the owner may retain the incidents of title and possession but not privacy . . . [O]nce a container has been found to a certainty to contain illicit drugs, the contraband becomes like objects physically within the plain view of the police, and the claim to privacy is lost. Consequently, the subsequent reopening of the container is not a "search" within the intendment of the Fourth Amendment. Illinois v. Andreas, — U.S. —, —, 103 S.Ct. 3319, 3324, 77 L.Ed.2d 1003, 1010 (1983).

In the *Andreas* case, the Court acknowledged that there are often unavoidable interruptions of control or surveillance of a container and that at some point after such an interruption, courts should recognize that the container may have been put to other uses, thereby reinstating the individual's legitimate expectation of privacy in the container. The Court decided that a workable, objective standard that limits the risk of intrusion on legitimate privacy interests when there is such an interruption is whether there is a substantial likelihood that the contents of the container have been changed during the gap in surveillance. If there is no such likelihood, the officer may legally open the container without a warrant.

Hot Pursuit Law enforcement officers who are lawfully on premises in hot pursuit of a dangerous person may seize items of evidence that fall within their plain view. In the 1967 U.S. Supreme Court case of *Warden v. Hayden,* the police were informed that an armed robbery had taken place and that a suspect, wearing a light cap and dark jacket had entered a certain house less than five minutes before they reached it. Several officers entered the house and began to search for the described suspect and for weapons that he had used in the robbery and might use against them. One officer, while searching the cellar, found in a washing machine clothing of the type that the fleeing man was said to have worn. The Court held that the seizure of the clothing was lawful:

> [T]he seizures occurred prior to or immediately contemporaneous with Hayden's arrest, as part of an effort to find a suspected felon, armed, within the house into which he had run only minutes before the police arrived. The permissible scope of search must, therefore, at the least, be as broad as may reasonably be necessary to prevent the dangers that the suspect at large in the house may resist or escape. 387 U.S. at 299, 87 S.Ct. at 1646, 18 L.Ed.2d at 787.

If, however, the felon had already been taken into custody when the officer looked into the washing machine, the seizure of the clothing would have been unlawful. There no longer would have been any danger of the fleeing felon using a weapon against the officers and, therefore, no reason to look for weapons in the washing machine.

To summarize, officers who enter a constitutionally protected area in hot pursuit of a fleeing felon are in a position in which they have a legal right to be and may seize items of evidence observed lying in plain view during the course of their pursuit and their protecting themselves from harm.

It should be noted that hot pursuit does not necessarily involve a violent crime or a dangerous person. The U.S. Supreme Court held that there was a hot pursuit when officers chased the defendant, who they had probable cause to believe had just purchased illegal drugs, from her doorway into her house. United States v. Santana, 427 U.S. 38, 96 S.Ct. 2406, 49 L.Ed.2d 300 (U.S. Supreme Court, 1976).

Responding to an Emergency Related to the hot pursuit situation is the situation in which an officer responds to an emergency and observes items of evidence in plain view. An example is a case in which two police officers responded to a report by citizens that a woman was screaming for help in a certain house. The officers went to the house. A man answered the door, said "Wait a minute," and then closed the door again. One officer heard shuffling inside the apartment and the other officer observed a man attempting to escape out a back window. After identifying himself and demanding admittance (which was not granted), the officer at the entrance to the house kicked in the door. While investigating the situation inside, he observed marijuana in plain view on a table.

The court found that the combination of circumstances presented to the officer justified his forced entry:

> The probability that a woman within the apartment was the unwilling victim of some criminal act was increased rather than lessened by the conduct of those within the apartment after the police presented themselves at the door; that conduct can only have had the effect of heightening the sense of emergency.

> * * *

> Having entered reasonably in an emergency "they did not have to blind themselves to what was in plain sight simply because it was disconnected with the purpose for which they entered." People v. Clark, 262 Cal.App.2d 471, 476–77, 68 Cal.Rptr. 713, 717 (California Court of Appeal, 1968).

An emergency will often justify a "protective search" of premises by law enforcement officers during which evidence may be observed in plain view. In People v. Sturgis, 76 Misc.2d 1053, 352 N.Y.S.2d 942 (Supreme Court of New York, 1973), law enforcement officers engaged in a gun battle with several suspects who were inside a home. The officers then entered the home and arrested several persons. To protect themselves, officers looked throughout the home for other persons. Narcotics were discovered lying open to view and were seized. The court held that the protective search by the officers was proper because of exigent circumstances, and that the seizure of the narcotics was lawful under the plain view doctrine.

The Supreme Court of California summarized the reasoning of many courts in cases involving "protective searches."

> During a lawful search of premises for persons believed to be in hiding, police officers may seize contraband evidence "in plain sight." . . . Under such circumstances there is, in fact, no search for evidence. People v. Block, 6 Cal.3d 239, 243, 103 Cal.Rptr. 281, 283, 499 P.2d 961, 963 (1971).

There is a temptation for law enforcement officers to attempt to justify otherwise illegal searches by resorting to this combination of the plain view doctrine and response to an emergency. Courts will look carefully at these types of cases and will rule the search illegal if a genuine emergency does not exist or if a search goes beyond what is necessary to respond to the emergency. On this issue the U.S. Supreme Court stated that "a warrantless search must be 'strictly circumscribed by the exigencies which justify its initiation,' . . . ." Mincey v. Arizona, 437 U.S. 385, 393, 98 S.Ct. 2408, 2414, 57 L.Ed.2d 290, 300 (1978). Again, when there is a question about the legality of a search or seizure, the officer should apply for a warrant.

The important thing to remember in all these cases, however, is that the officer must have a legal justification for the intrusion into a constitutionally protected area. If such a justification exists, and if the officer is in a position in which he or she has a right to be, any items observed lying open to view may be seized without violating the Fourth Amendment.

2. The officer must not unreasonably intrude on any person's reasonable expectation of privacy.

There are limits to the general rule that any observation made by a law enforcement officer after making a valid intrusion into a constitutionally protected area will not be a violation of the Fourth Amendment. In a California case, a law enforcement officer observed the defendant and another man go into the men's room of a city park and not come out for about five minutes. The officer then entered the plumbing access area of the rest room and observed the men performing illegal sexual acts. The officer had observed no other suspicious acts by the defendant before the defendant entered the men's room.

The court held that this was not a plain view observation by the officer but an illegal search. The language of the court in this case is worthy of quotation:

> The People here urge us to hold that clandestine observation of doorless stalls in public rest rooms is not a "search" and hence is not subject to the Fourth Amendment's prohibition of unreasonable searches. This would permit the police to make it a routine practice to observe from hidden vantage points the rest room conduct of the public whenever such activities do not occur within fully enclosed toilet stalls and would permit spying on the "innocent and guilty alike." Most persons using public rest rooms have no reason to suspect that a hidden agent of the state will observe them. The expectation of privacy a person has when he enters a rest room is reasonable and is not diminished or destroyed because the toilet stall being used lacks a door.
>
> Reference to expectations of privacy as a Fourth Amendment touchstone received the endorsement of the United States Supreme Court in Katz v. United States (1968) 389 U.S. 347, 88 S.Ct. 507, 19 L.Ed.2d 576. Viewed in the light of Katz, the standard for determining what is an illegal search is whether defendant's "reasonable expectation of privacy was violated by unreasonable governmental intrusion." People v. Triggs, 8 Cal.3d 884, 891, 106 Cal.Rptr. 408, 412–13, 506 P.2d 232, 236–37 (Supreme Court of California, 1973).

Therefore, what might seem on the surface to be a mere plain view observation becomes a *search* when it unreasonably intrudes upon a person's reasonable expectation of privacy. As a search, the officer's observations must be based on probable cause, at the minimum, in order to be reasonable. In this case, the officer's only suspicion was the defendant's prolonged stay in the rest room, which could have been consistent with innocent activity. This suspicion was not sufficient to provide probable cause. The officer's clandestine observations were, therefore, prompted only by a general curiosity to determine what, if anything, was going on within the rest room. As such, the observations were an illegal exploratory search under the Fourth Amendment.

This case and others following the *Katz* decision present problems for law enforcement officers with regard to the plain view doctrine. Officers must not only determine whether their intrusion into a constitutionally protected area is lawful, but they must also make sure that they are not intruding upon someone's reasonable expectation of privacy. The latter determination can be a difficult one and there are few guidelines to aid officers beyond their own common sense.

3. The officer must observe the item of evidence.

The law enforcement officer must actually *see* the item of evidence lying in the open in order to lawfully seize it under the plain view doctrine. At first this seems to be merely stating the obvious. A California case, however, held that officers who merely *smelled* fresh marijuana but did *not actually see* it lying in the open could not legally search for the marijuana and seize it without a warrant. In that case, officers had legally entered an apartment to arrest some suspects. They had therefore made a valid intrusion into a constitutionally protected area. They did not find any of the suspects in the apartment, but distinctly smelled fresh marijuana. They traced the smell to a closed bag inside a carton in the closet. The officers opened the bag, seized the marijuana, and arrested the defendant several hours later when he arrived back at the apartment.

The court held the seizure of the marijuana illegal. The court said that if the evidence had been in plain *sight,* the officers could have seized it, because the officers were rightfully on the premises looking for persons believed to be in hiding. In this case, however, the marijuana was *not* in plain sight. It was in cellophane bags inside a closed brown paper bag that was in an open box in an open closet. The officers, in smelling the marijuana and tracing it to the bag, had *probable cause* to believe that marijuana was in the bag. They could, therefore, have obtained a *search warrant* for the marijuana based on probable cause. They could *not,* however, legally go into the bag and seize the marijuana because the marijuana itself was not in plain view. In this case, there were no exigent circumstances to justify an immediate seizure of the marijuana.

The language of the Supreme Court of California is valuable here to try to clear up a point on probable cause that confuses many law enforcement officers:

> However strongly convinced officers may be that a search will reveal contraband, their belief, whether based on the sense of smell or other sources, does not justify a search without a warrant. The point of the Fourth Amendment, which often is not grasped by zealous officers, is not that it denies law enforcement the support of the usual inferences which reasonable men draw from evidence. Its protection consists in requiring that those inferences be drawn by a neutral and detached magistrate instead of being judged by the officer engaged in the often competitive enterprise of ferreting out crime. Any assumption that evidence sufficient to support a magistrate's disinterested determination to issue a search warrant will justify the officers in making a search without a warrant would reduce the Amendment to a nullity and leave the people's homes secure only in the discretion of police officers. People v. Marshall, 69 Cal.2d 51, 57, 69 Cal.Rptr. 585, 588–89, 442 P.2d 665, 668–69 (Supreme Court of California, 1968).

In a word, then, if an officer has made a valid intrusion into a constitutionally protected area and has probable cause to believe that an item of evidence is in a certain place, but does not *see* the item lying in plain view, the officer must obtain a search warrant before the item can be legally seized unless there are truly exigent circumstances.

4. The item of evidence must be lying in the open.

The requirement of the plain view doctrine that the evidence must be lying in the open has been expressed in several ways. Among the terms used by different courts are "in plain view," "in plain sight," "in open view," "open to view," and "in the open." All these mean substantially the same thing, but do not give much help to law enforcement officers in determining what items they may and may not seize. The best way to determine the meaning of these terms is to examine the cases interpreting them.

First of all, it is well settled that law enforcement officers may use mechanical or electrical aids to assist them in observing items of evidence, as long as they are in a position in which they have a legal right to be and are not intruding upon someone's reasonable expectation of privacy.   In one case, a law enforcement officer was told when he arrived at a drive-in restaurant that a car had been parked in the parking lot for an hour with its lights on and with a person lying in the back seat.   The officer went over to the car to see if anything was wrong.   He shined a flashlight into the car and observed defendant lying in the back with a sawed-off shotgun resting on the floorboard between his feet.   He arrested the defendant and seized the shotgun.

The court held that the observation of the shotgun by the officer was not a search.   The officer was in a position in which he had a legal right to be, and his use of the flashlight did not, in itself, make his observations unlawful:

> When the circumstances of a particular case are such that the police officer's observation would not have constituted a search had it occurred in daylight, then the fact that the officer used a flashlight to pierce the nighttime darkness does not transform his observation into a search.   Regardless of the time of day or night, the plain view rule must be upheld where the viewer is rightfully positioned, seeing through eyes that are neither accusatory nor criminally investigatory.   The plain view rule does not go into hibernation at sunset.   Marshall v. United States, 422 F.2d 185, 189 (5th Circuit Court of Appeals, 1970).

In another case, an officer stationed himself in a field about fifty yards from the defendant's house and with the aid of binoculars watched the activities of the defendant, a known liquor violator.   The officer observed the defendant placing two large cardboard boxes (each of which contained six gallons of untaxed whiskey) into a 1961 Buick.   The liquor was later found in the car while it was being operated on a public street by another person.   The court held that the officer's use of binoculars to observe defendant's activities did not constitute an illegal search.   United States v. Grimes, 426 F.2d 706 (5th Circuit Court of Appeals, 1970).

Another question that arises is how far an officer may go in examining an item more closely before the examination constitutes a search rather than a mere plain view observation.   In a case dealing with this question, police were lawfully in the defendant's apartment for the purpose of arresting him.   While they were looking for him, one officer observed a pair of shoes believed to have been worn by the defendant at the time of the murder.   The officer picked up the shoes and examined the heels.   After obtaining a search warrant, he returned and seized the shoes.   The shoes were introduced in evidence against the defendant.

The court held that the examination of the heels of the shoes was not an illegal search:

> Detective Shelby was lawfully in defendant's apartment.   He reasonably believed defendant to be hiding in the apartment and had every right, supported by probable cause, to search for the suspected killer.   Shelby's discovery of the shoes was not the result of a general search for evidence.   Rather, the pair of shoes was seen during the course of the search for Eddington.   In our view, Shelby's subsequent action in lifting the shoes and examining their heels involved no more than "legitimate and restrained investigative conduct undertaken on the basis of ample factual justification".   .   .   .   People v. Eddington, 387 Mich. 551, 564–65, 198 N.W.2d 297, 302 (Supreme Court of Michigan, 1972).

In another case involving closer examination of items, officers had valid warrants to arrest the defendant and to search his store for intoxicating liquors and apparatus used for manufacturing intoxicating liquors. Upon arrival at the store, the officers immediately arrested the defendant and seized a small quantity of beer. One officer then went to the upstairs residential area to search, and noticed two rifles leaning against a wall in a closet. The officer removed the rifles, took them downstairs to copy down their serial numbers, and returned them to the closet. The officers later learned that the rifles had been stolen, and they went back to the store and seized them under a second warrant.

The court held that the officer's removing the rifles from the closet and copying down their serial numbers was an illegal search. Although the search warrant for liquor and apparatus gave the officers a valid prior justification for their intrusion, the court held that the removal and examination of the rifles could be justified only if it was immediately apparent that the rifles were evidence of crime:

> Here, Officer Brodt inadvertently discovered the rifles in the upstairs clothes closet while searching for alcoholic beverages but it was not "immediately apparent" that the rifles were "evidence incriminating the accused." The rifles were not contraband; there was no nexus between the rifles and the crimes of selling or possessing intoxicating liquor without a license; nor did the officers at that time have any knowledge that the rifles were evidence of any other crimes. United States v. Gray, 484 F.2d 352, 355 (Sixth Circuit Court of Appeals, 1973).

It was only *after* the officer had copied down the serial numbers of the rifles and had checked them with the National Crime Information Center that he learned that they were stolen and therefore incriminating. (The requirement that it be immediately apparent to the law enforcement officer that the item to be seized is incriminating evidence is discussed under the fifth element of the plain view doctrine.)

For reasons similar to those in the previous case, an officer is not allowed to open a closed container lying in plain view in order to determine if there is incriminating evidence inside it, unless there is a genuine emergency. An example is a case in which officers were conducting a narcotics raid on an apartment, and they observed the defendant's purse lying on a table. One of the officers opened the purse and found a small bag of marijuana. When the defendant admitted that the purse was hers, she was arrested for possession of marijuana.

The court held that the seizure of the marijuana was illegal. Even though the purse was in plain view, the marijuana itself was not. The officer had to break into the purse to find the marijuana. This was an illegal search because the officer had no warrant, nor could he justify the search under any of the exceptions to the warrant requirement. State v. Keller, 255 La. 367, 231 So.2d 354 (Supreme Court of Louisiana, 1970).

Nevertheless, the U.S. Supreme Court allowed an examination of a partially closed container by government agents after the container had been opened and its contents examined by a private party. In United States v. Jacobsen, ___ U.S. ___, 104 S.Ct. 1652, 80 L.Ed.2d 85 (1984), employees of a freight carrier examined a damaged cardboard box wrapped in brown paper and found a white powdery substance in the innermost of four plastic bags that had been concealed in a tube inside the package. The employees notified the Drug Enforcement Administration (DEA), replaced the plastic bags in the tube, and placed the tube back in the box. A DEA agent arrived and removed the tube from the box and the plastic bags from the tube. When he saw the white powder, he opened the bags and removed a small amount of the white powder. He then subjected it to a field chemical test. The test indicated that the powder was cocaine.

The U.S. Supreme Court found that the initial invasion of the package by the freight carrier employees did not violate the Fourth Amendment because it was a private rather than a governmental action. The Court then analyzed the additional invasions of privacy by the DEA agent in terms of the degree to which they exceeded the scope of the private search. The Court found that even if the white powder was not itself in "plain view" because it was enclosed in so many containers and covered with papers, the DEA agent could be virtually certain that nothing else of significance was in the package and that a manual inspection of the tube and its contents would not tell him anything more than he already had been told by the freight carrier employees. The agent's reexamination of the contents of the package merely avoided the risk of a flaw in the employees' recollection, rather than further infringing on someone's privacy. The Court said:

> Respondents could have no privacy interest in the contents of the package, since it remained unsealed and since the Federal Express employees had just examined the package and had, of their own accord, invited the federal agent to their offices for the express purpose of viewing its contents. The agent's viewing of what a private party had freely made available for his inspection did not violate the Fourth Amendment. . . . Similarly, the removal of the plastic bags from the tube and the agent's visual inspection of their contents enabled the agent to learn nothing that had not previously been learned during the private search. It infringed no legitimate expectation of privacy and hence was not a "search" within the meaning of the Fourth Amendment. ___ U.S. at ___, 104 S.Ct. at 1659–60, 80 L.Ed.2d at 98.

The Court further held that the agent's assertion of dominion and control over the package and its contents was a "seizure," but that the seizure was reasonable, since it was apparent that the tube and plastic bags contained contraband and little else. The Court said that "it is well-settled law that it is constitutionally reasonable for law enforcement officials to seize 'effects' that cannot support a justifiable expectation of privacy without a warrant, based on probable cause to believe they contain contraband." ___ U.S. at ___, 104 S.Ct. at 1661, 80 L.Ed.2d at 99.

The Court then addressed the question of whether the additional intrusion occasioned by the field test, which had not been conducted by the freight carrier employees and therefore exceeded the scope of the private search, was an unlawful "search" or "seizure" within the meaning of the Fourth Amendment. The Court held that a chemical test that merely discloses whether or not a particular substance is cocaine, and no other arguably "private" fact, compromises no legitimate privacy interest. Furthermore, even though the test destroyed a quantity of the powder and thereby permanently deprived its owner of a protected possessory interest, the infringement was constitutionally reasonable. The Court reasoned that the law enforcement interests justifying the procedure were substantial and, because only a trace amount of material was involved, the "seizure" could have, at most, only a minimal effect on any protected property interest.

It appears, then, that a law enforcement officer may examine, without a warrant, a container whose contents are not open to view, if any privacy interest in the contents of the container has already been compromised by a private party and information about the contents has been made available to the officer by the private party.   In addition, it is constitutionally permissible for the officer to seize the contents of the container, if the officer has probable cause to believe the contents are contraband, and to conduct a chemical field test so long as only a trace amount of the substance is destroyed by the test.

As these cases indicate, it may not always be clear to officers whether they are allowed to examine an item more closely without it being considered a search. When in doubt, officers should obtain a search warrant, unless the situation presents an immediate danger of loss or destruction of evidence.

5. It must be immediately apparent to the officer that the item observed is evidence "subject to seizure."

The requirement that it be immediately apparent to the officer that the item observed is evidence "subject to seizure" simply means that the officer must have probable cause to believe that the item comes within one of the categories of property that are allowed to be seized under state law.   Texas v. Brown, 460 U.S. 730, 103 S.Ct. 1535, 75 L.Ed.2d 502 (U.S. Supreme Court, 1983).   These categories of property have been listed and discussed in Chapter 5.   They are:

1. Property stolen or embezzled; or

2. Property designed or intended for use or which is or has been used as a means of committing a criminal offense (instrumentalities); or

3. Property, the possession of which is unlawful (contraband); or

4. Property consisting of nontestimonial evidence that will aid in a particular apprehension or conviction ("mere evidence").

In a case illustrating this requirement of the plain view doctrine, a Massachusetts police officer arrested the defendant and two companions for trespassing.   They had parked their car on private property.   While waiting for assistance, the officer observed articles of clothing wrapped in cellophane lying inside the car.   Later, after the car had been removed to the police station, the officer learned through police channels that similar clothing had been recently stolen in Maine.   He obtained a search warrant and seized the clothing.

The court found the search warrant defective but upheld the seizure because the items of clothing were in the officer's plain view.   The court said:

> Even where .   .   . no search is necessary, the accompanying seizure must be accompanied by probable cause or reasonable grounds to believe that the property falls within a category which warrants the seizure.   State v. Mosher, 270 A.2d 451, 453 (Supreme Judicial Court of Maine, 1970).

In this case, the officer had reasonable grounds to believe that the articles of clothing were *stolen* (category 1 above), based on the report that similar articles had been stolen in Maine.

If, however, the Massachusetts officer in the *Mosher* case had seized the articles of clothing when he first observed them, the seizure would have been illegal. At that time, he had no reason to believe they were stolen or that they came under any other category of seizable property. It was only after he received the report that similar clothing had been stolen in Maine that he had probable cause to believe the property was seizable.

Officers may use their background and experience to evaluate the facts and circumstances in arriving at the probable cause determination. In Texas v. Brown, 460 U.S. 730, 103 S.Ct. 1535, 75 L.Ed.2d 502 (1983), an officer stopped the defendant's automobile at night at a routine driver's license checkpoint, asked him for his license, and shined his flashlight into the car. The officer observed an opaque, green party balloon, knotted about one-half inch from the tip and, after shifting his position, also observed several small plastic vials, quantities of loose white powder, and an open bag of party balloons in the open glove compartment. The U.S. Supreme Court held that the officer had probable cause to believe that the balloon contained an illicit substance:

> [The officer] testified that he was aware, both from his participation in previous narcotics arrests and from discussions with other officers, that balloons tied in the manner of the one possessed by [the defendant] were frequently used to carry narcotics. This testimony was corroborated by that of a police department chemist who noted that it was "common" for balloons to be used in packaging narcotics. In addition, [the officer] was able to observe the contents of the glove compartment of [the defendant's] car, which revealed further suggestions that [the defendant] was engaged in activities that might involve possession of illicit substances. The fact that [the officer] could not see through the opaque fabric of the balloon is all but irrelevant: the distinctive character of the balloon itself spoke volumes as to its contents—particularly to the trained eye of the officer. 460 U.S. at 742–43, 103 S.Ct. at 1543, 75 L.Ed.2d at 514.

In Shipman v. State, 291 Ala. 484, 282 So.2d 700 (Alabama Supreme Court, 1973), however, the object containing drugs was found to be insufficiently distinctive in character to justify its seizure. In that case, law enforcement officers detained several persons on a storeowner's complaint that they were acting in an unruly manner. As one of the persons (the defendant) was being confronted by an officer, the officer observed him transfer an object from one part of his person to the top of his boot. The object, though clearly not a weapon, was seized and was later determined to contain heroin. The court held that even though the object was in plain view its seizure was illegal because the officer did not have probable cause to believe it was contraband. The court said:

> The reason for this rule is apparent. If the rule were otherwise, an officer acting on mere groundless suspicion, could seize anything and everything belonging to an individual which happened to be in plain view on the prospect that on further investigation some of it might prove to have been stolen or to be contraband. It would open the door to unreasonable confiscation of a person's property while a minute examination of it is made in an effort to find something criminal. Such

practice would amount to the "general exploratory search from one object to another until something incriminating at last emerges" which was condemned in Coolidge v. New Hampshire . . . . Ex post facto justification of a seizure made on mere groundless suspicion, is totally contrary to the basic tenets of the Fourth Amendment.

* * *

For an item in plain view to be validly seized, the officer must possess some judgment at the time that the object to be seized is contraband and that judgment must be grounded upon probable cause.   291 Ala. at 488, 282 So.2d at 704.

6. The discovery of the item of evidence by the officer must be inadvertent.

The so-called "inadvertency" requirement of the plain view doctrine is best illustrated by the U.S. Supreme Court case of Coolidge v. New Hampshire, 403 U.S. 443, 91 S.Ct. 2022, 29 L.Ed.2d 564 (1971).   In that case, police went to the defendant's house to arrest him for murder.   They also had a warrant to search his Pontiac car for evidence of the murder.   They seized the car, which was parked and plainly visible in the driveway, and brought it back to the station where it was searched. Vacuum sweepings from the car were used as evidence at the defendant's trial, and he was convicted.

The search warrant was later found to be invalid and the prosecution attempted to justify the seizure of the automobile on the theory that, since the car was an "instrumentality of the crime," and was seized while lying in plain view, no warrant was needed.   The Court said that the plain view doctrine could not be used to justify the seizure in this case because the discovery of the evidence was not inadvertent:

> [T]he discovery of evidence in plain view must be inadvertent.   The rationale of the exception to the warrant requirement, as just stated, is that a plain-view seizure will not turn an initially valid (and therefore limited) search into a "general" one, while the inconvenience of procuring a warrant to cover an inadvertent discovery is great. *But where the discovery is anticipated, where the police know in advance the location of the evidence and intend to seize it, the situation is altogether different. The requirement of a warrant to seize imposes no inconvenience whatever, or at least none which is constitutionally cognizable in a legal system that regards warrantless searches as "per se unreasonable" in the absence of "exigent circumstances."* (emphasis supplied)   403 U.S. at 470–71, 91 S.Ct. at 2040, 29 L.Ed.2d at 585–86.

The significance of the inadvertency requirement for the law enforcement officer is that it reemphasizes the importance of obtaining a search warrant in situations in which the officer (1) expects to discover certain evidence, (2) knows its location in advance, and (3) intends to seize it.   Unless there are "exigent circumstances", a warrantless seizure in such circumstances will *not* be justified under the plain view doctrine.

The following is an example of a case in which the court found sufficient "exigent circumstances" to justify the use of the plain view doctrine to support the warrantless seizure of items whose location law enforcement officers already knew. Law enforcement agents on several occasions observed the defendant purchase laboratory equipment and chemicals used in the manufacture of amphetamine and carry them into his home. On one occasion, the agents entered the apartment with defendant's consent on the pretense of making an emergency phone call. They observed the laboratory equipment on a kitchen counter. The agents, stationed at a nearby apartment, also observed someone working in the laboratory, and they detected a smell of ether, which is employed in manufacturing amphetamine. Late one night, the agents observed the defendant dismantling the laboratory equipment. Believing that the defendant was attempting to flee, they called their superiors, who said they would attempt to obtain a search warrant. In the meantime, the agents at the scene went to "secure" the defendant's apartment while waiting for the delivery of the warrant. When they arrived at the apartment, they immediately arrested the defendant and seized the laboratory equipment, which was in plain view.

The defendant claimed that the seized equipment should not have been admitted into evidence because, although it was in plain view, the agents knew beforehand that the equipment was in the apartment. He cited the case of *Coolidge v. New Hampshire,* which held, as we have seen, that the "plain view" doctrine applies only when the discovery of the evidence is inadvertent, not where the discovery is anticipated, where the police know in advance the location of the evidence, and intend to seize it.

The court held that the warrantless seizure in this case was valid. The agents made efforts to obtain a search warrant—a warrantless seizure was not planned. When the agents saw the equipment being dismantled, however, they reasonably concluded that the defendant's flight was imminent and that incriminating evidence was about to be carried away. The situation having become acute, immediate action by the agents was required:

> *Coolidge* does not require suppression of evidence seized in plain view during an arrest where the circumstances have become exigent merely because prior knowledge of the evidence was acquired shortly before the seizure. United States v. Lisznyai, 470 F.2d 707, 710 (2d Circuit Court of Appeals, 1972).

This case indicates again the strong preference of the courts for warrants. It is likely that the court would have held the search illegal in this case had not the agents already begun the process of obtaining a search warrant when the emergency plain view search was made. Here, however, the attempt to obtain a warrant clearly showed that a warrantless seizure of the evidence in plain view was *not* planned, but was in response to an emergency.

In Ludlow v. State, 262 Ind. 266, 314 N.E.2d 750 (Supreme Court of Indiana, 1974), the court invalidated a warrantless seizure of narcotics because the seizure was anticipated. In that case law enforcement officers received information that certain narcotics were in a home in which there were five persons. When the officers discovered that they had arrest warrants for two of the five persons, they went to the home. The officers entered the home, discovered the narcotics lying open to view, and seized them. The court held that the discovery of the narcotics was not inadvertent because the entry to execute the arrest warrants was merely a pretext to search for the narcotics. Because the seizure of the narcotics was anticipated, the plain view doctrine did not apply and the seizure was unlawful.

SUMMARY

The plain view doctrine states that observation of items lying open to view by a law enforcement officer who has a right to be in a position to have that view is not a search, and the officer may seize the evidence without a warrant. The doctrine has six requirements, all of which must be satisfied before seizure of an item of evidence can be legally justified.

First, the officer, as a result of a prior valid intrusion into a constitutionally protected area, must be in a position in which he or she has a legal right to be. Some examples of situations in which an officer's intrusion is justified are: effecting an arrest or search incident to arrest; executing a search warrant; hot pursuit of a fleeing felon; and responding to an emergency.

Second, the officer must not unreasonably intrude on any person's reasonable expectation of privacy. In order to satisfy this requirement, the officer must use common sense to keep the investigation of crime within reasonable bounds.

Third, the officer must observe the item of evidence. This requirement means that the officer must actually see the item of evidence. If the officer merely has probable cause to believe that the item of evidence is in a particular place, a search warrant must be obtained before seizing it.

Fourth, the item of evidence must be lying in the open. The officer may use mechanical or electrical aids, such as a flashlight, to assist in observing the item, so long as this does not unreasonably intrude on someone's reasonable expectation of privacy. The officer may also examine items more closely, within limits. Opening of a container to determine if incriminating evidence is inside is prohibited, however, unless any privacy interest in the contents of the container has already been compromised by a private party and information about the contents has been made available to the officer by the private party.

Fifth, it must be immediately apparent to the officer that the item observed is evidence "subject to seizure." This simply means that the officer must have probable cause to believe that the item comes within one of the categories of property that are allowed to be seized under state law. An officer may use experience and background to assist in determining whether a particular item is seizable.

Sixth, the discovery of the item of evidence by the officer must be inadvertent. The plain view doctrine does not apply when the discovery of a particular item of evidence is anticipated, when the police know its location in advance, and when they intend to seize it. Nevertheless, if there are exigent circumstances, even a planned seizure of evidence in plain view may be justified, especially if efforts toward obtaining a search warrant have been made.

REVIEW AND DISCUSSION QUESTIONS

1. Should the requirement that the discovery of the item of evidence be inadvertent apply if the officer had insufficient time to obtain a search warrant after learning of the location of the item?

2. If law enforcement officers are in a place in which they have a right to be and they observe bottles that appear to contain illegal drugs, may they open the bottles and examine the contents further? May they use their senses of smell, taste, or touch to determine if items are subject to seizure when they are not sure?

3. Assume that law enforcement officers have a warrant to arrest the defendant for stealing guns four months ago. The officers suspect that the guns are at the defendant's home, but that suspicion is based on stale information insufficient to obtain a search warrant. May the officers seize guns found in plain view when they arrest the defendant? Would it make any difference if the officers could have easily found out if the guns were still at the defendants home by contacting a reliable informant?

4. May law enforcement officers take an item off the shelf in an antique store and examine it to determine if it is stolen? May officers do the same thing in a private home into which they have been invited by a person who does not know they are law enforcement officers?

5. Discuss the meaning of the following statement of the U.S. Supreme Court: " 'Plain view' is perhaps better understood . . . not as an independent 'exception' to the warrant clause, but simply as an extension of whatever the prior justification for an officer's 'access to an object' may be." Texas v. Brown, 460 U.S. 730, 738–39, 103 S.Ct. 1535, 1540–41, 75 L.Ed.2d 502, 511 (1983).

6. What problems are presented by an officer executing a search warrant for specified obscene materials, who seizes some magazines in plain view that were not specified in the warrant?

7. What are the limits on "protective searches?" May officers routinely look throughout a house for other suspects whenever they make an arrest or search? May officers go into other buildings on the premises? May officers go into neighboring homes? If an arrest is made in the hallway of a motel, may officers conduct a "protective search" of any or all of the rooms of the motel?

8. Does the plain view doctrine authorize a warrantless entry into a dwelling to seize contraband visible from outside the dwelling? Why? What if an officer observes contraband from the hallway of a motel through the open door to one of the rooms? What if an officer observes contraband lying on the desk in someone's office?

9. Would it be proper for officers executing a search warrant for stolen property to bring along victims of the theft to aid the officers in seizing other stolen items not named in the warrant that might be in plain view? Why?

10. If police officers are legitimately on premises, may they record the serial numbers of any objects that they suspect are stolen property? May they take photographs of the objects?

10

Search and Seizure of Vehicles and Containers

The same basic rules apply to the search of motor vehicles as to the search of fixed premises. For instance, it is well settled that an automobile is a personal "effect" within the meaning of the Fourth Amendment and as such is clearly protected against unreasonable searches and seizures. Therefore, law enforcement officers should obtain a warrant whenever they want to search a motor vehicle unless the situation falls within one of the exceptions to the warrant requirement discussed in this chapter or in other chapters of this book. Guidelines for obtaining a warrant can be found in Chapters 5 and 6.

Courts have created exceptions to the warrant requirement for motor vehicles because of the unique nature of motor vehicles. Some of their unique characteristics are their mobility, their use as transportation to and from scenes of crimes, and their employment in transporting dangerous weapons, stolen goods, contraband, and implements of crime. Also, a person has a lesser expectation of privacy in a motor vehicle because it travels public thoroughfares where its occupants and contents are open to view; it seldom serves as a residence or permanent place for personal effects; it is required to be registered and its occupant is required to be licensed; it is extensively regulated with respect to the condition and manner in which it is operated on public streets and highways; it periodically undergoes an official inspection; and it is often taken into police custody in the interests of public safety.

This chapter will discuss the exceptions to the warrant requirement for searches and seizures of motor vehicles and will present guidelines for law enforcement officers to give them a better understanding of their rights and limitations in this area.

THE CARROLL DOCTRINE

The *Carroll* doctrine holds that a warrantless search of a motor vehicle stopped on the highways or public streets by law enforcement officers who have probable cause to believe that the vehicle contains items subject to seizure is not unreasonable under the Fourth Amendment. The *Carroll* doctrine is sometimes referred to as the "automobile exception" to the search warrant requirement. The doctrine originated in the case of Carroll v. United States, 267 U.S. 132, 45 S.Ct. 280, 69 L.Ed. 543 (1925), in which federal prohibition agents obtained information that the defendant and another person were "bootleggers" who frequently traveled a certain road in a certain automobile. The officers later unexpectedly encountered the two men driving on that road in that automobile. The officers pursued and stopped the automobile on the highway. The automobile was thoroughly searched and the officers found several bottles of illegal liquor concealed in the automobile's upholstery. No warrant had been obtained for the search.

The U.S. Supreme Court held:

> On reason and authority the true rule is that if the search and seizure without a warrant are made upon probable cause, that is, upon a belief, reasonably arising out of circumstances known to the seizing officer, that an automobile or other vehicle contains that which by law is subject to seizure and destruction, the search and seizure are valid. The Fourth Amendment is to be construed in the light of what was deemed an unreasonable search and seizure when it was adopted, and in a manner which will conserve public interests as well as the interests and rights of individual citizens. 267 U.S. at 149, 45 S.Ct. at 283, 69 L.Ed. at 549.

Probable Cause

The controlling consideration in the search of a vehicle without a warrant is probable cause to believe that the vehicle contains items that are connected with criminal activity and thus are subject to seizure. This was emphasized in the *Carroll* decision:

> Having thus established that contraband goods concealed and illegally transported in an automobile or other vehicle may be searched for without a warrant, we come now to consider under what circumstances such search may be made. It would be intolerable and unreasonable if a prohibition agent were authorized to stop every automobile on the chance of finding liquor and thus subject all persons lawfully using the highways to the inconvenience and indignity of such a search. Travellers may be so stopped in crossing an international boundary because of national self protection reasonably requiring one entering the country to identify himself as entitled to come in, and his belongings as effects which may be lawfully brought in. But those lawfully within the Country, entitled to use the public highways, have a right to free passage without interruption or search unless there is known to a competent official authorized to search, probable cause for believing that their vehicles are carrying contraband or illegal merchandise. 267 U.S. at 153–54, 45 S.Ct. at 285, 69 L.Ed. at 551–52.

Probable cause is discussed in detail in Chapters 3 and 6. In vehicle search cases, as in all search and seizure cases, probable cause depends on the particular circumstances of each situation. The law enforcement officer's determination of probable cause must be based on objective facts that could justify the issuance of a warrant by a magistrate and not merely on the subjective good faith of the officer. Evidence seized from a vehicle that is not seized on the basis of probable cause will be inadmissible in court.

Impounding the Vehicle

The case of Chambers v. Maroney, 399 U.S. 42, 90 S.Ct. 1975, 26 L.Ed.2d 419 (1970), expanded the *Carroll* doctrine's grant of authority to law enforcement officers to search vehicles to include vehicles impounded and removed after being stopped on the highways or public streets. In that case, the police had information that armed robbers, carrying the fruits of the crime, had fled the robbery scene in a light blue compact station wagon. The vehicle was said to be carrying four men, one wearing a green sweater and another wearing a trench coat. The police stopped a vehicle fitting the description, arrested the four occupants, and drove the vehicle to the police station. The vehicle was thoroughly searched at the station and evidence was seized leading to the defendant's conviction.

The U.S. Supreme Court's decision upholding the search and seizure at the police station is worthy of quotation:

> In enforcing the Fourth Amendment's prohibition against unreasonable search-es and seizures, the Court has insisted upon probable cause as a minimum requirement for a reasonable search permitted by the Constitution. As a general rule, it has also required the judgment of a magistrate on the probable cause issue and the issuance of a warrant before a search is made. Only in exigent circum-stances will the judgment of the police as to probable cause serve as a sufficient authorization for a search. Carroll . . . holds a search warrant unnecessary where there is probable cause to search an automobile stopped on the highway; the car is movable, the occupants are alerted, and the car's contents may never be found again if a warrant must be obtained. Hence an immediate search is constitutionally permissible.
>
> Arguably, because of the preference for a magistrate's judgment, only the immobilization of the car should be permitted until a search warrant is obtained; arguably, only the "lesser" intrusion is permissible until the magistrate authorizes the "greater." But which is the "greater" and which the "lesser" intrusion is itself a debatable question and the answer may depend on a variety of circumstances. For constitutional purposes, we see no difference between on the one hand seizing and holding a car before presenting the probable cause issue to a magistrate and on the other hand carrying out an immediate search without a warrant. Given probable cause to search either course is reasonable under the Fourth Amendment.
>
> On the facts before us, the blue station wagon could have been searched on the spot when it was stopped since there was probable cause to search and it was a fleeting target for a search. The probable cause factor still obtained at the station house and so did the mobility of the car unless the Fourth Amendment permits a warrantless seizure of the car and the denial of its use to anyone until a warrant is secured. In that event there is little to choose in terms of practical consequences between an immediate search without a warrant and the car's immobilization until a warrant is obtained. 399 U.S. at 51–52, 90 S.Ct. at 1981, 26 L.Ed.2d 428–29.

Exigent Circumstances

In the passage quoted above from *Chambers v. Maroney,* the Supreme Court said that only in exigent circumstances will the judgment of the police as to probable cause serve as a sufficient authorization for a search. Some lower courts have taken this to mean that the police must be able to demonstrate specific facts establishing exigent circumstances, in addition to probable cause, before searching a vehicle stopped on the road. The U.S. Supreme Court, however, has made it clear that this is not necessary. In Michigan v. Thomas, 458 U.S. 259, 261, 102 S.Ct. 3079, 3081, 73 L.Ed.2d 750, 753 (1982), the Court said:

> In *Chambers v. Maroney* . . . we held that when police officers have probable cause to believe there is contraband inside an automobile that has been stopped on the road, the officers may conduct a warrantless search of the vehicle, even after it has been impounded and is in police custody. We firmly reiterated this holding in *Texas v. White,* 423 U.S. 67, 96 S.Ct. 304, 46 L.Ed.2d 209 (1975). . . . It is thus clear that the justification to conduct such a warrantless search does not vanish once the car has been immobilized; nor does it depend upon a reviewing court's assessment of the likelihood in each particular case that the car would have been driven away, or that its contents would have been tampered with, during the period required for the police to obtain a warrant.

It is thus apparent that the requirement of exigent circumstances before the police's judgment as to probable cause will justify a warrantless search is automatically satisfied in the case of a motor vehicle stopped on the road. Some state courts, however, may interpret their own constitutions to require stricter standards than the U.S. Supreme Court requires. Officers should be familiar with the laws and court decisions of their state in this area.

When a motor vehicle has not been stopped on the road, however, the requirement of exigent circumstances in addition to the requirement of probable cause must be established by the law enforcement officer before conducting a search or seizure. Usually, exigent circumstances is established by demonstrating specific facts showing either that the vehicle may be moved to an unknown location or out of the jurisdiction, making a search under authority of a warrant impossible, or that items subject to seizure may be removed from the vehicle and concealed or destroyed. For example, in Cardwell v. Lewis, 417 U.S. 583, 94 S.Ct. 2464, 41 L.Ed.2d 325 (1974), the U.S. Supreme Court found exigent circumstances justifying the warrantless seizure of the defendant's automobile from a commercial parking lot where he had left it prior to his appearance at the police station, where he was arrested. The defendant had been fully aware that he was under investigation for several months and he had told his attorney to see that his wife and family got the car. The Court based its finding on the possibility that the attorney or a family member might remove evidence from the car if the police delayed seizing it.

Also, if a vehicle or its contents present a potential danger to the public safety if not searched immediately, the "exigent circumstances" requirement of the *Carroll* doctrine may be satisfied, even though the car is not movable. In United States v. Cepulonis, 530 F.2d 238 (1st Circuit Court of Appeals, 1976), a law enforcement officer observed, through the window of an automobile, a sawed-off shotgun protruding from beneath the front seat. The court upheld the immediate warrantless seizure of the shotgun, finding probable cause and also finding that someone other than the car's owner (who was in custody) could have moved the car. The court went on to say:

> Moreover, a legitimate concern for public safety counselled against leaving the car, with a loaded shotgun visible through the window, unguarded in the Motel parking lot and "vulnerable to intrusion by vandals." . . . Under the circumstances the agents were faced with a choice whether to seize and hold the car while securing a warrant or to carry out an immediate warrantless search. 530 F.2d at 243.

In Coolidge v. New Hampshire, 403 U.S. 443, 91 S.Ct. 2022, 29 L.Ed.2d 564 (1971), the U.S. Supreme Court indicated that the exigent circumstances requirement would not be satisfied if there were no real possibility that someone would remove the car and conceal or destroy evidence within it. In the *Coolidge* case, the police had known for some time of the probable role of the defendant's automobile in a crime. The police went to the defendant's home, arrested him inside his house, and escorted his wife and children to another town to spend the night. There were no other adult occupants of the house. The vehicle was unoccupied and in the defendant's driveway. Police towed the vehicle to the station house and searched it there without a warrant.

The Court held that the search of the automobile could not be justified under the *Carroll* doctrine because the car was not movable, nor were there any other "exigent" circumstances to justify the search:

> [S]urely there is nothing in this case to invoke the meaning and purpose of the rule of Carroll v. U.S.—no alerted criminal bent on flight, no fleeting opportunity on an open highway after a hazardous chase, no contraband or stolen goods or weapons, no confederates waiting to move the evidence, not even the inconvenience of a special police detail to guard the immobilized automobile. In short, by no possible stretch of the legal imagination can this be made into a case where "it is not practicable to secure a warrant," . . . and the "automobile exception," despite its label, is simply irrelevant. 403 U.S. at 462, 91 S.Ct. at 2035–36, 29 L.Ed.2d at 580.

Entry Upon Private Premises

Courts have held that when law enforcement officers, acting on probable cause and following closely behind a vehicle, would have been authorized to stop and search the vehicle while on a public street, they may properly follow the vehicle onto private property and conduct the search there.

An example is a case in which an informant's tip and careful surveillance gave police officers probable cause to believe that a certain automobile contained contraband. The officers followed the auto until the defendant parked it in his garage. The subsequent warrantless search of the car in the garage was held valid by the Court:

> [I]t seems plain enough that just before he entered the garage the following officers properly could have stopped petitioner's car, [and] made search . . . .
> Passage of the car into the open garage closely followed by the observing officer did not destroy this right. Scher v. United States, 305 U.S. 251, 255, 59 S.Ct. 174, 176, 83 L.Ed. 151, 154 (U.S. Supreme Court, 1938).

Scope of Search

The permissible scope of a warrantless search of a motor vehicle under the *Carroll* doctrine has been defined in the case of United States v. Ross, 456 U.S. 798, 102 S.Ct. 2157, 72 L.Ed.2d 572 (1982). The *Ross* case involved the legitimate stopping of an automobile by police officers who had probable cause to believe that the automobile contained narcotics. During the search of the car, the searching officer found and opened a closed brown paper bag and a zippered leather pouch, discovering heroin in the bag and a large amount of money in the pouch. In holding the search legal, the U.S. Supreme Court said:

> [T]he scope of the warrantless search authorized by [the *Carroll*] exception is no broader and no narrower than a magistrate could legitimately authorize by warrant. If probable cause justifies the search of a lawfully stopped vehicle, it justifies the search of every part of the vehicle and its contents that may conceal the object of the search. 456 U.S. at 425, 102 S.Ct. at 2172, 72 L.Ed.2d at 572.

Emphasizing that the scope of a search under the *Carroll* doctrine depends entirely on the object of the search, the Court stated:

> The scope of a warrantless search of an automobile thus is not defined by the nature of the container in which the contraband is secreted. Rather, it is defined by the object of the search and the places in which there is probable cause to believe that it may be found. Just as probable cause to believe that a stolen lawnmower may be found in a garage will not support a warrant to search an upstairs bedroom, probable cause to believe that undocumented aliens are being transported in a van will not justify a warrantless search of a suitcase. Probable cause to believe that a container placed in the trunk of a taxi contains contraband or evidence does not justify a search of the entire cab. 456 U.S. at 824, 102 S.Ct. at 2172, 72 L.Ed.2d at 593.

It is clear then that, under the *Carroll* doctrine, if officers have probable cause to search an entire vehicle for a specific seizable item, they may search to the same extent as if they had a warrant to search for that item. But, if officers have only probable cause to search a particular movable container, which merely happens to be inside a motor vehicle, and not probable cause to search the entire vehicle, different rules apply. These rules will be discussed in the next section.

MOVABLE CONTAINERS

Although the rationale justifying a warrantless search of an automobile that is believed to be transporting items subject to seizure arguably applies with equal force to any movable container that is believed to be carrying such an item, the U.S. Supreme Court has squarely rejected that argument. In United States v. Chadwick, 433 U.S. 1, 97 S.Ct. 2476, 53 L.Ed.2d 538 (1977), federal railroad officials became suspicious when they noticed that a large footlocker loaded onto a train was unusually heavy and leaking talcum powder, a substance often used to mask the odor of marijuana. Narcotics agents met the train at its destination and a trained police dog signaled the presence of a controlled substance inside the footlocker. The agents did not seize the footlocker at this time. Instead, they waited until the defendant arrived and the footlocker was placed in the trunk of his automobile. Before the engine was started, the officers arrested the defendant and his two companions. The agents then removed the footlocker to a secure place, opened it without a warrant, and discovered a large quantity of marijuana.

The prosecution argued on appeal that the warrantless search was "reasonable" because a footlocker has some of the mobile characteristics that support warrantless searches of automobiles. The Supreme Court rejected the argument:

> "The factors which diminish the privacy aspects of an automobile do not apply to respondents' footlocker. Luggage contents are not open to public view, except as a condition to a border entry or common carrier travel; nor is luggage subject to regular inspections and official scrutiny on a continuing basis. Unlike an automobile, whose primary function is transportation, luggage is intended as a repository of personal effects. In sum, a person's expectations of privacy in personal luggage are substantially greater than in an automobile. 433 U.S. at 13, 97 S.Ct. at 2484, 53 L.Ed.2d at 549.

The Court noted that the practical problems associated with the temporary detention of a piece of luggage during the period of time necessary to obtain a warrant are significantly less than those associated with the detention of an automobile. In holding the warrantless search of the footlocker unjustified, the Court reaffirmed the general principle that closed packages and containers may not be searched without a warrant. Thus, the Court declined to extend the rationale of the "automobile exception" to permit a warrantless search of any movable container found in a public place.

In Arkansas v. Sanders, 442 U.S. 753, 99 S.Ct. 2586, 61 L.Ed.2d 235 (1979), a case similar to Chadwick, a police officer received information from a reliable informant that the defendant would arrive at the local airport on a specified flight that afternoon carrying a green suitcase containing marijuana. The officer went to the airport. The defendant arrived on schedule and retrieved a green suitcase from the airline baggage service. The defendant gave the suitcase to a waiting companion who placed it in the trunk of a taxi. The defendant and his companion drove off in the cab. Police officers followed and stopped the cab several blocks from the airport. The officers opened the trunk, seized the suitcase, and searched it on the scene without a warrant. The suitcase contained marijuana.

The U.S. Supreme Court ruled that the warrantless search of the suitcase was impermissible under the Fourth Amendment. As in Chadwick, the mere fact that the suitcase had been placed in the trunk of the vehicle did not render the automobile exception of Carroll applicable. The police had probable cause to seize the suitcase before it was placed in the trunk of the cab and did not have probable cause to search the cab itself. Since the suitcase had been placed in the trunk, no danger existed that its contents could have been hidden elsewhere in the vehicle. Furthermore, none of the practical difficulties associated with the detention of a vehicle on a public highway that made the immediate search in Carroll reasonable could justify the immediate search of the suitcase, since the officers had no interest in detaining the taxi or its driver. Again, the common thread in the Chadwick and Sanders cases is that in neither case did the police have probable cause to search the vehicle or anything in it except the footlocker in the former case and the green suitcase in the latter. Without probable cause to search the vehicle, the *Carroll* doctrine did not apply, and the searches should not have been conducted without a warrant.

IMPOUNDMENT AND INVENTORY OF VEHICLE

Impoundment

Some police departments have a policy requiring officers to impound a motor vehicle when the driver or owner is taken into custody or is incapacitated by intoxication, illness, or some other condition. The usual procedure involves the police taking possession of the vehicle and moving it to a garage or police lot for safekeeping. The main justification for such an impoundment policy is that the vehicle would otherwise be left unattended on a public street or highway, and would be an easy target for theft or vandalism, leaving the police open to potential liability.

Nevertheless, the right to impound a vehicle does not automatically follow upon the taking into custody or incapacitation of the driver or owner. Some courts have held that an impoundment of a vehicle must be necessary in order to be legal. In a case in which both occupants of an automobile were intoxicated, and there was no one else to drive or take care of it, the court favored impoundment over leaving the car unattended on the street. People v. Havenstein, 4 Cal.App.3d 710, 84 Cal.Rptr. 528 (California Court of Appeal, 1970).

If less intrusive alternate means of caring for the vehicle are available, however, they should be used. In a case involving a defendant arrested for driving under the influence, the defendant made arrangements to have his brother and mother take care of his car. The arresting officer, however, refused to relinquish the car and impounded it. The contents were later inventoried and LSD tablets were found. The court held that the impoundment of the car, and therefore the inventory search of it, was illegal. The court said:

> We hold that where police assumed custody of defendant's automobile for no legitimate state purpose other than safekeeping, and where defendant had arranged for alternate means, not shown to be unreasonable, for the safeguarding of his property, impoundment of defendant's automobile was unreasonable and, therefore, the concomitant inventory was an unreasonable search under the Fourth Amendment. State v. Goodrich, 256 N.W.2d 506, 507 (Supreme Court of Minnesota, 1977).

The removal of an unoccupied parked vehicle is clearly justified when the vehicle constitutes a traffic hazard or otherwise violates local parking ordinances. The U.S. Supreme Court specifically authorized impoundment of vehicles under such circumstances:

> In the interests of public safety and as part of what the Court has called "community caretaking functions," . . . automobiles are frequently taken into police custody. Vehicle accidents present one such occasion. To permit the uninterrupted flow of traffic and in some circumstances to preserve evidence, disabled or damaged vehicles will often be removed from the highways or streets at the behest of police engaged solely in caretaking and traffic control activities. Police will also frequently remove and impound automobiles which violate parking

ordinances which thereby jeopardize both the public safety and the efficient movement of vehicular traffic. The authority of police to seize and remove from the streets vehicles impeding traffic or threatening public safety and convenience is beyond challenge. South Dakota v. Opperman, 428 U.S. 364, 368–69, 96 S.Ct. 3092, 3096, 49 L.Ed.2d 1000, 1005 (1976).

Inventory

Assuming that a vehicle has been lawfully impounded, may the vehicle then be searched for incriminating evidence without a warrant? Unless the situation meets the requirements of the *Carroll* doctrine, discussed above, police have no authority to conduct a warrantless investigatory search of a lawfully impounded motor vehicle. Stated otherwise, police must obtain a search warrant to search an impounded vehicle unless they have probable cause to search a vehicle that was originally stopped on the highway or for which exigent circumstances make an immediate warrantless search necessary.

Nevertheless, the U.S. Supreme Court, in the case of South Dakota v. Opperman, 428 U.S. 364, 96 S.Ct. 3092, 49 L.Ed.2d 1000 (1976), approved a more limited type search of impounded motor vehicles—the routine practice of local police departments of securing and inventorying the vehicle's contents. This limited type of search is allowed for the following purposes:

1. The protection of the owner's property while it remains in police custody;

2. The protection of the police against claims or disputes over lost or stolen property; and

3. The protection of the police from potential danger.

This inventory procedure is not considered to be a search for purposes of the Fourth Amendment because its object is not to find incriminating evidence as part of a criminal investigation. Rather, it is considered to be a routine administrative-custodial procedure. As such, the inventory procedure may not be used as a pretext to conduct an exploratory search for incriminating evidence in order to circumvent the warrant requirement. Harris v. United States, 370 F.2d 477 (District of Columbia Circuit Court of Appeals, 1966).

Therefore, the scope of the inventory should be restricted to accessible areas of the vehicle in which the owner's or occupant's personal belongings might be vulnerable to theft or damage. Areas covered by the inventory would usually include an unlocked glove compartment, an unlocked trunk, the sun visors, the front and rear seat areas, and other places in which property is ordinarily kept. People v. Andrews, 6 Cal.App.3d 428, 85 Cal.Rptr. 908 (California Court of Appeal, 1970). As a part of the inventory, a notation should be made of the vehicle identification number, the motor number, and the make, model, and license plate number of the car in order that it may be readily identified later. Cotton v. United States, 371 F.2d 385 (9th Circuit Court of Appeals, 1967). Officers should not open locked glove compartments or locked trunks to make inventories of their contents because the protection of the property, themselves, and others would not ordinarily require it. Also inventorying locked areas may violate the owner's reasonable expectation of privacy. State v. Boster, 217 Kan. 618, 539 P.2d 294 (Kansas Supreme Court,

1975). But when officers reasonably believe that the contents of an automobile or the contents of a locked compartment in an automobile present a danger to themselves or others, they may make as extensive a search as necessary to end the danger.

The intensity of the inventory must also be limited according to its purpose. Thus, if officers dismantle the vehicle, look behind the upholstery, or in any other manner indicate that their purpose is other than to protect and secure the vehicle's contents, the courts will consider the inventory a pretext for a search designed to uncover evidentiary materials. In that event the inventory will be considered an illegal warrantless search and the fruits of the search will be inadmissible in court.

Likewise, if police delay making an inventory of the contents of an impounded vehicle for an unreasonable period of time, the inventory may be ruled an illegal search. An unreasonably delayed inventory indicates that police were not really concerned about safeguarding the owner's property or protecting themselves against claims or from danger, but were primarily interested in looking for evidence. A vehicle inventory should be conducted as soon as possible after the impoundment, taking into consideration the police agency's human resources, facilities, workload, and other circumstances. If the inventory is delayed for more than a day or two without good reason, it is likely to be declared illegal.

Each law enforcement agency should have standard procedures for inventorying impounded vehicles, or the inventories may be declared illegal. The U.S. Supreme Court, in upholding the validity of an inventory of an impounded car in *South Dakota v. Opperman,* emphasized that the police in that case were using a standai d inventory form pursuant to standard police procedures. The Court said, "The decisions of this Court point unmistakably to the conclusion reached by both federal and state courts that inventories pursuant to standard police procedures are reasonable." 428 U.S. at 372, 96 S.Ct. at 3098, 49 L.Ed.2d at 1007. The 9th Circuit Court of Appeals invalidated an inventory of a legally impounded automobile because the local police department did not have a standard procedure regarding the inventorying of an impounded vehicle's contents. The court said:

> [E]ven if an investigatory motive was not shown, our decision would be the same because the inventorying of impounded cars was not shown to be a routine practice and policy of *this* police department, as was the case in *Opperman* . . . . It is the inventorying practice and not the impounding practice that, if routinely followed and supported by proper noninvestigatory purposes, could render the inventory a reasonable search under *Opperman.* The fact that other police departments routinely follow such a practice may give support to the proposition that such a practice, if locally followed, is reasonable. It does not, however, render reasonable a search where the inventorying practice is not locally followed and the search, thus, is a departure from local practice. United States v. Hellman, 556 F.2d 442, 444 (1977).

Plain View Doctrine

While a law enforcement officer may not look for evidence of crime while conducting a bona fide inventory, if contraband or other items subject to seizure are unexpectedly discovered, they may lawfully be seized and are admissible in evidence. Since the officer is lawfully conducting an inventory in the vehicle and there has been no search in the Fourth Amendment sense, the situation is governed by the plain view doctrine discussed in Chapter 9.

In a case illustrating the application of the plain view doctrine to the inventory situation, local officers stopped a vehicle that was being operated without license plates. Neither of the occupants claimed to be the owner of the automobile nor did they know to whom it belonged. Furthermore, the driver's statement that he had borrowed the vehicle from a used car dealer was not consistent with information disclosed on the registration sticker. On the basis of these facts, the officers arrested the two men on a charge of auto theft. After the arrest, as a normal procedure before impounding the vehicle, the officers began an inventory of all personal property found in it. One of the officers picked up a jacket on the front seat where the defendant had been sitting and noticed in plain sight a burned cigarette. Since it appeared to him to be marijuana, the officer searched the jacket and found another such cigarette in the left-hand pocket. The defendant later admitted that he had purchased the cigarettes approximately one week earlier.

On appeal of the defendant's conviction for illegal possession of marijuana, the court held that the marijuana cigarette was legally obtained by the officer:

> In the course of making the inventory of the contents of the car, the officer merely removed the jacket from the front seat revealing in plain sight the narcotic. How it got there could not be determined but it is clear that when the officer picked up the jacket the cigarette was there for all to see. Actually, the officer's observation of the cigarette was not the result of a search, for it appeared in plain sight in the normal course of the reasonable and valid activity of the officer in making the inventory incidental to impounding the car. People v. Nebbitt, 183 Cal.App.2d 452, 460, 7 Cal.Rptr. 8, 13 (California Court of Appeal, 1960).

In another case illustrating the application of the plain view doctrine to an automobile inventory, officers came upon a closed satchel during an inventory of the contents of a lawfully impounded vehicle. They opened the satchel and found marijuana. The court held that the contents of the closed satchel did not come within the plain view doctrine and were inadmissible as evidence of a crime. Although the satchel itself was in plain view of the officer as he inventoried the contents of the vehicle, the contents of the satchel were not in his plain view. State v. Gwinn, 301 A.2d 291 (Delaware Supreme Court, 1972). Officers should obtain a search warrant before opening any closed container found during an inventory of the contents of a vehicle. (See the discussion of searches of containers earlier in this chapter.)

IMPOUNDMENT OF VEHICLE UNDER FORFEITURE STATUTES

Another ground for allowing a warrantless search of a vehicle by law enforcement officers is the seizure and impound of the vehicle under authority of a state forfeiture statute. In the case of Cooper v. California, 386 U.S. 58, 87 S.Ct. 788, 17 L.Ed.2d 730 (U.S. Supreme Court, 1967), the defendant was arrested for selling heroin wrapped in brown paper to a police informer. At the time of the arrest, the defendant's car was seized and impounded pursuant to a state forfeiture statute.

The statute required that any officer making an arrest for a narcotics offense involving the use of a vehicle must seize and hold the vehicle as evidence pending a judicial declaration of forfeiture or release. Evidence showed that the defendant used his vehicle in connection with his possession and transportation of narcotics. One week after the seizure, police searched the car and discovered a piece of brown paper in the glove compartment. The brown paper was later introduced at trial. The state had not acquired title to the car at the time of the search.

This search could not be justified under the *Carroll* doctrine because there were no exigent circumstances. The car had been in police custody for a week, during which time the police could easily have obtained a warrant. Nevertheless, the Court held the search legal. The Court said that the car was lawfully held by the police in connection with criminal activity under the state forfeiture statute. Since the car was to be held for a considerable period of time, and since the police could deny possession of the car to its owner, the police had possessory rights of their own for the limited purpose of searching the vehicle.

The *Cooper* case allows law enforcement officers to conduct a warrantless search of a vehicle, in the absence of exigent circumstances, when all the following conditions are met:

1. A state statute requires law enforcement officers to seize vehicles involved in certain offenses and hold them pending forfeiture proceedings.

2. A vehicle is seized by the officer in connection with an offense named in the state forfeiture statute, and impounded.

3. The search of the car is closely related to the reason the defendant was arrested, the reason the vehicle was impounded, and the reason it is being retained.

4. The officer expects that the car will be in police custody for a considerable time.

5. The officer can legally deny possession of the car to the owner.

The *Cooper* decision does not require that officers have probable cause to search a vehicle impounded under a forfeiture statute. Nevertheless, because of the general preference for warrants, if officers do have probable cause to search, they should obtain a search warrant.

INSTRUMENTALITY OF A CRIME

The motor vehicle is unique in that, besides its obvious use as a transporter of people and goods related to crime, it can itself be an instrumentality of crime. Some courts have expressed the viewpoint that for certain types of crimes the entire automobile may be seized as an instrumentality of the crime, much like the seizure of any other weapon. Then, the argument continues, a vehicle could be examined and tested, much like a weapon, for hair, bloodstains, soil, fingerprints, and other physical evidence. Weaver v. Lane, 382 F.2d 251 (7th Circuit Court of Appeals, 1967). This theory would be particularly useful in cases of rape, robbery, and other violent crimes in which the automobile itself may be the scene of the crime or an integral part of it. Some courts have shown an inclination toward this theory. For example, in the case of State v. Poulin, 268 A.2d 475 (Supreme Judicial Court of

Maine, 1970), the court gave as one of the reasons for justifying the seizure of an automobile that the automobile was an instrumentality of a probable crime. However, this is still a very unsettled area of the law, and the law enforcement officer should proceed on the basis of established principles and obtain a warrant rather than attempt to justify a warrantless seizure of a vehicle on the theory that it is an instrumentality of a crime.

EXPECTATION OF PRIVACY

In recent years, the U.S. Supreme Court and other courts have begun to analyze warrantless searches and seizures of vehicles in terms of whether they intrude upon a person's reasonable expectation of privacy. In Cardwell v. Lewis, 417 U.S. 583, 94 S.Ct. 2464, 41 L.Ed.2d 325 (1974), the U.S. Supreme Court held that, where probable cause exists, a warrantless examination of the exterior of a car is not unreasonable under the Fourth and Fourteenth Amendments. The Court said:

> One has a lesser expectation of privacy in a motor vehicle because its function is transportation and it seldom serves as one's residence or as the repository of personal effects. A car has little capacity for escaping public scrutiny. It travels public thoroughfares where both its occupants and its contents are in plain view. . . . This is not to say that no part of the interior of an automobile has Fourth Amendment protection; the exercise of a desire to be mobile does not, of course, waive one's right to be free of unreasonable governmental intrusion. But insofar as Fourth Amendment protection extends to a motor vehicle, it is the right to privacy that is the touchstone of our inquiry. 417 U.S. at 590–91, 94 S.Ct. at 2469–70, 41 L.Ed.2d at 335.

In South Dakota v. Opperman, 428 U.S. 364, 96 S.Ct. 3092, 49 L.Ed.2d 1000 (1976), the U.S. Supreme Court approved the warrantless inventory of an automobile impounded for parking violations. The Court said:

> Besides the elements of mobility, less rigorous warrant requirements govern because the expectation of privacy with respect to one's automobile is significantly less than that relating to one's home or office. In discharging their varied responsibilities for ensuring the public safety, law enforcement officials are necessarily brought into frequent contact with automobiles. Most of this contact is distinctly noncriminal in nature. . . . Automobiles, unlike homes, are subjected to pervasive and continuing governmental regulation and controls, including periodic inspection and licensing requirements. As an everyday occurrence, police stop and examine vehicles when license plates or inspection stickers have expired, or if other violations, such as exhaust fumes or excessive noise, are noted, or if headlights or other safety equipment are not in proper working order. 428 U.S. at 367–68, 96 S.Ct. at 3096, 49 L.Ed.2d at 1004.

The quoted passages indicate that the courts are imposing fewer restrictions on law enforcement officers with regard to warrantless searches of vehicles. Nevertheless, even though the reasonable expectation of privacy in one's vehicle is less than that in one's person, home, or office, officers must not violate that expectation when conducting searches or inventories of vehicles.

Electronic Beepers

A "beeper" is a radio transmitter, usually battery operated, that emits periodic signals that can be picked up by a radio receiver. A beeper neither records nor transmits any sounds other than its signal, but the signal can be monitored by directional finders, enabling law enforcement officers to determine the beeper's location. For the first time, the U.S. Supreme Court dealt with the Fourth Amendment implications of the use of beepers in the case of United States v. Knotts, 460 U.S. 276, 103 S.Ct. 1081, 75 L.Ed.2d 55 (1983). In that case, officers, with the consent of a chemical company, installed a beeper in a five-gallon container of chloroform, a substance used to manufacture illicit drugs. One of the defendant's codefendants purchased the container of chloroform and transported it by automobile to the defendant's secluded cabin in another state. Law enforcement officers monitored the progress of the automobile carrying the chloroform all the way to its destination. After three days of visual surveillance of the cabin, officers obtained a search warrant, searched the cabin, and found evidence of the illegal manufacture of drugs.

The Court held that the warrantless monitoring of the beeper by law enforcement officers to trace the location of the chloroform container did not violate the defendant's legitimate expectation of privacy:

> The governmental surveillance conducted by means of the beeper in this case amounted principally to the following of an automobile on public streets and highways. . . . A person travelling in an automobile on public thoroughfares has no reasonable expectation of privacy in his movements from one place to another. When [the codefendant] travelled over the public streets he voluntarily conveyed to anyone who wanted to look the fact that he was travelling over particular roads in a particular direction, the fact of whatever stops he made, and the fact of his final destination when he exited from public roads onto private property. 460 U.S. at 281, 103 S.Ct. at 1085, 75 L.Ed.2d at 62.

Although the defendant, as the owner of the cabin and surrounding premises, undoubtedly had a justifiable expectation of privacy within the cabin, that expectation did not extend to the visual observation of his codefendant's automobile arriving on his premises after leaving a public highway, nor to movements of objects such as the container of chloroform outside the cabin. That the officers relied not only on visual surveillance, but on the use of the beeper to locate the codefendant's automobile did not alter the situation. "Nothing in the Fourth Amendment prohibited the police from augmenting the sensory faculties bestowed upon them at birth with such enhancement as science and technology afforded them in this case." 460 U.S. at 282, 103 S.Ct. at 1086, 75 L.Ed.2d at 63.

The Court emphasized the limited use the officers made of the signals from the beeper. There was no indication that the beeper signal was received or relied upon after it had indicated that the chloroform container had ended its automotive journey at the defendant's camp. Moreover, there was no indication that the beeper was used in any way to reveal information as to the movement of the drum within the cabin, or in any way that would not have been visible to the naked eye from outside the cabin.

The U.S. Supreme Court case of United States v. Karo, ___ U.S. ___, 104 S.Ct. 3296, 82 L.Ed.2d 530 (1984), addressed the question of whether the monitoring of a beeper in a private residence, a location not open to visual surveillance, violates the Fourth Amendment rights of those who have a justifiable interest in the privacy of the residence. The Court found that the warrantless surreptitious use by the government of an electronic device to obtain information it could not have obtained by observation from outside the curtilage of a house was the same, for purposes of the Fourth Amendment, as a warrantless surreptitious entry of the house by a law enforcement officer to verify that the beeper was in the house. Even though the monitoring of a beeper inside a private residence is less intrusive than a full-scale search, it is illegal unless conducted under authority of a warrant. The Court said:

> Requiring a warrant will have the salutary effect of ensuring that use of beepers is not abused, by imposing upon agents the requirement that they demonstrate in advance their justification for the desired search. This is not to say that there are no exceptions to the warrant rule, because if truly exigent circumstances exist no warrant is required under general Fourth Amendment principles.

Therefore, the warrantless monitoring of a beeper is permissible only if the beeper, or the container containing the beeper, could have been observed from outside the curtilage of a house, or if there is an emergency. Otherwise, the monitoring of a beeper located in a place not open to visual surveillance is illegal without a warrant.

Searches by Dogs

In United States v. Solis, 536 F.2d 880 (9th Circuit Court of Appeals, 1976), the court held that the use of specially trained dogs to detect the smell of marijuana in a vehicle did not violate the reasonable expectation of privacy of the vehicle's owner. In that case, a drug agent suspected that marijuana was hidden in the floor of a certain semi-trailer parked at the rear of a gas station. The agent went to the gas station and found the semi-trailer with what appeared to be white talcum powder on its doors. The officer knew from his training and experience that marijuana was often smuggled in semi-trailer floors and that talcum powder was often used to conceal marijuana's odor. The agent notified the Customs office, which sent two Customs officers with specially trained marijuana sniffing dogs. The dogs, who were determined to be extremely reliable, reacted positively to marijuana in the semi-trailer. A search warrant was obtained and the marijuana was seized.

The court held that the use of the dogs to help the officers establish probable cause to search was reasonable and did not violate the defendant's reasonable expectation of privacy. The court said:

> The dogs' intrusion such as it was into the air space open to the public in the vicinity of the trailer appears to us reasonably tolerable in our society. There was no invasion of the "curtilage"—the trailer. No sophisticated mechanical or electronic devices were used. The investigation was not indiscriminate, but solely directed to the particular contraband. There was an expectation that the odor would emanate from the trailer. Efforts made to mask it were visible. The method used by the officers was inoffensive. There was no embarrassment to or search of the person. The target was a physical fact indicative of possible crime, not protected communications. We hold that the use of the dogs was not unreasonable under the

circumstances and therefore was not a prohibited search under the fourth amendment.   536 F.2d at 882–83.

Courts are in disagreement over the search and seizure implications of the use of drug-detecting dogs.   The safest procedure for law enforcement officers is to make sure drug-detecting dogs are reliable and to obtain a warrant before conducting a search based on a dog's reactions.

SUMMARY

Although the search and seizure of motor vehicles is generally governed by the warrant requirement of the Fourth Amendment, courts have created certain exceptions to the warrant requirement for motor vehicles, based on the differences between a motor vehicle and fixed premises.   A motor vehicle is mobile and is used to transport criminals, weapons, and fruits and instrumentalities of crime.   It seldom serves as a residence or a permanent repository of personal effects.   Also, a person has a reduced expectation of privacy in a motor vehicle because it travels public thoroughfares where its occupants and contents are open to view, and because it is subject to extensive governmental regulation, including periodic inspection and licensing.

The most important exception to the warrant requirement is the so-called automobile exception, as embodied in the *Carroll* doctrine.   The *Carroll* doctrine states that law enforcement officers may conduct a warrantless search of a motor vehicle if they have probable cause to believe that the vehicle contains items subject to seizure and if there are exigent circumstances that make obtaining a warrant impracticable.   If the vehicle is stopped on the road, the exigent circumstances requirement is automatically satisfied and the police need not provide supporting facts and circumstances to establish the existence of exigent circumstances.   Also, police may conduct a warrantless search of a vehicle stopped on the road even after it has been impounded and is in police custody.   The scope of the search is defined by the object of the search and the places in which there is probable cause to believe that it may be found.   If police have probable cause to believe that a particular seizable item is located somewhere in a vehicle that has been lawfully stopped on the road, they may search it as if they had a search warrant for the item.   This includes the right to open and search closed, opaque containers, located inside the vehicle, in which the seizable item might be contained.   If, however, police do not have probable cause to search the entire vehicle, but only probable cause to search a particular container inside the vehicle, police may not open and search the container without a warrant.   The only exceptions to this rule are:

1. If the contents of the container are open to plain view (in which case the container would be either not closed or not opaque), the officer may seize the contents without a warrant;

2. If the contents of the container can be inferred from its outward appearance (such as a kit of burglar tools or a gun case), the officer may seize the contents without a warrant;

3. If the officer has probable cause to believe that the container contains an immediately dangerous instrumentality, such as explosives, the officer may open the container and disarm the instrumentality or otherwise end the danger.

It should be noted that if a closed, opaque container is seized incident to the arrest of an occupant of a motor vehicle, the search and seizure of the contents of the container are governed by the case of *New York v. Belton,* discussed in Chapter 7.

The inventory of a lawfully impounded motor vehicle may also be conducted without a warrant. This procedure, however, is not considered to be a search for Fourth Amendment purposes, but merely an administrative procedure. The officer making the inventory may not look for incriminating evidence but may be concerned only with protecting the owner's property, protecting the police against claims or disputes over lost or stolen property, and protecting the police from potential danger. The inventory of a vehicle must be limited in scope and intensity by the purposes for which it is allowed. Nevertheless, evidence of crime found in "plain view" during the inventory may be seized and will be admissible in court.

Seizure and impoundment of a vehicle under a state forfeiture statute and seizure of a vehicle as an instrumentality of a crime may also provide legal justification for a warrantless search of the vehicle. Courts differ in their acceptance and application of these justifications, however, and the safer procedure for the officer is to apply for a search warrant.

Although still matters of some dispute, courts have generally approved the tracing of the location of a motor vehicle on public thoroughfares by means of an electronic "beeper," and the detection of drugs in a motor vehicle by means of sniffing by specially trained dogs. The allowance of both these limited types of intrusion is based upon the reduced expectation of privacy in motor vehicles.

REVIEW AND DISCUSSION QUESTIONS

1. Practically speaking, are there any situations left in which a warrant is required to search a motor vehicle? Isn't the warrant requirement the exception rather than the rule in automobile cases?

2. Do the legal principles in this chapter apply to vehicles such as bicycles, rowboats, motor homes, trains, or airplanes?

3. If a law enforcement officer has probable cause to believe a vehicle contains small concealable items such as drugs, jewels, or rare coins, to what extent can the vehicle be searched without a warrant under the *Carroll* doctrine? Can the upholstery be ripped open? Can the vehicle be dismantled? Can the tires be taken off to look inside them? Can pillows, radios, clothing, and other potential containers be dismantled or ripped apart?

4. Under the *Carroll* doctrine, the officer with probable cause to search a motor vehicle has the choice to either conduct the search immediately or impound the vehicle and search it later at the station house. What factors should be considered in making the choice?

5. Describe three situations in which there are exigent circumstances and probable cause to search a vehicle that has *not* been stopped on the highway.

6. If the postal service turns over to the police plastic bags believed to contain illegal drugs, may the police conduct chemical tests on the contents of the bags without a warrant?

7. Assume that a person is arrested for drunken driving late at night while driving alone on a city street. He tells the police that he doesn't want his car impounded and that a friend will pick up the car some time the next day. He says he will sign a statement absolving the police from any liability for any loss of or damage to the car or its contents. Should the police impound the car and inventory its contents?

8. Under the *Carroll* doctrine, do the police have to have probable cause to search the vehicle at the time it is stopped on the highway in order to search it later at the station. What if a person is arrested on the highway for a traffic violation and is told to accompany officers to the station to post bond. A routine check at the station reveals that the vehicle is stolen. May the officers search it without a warrant?

9. If officers have probable cause to search a vehicle stopped on the highway, but no probable cause to arrest the passengers of the vehicle, can the officers search the passengers also? Are the passengers "containers" under the ruling of the *Ross* case? Does the answer depend on the nature of the evidence the officers are looking for?

10. Is a warrantless installation of a "beeper" proper in the following circumstances?
    a. Attachment of the beeper to the outside of an automobile.
    b. Placement of the beeper somewhere inside an automobile.
    c. Opening a closed package or luggage to install a beeper.
    d. Attaching a beeper to the outside of a package or luggage.
    e. Placing a beeper with money taken in a bank robbery.

11

Open Fields and Abandoned Property

To open the discussion of the "open fields" and "abandoned property" exceptions to the search warrant requirement, we again refer to the Fourth Amendment to the U.S. Constitution. The Fourth Amendment guarantees "the right of the people to be secure in their persons, *houses,* papers, and effects, against unreasonable *searches* and seizures . . . . (emphasis supplied) U.S.C.A.Const. Amend. IV. The word "houses" and the word "searches" are italicized because the meaning of open fields depends upon court interpretation of the word "houses," and the meaning of abandoned property depends upon court interpretations of the word "searches." To introduce the legal meanings of these terms and their interrelationships, we begin with a summary of Hester v. United States, 265 U.S. 57, 44 S.Ct. 445, 68 L.Ed. 898 (U.S. Supreme Court, 1924). This case established the concepts of open fields and abandonment in the law of search and seizure.

HESTER v. U.S.

In *Hester v. U.S.,* revenue officers, investigating suspected bootlegging, went to the house of Hester's father. As they approached, they saw Henderson drive up to the house. The officers concealed themselves and observed Hester come out of the house and hand Henderson a quart bottle. An alarm was given. Hester went to a nearby car and removed a gallon jug, and he and Henderson fled across an open field. One of the officers pursued, firing his pistol. Henderson threw away his bottle, and Hester dropped his jug, which broke, keeping about one quart of its contents. A broken jar, still containing some of its contents, was found outside the house. The officers examined the jug, the jar, and the bottle and determined that they contained illicitly distilled whiskey. The officers had neither a search warrant nor an arrest warrant.

The defendant was convicted of concealing distilled spirits, and contended on appeal that the testimony of the two officers was inadmissible because their actions constituted an illegal search and seizure. The Court said:

> It is obvious that even if there had been a trespass, the above testimony was not obtained by an illegal search or seizure. The defendant's own acts, and those of his associates, disclosed the jug, the jar and the bottle—and there was no seizure in the sense of the law when the officers examined the contents of each after it had been *abandoned* . . . . The only shadow of a ground for bringing up the case is drawn from the hypothesis that the examination of the vessels took place upon Hester's father's land. As to that, it is enough to say that, apart from the justification, the special protection accorded by the Fourth Amendment to the people in their "persons, houses, papers and effects," is not extended to the *open fields*. The distinction between the latter and the house is as old as the common law. (emphasis supplied) 265 U.S. at 58–59, 44 S.Ct. at 446, 68 L.Ed. at 900.

The *Hester* decision has been heavily criticized, but has been applied and interpreted by many courts, and remains in effect today. The *Hester* case itself is not very helpful to the law enforcement officer, but the decisions of other courts following it have expanded upon and clarified its holdings. The remainder of this chapter will be devoted to setting out guidelines for the law enforcement officer on the search and seizure of open fields and abandoned property.

OPEN FIELDS

The open fields doctrine has been simply and clearly stated by the U.S. Supreme Court in the *Hester* case:

> [T]he special protection accorded by the Fourth Amendment to the people in their "persons, houses, papers and effects," is not extended to the open fields. 265 U.S. at 59, 44 S.Ct. at 446, 68 L.Ed. at 900.

The open fields doctrine is very important to law enforcement officers because it allows them to search for and seize evidence in the open fields without a warrant, probable cause, or any other legal justification. Even if officers trespass on the land of another while searching the open fields, the evidence they seize will not be inadmissible for that reason. Oliver v. U. S., ___ U.S. ___, 104 S.Ct. 1735, 80 L.Ed.2d 214 (1984). Furthermore, the officers themselves will not be held liable for trespass in a civil suit if the trespass was required in the performance of their duties. Giacona v. U.S., 257 F.2d 450 (5th Circuit Court of Appeals, 1958).

The problem for the law enforcement officer lies in determining where the area protected by the Fourth Amendment ends and the open fields begin. In order to make this determination, the officer must consult court decisions interpreting the word "houses" in the Fourth Amendment.

The word "houses" in the Fourth Amendment has been given a very broad meaning by the courts. Courts have held that the Fourth Amendment protects people in their homes, whether owned, rented, or leased. The term "houses" has also been held to include any quarters in which a person is staying or living, whether permanently or temporarily. Examples of other protected living quarters are hotel and motel rooms, apartments, rooming and boarding house rooms, and even hospital rooms. Furthermore, the protection of the Fourth Amendment is not restricted to places of residence, but extends to places of business also. United States v. Botsch, 364 F.2d 542, 547 (2nd Circuit Court of Appeals, 1966). The protection extended to places of business is limited, however, to those areas or sections that are not open to the public. As one court said:

> [A] private business whose doors are open to the general public is also to be considered open to entry by the police for any proper purpose not violative of the owner's constitutional rights—e.g., patronizing the place or surveying it to promote law and order or to suppress a breach of the peace. State v. La Duca, 89 N.J. Super. 159, 165, 214 A.2d 423, 426 (new Jersey Superior Court, 1965).

For purposes of convenience, the word "house" will be used in the remainder of this chapter to refer to either residential or commercial premises covered by the Fourth Amendment.

Courts have also extended the meaning of "houses" under the Fourth Amendment to include the "ground and buildings immediately surrounding a dwelling." Rosencranz v. United States, 356 F.2d 310, 313 (1st Circuit Court of Appeals, 1966). This area is commonly known as the "curtilage." The concept of curtilage is vital to the open fields doctrine because the open fields are considered to be all the space that is not contained within the curtilage. There are no well-defined guidelines to assist the law enforcement officer in determining the extent of the curtilage. Each case is decided by the courts on its own particular facts and circumstances. We turn now to a discussion of the facts and circumstances that courts rely on in determining the extent of the curtilage.

Determination of Curtilage

In order to determine whether property to be searched falls within the curtilage of a house (as house is defined under the Fourth Amendment), the law enforcement officer must consider "the factors that determine whether an individual reasonably may expect that an area immediately adjacent to the home will remain private." Oliver v. U. S., ___ U.S. ___, 104 S.Ct. 1735, 1742, 80 L.Ed.2d 214 (1984). As one court said:

> Whether the place to be searched is within the curtilage is to be determined from the facts, including its proximity or annexation to the dwelling, its inclusion within the general enclosure surrounding the dwelling, and its use and enjoyment as an adjunct to the domestic economy of the family. Care v. United States, 231 F.2d 22, 25 (10th Circuit Court of Appeals, 1956).

We will consider a variety of court decisions to clarify the meaning of this quote and to provide more specific guidelines for the law enforcement officer.

Residential Yard Courts differ as to whether the residential yard is within the curtilage. In one case, law enforcement officers investigating a robbery obtained a search warrant to search the defendant's premises. The officers searched the residence and an outbuilding and finally found a shotgun in the front yard, eight to ten feet from the street. The warrant was later held to be invalid. The court held that the front yard was within the curtilage of defendant's house and was subject to the same constitutional protection as the house itself. Since the officers' only justification for being on the premises was an invalid search warrant, the search was illegal. State v. Buchanan, Mo., 432 S.W.2d 342 (Supreme Court of Missouri, 1968).

In another case, however, the court held that entry into a residential yard, even if a trespass, and the observation of that which is open to view is not prohibited by the Fourth Amendment. An officer had received information that the defendant was growing marijuana under a fig tree outside his residence. The officer went to the defendant's residence to investigate. The premises were described by the court as a house that faced the street with a driveway that ran along the east of the house and terminated in a garage at the rear and east of the house. The defendant's residence was attached to the rear of the garage. The fig tree was about twenty feet from the defendant's door. The officer observed marijuana plants growing in a keg near the base of the tree, partially covered by the leaves and limbs of the tree.

In finding the seizure of the plants legal, the court said:

> [T]hey were located a scant 20 feet from defendant's door to which presumably delivery men and others came, and the front house, as well as defendant's house, apparently had access to the yard. Under the circumstances it does not appear that defendant exhibited a subjective expectation of privacy as to the plants. Furthermore, any such expectation would have been unreasonable. People v. Bradley, 1 Cal.3d 80, 85, 81 Cal.Rptr. 457, 459, 460 P.2d 129, 131 (Supreme Court of California, 1969).

The main difference between these two cases appears to be that the defendant's yard in the *Bradley* case was semi-public in nature because residents of the front house, people making deliveries, and others had access to it. Apparently, the defendant's yard in the *Buchanan* case did not allow such access. Judging by the different approaches taken by the courts in these two cases, it would be difficult to definitely say whether the residential yard is or is not to be considered part of the curtilage. The safest procedure for the law enforcement officer is to treat the residential yard of a house as part of the curtilage unless there are clear indications that the person residing in the house had no reasonable expectation of privacy in the yard. More importantly, since there is considerable doubt as to whether the residential yard falls within the curtilage, the officer should obtain a warrant for searches of this area when possible.

Fences   If the area immediately surrounding the house is enclosed by a fence, the area within the fence is usually defined as the curtilage. In a case illustrating this point, law enforcement officers investigating a murder learned that the defendant had been seen target shooting in a field outside his farm some time before the murder. The officers obtained a search warrant (which was later held invalid), went to the farm, and found spent bullets and shell casings outside a fence and about 250 feet from the dwelling house. The bullets and casings were used as evidence in convicting the defendant.

The court held that the search and seizure without a valid warrant was legal because it was conducted in the open fields, outside the curtilage. The court said:

> The evidence discloses that the area around the dwelling and outbuildings habitually used and necessary and convenient for family purposes was enclosed by a substantial fence. When such fence is erected it ordinarily defines the curtilage, particularly in a rural area. Patler v. Commonwealth, 211 Va. 448, 451, 177 S.E.2d 618, 620 (Supreme Court of Appeals of Virginia, 1970).

Nevertheless, if a piece of land is already outside the curtilage, erecting fences around it or taking other steps to protect privacy in the land will not establish that the expectation of privacy in the land is legitimate and bring it within the curtilage. In Oliver v. United States, the defendants, in order to conceal their criminal activities, planted marijuana upon secluded land and erected fences and "No Trespassing" signs around the property. The U.S. Supreme Court said:

> "[I]t may be that because of such precautions, few members of the public stumbled upon the marijuana crops seized by the police. Neither of these suppositions demonstrates, however, that the expectation of privacy was *legitimate* in the sense required by the Fourth Amendment. The test of legitimacy is not whether the individual chooses to conceal asserted 'private' activity. Rather, the correct inquiry is whether the government's intrusion infringes upon the personal and societal values protected by the Fourth Amendment. . . . [W]e find no basis for concluding that a police inspection of open fields accomplishes such an infringement." ___ U.S. at ___, 104 S.Ct. at 1743, 80 L.Ed.2d at 227.

Family Use Another factor that officers should consider in determining the extent of the curtilage is the area's use for family purposes in connection with the dwelling. As one court said, "curtilage has been held to include . . . such place as is necessary and convenient to a dwelling, and is habitually used for family purposes . . . ." United States v. Potts, 297 F.2d 68, 69 (6th Circuit Court of Appeals, 1961).

In the *Patler* case, discussed above under "Fences," the defendant claimed that the field outside the fence was part of the curtilage because it was used for family picnics, was regularly mowed, and the children played there. The court found that the family picnics were infrequent and that one would expect a non-grazing field to be regularly mowed. The evidence was therefore "insufficient to establish the necessity, convenience and habitual use for family purposes which would be required in order to extend the curtilage to include the field." 211 Va. at 451, 177 S.E.2d at 621.

Of course, it is often impossible for an officer to know if, and to what extent, a part of a person's premises are used for family purposes. Nevertheless, the officer can sometimes obtain this information by observation or by asking questions. Again, when there is doubt in the officer's mind whether the place to be searched is in the open fields, the officer should obtain a warrant.

Multiple Occupancy Dwellings   Multiple occupancy dwellings are treated somewhat differently from single occupancy dwellings for purposes of determining the extent of curtilage.   Some courts have held that the shared areas of multiple occupancy buildings such as common corridors, passageways, and yards, are not entitled to the protection of the Fourth Amendment because many people have access to them.   Nevertheless, there are many different types of multiple occupancy dwellings, and courts will look to all the facts and circumstances in determining the curtilage.   In an illustrative case, two law enforcement offices who had information that narcotics were beng sold on the defendant's premises were observing the defendant's behavior at his residence in a four-unit apartment building.   Over a forty-five-minute period, the officers observed several people enter the defendant's apartment, and each time the defendant would go into his back yard and remove a shaving kit from beneath some rubbish under a tree.   One of the officers then went into the back yard and seized the shaving kit while the other officer arrested the defendant.   Chemical analysis revealed that the shaving kit contained heroin.

The government argued that the defendant's back yard was an area common to or shared with other tenants and should not be entitled to the protection usually afforded the curtilage of a purely private residence.   The court held, however, that the back yard was a protected area and that the seizure and search of the shaving kit was illegal:

> The backyard of Fixel's home was not a common passageway normally used by the building's tenants for gaining access to the apartments. . . .   Nor is the backyard an area open as a corridor to salesmen or other businessmen who might approach the tenants in the course of their trade. . . .   This apartment was Fixel's home, he lived there and the backyard of the building was completely removed from the street and surrounded by a chain link fence. . . .   While the enjoyment of his backyard is not as exclusive as the backyard of a purely private residence, this area is not as public or shared as the corridors, yards or other common areas of a large apartment complex or motel.   Contemporary concepts of living such as multi-unit dwellings must not dilute Fixel's right to privacy any more than is absolutely required.   We believe that the backyard area of Fixel's home is sufficiently removed and private in character that he could reasonably expect privacy.   Fixel v. Wainwright, 492 F.2d 480, 484 (Fifth Circuit Court of Appeals, 1974).

Courts have also held that porches and fire escapes outside a person's apartment or unit in a multiple occupancy dwelling fall within the curtilage of the apartment or unit.   As one court reasoned:

> Unlike public halls or stairs which are public areas used in common by tenants and their guests or others lawfully on the property, a fire escape in a non-fireproof building is required outside of each apartment as a secondary means of egress for the occupants of that apartment.   While it is true that in the event of fire others might have occasion to lawfully pass over the fire escape of another, this would be the only time that one might be lawfully on the fire escape of another.   People v. Terrell, 53 Misc. 32, 38–39, 277 N.Y.S.2d 926, 933 (Supreme Court of New York, 1967).

Garages   Garages are usually held to be part of the curtilage, especially if they are near or attached to the dwelling house and used in connection with it.   Therefore, in a case in which a garage and a house were surrounded on three sides by a fence and the garage was close to the house, fifty to seventy-five feet from the street, the garage was held to be within the curtilage. Commonwealth v. Murphy, 353 Mass. 458, 233 N.E.2d 5 (Supreme Judicial Court of Massachusetts, 1968). A garage not used by its owner in connection with his residence, however, was held to be outside the curtilage. People v. Swanberg, 22 A.D.2d 902, 255 N.Y.S.2d 267 (Supreme Court of New York, 1964). Also a garage used in connection with a multi-unit dwelling was held to be outside the curtilage because it was used in common by many tenants of the dwelling. People v. Terry, 70 Cal.2d 410, 77 Cal.Rptr. 460, 454 P.2d 36 (Supreme Court of California, 1969).

Other Outbuildings In determining whether outbuildings are part of the curtilage, the courts consider such factors as distance from the dwelling house, presence or absence of a fence, and family use of the building. A barn was held to be within the curtilage where there was a driveway between the dwelling and the barn, tracks of vehicles and footprints were visible in the snow leading to both house and barn, and there were no separating barriers. Rosencranz v. United States, 356 F.2d 310 (1st Circuit Court of Appeals, 1966). In another case, a barn was held to be within the curtilage even though it was surrounded by a fence and separated from the house by a private driveway. The barn was seventy to eighty yards from the house, and there was a gap in the fence allowing entrance into the barnyard from the private driveway in front of the house. Walker v. United States, 225 F.2d 447 (5th Circuit Court of Appeals, 1955). A whiskey still located 250 yards from the back of a house on open land was held to be in the open fields, however. Atwell v. United States, 414 F.2d 136 (5th Circuit Court of Appeals, 1969). And a concrete outbuilding, which was located only 150 to 180 feet from the nearest residence, was held to be outside the curtilage of the residence, because it was separated by a fence and a gate. Brock v. United States, 256 F.2d 55 (5th Circuit Court of Appeals, 1958).

Very few definite guidelines for the law enforcement officer can be obtained from the cases in this area. It is strongly suggested that if the officer has any doubt whether an outbuilding is within the curtilage, a warrant should be obtained before searching the building.

Unoccupied Tracts An unoccupied, uncultivated, remote tract of land is almost always held to be outside the curtilage and in the open fields. The U.S. Supreme Court stated that "the term 'open fields' may include any unoccupied or undeveloped area outside of the curtilage. An open field need be neither 'open' nor a 'field' as those terms are used in common speech. For example . . . a thickly wooded area nonetheless may be an open field as that term is used in construing the Fourth Amendment." Oliver v. United States, __ U.S. __, __ n. 11, 104 S.Ct. 1735, 1742 n. 11, 80 L.Ed.2d 214, 225 n. 11 (1984). An example is a case in which police investigating a shooting incident obtained admissions from the defendant that he had left two guns in a vacant wooded area that he owned. The area was about one half mile from the scene of the shooting incident and was remote from human habitation. The police searched the area without a warrant and found the guns. The court held that the search was not constitutionally unreasonable because the area was an open field. People v. La Rosa, 25 A.D.2d 587, 267 N.Y.S.2d 235 (Supreme Court of New York, 1966). The Wisconsin Supreme Court held that the Fourth Amendment did not even apply to a local sheriff's warrantless digging in a field about 450 feet from the defendant's house in order to find the body of the defendant's wife, who had disappeared. The court said:

> Under the "open fields" doctrine, the fact that evidence is concealed or hidden is immaterial. The area [the open field] is simply not within the protection of the Fourth Amendment. If the field where the body was found does not have constitutional protection, the fact that the sheriff, rather than observing the evidence that might have been in plain view, dug into the earth to find the body and committed a trespass in so doing does not confer protection. Conrad v. State, 63 Wis.2d 616, 625, 218 N.W.2d 252, 257 (1974).

In a case involving an observation from an airplane of the defendant's open marijuana field surrounded by forests, the court said that the Fourth Amendment guards the privacy of human activity from aerial no less than terrestrial invasion. The court held, however, that one who establishes a three-quarter-acre tract of cultivation surrounded by forests exhibits no reasonable expectation of immunity from overflight. The court said:

> The contraband character of his crop doubtless arouses an internal, uncommunicated need for secrecy; the need is not exhibited, entirely subjective, highly personalized, and not consistent with the common habits of mankind in the use of agricultural and woodland areas. Aside from an uncommunicated need to hide his clandestine activity the occupant exhibits no reasonable expectation of privacy consistent with the common habits of persons engaged in agriculture. The aerial overflights which revealed petitioner's open marijuana field did not violate Fourth Amendment restrictions. Dean v. Superior Court, 35 Cal.App.3d 112, 117–18, 110 Cal.Rptr. 585, 589–90 (Court of Appeal of California, 1972).

A harder question is presented when the unoccupied area searched is not completely vacant but is being used as a building lot. Law enforcement officers had received a complaint that lumber, sacks of cement, and a cart had been stolen. Investigation led the officers to suspect the defendant. They went to the defendant's property, where he was laying the foundation for a house, searched it without a warrant, and found some of the stolen items.

The court held that the area searched came within the category of open fields, even though a house was in the process of construction on it:

> If the lot had been left completely untouched, there could be no doubt that it would fall within the ruling of the *Hester* case. That a large quantity of building material has been brought upon the lot and a foundation for a house dug out, or even completely laid, does not change the nature of the place. Not even the broad policy of protection against "invasion of 'the sanctity of a man's home and the privacies of life'," . . . is infringed by what took place here. Defendant's constitutional rights were not violated. People v. Grundeis, 413 Ill. 145, 152, 108 N.E.2d 483, 487 (Supreme Court of Illinois, 1952).

Reasonable Expectation of Privacy

In determining the legality of the search in many of the cases discussed above, courts have cosidered whether the person owning or inhabiting the premises had a reasonable expectation of privacy in the area searched. In this sense, reasonable expectation of privacy could be considered just another one of the facts and circumstances used to determine the extent of the curtilage. Since the U.S. Supreme Court decision in Katz v. United States, 389 U.S. 347, 88 S.Ct. 507, 19 L.Ed.2d 576 (1967), however, a person's reasonable expectation of privacy has taken on a whole new meaning and importance in the law of search and seizure. In the *Katz* case, a landmark opinion involving electronic eavesdropping, the U.S. Supreme Court stated that "the Fourth Amendment protects people, not places." 389 U.S. at 351, 88 S.Ct. at 511, 19 L.Ed.2d at 582. A later court decision said that *Katz*

> shifts the focus of the Fourth Amendment from "protected areas" to the individual's expectations of privacy. Whether the government's activity is considered a "search" depends upon whether the individual's reasonable expectations of privacy are disturbed. Davis v. United States, 413 F.2d 1226, 1232 (5th Circuit Court of Appeals, 1969).

In Oliver v. United States, a case involving a police seizure of marijuana from a secluded plot of land surrounded by fences and "No Trespassing" signs, the U.S. Supreme Court stated that "an individual may not legitimately demand privacy for activities conducted out of doors in fields, except in the area immediately surrounding the home." ___ U.S. at ___, 104 S.Ct. at 1741, 80 L.Ed.2d at 224. The Court went on to say:

> [O]pen fields do not provide the setting for those intimate activities that the [Fourth] Amendment is intended to shelter from government interference or surveillance. There is no societal interest in protecting the privacy of those activities such as the cultivation of crops, that occur in open fields. Moreover, as a practical matter these lands usually are accessible to the public and the police in ways that a home, an office or commercial structure would not be. It is not generally true that fences or no trespassing signs effectively bar the public from viewing open fields in rural areas. And . . . the public and police lawfully may survey lands from the air. For these reasons, the asserted expectation of privacy in open fields is not an expectation that 'society recognizes as reasonable.' ___ U.S. at ___, 104 S.Ct. at 1741, 80 L.Ed.2d at 224.

Although not all courts have specifically adopted the view that expectation of privacy is the primary factor to be considered in search and seizure cases, the trend is in that direction. The trend is particularly evident, for example, in cases in which the concepts of curtilage and open fields are difficult to apply. An example is a case in which law enforcement officers of the Forest Service were investigating the unauthorized cutting and removal of Christmas trees from Government lands. In connection with the investigation, the officers cut off the top portion of some stumps on the Government lands and attempted to match them with some trees stockpiled behind a motel. The stockpile was located about twenty to thirty-five feet from the motel and about five feet from a parking area used by personnel and patrons of the motel. The defendant operated and lived at the motel. The officers made several matches of stump cuts with trees, and the defendant was convicted of stealing the trees.

On appeal, the court held that the search and seizure was illegal because the officers had no warrant and the stockpile of trees was located within the curtilage of defendant's abode. The court applied the traditional tests for curtilage based upon proximity to the dwelling and inclusion within the general enclosure surrounding the dwelling.

The court went on, however, to further discuss the concepts of curtilage and privacy. Because the court's language indicates a growing trend in the law, it is quoted at length here:

> We wish to add, however, that it seems to us a more appropriate test in determining if a search and seizure adjacent to a house is constitutionally forbidden is whether it constitutes an intrusion upon what the resident seeks to preserve as private even in an area which, although adjacent to his home, is accessible to the public. . . .
>
> The "curtilage" test is predicated upon a common law concept which has no historical relevancy to the Fourth Amendment guaranty. In Jones v. U.S., 362 U.S. 257, 266, 80 S.Ct. 725, 733, 4 L.Ed.2d 697, the Supreme Court warned, in connection with another search and seizure problem that:
>
>> "[I]t is unnecessary and ill-advised to import into the law surrounding the constitutional right to be free from unreasonable searches and seizures subtle distinctions, developed and refined by the common law in evolving the body of private property law . . . . ."
>
> If the determination of such questions is made to turn upon the degree of privacy a resident is seeking to preserve as shown by the facts of the particular case, rather than upon a resort to the ancient concept of curtilage, attention will be more effectively focused on the basic interest which the Fourth Amendment was designed to protect. As the Supreme Court recently said in Camara v. Municipal Court of City and County of San Francisco, 387 U.S. 523, 528, 87 S.Ct. 1727, 1730, 18 L.Ed.2d 930:
>
>> "The basic purpose of this Amendment, as recognized in countless decisions of this Court, is to safeguard the privacy and security of individuals against arbitrary invasions by governmental officials."
>
> Wattenburg v. U.S., 388 F.2d 853, 857–58 (9th Circuit Court of Appeals, 1968).

The court also found the search and seizure of the Christmas trees illegal under the "reasonable expectation of privacy" test.

The "reasonable expectation of privacy" test may be difficult for law enforcement officers to apply because it involves determining a person's state of mind. It is suggested that in order to determine whether a place may be legally searched without a warrant, law enforcement officers apply the traditional tests for determining the extent of the curtilage discussed above. In addition, however, officers should put themselves in the position of a person owning property, and ask themselves if they would reasonably expect to be free from governmental intrusion in the particular area of the property to be searched. If officers have any doubt whether or not a person is seeking to preserve privacy in the area to be searched, they should obtain a warrant.

Open Fields, Plain View, and Observations into Constitutionally Protected Areas

The open fields and plain view doctrines are often confused by law enforcement officers. The plain view doctrine states that if a law enforcement officer, as the result of a prior valid intrusion into a constitutionally protected area, is in a position in which he or she has a legal right to be, items of evidence lying open to view may be seized (see Chapter 9). The open fields doctrine differs from the plain view doctrine in that, under the open fields doctrine, a law enforcement officer need not be concerned with the validity of the prior intrusion into a constitutionally protected area. In the open fields, therefore, the officer may not only seize items that are open to view, but may search for items hidden from view and seize them. Furthermore, the officer, from a vantage point in the open fields, may make observations into constitutionally protected areas to detect criminal activity or criminal evidence. Such observations may be used as a basis for probable cause to make an arrest or to obtain a search warrant. An example is a case in which law enforcement officers obtained a search warrant on the basis of observations of illicit whiskey containers from a vantage point in the open fields. The court in that case said:

> [I]t is of no significance that the object of the agents' observations was within the curtilage, so long as the observations were made from without the curtilage. The protection of the Fourth Amendment extends only to the curtilage, and observations made from without the curtilage thus do not violate the Amendment whether made from an open field belonging to the defendant or from the public street. United States v. Sims, 202 F.Supp. 65, 67 (U.S. District Court, Eastern District of Tennessee, 1962).

In this type of situation, however, the officer may *not enter* into the constitutionally protected area to make a warrantless seizure of the items observed, or to conduct a warrantless search for other items, unless the situation falls within the *Carroll* doctrine (see Chapter 10).

In recent cases involving observations into constitutionally protected areas, courts have begun emphasizing the reasonable expectation of privacy of the person whose premises or activities are being observed by law enforcement officers. An example is a case in which a narcotics officer was investigating a tip about heroin dealing. He went to the place where the dealing was said to be taking place. It was a single family dwelling, seventy feet from the sidewalk, with access from the west. There were no doorways or defined pathways on the east side of the house, and a strip of land covered with grass and dirt separated the east side of the house from the driveway of the apartment next door. The officer went to the east side of the house, peeked through a two-inch gap under the partially drawn shade of a closed window, and observed indications of criminal activity.

The court held that the officer's observations constituted an illegal search. The court initially analyzed the problem in terms of whether the officer was standing upon a part of the property surrounding the house that had been opened, expressly or impliedly, to public use. Under the facts, the officer was found to have made his observations from a position in which he had no right to be. Since neither a warrant nor one of the established exceptions to the warrant requirement justified the intrusion, it was unlawful.

The court went on, however, to discuss the officer's actions at length, in terms of the defendant's reasonable expectation of privacy:

> [T]he generic *Katz* rule permits the resident of a house to rely justifiably upon the privacy of the surrounding areas as a protection from the peering of the officer unless such residence is "exposed" to that intrusion by the existence of public pathways or other invitations to the public to enter upon the property. This justifiable reliance on the privacy of the property surrounding one's residence thus leads to the *particular* rule that searches conducted without a warrant from such parts of the property *always* are unconstitutional unless an exception to the warrant requirement applies. . . .
>
> Pursuant to the principles of *Katz,* therefore, we do not rest our analysis exclusively upon such abstractions as "trespass" or "constitutionally protected areas" or upon the physical differences between a telephone booth and the land surrounding a residence; we do, however, look to the conduct of people in regard to these elements. Taking into account the nature of the area surrounding a private residence, we ask whether that area has been opened to public use; if so, the occupant cannot claim he expected privacy from all observations of the officer who stands upon that ground; if not, the occupant does deserve that privacy. Since the eavesdropping officer in the case before us stood upon private property and since such property exhibited no invitation to public use, we find that the officer violated petitioner Lorenzana's expectations of privacy, and hence, his constitutional rights. Lorenzana v. Superior Court of Los Angeles County, 9 Cal.3d 626, 638, 108 Cal. Rptr. 585, 594, 511 P.2d 33, 42 (Supreme Court of California, 1973).

It is difficult to formulate rules to guide law enforcement officers in determining when they are violating a person's reasonable expectation of privacy. Common sense will often aid the officer in making that determination. Nevertheless, broad principles can be stated to help the officer balance the need to investigate crime with the need to respect the reasonable expectation of privacy of all persons.

In general, if an officer gathers information while situated in a public place or in a place where an ordinary citizen with legitimate business might be expected to be, the officer will not be invading anyone's reasonable expectation of privacy. Therefore, an officer's observations from an ordinary means of access to a dwelling, such as a front porch or side door, will not ordinarily violate a person's reasonable expectation of privacy. People v. Willard, 238 Cal.App.2d 292, 47 Cal.Rptr. 734 (California District Court of Appeal, First District, 1966).

Once officers are in a place in which they have a legitimate right to be, they may look around and peer through windows or other openings. The Supreme Court of California stated:

> Peering through a window or a crack in the door or a keyhole is not, in the abstract, genteel behavior, but the Fourth Amendment does not protect against all conduct unworthy of a good neighbor. . . . [I]t is the duty of a policeman to investigate, and *we cannot say that . . . the Fourth Amendment itself draws the blinds the occupant could have drawn and did not.* People v. Berutko, 71 Cal.2d 84, 93, 77 Cal.Rptr. 217, 222, 453 P.2d 721, 726 (Supreme Court of California, 1969).

Also, so long as officers are where they have a right to be, they may listen at doors or gather evidence with their other senses.   In United States v. Perry, 339 F.Supp. 209 (U.S. District Court, Southern District of California, 1972), the court said:

> The general rule is that information obtained by an officer using his natural senses, where the officer has a right to be where he is, is admissible evidence.   The fact that the information is in the form of conversations emanating from a private space, such as a hotel room, is not a bar to its admissibility.   339 F.Supp. at 213.

A great number of cases illustrating these basic principles have been decided throughout the country.   It would serve no purpose to present further examples of these cases because courts in every jurisdiction differ in their interpretations of the meaning of "reasonable expectation of privacy."   Officers investigating crime should become very sensitive to the reasonable expectations of privacy of all persons. When in doubt about the legality of any kind of intrusion, officers should obtain a search warrant.

ABANDONED PROPERTY

As stated earlier, the meaning of the term abandoned property depends upon the interpretation given to the word "searches" in the Fourth Amendment.   Courts have held that no search occurs when a law enforcement officer observes property voluntarily discarded by a person.   And it is not an illegal seizure to pick up such property and use it as evidence against the person in court.   The Fourth Amendment's protection does not extend to such property because a person who abandons property brings any right to privacy in it to an end.   A person cannot complain about the seizure of property no longer in that person's possession or about the property's use as evidence in court.

Abandoned property is treated by the courts similarly to seizable property found lying in plain view.   Since no search under the Fourth Amendment is involved, officers may lawfully seize the property without a warrant or probable cause.   The main difference between the abandonment doctrine and the plain view doctrine turns on the nature of the place from which the officer seizes an object.   Under the plain view doctrine, if a law enforcement officer, as the result of a prior *valid* intrusion into a constitutionally protected area, is in a position in which he or she has a legal right to be, items of evidence lying open to view may be seized.   The plain view doctrine is only applicable *after* the law enforcement officer has lawfully entered into a *constitutionally protected area*.   If a law enforcement officer, acting lawfully, seizes objects that have been discarded on the street, in a public park, or in some other place *not* protected by the Fourth Amendment to the Constitution, the seizure is legal under the abandonment doctrine.   The abandonment doctrine, unlike the plain view doctrine, involves *no intrusion into a constitutionally protected area*.   It is important for the law enforcement officer to learn this distinction because in order to lawfully seize items that have been discarded within a constitutionally protected area, the officer must be lawfully present in the constitutionally protected area.   Otherwise, the plain view doctrine is not satisfied, and any item of evidence seized will be inadmissible in court.

When law enforcement officers attempt to justify a seizure of property on the ground that it was abandoned, they must be prepared to prove it. Abandonment is never presumed by the courts but must be established by the prosecution. It is very important, therefore, for law enforcement officers to carefully note all the circumstances surrounding the seizure of property on the basis of abandonment. Officers may have to justify the seizure later at a trial or hearing.

In order to properly testify, the officer needs to know what factors the courts consider important in determining whether property has been abandoned. The remainder of this chapter will be devoted to a discussion of specific facts and circumstances bearing upon the issue of abandonment, as illustrated by decisions of courts throughout the country.

Factors Determining Abandonment

The factors that the courts consider in determining whether property has been abandoned can be classified into four broad categories:

1. Nature of the place in which the property was left;

2. Indications of intent to abandon property;

3. Lawfulness of police behavior; and

4. Reasonable expectation of privacy in the property.

Most cases dealing with the issue of abandonment will involve circumstances falling into more than one of the four categories. For example, the nature of the place in which an object is left is usually a strong indication of a person's intent to abandon the property and also of the person's expectation of privacy in it. Nevertheless, there are usually one or two circumstances in each case that provide the primary basis for a court's decision on the issue of abandonment. These are the circumstances that will be emphasized in the cases discussed under each category.

Nature of Place in Which Property Left   The nature of the place in which property is left is an important determinant of whether or not the property has been abandoned. In *Hester v. United States*, summarized above, the U.S. Supreme Court held that it was proper for law enforcement officers to retrieve property discarded by the defendant in an open field. The Court said that the protection of the Fourth Amendment did not extend to the open fields. Although it is not clear whether the primary basis for the Court's decision in *Hester* was abandonment or the "open fields" doctrine, it is clear that the place of discard had a bearing on the Court's determination of abandonment. The Court specifically noted that the evidence was not obtained by entry into the house.

It follows logically that if an object discarded in the open fields of a person's private property is considered abandoned, an object discarded in a public place will also be considered abandoned. An example is a case in which law enforcement officers had the defendant under surveillance for violation of federal narcotic laws. As the defendant disembarked from an airplane at a public airport, he apparently recognized one of the officers, and he discarded contraband narcotics. The officers retrieved the narcotics and immediately arrested the defendant. The court held that the discarded narcotics were admissible in court. There had been no illegal search because the narcotics were abandoned. Vincent v. United States, 337 F.2d 891 (8th Circuit Court of Appeals, 1964).

In another case, the defendant threw a package of heroin into the courtyard of a six-story apartment building. The defendant's only rights in the courtyard were to use it in common with other tenants and with members of the public who had business there. The court held that the warrantless seizure of the abandoned package from the courtyard was legal. United States v. Lewis, 227 F.Supp. 433 (U.S. District Court, Southern District of New York, 1964).

When, however, an object is discarded in response to illegal police activity, and falls within the curtilage of a person's home or business, a warrantless seizure of the object will be illegal. In an illustrative case, officers went to a woman's residence to arrest her without a warrant for a narcotics violation. Her husband, the defendant, came to the door but retreated without opening it. The defendant's wife then came to the door, clad only in a slip, and asked the officer to wait until she dressed. Meanwhile, the defendant ran upstairs and threw a package out of the window into an enclosed back yard. The officers then broke into the house, allegedly to arrest the defendant's wife, and without knowing the contents of the thrown package. The package was seized by another officer stationed outside and was found to contain heroin. The court held that the seizure of the package was illegal, stating that the enclosed back yard in which the thrown package landed was part of the curtilage of the defendant's home and was entitled to the same protection as the home itself. It should be noted that a major reason for the court's holding the seizure illegal was the court's finding that the officers entered the residence illegally. If the police had entered legally, the seizure of the package would probably have been upheld under the plain view doctrine. Hobson v. United States, 226 F.2d 890 (8th Circuit Court of Appeals, 1955).

Therefore, if an object is voluntarily discarded outside the curtilage of a house, it will be considered abandoned; if discarded inside the curtilage, the legality of its seizure will be governed by the plain view doctrine.

Under certain circumstances, however, a law enforcement officer may search for and seize objects inside a house, without a warrant or probable cause and without satisfying any of the exceptions to the warrant requirement. When a person has abandoned or vacated premises, officers may search for and seize items of evidence or any other items left on the premises. The leading case on this point is the U.S. Supreme Court case of Abel v. United States, 362 U.S. 217, 80 S.Ct. 683, 4 L.Ed.2d 668 (1960). In the *Abel* case, officers of the Immigration and Naturalization Service arrested the defendant in his hotel room, under an administrative arrest warrant, and charged him with being illegally in this country. Before he was escorted out of his room, the defendant was permitted to pack his personal belongings. He packed nearly everything in the room except for a few things that he left on a window sill and put in a wastebasket. He then checked out of the hotel, turned in his keys, and paid his bill. Shortly thereafter, an FBI agent, with the permission of the hotel management, searched the defendant's room without a warrant. In the wastebasket, the FBI agent found a hollow pencil containing microfilm and a block of wood containing a "cipher pad."

The Court held that the search for and seizure of the pencil and block of wood was legal:

> These two items were found by an agent of the F.B.I. in the course of a search he undertook of petitioner's hotel room, immediately after petitioner had paid his bill and vacated the room. They were found in the room's wastepaper basket, where petitioner had put them while packing his belongings and preparing to leave. No pretense is made that this search by the F.B.I. was for any purpose other than to gather evidence of crime, that is, evidence of petitioner's espionage. As such, however, it was entirely lawful, although undertaken without a warrant. This is so for the reason that at the time of the search petitioner had vacated the room. The hotel then had the exclusive right to its possession, and the hotel management freely gave its consent that the search be made. Nor was it unlawful to seize the entire contents of the wastepaper basket, even though some of its contents had no connection with crime. So far as the record shows, petitioner had abandoned these articles. He had thrown them away. So far as he was concerned, they were bona vacantia. There can be nothing unlawful in the Government's appropriation of such abandoned property. . . .   The two items which were eventually introduced in evidence were assertedly means for the commission of espionage, and were themselves seizable as such. These two items having been lawfully seized by the Government in connection with an investigation of crime, we encounter no basis for discussing further their admissibility as evidence. 362 U.S. at 241, 80 S.Ct. at 698, 4 L.Ed.2d at 687–88.

It is important to note that if the defendant in the *Abel* case had not vacated his room, the hotel management could not have given consent to search the room. (See Chapter 8 on "Consent Searches.") The key question, then, for the law enforcement officer who wants to search a house without a warrant, probable cause, or other justification, is whether the person residing there intended to abandon it. Various indications of intent to abandon, relied upon by the courts, are discussed in the next section.

Indications of Intent to Abandon Property   One of the main circumstances relied upon by courts in determining whether property has been abandoned is the *intent* of the person vacating or discarding property to relinquish all title, possession, or claim to it. Sometimes intent to abandon is fairly easy to establish, as when a person voluntarily throws an object away, without any inducement by the police. There are many situations, however, in which a person's intent to abandon property is not so easily established. In these situations, the law enforcement officer must carefully note all indications of intent to abandon in case the search or seizure is later challenged at a trial or suppression hearing. The following discussion will highlight the various indications of intent relied upon by the courts in determining abandonment. The discussion will be divided into three parts—premises, objects, and motor vehicles—because intent to abandon is determined in different ways for each kind of property.

Premises   In *Abel v. United States,* summarized above, the Court found that a hotel room had been abandoned when the person moved his personal belongings out of the room, paid his bill, checked out, and turned in his key. In another case involving a hotel room, a court found that the defendant had abandoned a room that he had rented on March 23, when he failed to pay his bill on March 28, and did not return to or communicate with the hotel prior to his arrest on April 8. At the time he rented the room, the defendant said he intended to stay only one night. A search of the defendant's baggage left in the room was therefore held not to violate his property rights. United States v. Cowan, 396 F.2d 83 (2nd Circuit Court of Appeals, 1968).

In a case involving abandonment of an *apartment*, law enforcement officers were allowed to search defendant's apartment without a warrant, even though the defendant had three days to go on his lease period. The court said:

> What were the circumstances showing abandonment? Baggett quit his job, received pay for one day's work, told several people that he was going to New Orleans to get a job, paid all bills that he owed except one, told his friends in Little Rock good-bye on the 11th, turned the apartment keys over to the owner, and took all personal belongings to New Orleans with him. Of course, had he returned within the two days before his rent came due, he could not have gone into his apartment for Ballard [the landlord] had the keys. The fact that the rent was paid up for three days after Baggett left does not mean that the apartment had not been abandoned. Baggett v. State, 254 Ark. 553, 554, 494 S.W.2d 717, 719 (Supreme Court of Arkansas, 1973).

The following quote from a case involving a warrantless search of a house illustrates other indications of intent to abandon:

> [I]t was clearly established that even though the Mannings had rented the . . . house for thirty days, they departed after the first day leaving no personal belongings. The door was unlocked, food was on the table, and dishwater was in the sink. Thirty days later the same condition prevailed. Moreover, the decayed food created a stench, the grass was uncut, and the weeds had grown high.
>   These circumstances strongly indicate that the Mannings had abandoned the house . . . . United States v. Manning, 440 F.2d 1105, 1111 (5th Circuit Court of Appeals, 1971).

As mentioned earlier, the non-public areas of a business office come within the Fourth Amendment's protection against unreasonable searches and seizures. If the office is abandoned by its occupant, however, it no longer has this protection. The indications of intent to abandon an office are similar to those for a room or house. An example is a case in which U.S. postal inspectors, without a warrant, searched for and seized business records from an office that had previously been rented by the defendant. The defendant claimed that the search and seizure was illegal because he did not intend to abandon the office and the records kept there. The court found that the facts indicated an intent to abandon. The search and seizure were made on June 12, 1972. Defendant had rented the office from May 1, 1971 through October 31, 1971, but had left the state in August 1971. No rent had been paid for the office beginning November 1, 1971, nor did defendant, his wife, or any business associate or employee visit the office after November 1, 1971. Finally, the office had been padlocked by the U.S. District Attorney during February 1972. Mullins v. United States, 487 F.2d 581 (8th Circuit Court of Appeals, 1973).

The mere absence of a person from premises does not make the premises abandoned, unless the person had an *intent* to abandon the premises. Therefore, in a case in which the defendant's absence from his apartment was involuntary because of his arrest and incarceration, the court held that the prosecution should bear an especially heavy burden of showing that he intended to abandon it. The prosecution did not satisfy this burden by merely showing defendant's absence without showing any other indications of intent to abandon. United States v. Robinson, 430 F.2d 1141 (6th Circuit Court of Appeals, 1970).

Objects   Some of the indications of intent to abandon premises are also applicable to objects. Objects, however, can be moved from place to place, and many can be carried on the person. Therefore, courts consider different factors in determining intent to abandon objects.

A strong indication of a person's intent to abandon property is leaving the property unattended and unclaimed for a long period of time. An example is a case in which two men left a U-Haul trailer at a service station, asking permission to leave it there for two or three days. The men stated that "everything we own is in the trailer." Ten days later, the men not having returned, the service station attendant called law enforcement authorities. The trailer was searched without a warrant and stolen whiskey was found. The court held that the search was legal because the property had been abandoned. United States v. Gulledge, 469 F.2d 713 (5th Circuit Court of Appeals, 1972).

In other cases involving warrantless searches and seizures of objects, the object is often picked up by a law enforcement officer immediately after it is dropped, thrown away, or otherwise discarded by a person. In these cases, courts cannot rely on the length of time the object has been left alone to determine whether it has been abandoned. Courts must look to other circumstances such as the conduct of the defendant and the manner of disposal of the object. In an illustrative case, a police officer approached the defendant without probable cause to make an arrest, and the defendant dropped a tin box to the ground. The officer immediately picked up the box, opened it, and found heroin. The court held that the evidence was insufficient to constitute an abandonment:

> There is no proof that the defendant threw it away or attempted to dispose of it in any manner which might have manifested the requisite intention to abandon. Moreover, the police officer's testimony reveals that he picked up the box so soon after it had been dropped that it is impossible to determine whether or not the defendant, if given the opportunity, would have picked up the box himself. Absent any such proof, the seizure of the tin box under the circumstances of this case cannot be sustained. People v. Anderson, 24 N.Y.2d 12, 14, 298 N.Y.S.2d 698, 699, 246 N.E.2d 508, 509 (Court of Appeals of New York, 1969).

However, when the manner of disposal indicates that the defendant intended to permanently relinquish possession of the property because of consciousness of guilt or fear of potential apprehension, the courts usually find abandonment. One example is a case in which the defendant threw packages out of an automobile he was driving when he noticed he was being pursued by a car with flashing lights and a siren. Law enforcement officers were lawfully chasing the defendant's auto because they had seen it pick up a man whom the officers had probable cause to arrest. The packages were recovered and were found to be stolen goods. The court held the seizure legal and allowed the introduction of the packages in evidence against the defendant. Stack v. United States, 368 F.2d 788 (1st Circuit Court of Appeals, 1966). It should be noted that there was no illegal activity on the part of law enforcement officers in this case.

When there is evidence that an object was intentionally concealed, courts will usually find there was no intent to abandon the object and therefore no abandonment. In an illustrative case, officers seized a bottle in a barrel located in a garage underneath the defendant's residence. The prosecution claimed the bottle had been abandoned. The court disagreed saying that "[t]he position of the bottle well down in the barrel and covered with trash and paper strongly suggests that it was intentionally hidden and concealed there." State v. Chapman, 250 A.2d 203, 212 (Supreme Judicial Court of Maine, 1969).

Sometimes courts find an intent to abandon property when the defendant fails to object or take any other affirmative action, but merely allows evidence to be seized in the ordinary course of events. The defendant was in jail, having been arrested for bank robbery. He was given a haircut pursuant to routine jail procedures, and the hair clippings were turned over to the FBI, at their request, and used as evidence. In response to defendant's claim of an illegal search and seizure, the court said:

> At no time has defendant objected to the legality of the prison procedures under which he received his haircut. He has never claimed that the haircut was illegally or improperly given. The thrust of his contention is rather that a warrant should have been obtained before the shorn locks were appropriated by the state officer for analysis. Cox, however, never indicated any desire or intention to retain possession of the hair after it had been scissored from his head. Clippings such as those preserved in the instant case are ordinarily abandoned after being cut. Cox in fact left his hair and has never claimed otherwise. The deputy sheriff was not obliged to inform him that, if abandoned, his hair would be taken and analyzed. Having voluntarily abandoned his property, in this case his hair, Cox may not object to its appropriation by the government. United States v. Cox, 428 F.2d 683, 687–88 (Seventh Circuit Court of Appeals, 1970).

Before seizing a discarded object without a warrant, law enforcement officers should attempt to determine whether the discarding person intended to abandon the property. Courts usually find an intent to abandon when an object has been left unattended and unclaimed for an unreasonable length of time, or when the object was discarded out of consciousness of guilt or fear of apprehension. However, when the facts indicate that the person accidentally dropped or intentionally concealed an object, courts will usually not find an intent to abandon. No particular affirmative action by a person is required to indicate an intent to abandon, and such an intent may be found when a person merely fails to object to the seizure of property in the ordinary course of events.

Motor Vehicles Motor vehicles are unique for purposes of abandonment in that they are treated both as premises and as objects. In a case in which the defendant, who was tampering with a cigarette machine, left his car in the street and fled on foot to avoid apprehension by an officer, the court said:

> Sometimes an automobile takes on the characteristics of a man's castle. Other times an automobile takes on the characteristic of an overcoat—that is, it is movable and can be discarded by the possessor at will. If appellant in his endeavors to avoid the clutches of the law had discarded his overcoat to make his flight more speedy, no one would think that an officer was unreasonably invading his privacy or security in picking up the overcoat and searching it thoroughly. In that situation most people would agree that the fleeing suspect had abandoned his coat as a matter of expediency as well as any rights relative to its search and seizure. What difference can there be when a fleeing burglar abandons his automobile to escape the clutches of the law? We can see no distinction and consequently hold that when property is abandoned officers in making a search thereof do not violate any rights or security of a citizen guaranteed under the Fourth Amendment. Thom v. State, 248 Ark. 180, 182, 450 S.W.2d 550, 552 (Supreme Court of Arkansas, 1970).

If an officer has probable cause to search a motor vehicle, he may also be able to justify a search of the vehicle under the *Carroll* doctrine (see Chapter 10).

Lawfulness of Police Behavior In many of the cases discussed above, property was left or discarded in response to either the presence or the activities of law enforcement officers. In determining whether such property is abandoned, courts examine very closely the lawfulness of the law enforcement officer's role in each incident. If a person discards evidence as a direct result of the unlawful presence or activity of a law enforcement officer, the courts will not consider the act a voluntary abandonment, but rather a forced response to the unlawful police behavior.

There are numerous examples of cases in which a person discarded an object in response to the lawful activities of the police, and courts have considered the object abandoned, and therefore seizable without a warrant or other justification. Examples include the following situations:

1. Officers arrested the defendant on authority of a warrant and, while escorting him to the police car, defendant threw away a marijuana cigarette. Oliver v. State, 85 Nev. 10, 449 P.2d 252 (Supreme Court of Nevada, 1969).

2. An officer with probable cause to arrest the defendant was pursuing the defendant's car and contraband was thrown from the car. Capitoli v. Wainwright, 426 F.2d 868 (5th Circuit Court of Appeals, 1970).

3. Officers were lawfully approaching the defendant for questioning, and defendant dropped a bundle of marijuana cigarettes. People v. Blackmon, 276 Cal.App.2d 346, 80 Cal.Rptr. 862 (Court of Appeal of California, 1969).

4. Officers, attempting to execute a valid search warrant, temporarily detained the defendant at the scene of the search, and the defendant discarded a package containing incriminating evidence. State v. Romeo, 45 N.J. 188, 203 A.2d 23 (Supreme Court of New Jersey, 1964).

Examples should also be given of cases in which unlawful police activity caused the court to rule that a discarded object was not voluntarily abandoned. In a case involving an arrest and search, a law enforcement officer received an anonymous phone call informing him that the defendant could be apprehended at a given place and time with narcotics in his possession. Officers went to the designated place and observed the defendant in his car. The officers told him he was under arrest and to get out of his car and place his hands on top of it. As the defendant did this, he flipped into the street a plastic vial containing narcotics, which the officers retrieved.

The court held that the arrest was unlawful for lack of probable cause. The court also refused to find that the plastic vial was abandoned, because it was thrown away as a result of a *threat* of an illegal search:

> Had the appellant here thrown the item away before the search had been threatened the argument of abandonment might well be persuasive. Here however he threw the vial away only after being told to turn and place his hands atop his vehicle, the position commonly known to be employed by police in searching a suspect for weapons. The vial, as evidenced by the record, was not seen by the officers until it was thrown by appellant. Had it been seen before the threat of an illegal search had been made, even in appellant's hand, the plain view doctrine *may* have applied. But that is not this case. The vial was seen and secured only as a result of the threat of a search, an illegal search. Clearly it was the fruit of illegal activity by the police and ought to have been excluded. Bowles v. State, 256 Ind. 27, 31–32, 267 N.E.2d 56, 59 (Supreme Court of Indiana, 1971).

In another case, an officer was investigating a window smashing incident at a hotel. He spotted, at another hotel, a car believed to have been involved in the incident, and he went to the room occupied by its owner in order to interview the owner. The officer had neither a warrant nor probable cause to arrest, and he did not intend to make an arrest. After knocking twice and receiving no response, the officer kicked in the door only to find that the defendants had escaped through a window. They were apprehended shortly thereafter. Stolen jewelry was found beneath the window where it had been thrown when the officer began kicking down the door.

The court held that there was no voluntary abandonment of the jewelry:

> [S]ince the initial entry was improper and the items were thrown out of the window as a direct result of that illegality, the police were not entitled to the fruits and the admission of the jewelry in evidence was reversible error. Fletcher v. Wainwright, 399 F.2d 62, 64–65 (5th Circuit Court of Appeals, 1968).

In a third case involving illegal police activity, the defendant was walking down the street when he observed police officers in an unmarked car. He quickened his pace, and one of the officers got out of the car and began to pursue him. The defendant then began to run, and the officer, while giving chase, observed him throw a cigarette pack under a parked automobile. The defendant was apprehended, and the cigarette pack was recovered and found to contain heroin.

The court held that the officers had no justification to arrest the defendant or to stop him under the *Terry* rule (discussed in Chapter 12). The only conduct of the defendant observed by the police was his quickening pace when he observed the officers. This alone could not provide probable cause to arrest nor would it justify a stop of the defendant because it was not sufficient to give rise to a reasonable belief that criminal activity was afoot. Since the discarding of the cigarette pack was a direct result of the unlawful and coercive action of the police in chasing the defendant, the court held there was no voluntary abandonment. Commonwealth v. Jeffries, 454 Pa. 320, 311 A.2d 914 (Supreme Court of Pennsylvania, 1973).

Reasonable Expectation of Privacy   As we have seen in the discussion of the open fields doctrine, since the U.S. Supreme Court decision in *Katz v. U.S.,* the courts increasingly have analyzed the legality of warrantless searches and seizures in terms of their intrusion upon the defendant's reasonable expectation of privacy. This trend has extended also to cases involving vacated or discarded property. The Minnesota Supreme Court explained:

> In the law of property, the question .   .   . is whether the owner has voluntarily, intentionally, and unconditionally relinquished his interest in the property so that another, having acquired possession, may successfully assert his superior interest. In the law of search and seizure, however, the question is whether the defendant has, in discarding the property, relinquished his reasonable expectation of privacy so that its seizure and search is reasonable within the limits of the Fourth Amendment. In essence, what is abandoned is not necessarily the defendant's property, but his reasonable expectation of privacy therein. City of St. Paul v. Vaughn, 306 Minn. 337, 346, 237 N.W.2d 365, 370–71 (Minnesota Supreme Court, 1975).

In a case involving supposedly vacated premises, law enforcement officers were investigating a possible arson in a building gutted by fire. The fire occurred on April 14, 1968, and the officers entered the building, made observations, and took photographs on April 24, 1968. Evidence showed that the house had been boarded up on April 14. Thereafter the owner went to the house every day, and both she and the defendant kept some of their personal effects in the house. The defendant claimed that the observations and photographs of the officers were a product of an illegal search and seizure.

The court said:

> The uncontradicted evidence before the court was that the building was not abandoned. On April 24, 1968, it still contained personal effects and had been boarded up to keep the public out.
>   The test to be used in determining whether a place is a constitutionally protected area within the meaning of the Fourth Amendment is .   .   . "whether the person has exhibited a reasonable expectation of privacy, and, if so, whether that expectation has been violated by unreasonable governmental intrusion." In the instant matter the owner of the dwelling house clearly demonstrated her expectation of privacy as to the interior of the house and its contents by boarding up the doorways, which were damaged by fire. That expectation was violated by the intrusion of the police on April 24, 1968. Swan v. Superior Court, County of Los Angeles, 8 Cal.App.3d 392, 396, 87 Cal.Rptr. 280, 282 (California Court of Appeal, 1970).

The question of the extent of a person's reasonable expectation of privacy in discarded *objects* has been the subject of differing opinions by the courts. The controversy has centered around the search and seizure of trash or garbage by law enforcement officers. In one of the leading cases in this area, law enforcement officers, acting without a warrant, found marijuana in a trash can in the open back yard area of the defendant's residence.   The court held that the marijuana in the trash can was not abandoned for the following reasons:

> As we have seen, the trash can was within a few feet of the back door of defendants' home and required trespass for its inspection.   It was an adjunct to the domestic economy. . . .   Placing the marijuana in the trash can, so situated and used, was not an abandonment unless as to persons authorized to remove the receptacle's contents, such as trashmen. . . .   The marijuana itself was not visible without "rummaging" in the receptable.   So far as appears defendants alone resided at the house.   In the light of the combined facts and circumstances it appears that defendants exhibited an expectation of privacy, and we believe that expectation was reasonable under the circumstances of the case.   We can readily ascribe many reasons why residents would not want their castaway clothing, letters, medicine bottles or other telltale refuse and trash to be examined by neighbors or others, at least not until the trash has lost its identity and meaning by becoming part of a large conglomeration of trash elsewhere.   Half truths leading to rumor and gossip may readily flow from an attempt to "read" the contents of another's trash.   People v. Edwards, 71 Cal.2d 1096, 1104, 80 Cal.Rptr. 633, 638, 458 P.2d 713, 718 (Supreme Court of California, 1969).

Other courts have generally agreed with the holding in the *Edwards* case, and found a violation of the defendant's reasonable expectation of privacy where the trash can was located within the curtilage of the defendant's house.   Ball v. State, 57 Wis. 653, 205 N.W.2d 353 (Supreme Court of Wisconsin, 1973).

Where the trash can is placed adjacent to the street for collection, however, courts have differed greatly as to whether a person has a reasonable expectation of privacy in the trash.   One court, relying on the *Edwards* case, said that placement of trash on the sidewalk for collection is not necessarily an abandonment of it to the police or the general public.   Among the court's reasons for not considering contraband found in the barrels abandoned was that the contraband was concealed in paper sacks within the barrels and it was not visible without emptying or searching through the barrels.   Also, the court said that many municipal ordinances prohibit unauthorized persons from tampering with trash containers, refuting the view that the contents of one's trash barrels become public property when placed on the sidewalk for collection.   People v. Krivda, 5 Cal.3d 357, 96 Cal.Rptr. 62, 486 P.2d 1262 (Supreme Court of California, 1971).

Another court took the opposite view and, in a similar fact situation, held that the defendant abandoned the property.   "The town ordinance simply cannot change the fact that he 'threw [these articles] away' and thus there 'can be nothing unlawful in the Government's appropriation of such abandoned property.' "   United States v. Dzialak, 441 F.2d 212, 215 (2d Circuit Court of Appeals, 1971).

It is difficult to set forth any definite guidelines for the law enforcement officer with regard to the determination of a person's reasonable expectation of privacy in discarded or vacated property.   Before officers conduct a warrantless search and seizure of the property, they should look for any indications that a person expects privacy in the property, and determine as best they can whether that expectation is reasonable.   It is strongly recommended that officers obtain a search warrant before searching for and seizing objects in trash cans that are located within the curtilage of a house.   The same advice applies to trash cans located outside the curtilage or that have been set out for collection, unless there is an emergency, or there are clear indications that the trash has been completely abandoned.

SUMMARY

A law enforcement officer may search for and seize items of evidence lying in the open fields without probable cause, search warrant, or other legal justification without violating a person's Fourth Amendment rights. An officer may also legally make observations from a vantage point in the open fields into constitutionally protected areas, in order to detect criminal activity or evidence. The open fields are the area lying outside the curtilage of a person's home or business. Whether or not a piece of land or building falls within the curtilage can be determined by consideration of the following factors:

1. Inclusion within the residential yard;
2. Enclosure by a fence;
3. Use in connection with the dwelling for family purposes;
4. Distance or remoteness from main dwelling; and
5. Use or invitation to use by the public.

Since the 1967 U.S. Supreme Court decision in *Katz v. U.S.,* which held that "the Fourth Amendment protects people, not places," courts have increasingly analyzed the legality of warrantless searches in terms of the defendant's reasonable expectation of privacy, in addition to the concepts of curtilage and open fields. Law enforcement officers, therefore, must be careful to avoid warrantless intrusions not only into the curtilage of a person's house, but also into any area that the person reasonably seeks to preserve as private.

A law enforcement officer, without probable cause, warrant, or other legal justification may retrieve items of evidence that have been abandoned by their owners without violating Fourth Amendment rights. Property has been abandoned when the owner has voluntarily relinquished all title, possession, or claim to it. Among the factors that the courts rely on in determining whether a given object has been abandoned by its owner are the following:

1. Place in which property was left—As a general rule, if an object is voluntarily discarded inside the curtilage, it will not be considered abandoned; if discarded outside the curtilage, it will be considered abandoned. Objects left on premises, however, may be considered abandoned if the premises themselves have been voluntarily vacated or abandoned.

2. Indications of intent to abandon—Indications of intent to abandon *premises* can be divided into positive acts and omissions. Positive indications of intent to abandon include removing personal belongings, paying final rent and other bills, turning in keys, quitting local employment, and taking leave of friends. Omissions indicating intent to abandon include failing to pay rent for a long time, long absence from premises, failure to communicate with anyone regarding premises, and failure to attend to or care for premises. Intent to abandon an *object* is indicated by

leaving the object unattended for an unreasonable period of time, discarding the object out of consciousness of guilt or fear of apprehension, and allowing the object to be taken away in the ordinary course of events, without objection. Intentional concealment of an object is not considered an indication of intent to abandon. Intent to abandon *vehicles* is determined by the same considerations as those for premises and objects.

3. Lawfulness of police behavior—Objects discarded as a direct result of the unlawful presence or activity of a law enforcement officer will not be considered voluntarily abandoned.

4. Reasonable expectation of privacy in the property—Even though property has been vacated or thrown away, under certain circumstances, a person may reasonably retain an expectation of privacy with respect to the property. Such property is not considered abandoned and a search and seizure of it, without a warrant or probable cause, will be illegal.

Determining whether property is abandoned is similar to determining whether it is in the open fields, in that both require a consideration not only of a person's property rights, but also of the person's rights of privacy. Such determinations will always be difficult for the courts as well as for law enforcement officers. It is recommended that in the absence of an emergency officers obtain a search warrant whenever possible.

REVIEW AND DISCUSSION QUESTIONS

1. Does "open fields" include any place that is "public," including forests, lakes, city streets, and stadiums?

2. Would any of the following be considered a "house" for purposes of the Fourth Amendment?
   a. A tent.
   b. A lean-to.
   c. A motor home.
   d. A sailboat.
   e. A cave.

3. Would an aerial observation of marijuana plants growing in a greenhouse on the defendant's roof violate the defendant's reasonable expectation of privacy?

4. Would a person's Fourth Amendment rights be violated by law enforcement officers who, after illegally arresting the person, entered the person's fenced and posted rural property to observe a marijuana field surrounded by a forest?

5. Compare the plain view doctrine, the open fields doctrine, and the abandonment doctrine with respect to the reasonable expectation of privacy.

6. If a person abandons property inside the curtilage of someone else's property, may a law enforcement officer seize the abandoned property?

7. Is observation of activities inside a house in the country by looking into a window with binoculars from a field or forest any different from observing activities in a tenth-story apartment from a window in an adjacent apartment building?

8. Does the value of an object have any bearing on the question of whether a person abandoned it? Can a person who runs away from his or her automobile to avoid apprehension by the police be said to give up all reasonable expectations of privacy in the vehicle? What if the person locks the vehicle before fleeing?

9. What indications of intent to abandon each of the places listed in question number two above would give a law enforcement officer authority to search for and seize items left at the place?

10. If a person seeks medical attention after being shot while driving an automobile, has the person abandoned:

    a. Clothing worn at the time of the shooting?
    b. Wallets and other items in the pockets of the clothing?
    c. Bullets surgically removed?
    d. The automobile?

12

Stop and Frisk

In recent years, "stop and frisk" has become a major subject of comment and controversy in the field of law enforcement. This is not because it is a new procedure. In fact, it has been a long recognized procedure for law enforcement officers to stop suspicious persons for questioning and, occasionally, to search these persons for dangerous weapons. Nevertheless, it has taken the law and the courts a long time to respond to this practice, and, as a result, the limited warrantless "seizure" and "search" involved in a "stop and frisk" have only relatively recently been given judicial approval by the U.S. Supreme Court. This approval was given in the case of Terry v. Ohio, 392 U.S. 1, 88 S.Ct. 1868, 20 L.Ed.2d 889 (1968), and its companion cases of Sibron v. New York and Peters v. New York, 392 U.S. 40, 88 S.Ct. 1889, 20 L.Ed.2d 917 (U.S. Supreme Court, 1968).

Before discussing these three cases, "stop and frisk" should be tentatively defined and distinguished from arrests and other encounters between the police and citizens. In Chapter 4 we defined a technical arrest as "the apprehension or detention of the person of another in order that he may be forthcoming to answer for an alleged or supposed crime." We also spoke of seizures tantamount to arrest in which, although an officer has no intention to take a person into custody and charge the person with a crime, the circumstances surrounding the detention are indistinguishable from an arrest in important respects. "Stop and frisk" also involves a detention or restraint of a person, but a much briefer and less intrusive detention or restraint. As a preliminary definition, "stop and frisk" is a police practice involving the temporary detention, questioning, and limited search of a person suspected of criminal activity. It is initiated on a reasonable suspicion of crime amounting to less than probable cause for the purposes of crime prevention and investigation and for the protection of the law enforcement officer carrying out the investigation. It is important to point out that a "stop and frisk" that is initially justifiable may become a seizure tantamount to arrest if the detention and search exceed their allowable purposes or if the extent of the intrusion goes beyond what is reasonably necessary.

Stop and frisk should also be distinguished from the common situation, also described in Chapter 4, in which the law enforcement officer approaches a person in a public place and asks if the person is willing to answer questions. In this situation, the officer needs no justification or level of suspicion to approach the person and the officer has no authority to detain the person even momentarily, whether or not the person agrees to cooperate. Of course, if an initially friendly and neutral encounter somehow provides the officer with reason to suspect criminal activity, the officer may be justified in making the more significant intrusion of a stop and frisk.

The definition of "stop and frisk" will be refined throughout the chapter through the discussion of the *Terry, Sibron,* and *Peters* cases and several others that have followed from 1968 to the present. An attempt will be made to set forth guidelines for the law enforcement officer in this area. However, officers should remember that this is a very sensitive and complex area of the law and many questions regarding stop and frisk still have not been answered. As a result, clearcut procedures for all situations are not available. These problem areas will have to be dealt with in the future as the courts resolve them on a case by case basis.

DISCUSSION OF THE TERRY, SIBRON, AND PETERS CASES

Terry v. Ohio

In the *Terry* case, a police detective with thirty-nine years' experience observed two men alternately pacing back and forth five or six times in front of a store window, each time peering into the store and returning to a corner to confer. The two men were joined briefly by a third man. When he walked away, the first two resumed their pacing, peering, and conferring. When the third man rejoined them again, the detective, suspecting that the men were "casing" the store for an armed robbery, approached them, identified himself, and asked their names. When the men "mumbled something," the detective grabbed Terry, spun him around in order to place him between the other two suspects and himself, and patted down the outside of his clothing. Feeling a pistol in Terry's coat pocket, the officer seized it and patted down the outer clothing of the other two men. One more weapon was found. Terry and the other man were arrested and convicted of carrying concealed weapons. They appealed, claiming that the weapons were obtained by means of an unreasonable search and should not have been admitted into evidence at their trial.

The U.S. Supreme Court affirmed the convictions. The Court said that even though "stop" and "frisk" represented a lesser restraint than a traditional "arrest" and "search," the procedure is still governed by the Fourth Amendment. However, stop and frisk is not subject to as stringent a limitation as a traditional full arrest and search. Instead of applying the "probable cause" standard to stop and frisk, the Court applied the fundamental test of the Fourth Amendment—the "reasonableness" in all the circumstances of the particular governmental invasion of a citizen's personal security.

In discussing the reasonableness of the officer's actions in this case, the Court first mentioned the long tradition of armed violence of American criminals and the number of law enforcement officers killed or wounded in action. In light of this, the Court recognized law enforcement officers' need to protect themselves when suspicious circumstances indicate possible criminal activity by potentially dangerous persons, but when probable cause for an arrest is lacking. In these situations, the Court felt it would be unreasonable to deny an officer the authority to take necessary steps to determine whether a suspected person is armed and to neutralize the threat of harm. The Court concluded that

> where a police officer observes unusual conduct which leads him reasonably to conclude in light of his experience that criminal activity may be afoot and that the persons with whom he is dealing may be armed and presently dangerous, where in the course of investigating this behavior he identifies himself as a policeman and makes reasonable inquiries, and where nothing in the initial stages of the encounter serves to dispel his reasonable fear for his own or others' safety, he is entitled for the protection of himself and others in the area to conduct a carefully limited search of the outer clothing of such persons in an attempt to discover weapons which might be used to assault him. 392 U.S. at 30, 88 S.Ct. at 1884–85, 20 L.Ed.2d at 911.

Sibron v. New York

The *Sibron* case arose from another instance of police surveillance, in which a uniformed patrolman observed Sibron in the company of several known drug addicts during an eight-hour period. The officer did not see anything pass between Sibron and the others, nor did he hear any of their conversation. Sibron later entered a restaurant where he spoke to three other known addicts but again nothing was observed to pass between them.

On the basis of these actions alone, the policeman accosted Sibron with the remark, "You know what I am after." Sibron mumbled a reply and began to reach into his pocket. The policeman intercepted his hand, reached into the same pocket, and discovered envelopes containing heroin. Sibron was convicted of unauthorized possession of narcotics and appealed on the basis that the seizure was made in violation of his Fourth Amendment rights.

The Supreme Court found that the policeman in the *Sibron* case did not have probable cause to make an arrest and therefore could not justify the search as incident to arrest. The officer knew nothing of the conversations between Sibron and the others, and saw nothing pass between them. All he had to go on was the fact that the others were addicts. This was not enough. "The inference that persons who talk to narcotics addicts are engaged in criminal traffic in narcotics is simply not the sort of reasonable inference required to support an intrusion by the police upon an individual's personal security." 392 U.S. at 62, 88 S.Ct. at 1902, 20 L.Ed.2d at 934. There was no basis to arrest until after the unlawful search.

Moreover, nothing in the record gave the slightest indication that the officer thought that Sibron might be armed. The officer, therefore, could not justify his actions on the grounds of self-protection. The *Terry* case certainly did not authorize a routine frisk of everyone seen on the street or encountered by an officer. The officer in *Sibron* was apparently after narcotics and nothing else. His search was therefore unreasonable under the standards announced in the *Terry* case. Since there was neither probable cause to arrest nor sufficient justification to frisk, the heroin seized by the officer was not admissible in evidence and the conviction of Sibron was reversed.

Peters v. New York

In the *Peters* case, an off-duty patrolman heard a noise outside his apartment door. He saw two men tiptoeing furtively about the hallway, neither of whom he recognized although he had lived in the building for twelve years. After telephoning the police, he entered the hallway with his gun drawn, slamming the door behind him. The two suspects fled down the stairs and the patrolman gave chase. He caught up with the defendant, questioned him, and patted down his clothing. In the course of the frisk, the officer discovered a hard object that he believed could be a weapon. It turned out to be an envelope containing burglar's tools. Peters was convicted of possessing burglar's tools.

The Supreme Court affirmed the conviction of Peters. However, the decision was not based upon the officer's authority to "stop and frisk." Rather, the Court found the facts sufficient to give the officer probable cause to *arrest* the defendant for attempted burglary, and for purposes of the Fourth Amendment the search was properly incident to a lawful arrest. Emphasis was placed by the Court on the defendant's furtive action and his flight in establishing probable cause. The Court said:

> It is difficult to conceive of stronger grounds for an arrest, short of actual eyewitness observation of criminal activity. . . . [D]eliberately furtive actions and flight at the approach of strangers or law officers are strong indicia of *mens rea*, and when coupled with specific knowledge on the part of the officer relating the suspect to the evidence of crime, they are proper factors to be considered in the decision to make an arrest. 392 U.S. at 66–67, 88 S.Ct. at 1904, 20 L.Ed.2d at 937.

The Court did not examine the reasonableness of the stop and the frisk because there was probable cause to arrest and the search was justified as incident to the arrest.

We turn now to a discussion of some general principles regarding "stop and frisk" that can be derived from the *Terry, Sibron,* and *Peters* decisions. When possible, guidelines and suggestions to aid the law enforcement officer in determining what action to take, if any, in a stop and frisk situation will be presented. Direct quotations from the *Terry, Sibron,* and *Peters* decisions will be used whenever appropriate because it is important that law enforcement officers become familiar with the exact language of the Court in these important cases.

THE REASONABLENESS STANDARD

In order to fully understand the reasons for the restrictions placed on law enforcement officers in stop and frisk situations, the law enforcement officer must realize that "stop and frisk" procedures are serious intrusions upon an individual's privacy and therefore are governed by the Fourth Amendment to the Constitution prohibiting unreasonable searches and seizures. As the Supreme Court stated in the *Terry* case:

> It is quite plain that the Fourth Amendment governs "seizures" of the person which do not eventuate in a trip to the station house and prosecution for crime—"arrests" in traditional terminology. It must be recognized that whenever a police officer accosts an individual and restrains his freedom to walk away, he has "seized" that person. And it is nothing less than sheer torture of the English language to suggest that a careful exploration of the outer surfaces of a person's clothing all over his or her body in an attempt to find weapons is not a "search." Moreover, it is simply fantastic to urge that such a procedure performed in public by a policeman while the citizen stands helpless, perhaps facing a wall with his hands raised, is a "petty indignity." It is a serious intrusion upon the sanctity of the person, which may inflict great indignity and arouse strong resentment, and it is not to be undertaken lightly. 392 U.S. at 16–17, 88 S.Ct. at 1877, 20 L.Ed.2d at 903.

Although a stop and frisk is a lesser form of intrusion or interference, it is still constitutionally protected. However, the Fourth Amendment does not apply to stop and frisk in the same way that it does in traditional search and seizure law. In a traditional search and seizure or arrest situation, law enforcement officers must determine whether probable cause exists before they can justify a particular search, seizure, or arrest, whether a warrant is being sought or whether the situation falls within certain exceptions to the warrant requirement.

This is not the case, however, with stop and frisk. Here we deal with the many and varied situations in which a law enforcement officer must take swift action based on brief on-the-scene observations. This type of police conduct has not historically been subjected to the warrant procedure, nor could it be as a practical matter. The police conduct in a stop and frisk situation must therefore be tested, not by a probable cause standard, but under the Fourth Amendment's general prohibition against unreasonable searches and seizures.

The question for the law enforcement officer then becomes whether or not it is reasonable, in a particular set of circumstances, for the officer to seize a person and subject the person to a limited search when there is no probable cause to arrest.

Competing Interests

In determining reasonableness, it is helpful to consider the competing interests involved in a stop and frisk situation. On one side there is the individual's privacy and the right to be free from unreasonable searches and seizures. In the words of the Supreme Court:

> Even a limited search of the outer clothing for weapons constitutes a severe, though brief, intrusion upon cherished personal security, and it must surely be an annoying, frightening, and perhaps humiliating experience. 392 U.S. at 24–25, 88 S.Ct. at 1881–82, 20 L.Ed.2d at 908.

On the other side are the governmental interests involved. One of these is effective crime prevention and detection. The other governmental interest, and the one with which the *Terry* Court was most concerned, is the interest of police officers in taking steps to assure themselves that the person with whom they are dealing is not armed with a weapon that could unexpectedly be used against them:

> Certainly it would be unreasonable to require that police officers take unnecessary risks in the performance of their duties. American criminals have a long tradition of armed violence, and every year in this country many law enforcement officers are killed in the line of duty, and thousands more are wounded. 392 U.S. at 23, 88 S.Ct. at 1881, 20 L.Ed.2d at 907.

With these competing interests in mind, law enforcement officers must evaluate each situation and determine for themselves what action, if any, is justified by the circumstances. This determination can be broken down into two considerations:

1. Whether *any* police interference at all is justified by the circumstances; and

2. If so, *how extensive* an interference do those circumstances justify.

In setting out guidelines to help the law enforcement officer answer these questions, the "stop" aspect and the "frisk" aspect will be considered separately because the "stop" and the "frisk" each have different purposes behind them, different sets of circumstances that will justify them, and different consequences for the individual who is subjected to the procedure.

DETERMINATION OF WHETHER TO STOP

The Supreme Court recognized that stopping persons for the purpose of investigating possible criminal activity is necessary to the government's interest in effective crime prevention and detection:

> [I]t is this interest which underlies the recognition that a police officer may in appropriate circumstances and in an appropriate manner approach a person for purposes of investigating possibly criminal behavior even though there is no probable cause to make an arrest. 392 U.S. at 22, 88 S.Ct. at 1880, 20 L.Ed.2d at 906–07.

Given this authority, law enforcement officers must determine under what circumstances it is appropriate for them to stop a person for investigation. Officers may consider many factors. The following is a partial list of possible indications of criminal behavior that officers should consider in deciding to make the initial stop:

1. The suspect is known to have a felony record.

2. The suspect fits a "wanted" notice.

3. The suspect makes furtive or evasive movements.

4. The suspect's actions are unusual for the time of day or night.

5. The suspect's clothing is peculiar or inappropriate, e.g., a coat on a hot day.

6. The suspect's vehicle is peculiar in some respect, e.g., clean license on a dirty car.

7. The suspect is in an unusual place or is acting strangely.

Any one of these things alone may not give an officer sufficient grounds to stop a person. However, a combination of some of these factors and others, evaluated in light of the officer's experience, may cause the officer to decide that an investigation is warranted.

Most importantly, the officer must be able to justify any investigative stop by showing concrete facts and circumstances indicating possible criminal activity that caused the officer to decide to take action. As the Supreme Court said in *Terry:*

> [I]n justifying the particular intrusion the police officer must be able to point to specific and articulable facts which, taken together with rational inferences from those facts, reasonably warrant that intrusion. 392 U.S. at 21, 88 S.Ct. at 1880, 20 L.Ed.2d at 906.

This means that a court will not accept an officer's mere statement or conclusion that criminal activity was suspected. The officer must be able to back up such a conclusion by reciting the specific facts that led to that conclusion. Furthermore, the officer's decision to initiate a stop will be judged against the following objective standard:

> [W]ould the facts available to the officer at the moment of the seizure or the search "warrant a man of reasonable caution in the belief" that the action taken was appropriate? 392 U.S. at 21–22, 88 S.Ct. at 1880, 20 L.Ed.2d at 906.

This objective standard is very similar to the standard imposed upon law enforcement officers in traditional search and seizure or arrest situations. For example, assume that an officer is attempting to obtain a warrant for a person's arrest. Since probable cause is required to obtain the warrant, the officer must produce specific facts sufficient to support a reasonable belief *that a specific crime has been or is being committed.* In the stop and frisk situation, no crime has been committed—there is only a possibility that criminal activity is under way, perhaps only in the planning stage. However, the officer must still come up with specific facts indicating a *possibility of impending criminal activity* to justify the initial intrusion. The element common to the two situations is that officers must be able to justify their action with specific facts. The only difference is in the nature of the information to be given, and for an investigative stop, the officer need only show facts indicating the possibility that criminal behavior is afoot.

Extent of Stop

Once an officer has determined that the circumstances justify interfering with an individual to investigate possible criminal activity, to what extent do those circumstances allow the officer to interfere? In other words, how long may the person be detained, how much force may be used, and how much questioning may the person be subjected to? In Florida v. Royer, 460 U.S. 491, 500, 103 S.Ct. 1319, 1325, 75 L.Ed.2d 229, 238 (1983), the U.S. Supreme Court said:

> The predicate permitting seizures on suspicion short of probable cause is that law enforcement interests warrant a limited intrusion on the personal security of the suspect. The scope of the intrusion permitted will vary to some extent with the particular facts and circumstances of each case. This much, however is clear: an

investigative detention must be temporary and last no longer than is necessary to effectuate the purpose of the stop. Similarly, the investigative methods employed should be the least intrusive means reasonably available to verify or dispel the officer's suspicion in a short period of time. . . . It is the State's burden to demonstrate that the seizure it seeks to justify on the basis of a reasonable suspicion was sufficiently limited in scope and duration to satisfy the conditions of an investigative seizure.

An investigative stop can range from a friendly encounter with minimal intrusion to an angry confrontation resulting in the use of force or violence. Officers must be able to point to specific facts and circumstances to indicate that the extent of the interference with an individual was reasonable.

For example, an officer's initial questioning of a suspect may assure the officer that no further investigation is necessary. A law enforcement officer observed a young man carrying a flashlight and a small box walking on the sidewalk of a residential street at 2:40 A.M. The officer passed him in the patrol car and then stopped to ask him what he was doing. He replied that he was collecting night crawlers for fishing bait. The officer wished him luck and drove on.

On the other hand, the answers given by the stopped person may cause the officer to believe more strongly that something is amiss. In this situation the officer is permitted to investigate further or, if probable cause exists, to arrest the person. For example, an officer saw the defendant wearing one topcoat and carrying another. The defendant seemed to be attempting to hide something under the coat he carried. Considering this behavior suspicious, the officer stopped the defendant and asked him what he had under his coat. The defendant replied that he had a tape recorder. When the officer asked him to identify himself he handed the officer a driver's license describing an older person of a different race. The officer then arrested the defendant.

The court held that the initial suspicious circumstances justified at least the mere questioning of the defendant by the officer. Then, when the officer checked the license, he had "probable cause not only to investigate further but to place the appellant under arrest with the very reasonable belief that the appellant's possession indicated, at the least, receiving stolen goods." Commonwealth v. Howell, 213 Pa. Super. 33, 41, 245 A.2d 680, 684 (Superior Court of Pennsylvania, 1968).

Other cases dealing with the extent of the stop will be discussed later in the chapter.

DETERMINATION OF WHETHER TO FRISK

The determination by a law enforcement officer of whether or not to "frisk" a suspect is a separate issue from the determination of whether or not to stop. There is a different governmental interest to be served and there is a different set of factors to be considered by the officer. The governmental interest that is served by giving police the authority to frisk is that of protecting the officer and others from possible violence by persons being investigated for crime. As the Supreme Court said:

[W]e cannot blind ourselves to the need for law enforcement officers to protect themselves and other prospective victims of violence in situations where they may lack probable cause for an arrest. 392 U.S. at 24, 88 S.Ct. at 1881, 20 L.Ed.2d at 907–08.

Balanced against this interest is the citizen's right to privacy that would necessarily be invaded by giving police the right to frisk suspects. The Supreme Court expressed its concern for this in the following language:

> We must still consider, however, the nature and quality of the intrusion on individual rights which must be accepted if police officers are to be conceded the right to search for weapons in situations where probable cause to arrest for crime is lacking. 392 U.S. at 24, 88 S.Ct. at 1881, 20 L.Ed.2d at 908.

As we noted earlier, the Court considers the stop and frisk procedure to be a serious intrusion on a person's rights, possibly inflicting great indignity and arousing strong resentment.

Taking both sides of the issue into consideration, the Court set out a limited authority for a protective frisk by law enforcement officers in the following terms:

> Our evaluation of the proper balance that has to be struck in this type of case leads us to conclude that there must be a narrowly drawn authority to permit a reasonable search for weapons for the protection of the police officer, where he has reason to believe that he is dealing with an armed and dangerous individual, regardless of whether he has probable cause to arrest the individual for a crime. 392 U.S. at 27, 88 S.Ct. at 1883, 20 L.Ed.2d at 909.

Limited Authority

The most important thing for law enforcement officers to remember is that their authority to frisk is a limited and narrowly drawn authority. Officers may not frisk everyone that they stop to investigate the possibility of criminal activity. Before deciding to conduct any frisk, an officer must have "reason to believe that he is dealing with an armed and dangerous individual." The officer need not be absolutely certain that the individual is armed. Rather the issue is "whether a reasonably prudent man in the circumstances would be warranted in the belief that his safety or that of others was in danger. . . ." 392 U.S. at 27, 88 S.Ct. at 1883, 20 L.Ed.2d at 909.

Thus, officers are governed by an objective standard as they are in determining whether to stop. An officer must be able to justify a search or frisk of the individual by pointing to specific facts and "specific reasonable inferences which he is entitled to draw from the facts in light of his experience." 392 U.S. at 27, 88 S.Ct. at 1883, 20 L.Ed.2d at 909.

Many factors may be taken into consideration in deciding whether or not it is appropriate to frisk a person. Some things will carry more weight with one officer than another because of differences in experience and knowledge. The following is a partial list of things to consider in deciding whether or not to frisk an individual.

1. The suspected crime involves the use of weapons.

2. The suspect is nervous or "rattled" over being stopped.

3. There is a bulge in the suspect's clothing.

4. The suspect's hand is concealed in a pocket.

5. The suspect does not present satisfactory identification or an adequate explanation for suspicious behavior.

6. The area the officer is operating in is known to contain armed persons.

Any one of these things taken alone may not give sufficient grounds to frisk a suspect, but a combination of some of these elements or others, evaluated in light of the officer's knowledge and experience, might provide a justification to frisk. Specific cases dealing with authority to stop will be discussed later in this chapter.

Scope of Search

The Supreme Court requires a frisk to be "a *reasonable* search for weapons for the protection of the police officer." (emphasis supplied) 392 U.S. at 27, 88 S.Ct. at 1883, 20 L.Ed.2d at 909. Since the *only* justifiable purpose of a frisk is the protection of the officer and others, the search must be limited to what is minimally necessary for this protection. Therefore, the frisk must initially be limited to a pat-down of the *outer* clothing. There is no authority to reach inside clothing or into pockets in the *initial* stages of a frisk. During the pat-down, if the officer detects an object that feels as if it might be a weapon, the officer may then reach inside the clothing or pocket and seize it. If it turns out that it is not a weapon, but instead some other implement of crime (such as burglar's tools) that implement would be admissible in evidence for the crime to which it related (e.g., attempted burglary). However, if the officer does not feel an object that could be a weapon, but instead feels a package or bulge that he believes might be evidence of some other crime (such as possession of narcotics or lottery tickets), the officer may not seize the package or object. The search must end at this point because the only authorized purpose for a frisk is the protection of the officer and others, *not* to obtain evidence for use at a subsequent trial. If the officer feels no weapon-like object during the course of the pat-down, there can no longer be any reasonable fear that the person is armed. Therefore, any further search without probable cause would exceed the purpose of the frisk, namely, the protection of the officer. Such a search would be unreasonable under the Fourth Amendment and any evidence obtained through it would be inadmissible.

The U.S. Supreme Court has approved an extension of the permissible scope of a protective search for weapons beyond the person of the suspect to include the passenger compartment of an automobile. The Court said:

> [T]he search of the passenger compartment of an automobile, limited to those areas in which a weapon may be placed or hidden, is permissible if the police officer possesses a reasonable belief based on "specific and articulable facts which, taken together with the rational inferences from those facts, reasonably warrant" the officers in believing that the suspect is dangerous and the suspect may gain immediate control of weapons. Michigan v. Long, — U.S. —, —, 103 S.Ct. 3469, 3480, 77 L.Ed.2d 1201, 1220 (1983).

In reaching this decision, the Court recognized that roadside encounters between police and suspects are especially hazardous, and that danger may arise from the possible presence of weapons in the area surrounding a suspect. The Court stressed, however, that its decision does not mean that the police may conduct automobile searches whenever they conduct an investigative stop. Since the sole justification for a *Terry* search is the protection of police officers and others nearby, officers may conduct such a search only when they have a reasonable suspicion that the suspect is dangerous. Unlike a warrantless search incident to a lawful arrest, a *Terry* search is not justified by any need to prevent the disappearance or destruction of evidence of crime.

SPECIFIC CIRCUMSTANCES IN STOP AND FRISK

Since the term "stop and frisk" covers an infinite variety of possible situations, a mere statement of general guidelines may not be sufficient to clearly indicate what behavior is or is not appropriate for a law enforcement officer in a given situation. Therefore, we will now consider specific fact situations involving "stop and frisk" and discuss the ways in which courts throughout the country have responded to these situations. We will cite actual court cases and discuss the court's reasons for deciding that the actions of the law enforcement officer in each case were either reasonable or unreasonable. In each situation, we will emphasize (1) the indications of possible criminal behavior that caused the officer to stop the suspect in the first place and (2) the circumstances that caused the officer to reasonably believe that his or her safety or that of others was in danger, thus necessitating a frisk of the suspect.

The cases to be discussed will be grouped under various headings, each indicating the chief factor that caused a law enforcement officer either to stop or to frisk a suspect. In most cases, this will not be the only factor present, but it is a convenient way of classifying the cases and should help to make the presentation more meaningful.

Bulge

In a District of Columbia case, two officers in plain clothes approached the entrance of a delicatessen to investigate a robbery of an earlier date. On their way into the store they passed the defendant who was standing outside. Inside the store, the officers overheard the store owner and some other people discussing the defendant and a companion, who was concealed behind a truck nearby. It was mentioned that they were acting in a suspicious manner. The owner went outside and told the defendant that everyone was watching him and that he had better leave.

The officers then approached the defendant, identified themselves, and asked for his identification. The defendant said, "Why? My name is Lee." When the officers again requested some identification, the defendant reached back with his left hand into his left rear pocket to get his wallet. At this point a bulge was observed under the defendant's shirt, sticking in the waistband of his pants. The object was immediately seized and it turned out to be a loaded pistol.

The court found the "stop and frisk" to be reasonable. With respect to the "stop," the court said that the action of the officers here

> is the kind of momentary contact which is and must be recognized as necessary to a sound police-community relationship and its commensurate effective law enforcement. It cannot be said that the accused was so inconvenienced or restricted that the delicate balance between individual freedom and legitimate police activity has been unduly weighted against him. United States v. Lee, D.C.App., 271 A.2d 566, 567–68 (District of Columbia Court of Appeals, 1970).

In approving the seizure of the gun, the court stated that the officer

> had no other choice. He was justifiably concerned for his own safety when the accused revealed that he had something concealed under his waistband. . . . Surely then, under the considerations discussed in Terry v. Ohio, supra, the in-depth search for and seizure of the gun was reasonable—clearly as reasonable as the in-depth search for and seizure of Terry's gun when its presence was discovered by Officer McFadden's sense of touch during the so-called "frisk." 271 A.2d at 568.

Hand Concealed in Pocket

During a routine investigation for a traffic violation, an officer was informed from police headquarters via radio that the car and driver he was investigating were carrying forged prescriptions for narcotic drugs. The defendant, a passenger in the car, while talking with the officer, voluntarily got out of the car with his right hand concealed in his coat pocket. The officer asked the defendant to remove his hand from his pocket. Upon his refusal, the officer removed the hand and frisked the defendant. At no time did the officer go into any hidden places upon the defendant's person. However, clutched in the removed hand was a small yellow envelope, which the officer seized. Upon observing its contents, the officer arrested the defendant for the possession of heroin.

This case presents no problems as far as the initial stop is concerned. The facts indicate that it was a routine traffic investigation. The information received over the police radio certainly gave the officer good reason at least to investigate further.

The real issue was the reasonableness of the frisk. The court said:

> A person does not ordinarily alight from an automobile with a hand inserted in a pocket. When the hands are free such person has better maneuverability to accomplish this task. Thus when the hand didn't come out after one or more routine questions by the officer, he certainly by this time had probable cause to initiate reasonable precaution for his own safety. Under such facts and circumstances the frisk for weapons was not unreasonable. State v. Henry, 23 Ohio Misc. 367, 368, 256 N.E.2d 269, 270 (Court of Common Pleas of Ohio, 1969).

Thus, based upon all the facts and circumstances presented, the court found that the officer had reasonable grounds to believe that the defendant was armed and dangerous. Furthermore, the court held that the heroin taken from the defendant was admissible in evidence against him because, as a result of a reasonable frisk, the defendant *himself* brought the envelope containing the heroin from his pocket, after which it was then in plain view.

Admission by Defendant

While driving an automobile, the defendant was stopped by a police officer for speeding. After stopping the vehicle, the officer walked up to it. The defendant got out holding his right hand in the pocket of his knee-length coat. The pocket was baggy and sagged. The officer grabbed the defendant's arm and asked him if he had a gun. The defendant answered "yes." The officer then removed the gun and arrested the defendant.

Here, again, the court assumed without discussion that the stop was reasonable because it was a routine traffic stop. In dealing with the frisk, the court cited *Terry v. Ohio:*

> Terry v. Ohio .   .   . tells us that when a police officer has reason to believe that he is dealing with an armed individual he has a right to search for weapons regardless of whether he has probable cause to arrest that individual for a crime. Here the officer did not merely think he was dealing with an armed person—he knew he was. State v. Hall, 4 Or.App. 30, 31, 476 P.2d 930, 931 (Court of Appeals of Oregon, 1970).

The gun was held to be admissible in evidence and the defendant's concealed firearm conviction was upheld.

Information from Informants

In Adams v. Williams, 407 U.S. 143, 92 S.Ct. 1921, 32 L.Ed.2d 612 (U.S. Supreme Court, 1972), a law enforcement officer on patrol in his cruiser was approached by a person known to him and was told that a man seated in a nearby vehicle had a gun at his waist and was carrying narcotics. The officer approached the vehicle, tapped on the window, and asked the occupant (the defendant) to open the door. When the defendant rolled down the window instead, the officer reached in, removed a pistol from the defendant's waistband, and then arrested him.

The Court held that the officer acted justifiably in responding to the informant's tip:

> The informant was known to him personally and had provided him with information in the past. This is a stronger case than obtains in the case of an anonymous telephone tip. The informant here came forward personally to give information that was immediately verifiable at the scene. Indeed, under Connecticut law, the informant herself might have been subject to immediate arrest for making a false complaint had Sgt. Connolly's investigation proven the tip incorrect. Thus, while the Court's decisions indicate that this informant's unverified tip may have been insufficient for a narcotics arrest or search warrant, the information carried enough indicia of reliability to justify the officer's forcible stop of Williams.
>
> In reaching this conclusion, we reject respondent's argument that reasonable cause for a stop and frisk can only be based on the officer's personal observation, rather than on information supplied by another person. Informants' tips, like all other clues and evidence coming to a policeman on the scene, may vary greatly in their value and reliability. One simple rule will not cover every situation. Some tips, completely lacking in indicia of reliability, would either warrant no police response or require further investigation before a forcible stop of a suspect would be authorized But in some situations—for example, when the victim of a street crime seeks immediate police aid and gives a description of his assailant, or when a

credible informant warns of a specific impending crime—the subtleties of the hearsay rule should not thwart an appropriate police response. 407 U.S. at 146–47, 92 S.Ct. at 1923–24, 32 L.Ed.2d at 617–18.

Under the *Adams v. Williams* case, an officer may stop a person suspected of possible criminal activity based on an informant's tip if the tip carries "enough indicia of reliability." This standard is less than the probable cause standard discussed in Chapter 6. Nevertheless, the officer must be able to give specific reasons why the tip was believed to be reliable. As the *Adams v. Williams* case indicated, an anonymous telephone tip might not be sufficiently reliable without corroboration.

Officers may rely upon a police radio dispatch to obtain facts to justify the stop of a person or vehicle. If, however, it is later determined that the person relaying the information over the radio had no factual foundation for the message, the stop will be ruled illegal. In United States v. Robinson, 536 F.2d 1298 (9th Circuit Court of Appeals, 1976), the court said:

> We recognize that effective law enforcement cannot be conducted unless police officers can act on directions and information transmitted by one officer to another and that officers, who must often act swiftly, cannot be expected to cross-examine their fellow officers about the foundation for the transmitted information. The fact that an officer does not have to have personal knowledge of the evidence supplying good cause for a stop before he can obey a direction to detain a person or a vehicle does not mean that the Government need not produce evidence at trial showing good cause to legitimate the detention when the legality of the stop is challenged. If the dispatcher himself had had founded suspicion, or if he had relied on information from a reliable informant who supplied him with adequate facts to establish founded suspicion, the dispatcher could properly have delegated the stopping function to Officer Holland. But if the dispatcher did not have such cause, he could not create justification simply by relaying a direction to a fellow officer to make the stop. 536 F.2d at 1299–1300.

Frisk of Traffic Offender's Passengers

When an officer makes a stop for a traffic offense and has sufficient specific facts to support a belief that a dangerous situation is present, he or she may frisk the traffic offender's passengers for weapons. The court in United States v. Tharpe, 536 F.2d 1098 (5th Circuit Court of Appeals, 1976), found sufficient facts to justify such a frisk under the following circumstances: (1) The driver showed the officer a false license; (2) The driver admitted being the "bad check" suspect of whom the officer had just been informed by radio; (3) The officer recognized the two passengers as burglary suspects; (4) The officer was alone; and (5) The encounter occurred late at night.

Routine Vehicle Checks

In Delaware v. Prouse, 440 U.S. 648, 663, 99 S.Ct. 1391, 1401, 59 L.Ed.2d 660, 673 (1979), the U.S. Supreme Court held "that except in those situations in which there is at least articulable and reasonable suspicion that a motorist is unlicensed or that an automobile is not registered, or that either the vehicle or an occupant is otherwise subject to seizure for violation of law, stopping an automobile and detaining the driver in order to check his driver's license and the registration of the automobile are unreasonable under the Fourth Amendment." The Court expressed its concern that random vehicle checks presented a potential danger of arbitrary or discriminatory enforcement of the law.

Nevertheless, the Court stressed that it was not precluding states from developing methods for spot checks that involve less intrusion or that do not involve the unconstrained exercise of discretion. The Court suggested as one possible alternative the questioning of all oncoming traffic at roadblock-type stops. In U.S. v. Prichard, 645 F.2d 854 (10th Circuit Court of Appeals, 1981), a police roadblock that stopped all vehicles for a license and registration check was held reasonable, even though some vehicles were allowed to pass through when the traffic congestion became too heavy.

Ordering Driver Out of Vehicle

Once an officer has lawfully stopped a motor vehicle for a traffic violation, the officer may, for personal safety reasons, order the driver out of the vehicle. The officer may do so even though there is no reason to suspect foul play from the particular driver at the time of the stop. The U.S. Supreme Court said:

> We think this additional intrusion can only be described as de minimis. The driver is being asked to expose to view very little more of his person than is already exposed. The police have already lawfully decided that the driver shall be briefly detained; the only question is whether he shall spend that period sitting in the driver's seat of his car or standing alongside it. Not only is the insistence of the police on the latter choice not a "serious intrusion upon the sanctity of the person," but it hardly rises to the level of a " 'petty indignity.' " .   .   . What is at most a mere inconvenience cannot prevail when balanced against legitimate concerns for the officer's safety. Pennsylvania v. Mimms, 434 U.S. 106, 111, 98 S.Ct. 330, 333 54 L.Ed.2d 331, 337 (1977).

Once the driver is out of the car, the officer may, of course, frisk the person if the officer has reason to believe that the person is armed and dangerous.

Violent Crime

Police received a report of an armed robbery minutes after it happened. The time was about 3:30 A.M. and the officers on patrol in the area of the robbery had seen only one moving car in the vicinity. Police approached the car and noticed that one of the passengers fit the description of the robber given to them over the radio. The car was stopped and the two occupants were instructed to get out. No questions were asked at this moment, but one of the officers immediately began a pat-down search of the defendant for weapons. Bullets were found and the defendant was arrested.

The court found that the stop was justified by the information that the police had received over the radio:

> It is well established that circumstances short of probable cause to make an arrest may justify an officer's stopping motorists for questioning, and, if the

circumstances warrant it, the officer may in self-protection request a suspect to alight from an automobile and to submit to a superficial search for concealed weapons. People v. Anthony, 7 Cal.App.3d 751, 760, 86 Cal.Rptr. 767, 773 (California Court of Appeal, 1970).

The important point in this case, however, is that the court authorized an immediate frisk for weapons without any questions being asked:

If the reason for the stop is an articulate suspicion of a crime of violence, and the officer has reason to fear for his personal safety, he may immediately proceed to make a pat-down search for weapons without asking any prior questions . . . " ' There is no reason why an officer, rightfully but forcibly confronting a person suspected of a serious crime, *should have to ask one question and take the risk that the answer might be a bullet.'* " 7 Cal.App.3d at 760, 86 Cal.Rptr. at 773.

Therefore, officers need not ask questions before frisking a suspect if the nature of the crime being investigated is violent and they have a reasonable fear for their own safety.

Questionable Objects Felt in Frisk

Police had a certain residence under surveillance as a receiving point for marijuana shipments. They also had probable cause to arrest its occupant, although he was absent at the time. The defendants entered the driveway of the residence in a car, proceeded up the driveway, and were attempting to back out when the police stopped them. The officers knew that the defendants were not occupants of the residence nor were they subjects of the investigation. Nevertheless, they caused the defendants to be spread-eagled against the car and searched. One of the officers patted down the defendants' outer clothing and frisked the defendants' inner clothing. During the patdown and frisk of one defendant, the officer felt a lump in his shirt pocket. A further search disclosed that the lump was a plastic baggie containing marijuana seeds and a package of roll-your-own cigarette papers. Defendants were arrested and convicted of possession of marijuana.

The court approved the stop, stating:

Admittedly the police officers would have been derelict in their duty had they not stopped the defendants' vehicle to determine whether the occupant of the residence, or any other known subject of the investigation, was in the car. Likewise, the officers could have detained the defendants long enough to ascertain why they were on the premises. People v. Navran, 174 Colo. 222, 226, 483 P.2d 228, 230 (Supreme Court of Colorado, 1971).

However, the court found the frisk unreasonable:

It is apparent that the search conducted herein was not the "reasonable search for weapons" contemplated by the *Terry* case. . . . The right to "stop and frisk" is not an open invitation to conduct an unlimited search incident to arrest or a means to effect a search to provide grounds for an arrest. Rather, it is a right to conduct a limited search for weapons. . . . The seeds and cigarette papers seized were not shown by any evidence produced at the hearing to have been taken from the defendants under circumstances which would permit a search for weapons. 174 Colo. at 229, 483 P.2d at 232.

In another case involving objects felt in a frisk, an officer received a broadcast that a murder had just been committed at a certain intersection. The officer proceeded to the scene of the crime and spotted the defendant, who fit the description that the officer had received on his radio. The officer stopped the defendant and conducted a frisk for offensive weapons. Just after he started the search around the defendant's waistband, defendant abruptly grabbed his outside upper jacket pocket. The officer moved the defendant's hand away from the pocket and from the outside felt a round cylindrical object that he thought to be a 12 gauge shotgun shell. He reached into the pocket to remove it and at the same time pulled out a marijuana cigarette. The cylindrical object turned out to be a lipstick container. The defendant was convicted of unauthorized possession of marijuana.

The reasonableness of the stop was not in question. Certainly, the officer had a duty to investigate the defendant on the basis of the description given over his police radio. The court addressed itself therefore to the reasonableness of the frisk. Without deciding if a shotgun shell alone could be used as a weapon, the court found that the officer could have reasonably believed that his safety was in danger and that the frisk was justified:

> Though there is some confusion in the record it is susceptible of the inference that at the moment the officer had not yet eliminated the possibility that defendant was hiding a relatively short shotgun under his jacket. In any event a shotgun was not necessarily the only object which, in combination with a shell, could be used as a weapon. The officer could reasonably believe that any sharp object could be used as a detonator. People v. Atmore, 13 Cal.App.3d 244, 247, 91 Cal.Rptr. 311, 313–14 (Court of Appeal of California, 1971).

The court further stated:

> Hindsight may suggest that, in order to combine maximum personal safety for the officer with a minimum invasion of defendant's privacy, the officer should first have ascertained what else defendant was carrying. We do not believe, however, that under the circumstances the officer was required to proceed in the coldly logical sequence which may suggest itself after the event. It appears from the record that his reaching into the pocket was almost a reflexive motion, provoked by defendant's sudden gesture toward the pocket and his own feeling of the contents. We cannot say that under all of the circumstances defendant's constitutional rights were violated. 13 Cal.App.3d at 247–48, 91 Cal.Rptr. at 314.

Other Unusual Circumstances

After a high speed chase, an officer stopped the defendant's vehicle for speeding. The officer went to the passenger side of the vehicle and asked the defendant to get out of the vehicle. While the officer was at the car, he could smell alcohol. The defendant started to unbutton his coat. He turned towards the police officer and proceeded to take off his coat while he was still seated in the car. As he got out of the car he dropped the coat on the passenger seat where he had been sitting.

Since it was a cold November night, the officer thought it was peculiar for the defendant to remove his coat and the officer grabbed the coat as the defendant was getting out. As the officer started to follow the defendant, he noticed a pistol on the passenger seat, which had been covered by the coat. The pistol was introduced as evidence at defendant's trial and defendant was convicted of carrying a concealed deadly weapon.

On appeal, the court analyzed the reasonableness of both the stop and the frisk:

> The question then becomes whether or not the policeman acted legally when he reached into the car and picked up the defendant's coat. It should be noted that this case involves an incident where the police had a duty to act in stopping the vehicle. It is not a case of general exploratory investigation. Since the police had a duty to act, they also had a right to take reasonable measures to see that their safety was not endangered. . . . In view of the lateness of the hour, the high speed chase, the number of men in the car [3], the fact that the men had been drinking, the police acted reasonably in self protection in asking the gentlemen to get out of the car. Moreover, under these facts, it was reasonable for the police to conduct a limited pat-down search for weapons. A person cannot avoid such a search of his clothing by removing his clothing when it necessarily remains in the general vicinity where he is to remain. The police do not have to risk watching three men to make sure that they did not at any time go back to the clothing left in the car. And the mere fact that the coat was removed is another circumstance justifying a self protection frisk search. Modesti v. State, Del.Super., 258 A.2d 287, 288 (Superior Court of Delaware, 1969).

In another case, two police officers had received information over the police radio that a shooting had occurred. The suspects were described as two black men in dark clothing and one Puerto Rican in light clothing. The officers proceeded to the area of the shooting and spotted a black man in dark clothing and a Puerto Rican in light clothing, walking together near the scene, acting normally. The only reason the police had to connect them with the reported shooting was that they were walking in the general area and they fit the limited description police had been given. The police had no information of the physical makeup or characteristics of the men they were seeking.

The officers stopped the two men and frisked them on the spot. A gun was found in the defendant's belt and he was convicted of carrying a concealed deadly weapon.

The court discussed the "stop and frisk" aspects of the case together:

> A policeman may legally stop a person and question him. But he may not without a warrant restrain that person from walking away and "search" his clothing, unless he has "probable cause" to arrest that person or he observes such unusual and suspicious conduct on the part of the person who is stopped and searched that the policeman may reasonably conclude that criminal activity may be afoot, and that the person with whom he is dealing may be armed and dangerous. Commonwealth v. Berrios, 437 Pa. 338, 340, 263 A.2d 342, 343 (Supreme Court of Pennsylvania, 1970).

The court found that the circumstances of this case would *not* warrant a reasonably prudent man in the belief that his safety or that of others was in danger:

> If the policemen were constitutionally justified in searching Berrios under these circumstances, then every Puerto Rican wearing light clothing and walking with a negro in this area could likewise be validly searched. This, we cannot accept. 437 Pa. at 342, 263 A.2d at 344.

MISCELLANEOUS ISSUES IN STOP AND FRISK

Stop and Frisk and Miranda

As discussed in Chapter 13, the *Miranda* warnings must be given before any questioning of a person in custody or otherwise deprived of freedom of action in any *significant* way. The question arises whether the warnings are required to be given before questioning in connection with a "stop and frisk."

Most courts agree that a short period of on-the-scene questioning pursuant to a "stop and frisk" does not require the *Miranda* warnings because the *Miranda* decision was designed to protect against the dangers of compulsion arising when a suspect is swept from familiar surroundings and questioned in a coercive, police-dominated atmosphere. This compelling atmosphere is usually not present in a stop and frisk situation. First of all, the questions in a stop and frisk situation are not considered to be interrogative but rather are usually neutral and brief in scope. Secondly, an ordinary stop and frisk situation does not involve taking a person into custody, nor does it involve a significant deprivation of the person's freedom of action. The key word here is *significant*. Although there is definitely a deprivation of a person's freedom of action, because the detention and questioning is brief, casual, and limited in scope, courts have usually not considered it significant enough to require the *Miranda* warnings.

This is not to say that questioning in connection with a stop and frisk could never require the warnings. Circumstances might develop that would create a coercive and compelling atmosphere resulting in a significant deprivation of a person's freedom of action. For example, if the police outnumber the suspects, questioning is sustained and accusatory, force is used, or other coercive factors are present, alone or in combination, then very likely the warnings would be required.

There are no definite rules for determining when questioning in connection with a stop and frisk will require the *Miranda* warnings. The following cases should give some guidance, however.

Police officers had been alerted via radio to be on the lookout for a white Mustang with California license plates believed to be driven by a person involved in a robbery in a nearby town. When the officers spotted a car fitting that description, they stopped the defendant, asked him for identification, and asked if he had been in the town where the robbery occurred. Defendant replied that he had. No *Miranda* warnings had been given prior to the questions. Defendant was convicted of robbery and appealed.

The court found nothing in the questioning that amounted to an in-custody interrogation calling for *Miranda* warnings:

> *Miranda* does not bar all inquiry by authorities without previous warnings. . . . In our opinion *Miranda* was not intended to prohibit police officers from asking suspicious persons such things as their names and recent whereabouts without fully informing them of their constitutional rights. Utsler v. State, 84 S.D. 360, 368, 171 N.W.2d 739, 743 (Supreme Court of South Dakota, 1969).

Another case illustrates that law enforcement officers need not give the *Miranda* warnings before asking questions related to their immediate physical protection. The police had evidence that the defendant had robbed a store at gunpoint and they were looking for him. By luck, several days after the robbery, one of the robbery eye-witnesses recognized the defendant in public and informed police of his whereabouts. Police then broke into the defendant's apartment and placed him under arrest. One officer handcuffed the defendant while the other proceeded to give him *Miranda* warnings. A third officer interrupted asking, "Do you have the gun?" The defendant replied "I don't have the gun. I wouldn't be dumb enough to have it here." A jury subsequently found him guilty of armed robbery.

The defendant claimed on appeal that this potentially incriminating statement should not have been admitted in court because he had not been given the *Miranda* warnings. The court found however, that the questions were not designed to elicit incriminating information but were apparently for one reason only—the physical protection of the police. The police had good reason to believe the defendant was armed and dangerous because he had an extensive past history of robbery and burglary.

The court cited the following passage from Terry v. Ohio:

> "[I]t would appear to be clearly unreasonable to deny the officer the power to take necessary measures to determine whether the person is in fact carrying a weapon and to neutralize the threat of physical harm." State v. Lane, 77 Wn.2d 860, 863, 467 P.2d 304, 306 (Supreme Court of Washington, 1970).

The court went on to say:

> Although Terry v. Ohio involved a "stop and frisk" situation which was tested by the reasonableness standard of the Fourth Amendment, we believe the concern there expressed is equally applicable when the Fifth Amendment is involved. Accordingly, we hold that it is not a violation of either the letter or spirit of *Miranda* for police to ask questions which are strictly limited to protecting the immediate physical safety of the police themselves and which could not reasonably be delayed until after warnings are given. 77 Wn.2d at 863, 467 P.2d at 306.

Frisking of Persons of the Opposite Sex

The frisking of a person of the opposite sex presents a very delicate situation for which there are few specific guidelines. On the one hand, there are certainly situations in which a law enforcement officer could reasonably fear that a person of the opposite sex presents a danger to the officer or to other persons. On the other hand, if routine frisk procedures are used on a person of the opposite sex, the officer may be subjected to a claim of indecent handling or the embarrassment of a lawsuit. Therefore, an examination of the outer clothing of a person of the opposite sex should not be undertaken without some degree of certainty that the person is armed. The officer may ask a person to remove an overcoat or other covering, and the officer may squeeze handbags or shoulder bags. Bags should not be opened unless a weapon-like object is felt. Of course, if the person is arrested, the search and seizure of clothing, pockets, bags, and bundles is governed by the law of search incident to arrest (see Chapter 7).

Luggage and Other Containers

In United States v. Place, —— U.S. ——, 103 S.Ct. 2637, 77 L.Ed.2d 110 (1983), the U.S. Supreme Court held that the principles of the *Terry* case apply to the warrantless seizure and limited investigation of personal luggage. In that case, Drug Enforcement Administration (DEA) agents at a New York airport, based on information from law enforcement officers in Miami, believed that the defendant might be carrying narcotics. Upon the defendant's arrival at the airport, the agents approached him, informed him of their suspicion, and requested and received identification from him. When the defendant refused to consent to a search of his luggage, one of the agents told him that they were going to take the luggage to a federal judge to try to obtain a search warrant. The agents then took the luggage to another airport where they subjected it to a "sniff test" by a trained narcotics detection dog, which reacted positively to one of the bags. At this point, approximately ninety minutes had elapsed since the seizure of the luggage. The agents later obtained a search warrant for the luggage and, upon opening it, discovered a large quantity of cocaine.

As in the *Terry* case, the Court balanced the nature and quality of the intrusion on the individual's Fourth Amendment interests against the importance of the governmental interests alleged to justify the intrusion. The court found a substantial governmental interest in detecting drug trafficking, a unique problem because it is highly organized and conducted by sophisticated criminal syndicates, the profits are enormous, and drugs are easily concealed. The Court said:

> The context of a particular law enforcement practice, of course, may affect the determination whether a brief intrusion on Fourth Amendment interests on less than probable cause is essential to effective criminal investigation. Because of the inherently transient nature of drug courier activity at airports, allowing police to make brief investigative stops of persons at airports on reasonable suspicion of drug-trafficking substantially enhances the likelihood that police will be able to prevent the flow of narcotics into distribution channels. —— U.S. at ——, 103 S.Ct. at 2643, 77 L.Ed.2d at 119.

With respect to the intrusion on Fourth Amendment rights, the Court found that seizures of property can vary in intrusiveness and that some brief detentions of personal effects may be so minimally intrusive that strong countervailing governmental interests will justify a seizure based only on specific articulable facts that the property contains contraband or evidence of a crime. The Court held:

> [W]hen an officer's observations lead him reasonably to believe that a traveler is carrying luggage that contains narcotics, the principles of Terry and its progeny would permit the officer to detain the luggage briefly to investigate the circumstances that aroused his suspicion, provided that the investigative detention is properly limited in scope. —— U.S. at ——, 103 S.Ct. at 2644, 77 L.Ed.2d at 120.

In addition, the Court specifically found that the brief investigation of the luggage could include a "canine sniff" by a well-trained narcotics detection dog. This procedure was found to be uniquely limited in nature because it does not require opening the luggage, it does not expose noncontraband items to view, and it discloses only the presence or absence of narcotics, a contraband item.

Nevertheless, the Court found that the scope of the investigative detention of the luggage in the *Place* case exceeded the limits established in the *Terry* case, primarily because of the length of the detention. The Court said:

> Although the 90-minute detention of respondent's luggage is sufficient to render the seizure unreasonable, the violation was exacerbated by the failure of the agents to accurately inform respondent of the place to which they were transporting his luggage, of the length of time he might be dispossessed, and of what arrangements would be made for return of the luggage if the investigation dispelled the suspicion. In short, we hold that the detention of respondent's luggage in this case went beyond the narrow authority possessed by police to detain briefly luggage reasonably suspected to contain narcotics. —— U.S. at ——, 103 S.Ct. at 2646, 77 L.Ed.2d at 122.

It is important to note that, although the Court did not establish any rigid time limitation on an investigative detention, it clearly indicated that efforts of officers to minimize the intrusion on Fourth Amendment rights would be considered in determining the reasonableness of the detention.

Other types of containers, besides luggage, can also be detained for investigative purposes. In a rather unusual U.S. Supreme Court case, a postal clerk advised a policeman that he was suspicious of two packages of coins that had just been mailed. The policeman immediately noted that the return address was fictitious and that the person who mailed the packages had Canadian license plates. Later investigation disclosed that the addresses (one in California, the other in Tennessee) were under investigation for trafficking in illegal coins. Upon this basis, a search warrant for both packages was obtained, but not until the packages had been detained for slightly more than a day. The defendants were convicted of trafficking in illegal coins.

The Court upheld the warrantless detention of the packages while the investigation was made, recognizing nevertheless that a detention of mail could at some point become an unreasonable seizure of "papers" or "effects" within the meaning of the Fourth Amendment. The Court emphasized, however, that the investigation was conducted promptly and that most of the delay was attributable to the fact that the Tennessee authorities could not be reached until the following day because of the time zone differential. United States v. Van Leeuwen, 397 U.S. 249, 90 S.Ct. 1029, 25 L.Ed.2d 282 (U.S. Supreme Court, 1970). As in the *Place* case, the length of time of the detention was an important determinant of its reasonableness.

SUMMARY

A law enforcement officer may intrude upon a person's freedom of action and "stop" the person for purposes of investigating possible criminal behavior even though the officer does not have probable cause to arrest the person. The officer must, however, be able to point to specific circumstances indicating that possible criminal activity was afoot. This investigative detention must last no longer than necessary to achieve its purpose, and the investigative methods used must be the least intrusive means reasonably available to verify or dispel the officer's suspicion.

A law enforcement officer may, upon less than probable cause, intrude upon a person's privacy for purposes of conducting a protective search for weapons or a "frisk." A frisk is not automatically authorized whenever there is a stop. The officer must be able to demonstrate that the circumstances reasonably indicated that the person might be armed and dangerous. Also, the frisk must be very strictly limited to a protective purpose, although evidence of a crime obtained during a properly conducted frisk will be admissible in court.

The standard to be applied for both the stop and the frisk is whether the action taken by the officer was reasonable at its inception and limited in scope to what is minimally necessary for the accomplishment of the lawful purpose. This standard was developed by the U.S. Supreme Court as a result of a careful balancing of the needs of the police to prevent and investigate crime and to protect themselves and others from danger against the constitutional rights of individuals to their privacy, security, and freedom of action. Achieving an equitable balance in the infinite variety of encounters between police and citizens requires a careful consideration of the totality of the facts and circumstances.

REVIEW AND DISCUSSION QUESTIONS

1. Name some of the factors that might distinguish a *Terry*-type investigative stop from a seizure tantamount to an arrest.

2. In determining whether an officer has a reasonable suspicion that criminal activity is afoot, must the officer have a particular crime in mind?

3. Is less evidence required to support an investigative stop for a suspected serious violent crime than for a minor misdemeanor?

4. If an officer reasonably believes that a person is armed and dangerous, may the officer "frisk" the person regardless of the circumstances? Will any weapons found be admissible in evidence?

5. How does the "indicia of reliability" test for evaluating an informant's tip in the stop and frisk situation differ from the "totality of the circumstances" test of the *Gates* case discussed in Chapter 6? Why should there be different tests?

6. Must there be an *immediate* possibility of criminal activity to justify a *Terry*-type investigative stop, or would a possibility of criminal activity at some time in the future suffice?

7. Assuming that a frisk of a person is warranted, how extensive a search is permitted? Can the officer look for razor blades, nails, vials of acid, or mace containers? Can the officer look into briefcases, shopping bags, purses, hatbands, and other containers?

8. Since the only allowable purpose of a frisk is to discover a dangerous concealed weapon, should any other evidence found be admissible in court? What about items discovered in plain view as a result of a properly limited frisk?

9. Assuming that a law enforcement officer reasonably believes that a suspect is dangerous and may gain immediate control of weapons from an automobile, how extensive a protective search of the automobile may be made? May the officer look into suitcases and other containers?

10. If law enforcement officers have a reasonable suspicion that a package contains contraband, does the length of time that they may detain the package for investigation depend upon whether a person is carrying the package?

PART FOUR

Admissions and Confessions, Pre-trial Identification, and Electronic Surveillance

13

Admissions and Confessions

Since the U.S. Supreme Court decision in the case of Miranda v. Arizona, 384 U.S. 436, 86 S.Ct. 1602, 16 L.Ed.2d 694 (1966), the name *Miranda* has become very familiar to law enforcement personnel throughout the United States. The *Miranda* decision radically changed the course of law enforcement in the area of admissions, confessions, and interrogations, and in the process created a great deal of turmoil. The multitude of lower court decisions interpreting various aspects of the *Miranda* decision indicates the degree of confusion and misunderstanding that followed in its wake.

Although many of the questions arising from the *Miranda* decision have not been resolved by the courts, there is still a great deal of misunderstanding concerning the practical applications of *Miranda*. This chapter will discuss the *Miranda* case, its background, its meaning, and its implications for law enforcement officers. A large number of court decisions will be cited, and it is strongly suggested that the law enforcement officer read the *Miranda* decision as well as several of the lower court decisions in order to fully appreciate the way in which the courts handle problems in this area of the law.

HISTORICAL BACKGROUND

Prior to 1964, the test for the admissibility of a defendant's admission or confession was its "voluntariness." An involuntary statement was ruled inadmissible because it violated the due process clause of the Fourteenth Amendment to the Constitution. Three basic rationales are given for holding involuntary statements violations of due process. First, an involuntary statement is considered to be inherently untrustworthy or unreliable, and convictions based on unreliable evidence violate due process. Second, coercive police practices are a violation of "fundamental fairness," an essential element of due process. Therefore, a confession coerced by the police violates due process, even if it is otherwise reliable. Finally, free choice is an essential aspect of due process, and an involuntary confession cannot be the product of a person's free and rational choice.

The voluntariness test was established in Brown v. Mississippi, 297 U.S. 278, 56 S.Ct. 461, 80 L.Ed. 682 (1936), in which the U.S. Supreme Court held that a confession coerced from a defendant by means of police brutality violated due process of law. Later cases established that various other forms of police coercive conduct, including the more subtle psychological pressures, might render a resulting confession involuntary and thus violative of due process. In addition to outright brutality and violence, the following kinds of police conduct were found to violate due process:

1. Threats of violence—State v. Jennings, 367 So.2d 357 (Louisiana Supreme Court, 1979);

2. Confinement of the suspect in a small space until the suspect confessed—United States v. Koch, 552 F.2d 1216 (7th Circuit Court of Appeals, 1977);

3. Deprivation of food or sleep—Robinson v. Smith, 451 F.Supp. 1278 (U.S. District Court, Western District of New York, 1978);

4. Extended periods of incommunicado interrogation—Ashcraft v. Tennessee, 322 U.S. 143, 64 S.Ct. 921, 88 L.Ed. 1192 (U.S. Supreme Court, 1944), Davis v. North Carolina, 384 U.S. 737, 86 S.Ct. 1761, 16 L.Ed.2d 895 (U.S. Supreme Court, 1966);

5. Promises of leniency—Brady v. United States, 397 U.S. 742, 90 S.Ct. 1463, 25 L.Ed.2d 747 (U.S. Supreme Court, 1970)

6. Trickery or deception—Spano v. New York, 360 U.S. 315, 79 S.Ct. 1202, 3 L.Ed.2d 1265 (U.S. Supreme Court, 1959), although some courts have adopted the view of the District of Columbia Court of Appeals that "[c]onfessions generally are not vitiated when they are obtained by deception or trickery, as long as the means employed are not calculated to produce an untrue statement." Matter of D.A.S., 391 A.2d 255 (1978);

7. Obtaining of a statement during a period of unnecessary delay between arrest and arraignment—McNabb v. United States, 318 U.S. 332, 63 S.Ct. 608, 87 L.Ed. 819 (U.S. Supreme Court, 1943); Mallory v. United States, 354 U.S. 449, 77 S.Ct. 1356, 1 L.Ed.2d 1479 (U.S. Supreme Court, 1957). The *McNabb* and *Mallory* cases apply only to federal courts and hold that any admission or confession obtained during an unreasonable delay between arrest and appearance before a magistrate will be inadmissible in court. Some states have adopted similar rules and some have not.

Courts have also examined the personal characteristics of defendants in determining the voluntariness of an admission or confession. Some of the characteristics considered important are age, mental capacity, education level, physical or mental impairment from illness, injury, or intoxication, and prior experience in dealing with the police. The U.S. Supreme Court said that these personal characteristics are "relevant only in establishing a setting in which actual coercion might have been exerted to overcome the will of the suspect." Procunier v. Atchley, 400 U.S. 446, 453–54, 91 S.Ct. 485, 489, 27 L.Ed.2d 524, 531 (1971). Therefore, absent coercive conduct by the police, even an inexperienced young person with a mental disorder could be found to have made a voluntary confession.

The determination of the voluntariness of an admission or confession is, therefore, based on an evaluation of the "totality of the circumstances" surrounding the giving of the statement. The approach is similar to that used in determining the voluntariness of a consent to search. With the exception of the actual use of violence, no single fact or circumstance is solely determinative.

In 1964, a major change in the law took place. In the case of Escobedo v. Illinois, 378 U.S. 478, 84 S.Ct. 1758, 12 L.Ed.2d 977 (1964), the U.S. Supreme Court held:

> [W]here . . . the investigation is no longer a general inquiry into an unsolved crime but has begun to focus on a particular suspect, the suspect has been taken into police custody, the police carry out a process of interrogations that lends itself to eliciting incriminating statements, the suspect has requested and been denied an opportunity to consult with his lawyer, and the police have not effectively warned him of his absolute constitutional right to remain silent, the accused has been denied "the Assistance of Counsel" in violation of the Sixth Amendment to the Constitution as "made obligatory upon the States by the Fourteenth Amendment," . . . and that no statement elicited by the police during the interrogation may be used against him at a criminal trial. 378 U.S. at 491, 84 S.Ct. at 1765, 12 L.Ed.2d at 986.

The *Escobedo* case was significant, not only because it shifted the area of inquiry from due process to the Sixth Amendment, but also because it did not follow a "totality of the circumstances" approach. Instead, the Court took a single circumstance and made it the single determinative factor in all cases in which it occurred. The Court said:

> [W]hen the process shifts from investigatory to accusatory—when its focus is on the accused and its purpose is to elicit a confession . . . the accused must be permitted to consult with his lawyer. 378 U.S. at 492, 84 S.Ct. at 1766, 12 L.Ed.2d at 987.

This has come to be known as the *Escobedo* "focus of investigation" test.

Miranda v. Arizona, decided two years later in 1966, again rejected the "totality of the circumstances" approach, extended the *Escobedo* decision, and shifted the area of inquiry to the Fifth Amendment. In short, the *Miranda* case held that "the prosecution may not use statements, whether exculpatory or inculpatory, stemming from custodial interrogation of the defendant unless it demonstrates the use of procedural safeguards effective to secure the privilege against self-incrimination." 384 U.S. at 444, 86 S.Ct. at 1612, 16 L.Ed.2d at 706. The statements may not be used to prove the case against the defendant even if the statements were otherwise voluntary. Of course, if an admission or confession is involuntary for whatever reason, it will be inadmissible in court despite compliance with the *Miranda* requirements. Courts will carefully evaluate all the circumstances of an interrogation in determining voluntariness, and, even though *Miranda* requirements are met, a statement obtained through force, threat, promises, or any other form of coercion will be involuntary and therefore inadmissible for any purpose.

Admissibility of admissions and confessions is therefore treated differently from admissibility of evidence seized as the result of a consent search. Evidence resulting from a consent search is admissible if the "totality of the circumstances" shows that the consent was voluntary. An admission or confession is admissible if (1) the "totality of the circumstances" shows that the statement was voluntary, *and* (2) the *Miranda* requirements have been complied with.

We turn now to a discussion of the requirements outlined in the *Miranda* decision.

MIRANDA—FACTS AND HOLDING

The Court's opinion in *Miranda v. Arizona* actually covers three other cases besides *Miranda,* all dealing with the admissibility of statements obtained from an individual who is subjected to custodial police interrogation. A brief description of the facts of each case is helpful in understanding the scope of the opinion.

In *Miranda v. Arizona,* the defendant was arrested at his home for rape and taken to a police station where he was identified by the complaining witness. There he was interrogated and within two hours signed a written confession. At no time was he informed of his right to consult with an attorney, to have an attorney present during the interrogation, or of his right not to be compelled to incriminate himself. In *Vignera v. New York,* the defendant was picked up in connection with a robbery and taken to detective squad headquarters where he was interrogated and confessed. He was then locked up. He was questioned again about eight hours later and at that time gave a written statement. At no time was he informed of any of his rights. In *Westover v. U.S.,* the defendant was arrested by municipal police as a robbery suspect. The FBI conducted an interrogation that same afternoon in an interrogation room in the municipal police department. After two hours, the defendant signed two confessions. The Court noted that the FBI interrogation was conducted following the interrogation by municipal police in the same police station—in the same compelling surroundings. In *California v. Stewart,* the defendant was arrested at his home where police found robbery proceeds. He was then taken to a police station and placed in a cell where over a period of five days he was interrogated nine times. The Court noted that the defendant was isolated with his interrogators at all times except when he was being confronted by an accusing witness.

The purpose of the above fact summaries is to indicate the type of situation to which the Court was addressing itself. In each case the defendant was questioned by police officers, detectives, or a prosecuting attorney in a room in which he was cut off from the outside world. In none of the cases was the defendant given a full and effective warning of his rights at the outset of the interrogation process. In all of the cases, the questioning elicited oral statements, and in three of them, signed statements resulted as well. These statements were admitted into evidence at trial. Thus, all the cases shared the features of incommunicado interrogation of individuals in a police-dominated atmosphere, resulting in self-incriminating statements without full warnings of constitutional rights.

The *Miranda* Court, having reviewed the facts in each case, then discussed specific police interrogation techniques as prescribed in police manuals. In condemning these techniques, the Court said:

> It is obvious that such an interrogation environment is created for no purpose other than to subjugate the individual to the will of his examiner. This atmosphere carries its own badge of intimidation. To be sure, this is not physical intimidation, but it is equally destructive of human dignity. The current practice of incommunicado interrogation is at odds with one of our Nation's most cherished principles—that the individual may not be compelled to incriminate himself. Unless adequate protective devices are employed to dispel the compulsion inherent in custodial surroundings, no statement obtained from the defendant can truly be the product of his free choice. 384 U.S. at 457–58, 86 S.Ct. at 1619, 16 L.Ed.2d at 714.

The Court then went on to establish procedural safeguards to protect the individual's privilege against self-incrimination. These safeguards take the form of the *Miranda* warnings so familiar to all law enforcement personnel.

The *Miranda* case requires that, whenever persons are taken into custody or otherwise deprived of their freedom of action by law enforcement officers in any significant way, they must be given the following warnings before any questioning takes place:

1. They must be informed clearly and unequivocally that they have the right to remain silent.

2. They must be told that any statement they make can and will be used against them in court.

3. They must be informed that they have the right to consult with a lawyer and to have the lawyer with them during interrogation.

4. They must be told that if they are indigent and cannot afford a lawyer, a lawyer will be appointed to represent them.

The person in custody must be given the opportunity to exercise these rights throughout the course of the interrogation. After the warnings and opportunity to exercise them have been given, the person may knowingly and intelligently waive these rights and agree to answer questions or make a statement. Until sufficient proof of adequate warnings and waiver are demonstrated by the prosecution at a trial or suppression hearing, however, no evidence obtained as a result of interrogation can be used against the person.

MIRANDA—ISSUES

The *Miranda* decision has raised many questions, but in general, the issues can be divided into two categories:

1. The first category is whether *Miranda* requirements apply to the particular case. Under this general heading the issues are whether the defendant was in custody, whether the defendant's statements were the result of interrogation, whether the interrogator was a law enforcement officer or agent, and whether the seriousness of the offense has any bearing.

2. The second category is whether *Miranda* requirements have been met in cases in which they apply. Under this general heading the issues are whether the warnings were adequate, whether rights were clearly waived, whether the suspect was competent to waive the rights, and whether more than one interrogation is allowed under *Miranda.*

In short, the major issues of *Miranda* can be said to center around the meaning of four words: "custody," "interrogation," "warning," and "waiver." The remainder of this chapter will be devoted to a discussion of these issues as well as some additional miscellaneous issues.

CUSTODY

Law enforcement officers often have difficulty determining when a person is in "custody" or is "deprived of his freedom of action in any significant way" so as to entitle the person to the *Miranda* warnings. One of the reasons for this difficulty is that the meaning of the word custody depends upon a consideration of a variety of circumstances. A safe policy to follow is to give the warnings whenever there is any doubt whether or not they apply. However, there are several situations under which the warnings are clearly not required. The following discussion of particular facts and circumstances should help clarify this issue for the law enforcement officer.

Focus of Investigation

The *Miranda* decision has been generally understood to have abandoned the "focus of investigation" test of the *Escobedo* case to determine when an interrogated suspect is entitled to warnings. Lowe v. United States, 407 F.2d 1391, 1396 (9th Circuit Court of Appeals, 1969). The test now, under *Miranda,* is whether the individual being questioned is in custody or has been deprived of freedom of action in any significant way. Therefore, it has generally been held that even though (1) an officer knows the suspect committed the crime, or (2) the officer intends to arrest the suspect at the end of the questioning, or (3) the officer would not allow the suspect to leave if he or she tried, *Miranda* warnings need not be given if the interview is not otherwise custodial. State v. Hall, 12 Ariz.App. 147, 468 P.2d 598 (Court of Appeals of Arizona, 1970); People v. Hazel, 252 Cal.App.2d 412, 60 Cal. Rptr. 437 (California Court of Appeal, 1967). The U.S. Supreme Court specifically held that, even though a suspect is clearly the focus of a criminal investigation, the suspect need not be given *Miranda* warnings if not otherwise in custody or deprived of freedom of action in any significant way.   Beckwith v. United States, 425 U.S. 341, 96 S.Ct. 1612, 48 L.Ed.2d 1 (1976).

Many courts have adopted an "objective" test of custody, i.e., whether under the circumstances of the case, a reasonable person would reasonably believe that he or she was in custody or deprived of freedom of action in any significant way.   Under this "objective" test, a court will not accept a suspect's mere assertion of belief of being in custody or deprived of freedom of action, but will look at all the circumstances to determine the reasonableness of this belief.   Freije v. United States, 408 F.2d 100 (1st Circuit Court of Appeals, 1969).

The focus concept may still have some vitality as one of the circumstances to be considered by the court in determining the custody issue.   In a case in which three agents interviewed a suspect in his home, the court, discussing the custody issue, said that in the absence of actual arrest, something must be said or done by the authorities, either in their manner or approach or in the tone or extent of their questioning, that indicates that they would not have heeded a request to depart or allowed the suspect to do so.   The court went on to say:

> This is not to say that the amount of information possessed by the police and the consequent acuity of their "focus," is irrelevant.   The more cause for believing the suspect committed the crime, the greater the tendency to bear down in interrogation and to create the kind of atmosphere of significant restraint that triggers Miranda . . . .   United States v. Hall, 421 F.2d 540, 545 (2d Circuit Court of Appeals, 1969).

Therefore, it would seem that an interview with a suspect could initially be non-custodial in all respects.   However, as the questioning became more intense and pointed, a reasonable person might feel no longer free to go about personal and business affairs.   A court might decide that, at this time, the person was significantly deprived of freedom of action and thus entitled to *Miranda* warnings.

To summarize, in evaluating the necessity for *Miranda* warnings, the existence of "custody" or "deprivation of freedom of action in a significant way" is determined by consideration of all the facts and circumstances, one of which may be the "focus" of the investigation on the suspect.   We turn now to the various other facts and circumstances upon which a determination of custody may be based.

Place of Interrogation

Court decisions interpreting the *Miranda* requirements have indicated that the place of interrogation is a vital, though not conclusive, factor in determining custody.   The following is a discussion of cases that have placed strong reliance on the place of interrogation in determining the question of custody.

Police Stations and Police Vehicles   In all four of the cases decided in the *Miranda* opinion (discussed earlier), the suspect was questioned in a police station after arrest.   There would seem to be little question that custody exists in this type of situation. Other courts have held that even if the person is not arrested but is present at a police station for questioning at the command of the police, the person is in custody for purposes of *Miranda*. United States v. Pierce, 397 F.2d 128 (4th Circuit Court of Appeals, 1968).

Nevertheless, numerous cases have held that the presence of a suspect at a police station was clearly non-custodial. Police station interrogation was held non-custodial where the person questioned was present as a witness. Clark v. United States, 400 F.2d 83 (9th Circuit Court of Appeals, 1968). In Oregon v. Mathiason, 429 U.S. 492, 97 S.Ct. 711, 50 L.Ed.2d 714 (1977), the U.S. Supreme Court held that a suspect is not necessarily in custody even when questioned in a police station. In that case the defendant, a parolee, was a suspect in a burglary. A state police officer asked him to come to the state police offices "to discuss something." When the defendant arrived, the officer took him into a closed office and told him that he was not under arrest. The officer then informed him that he was a suspect in the burglary and falsely stated that his fingerprints had been found at the scene. Within five minutes, the defendant confessed to the burglary. He left the office one half-hour later.

The Court held that the *Miranda* warnings were not required because the defendant was not in custody.

> In the present case, however, there is no indication that the questioning took place in a context where respondent's freedom to depart was restricted in any way. He came voluntarily to the police station, where he was immediately informed that he was not under arrest. At the close of a one half-hour interview respondent did in fact leave the police station without hindrance. It is clear from these facts that Mathiason was not in custody "or otherwise deprived of his freedom of action in any significant way."

> *   *   *

> Any interview of one suspected of a crime by a police officer will have coercive aspects to it, simply by virtue of the fact that the police officer is part of a law enforcement system which may ultimately cause the suspect to be charged with a crime. But police officers are not required to administer Miranda warnings to everyone whom they question. Nor is the requirement of warnings imposed simply because the questioning takes place in the station house, or because the questioned person is one whom the police suspect. Miranda warnings are required only where there has been such a restriction on a person's freedom as to render him "in custody." It was that sort of coercive environment to which Miranda by its terms was made applicable, and to which it is limited. 429 U.S. at 495, 97 S.Ct. at 714, 50 L.Ed.2d at 719.

Cases dealing with the questioning of suspects in police vehicles have provided few guidelines for the law enforcement officer. The safest policy to follow in the police station or vehicle interrogation situation is to give the *Miranda* warnings, unless the individual is clearly there voluntarily.

Jails Generally, a suspect who is incarcerated in a jail or prison is in custody for purposes of any interrogation. Thus, a person who was incarcerated in a penitentiary for one offense was held to be in custody for purposes of interrogation conducted by IRS agents with respect to another offense. Mathis v. United States, 391 U.S. 1, 88 S.Ct. 1503, 20 L.Ed.2d 381 (U.S. Supreme Court, 1968).

Homes   Ordinarily, interrogation in a suspect's home is non-custodial because the person is in familiar surroundings and there is an absence of a "police-dominated atmosphere." However, this principle is not absolute. In Orozco v. Texas, 394 U.S. 324, 89 S.Ct. 1095, 22 L.Ed.2d 311 (U.S. Supreme Court, 1969), a suspect was questioned at 4:00 a.m. in his bedroom by four officers, one of whom later testified that the suspect was under arrest. The Court held that even though the questioning was brief and the suspect was in familiar surroundings, there was a custodial interrogation. The key reasons for the decision were the time of the interrogation, the number of officers present, and the somewhat unclear evidence of formal arrest.

Usually cases of interrogation in homes involve less severe circumstances than those of the *Orozco* case. Courts generally hold that questioning suspects in their own home without arrest is not custodial interrogation so long as there has been no coercive conduct by law enforcement officers. United States v. Agy, 374 F.2d 94 (6th Circuit Court of Appeals, 1967).

Places of Business   Interrogation of suspects at their place of business is usually held to be non-custodial. Like the home, the place of business represents a familiar surrounding. Archer v. United States, 393 F.2d 124 (5th Circuit Court of Appeals, 1968).

Stores, Restaurants, and Other Public Places   Public places such as stores, restaurants, and bars are considered less familiar to a suspect than a home or office. Nevertheless, courts usually find that an interrogation conducted in these places is non-custodial. The reasons usually given are that the suspect is in a place of personal choice and is not isolated from the outside world. Also there is generally an absence of a police-dominated atmosphere in public places. Lucas v. United States, 408 F.2d 835 (9th Circuit Court of Appeals, 1969).

Hospitals   Questioning of a suspect confined in a hospital as a patient but not under arrest is not usually held to be a custodial interrogation. State v. Zucconi, 50 N.J. 361, 235 A.2d 193 (New Jersey Supreme Court, 1967). The reasons usually relied on are the lack of a compelling atmosphere, the routine nature of the questioning, and the lack of any deprivation of freedom. However, this is not a hard and fast rule, and factors such as intense and pointed questioning or a very sick or highly drugged suspect might cause a hospital interview to be held custodial in nature. State v. Ross, 183 Neb. 1, 157 N.W.2d 860 (Supreme Court of Nebraska, 1968).

Automobiles   Most questioning of a suspect in an automobile is dealt with as "on-the-scene" questioning or as a traffic stop. Both these situations are discussed later in the chapter. Some cases emphasize that suspects in their own cars are in familiar surroundings.   Under any of these rationales, the courts generally find a lack of custody.

Crime Scenes   The *Miranda* decision itself gives some guidance to the law enforcement officer regarding the necessity for warnings when investigating the scene of a crime.   The Court said that its decision was:

> not intended to hamper the traditional function of police officers in investigating crime. . . .   General on-the-scene questioning as to facts surrounding a crime or other general questioning of citizens in the fact-finding process is not affected by our holding.   It is an act of responsible citizenship for individuals to give whatever information they may have to aid in law enforcement.   In such situations the compelling atmosphere inherent in the process of in custody interrogation is not necessarily present.   384 U.S. at 477–78, 86 S.Ct. at 1629–30, 16 L.Ed.2d at 725–26.

In general, courts have held that the questioning of a suspect near the scene of a crime prior to arrest is not custodial interrogation.   People v. Schwartz, 30 A.D.2d 385, 292 N.Y.S.2d 518 (Supreme Court of N.Y., Appellate Division, 1968).   An example of crime scene questioning in a homicide situation is a case in which the defendant shot the victim in the defendant's home.   The police arrived at the scene and asked what happened.   The defendant replied that he shot the victim.   The court held that the defendant was not in custody or deprived of his freedom in any significant way and that *Miranda* warnings were not required.   "We do not interpret this important decision [*Miranda*] to exclude statements made at the scene of an investigation when nobody has been arrested, detained, or charged."   State v. Oxentine, 270 N.C. 412, 415, 154 S.E.2d 529, 531 (Supreme Court of North Carolina, 1967).

It is likely that a law enforcement officer would be allowed to briefly detain all potential witnesses at the scene of a crime for questioning without triggering *Miranda*.   Innocent citizen witnesses directed by an officer not to leave the scene of a crime are not likely to consider themselves in-custody or under arrest and it is unlikely that a court would so consider them.   Arnold v. United States, 382 F.2d 4 (9th Circuit Court of Appeals, 1967).

Brief Street Encounters   Another form of investigative questioning occurs when an officer makes inquiries of persons who are acting suspiciously.   An example is a case in which a suspect was walking on a highway near a car known to be stolen and officers stopped him and asked him if the car was his.   The suspect made incriminating statements in response.   The court held that this situation did not require the giving of *Miranda* warnings, and the statements were admissible in court.   State v. Whitney, 72 Wn.2d 122, 431 P.2d 711 (Supreme Court of Washington, 1967).

For several reasons, courts do not require *Miranda* warnings before brief "on-the-scene" questioning during a street encounter.   One basic reason is that law enforcement officers should be allowed to resolve suspicious situations by asking simple questions of suspects, without having to explain all their rights to them. Also, there is usually an absence of a compelling police-dominated atmosphere in a brief street encounter and the questioning is brief and non-focused. See Chapter 12 for a discussion of "Stop and Frisk and Miranda."

It is important to emphasize that the place where the interrogation occurs is only one factor to be considered in determining whether the person questioned is in custody for purposes of *Miranda*. Many of the cases cited above might have been decided differently if other surrounding facts and circumstances had been different. We turn now to a discussion of some of those other facts and circumstances.

Time of Interrogation

An interrogation conducted during business hours is less likely to be considered custodial than one carried out in the late evening or early morning. For example, the time of the interrogation was a significant reason for holding the interrogation at the suspect's home to be custodial in the *Orozco* case (see above under "Homes"). Had the questioning of the suspect taken place during business hours, the decision might have gone the other way. It is not unlikely that reasonable persons would consider their freedom significantly restrained when approached by police for questioning in the early hours of the morning.

Presence of Other Persons

The *Miranda* decision expressly indicated a concern for the suspect who is "cut off from the outside world." 384 U.S. at 445, 86 S.Ct. at 1612, 16 L.Ed.2d at 707. Courts have taken this to mean that the presence of family, friends, or neutrals during the questioning of a suspect may cause it to be considered non-custodial. People v. Butterfield, 258 Cal.App.2d 586, 65 Cal.Rptr. 765 (California Court of Appeal, 1968). Correspondingly, the deliberate removal of a suspect from the presence of family and friends is indicative of custody. Commonwealth v. Sites, 427 Pa. 486, 235 A.2d 387 (Pennsylvania Supreme Court, 1967). Some courts speak of a "balance of power" and find custody to exist in cases in which the sheer number of police indicates a police-dominated atmosphere. State v. Ross, 183 Neb. 1, 157 N.W.2d 860 (Nebraska Supreme Court, 1968); Orozco v. Texas, 394 U.S. 324, 89 S.Ct. 1095, 22 L.Ed.2d 311 (U.S. Supreme Court, 1969).

Suspect Under Arrest or Restraint

If suspects are told they are under arrest, then they are definitely in custody for *Miranda* purposes. Duckett v. State, 3 Md.App. 563, 240 A.2d 332 (Court of Special Appeals of Maryland, 1968). Of course, the reverse is also true, and the officer who tells a suspect that he or she is not under arrest and is free to leave at any time generally creates a non-custodial setting for an interrogation. U.S. v. Manglona, 414 F.2d 642 (9th Circuit Court of Appeals, 1969).

Short of actual arrest, the courts have generally recognized that the physical restraint of the suspect is a significant factor in determining questions of custody. In cases in which physical restraint was present, courts have almost invariably found custody. State v. Saunders, 102 Ariz. 565, 435 P.2d 38 (Supreme Court of Arizona, 1967). By the same token, an absence of physical restraint has led several courts to conclude that the defendant was not in custody. People v. Merchant, 260 Cal.App.2d 875, 67 Cal.Rptr. 459 (California Court of Appeal, 1968).

If an officer holds a gun on a suspect, the officer clearly creates a custodial situation. People v. Shivers, 21 N.Y. 118, 233 N.E.2d 836 (N.Y. Court of Appeals, 1967). However, if the suspect is also armed, a court is unlikely to find that the suspect was in custody. Yates v. United States, 384 F.2d 586 (5th Circuit Court of Appeals, 1967). This is a potentially important situation because armed offenders often make damaging admissions while holding off the police.

The absence of other incidents of arrest such as handcuffing, searching, fingerprinting, photographing, and other booking procedures tends to indicate a non-custodial interview. Hicks v. United States, 382 F.2d 158 (District of Columbia Circuit Court of Appeals, 1967); United States v. Thomas, 396 F.2d 310 (2d Circuit Court of Appeals, 1968). The use of these procedures may of course lead to the contrary conclusion. People v. Ellingsen, 258 Cal.App.2d 535, 65 Cal.Rptr. 744 (California Court of Appeal, 1968).

A probationer, although subject to a number of restrictive conditions governing various aspects of life, is not in custody for purposes of *Miranda* simply by reason of the probationer status. Furthermore, an interview between a probationer and probation officer, which is non-custodial in all respects, does not become custodial for *Miranda* purposes, even though the probation officer could compel attendance and truthful answers at the interview. Minnesota v. Murphy, ___ U.S. ___, 104 S.Ct. 1136, 79 L.Ed.2d 409 (1984).

Duration and Nature of Questioning

The duration and nature of the interrogation is very significant in determining custody for purposes of *Miranda*. Most of the cases that allowed questioning without warnings at crime scenes and during brief street encounters emphasized that the questioning was of short duration and involved only a few general investigative questions. Such brief, routine police inquiries generally indicate a non-custodial interview for the purpose of clarifying a suspicious situation.

An example is a case in which an officer stopped a car being driven by defendant in an unusual manner. A passenger in the car was injured and bleeding. The defendant gave suspicious answers to the officer's questions. When the officer asked the passenger if he had been beaten and by whom, the passenger mumbled something and pointed at the defendant. The officer then asked the defendant if he had beaten the passenger and the defendant said yes. The court held that the officer acted properly by asking routine questions to clarify the situation. The court found that *Miranda* warnings were unnecessary, pointing out that warnings hamper and perhaps demean routine police investigation, and make cooperative citizens nervous. Allen v. United States, 390 F.2d 476 (District of Columbia Circuit Court of Appeals, 1968).

Interview Initiated by Suspect

If a suspect summons the police or initiates the interview, or both, a court is likely to hold that subsequent police interrogation is non-custodial. The element of compulsion is lacking and the statements are not entirely the product of police action.

An example is a case in which the defendant waved down a police car, voluntarily got into the car, and told the police that he had just shot a person attempting a robbery. The court held that police questioning of the defendant about the incident, in the police car, was not custodial and did not require *Miranda* warnings. People v. Lee, 33 A.D.2d 397, 308 N.Y.S.2d 412 (N.Y. Court of Appeals, 1970).

Statements to Undercover Agents or Informants

Suspects who do not know they are speaking to a law enforcement officer cannot have a reasonable belief that they are in custody. Therefore, situations involving undercover agents or informants are clearly non-custodial. Hoffa v. United States, 385 U.S. 293, 87 S.Ct. 408, 176 L.Ed.2d 374 (U.S. Supreme Court, 1966); People v. Ward, 266 Cal.App.2d 241, 72 Cal.Rptr. 46 (California Court of Appeal, 1968).

Traffic Stops

The questioning of a driver of a vehicle stopped for traffic violations is generally held by courts to be non-custodial. A traffic stop is very similar to an "on-the-scene" street encounter in that the questions are usually brief and general. Also, for most drivers, being stopped for a traffic violation is a fairly common occurrence, and it is not likely that drivers would reasonably believe themselves to be under arrest or in custody in such a situation. Lowe v. United States, 407 F.2d 1391 (9th Circuit Court of Appeals, 1969).

Statements Arising Out of a Stop and Frisk

Most courts agree that brief questioning of a suspect in connection with an investigative stop or frisk authorized by *Terry v. Ohio* (see Chapter 12) does not require *Miranda* warnings. This type of stop is similar to general on-the-scene questioning at a crime scene in that the setting is usually a public place and the questions are brief. Although a detention of a suspect occurs, a compelling police atmosphere is usually not present, and the deprivation of the suspect's freedom of action is not significant enough to require the protection of the *Miranda* warnings. People v. Manis, 268 Cal.App.2d 653, 74 Cal.Rptr. 423 (California Court of Appeal, 1969). *Miranda* issues in the stop and frisk situation are discussed in further detail in Chapter 12.

Determination of Custody—Summary

The determination of whether an interrogation is custodial for purposes of *Miranda* requires a consideration of many factors. No one can predict for certain how a court will interpret a given set of facts and circumstances in deciding whether

Miranda warnings are required. The safe procedure is to give the warnings whenever there is doubt as to whether they apply.

Miranda is designed to protect individuals and inform them of their rights, but it is not intended to hamper effective law enforcement. The cases discussed above clearly indicate that law enforcement officers may ask routine questions, investigate suspicious circumstances, enlist the aid of cooperative citizens, etc., without being required to give *Miranda* warnings in every instance. Making the proper decision in borderline cases will require a combination of knowledge, experience, and confidence.

INTERROGATION

Once it has been determined whether or not a suspect is in custody for *Miranda* purposes, the question arises whether any statements made are the product of interrogation. In Rhode Island v. Innis, 446 U.S. 291, 100 S.Ct. 1682, 64 L.Ed.2d 297 (1980), the U.S. Supreme Court explained the meaning of "interrogation" for purposes of the *Miranda* cases. The Court said:

> [T]he Miranda safeguards come into play whenever a person in custody is subjected to either express questioning or its functional equivalent. That is to say, the term "interrogation" under Miranda refers not only to express questioning, but also to any words or actions on the part of police (other than those normally attendant to arrest and custody) that the police should know are reasonably likely to elicit an incriminating response from the suspect. 446 U.S. at 300–01, 100 S.Ct. at 1689, 64 L.Ed.2d at 307–08.

The Court further clarified the definition by stating that an incriminating response is any response—whether inculpatory or exculpatory—that the prosecution may seek to introduce at trial. Despite this broad definition of interrogation, there are many situations in which a person converses with or gives information to law enforcement officers that are not considered to be "interrogation" for *Miranda* purposes and thus do not require the *Miranda* warnings.

Volunteered Statements

The most obvious case in which *Miranda* warnings are not required is the volunteered statement—the statement made either without, or not in response to, questioning by a law enforcement officer. In the *Miranda* opinion, the Court stated that "[v]olunteered statements of any kind are not barred by the Fifth Amendment and their admissibility is not affected by our holding today." 384 U.S. at 478, 86 S.Ct. at 1630, 16 L.Ed.2d at 726.

Volunteered statements sometimes occur when a person simply walks up to a police officer on the street or into a police station and makes damaging admissions. People v. Hines, 66 Cal.2d 348, 57 Cal.Rptr. 757, 425 P.2d 557 (California Supreme Court, 1967). Volunteered statements occur more frequently, however, when a person is in custody, either before, during, or after interrogation. Dick v. United States, 395 F.2d 89 (9th Circuit Court of Appeals, 1968). Volunteered statements may occur during interrogation when the suspect makes a damaging statement that does not respond to an officer's question. For example, an officer asked the defendant where the key to his car was, so the car could be moved off the street and put in storage. Defendant replied that the car had been stolen. The court held that the statement that the car was stolen was not responsive to the inquiry about the key and was completely voluntary. Parson v. United States, 387 F.2d 944 (10th Circuit Court of Appeals, 1968).

Furthermore, officers need not interrupt a volunteered statement in order to warn a suspect of *Miranda* rights. The *Miranda* decision specifically states that "[t]here is no requirement that police stop a person who enters a police station and states that he wishes to confess to a crime, or a person who calls the police to offer a confession or any other statement he desires to make." 384 U.S. at 478, 86 S.Ct. at 1630, 16 L.Ed.2d at 726.

Clarifying Questions

Since most volunteered admissions are unspecific, an officer may try to clarify exactly what is being said. Courts have held that a statement is volunteered even if some questions are asked by police. The questions, however, must not be designed to expand upon what the person originally intended to say, but merely to clear up or explain the person's statement. People v. Sunday, 275 Cal.App.2d 473, 79 Cal. Rptr. 752 (California Court of Appeal, 1969).

An example is a case in which a man walked into a police station and said "I done it; I done it; arrest me; arrest me." The officer asked him what he had done and the man said he killed his wife. Then the officer asked him how, and he replied, "With an axe, that's all I had." The court held that this type of clarifying questioning without warnings was permitted by *Miranda*. People v. Savage, 102 Ill. App.2d 477, 479, 242 N.E.2d 446, 447 (Illinois Court of Appeals, 1968).

Brief and Routine Questions

In the discussion of "custody" earlier, the brief and routine nature of questioning was usually indicative of a lack of custody. Courts have also held that brief and routine questioning is not "interrogation" under *Miranda,* even if the suspect is in custody.

Routine questions asked during the booking of a suspect by the booking officer have usually been held to be non-interrogative in nature. Toohey v. United States, 404 F.2d 907 (9th Circuit Court of Appeals, 1968). However, this is not a hard and fast rule, and since the suspect is in a police station, probably involuntarily, it is safer to give the *Miranda* warnings in this situation.

Brief routine questions are asked by officers in a great variety of situations. Most courts have taken the view that *Miranda* warnings are only required when law enforcement officers demand answers in an authoritative manner from persons in custody. State v. Travis, 25 Or. 213, 441 P.2d 597 (Oregon Supreme Court, 1968). Therefore, the simple, everyday investigative question does not constitute interrogation. Usually, if an officer is not trying to elicit an incriminating response, the courts will not require *Miranda* warnings.

Spontaneous Questions

When law enforcement officers ask questions spontaneously, impulsively, or in response to emergency circumstances, the questions are usually held to be non-interrogative. An example is a case in which a jailer and a guard were called to a cell area where they found one prisoner near death from strangling. While tending to the injured prisoner, they asked the defendant, who was also a prisoner, about the incident and received incriminating replies. The court held that this questioning was not a deliberate effort to elicit damaging evidence but rather was spontaneous on-the-scene questioning by an astonished jailer. People v. Morse, 70 Cal.2d 711, 452 P.2d 607 (California Supreme Court, 1969).

Questions Related to Public Safety

Closely related to spontaneous questions are questions by a law enforcement officer arising out of a concern for public safety. In New York v. Quarles, ___ U.S. ___, 104 S.Ct. 2626, 81 L.Ed.2d 550 (1984), two police officers were approached by a woman who told them that she had just been raped and that her assailant had just entered a nearby supermarket and was carrying a gun. One of the officers entered the store and spotted the defendant, who matched the description given by the woman. The officer pursued the defendant with a drawn gun and ordered the defendant to stop and put his hands over his head. The officer frisked him and discovered that he was wearing an empty shoulder holster. After handcuffing him, the officer asked him where the gun was and the defendant nodded toward some empty cartons and responded that "the gun is over there."

Although the defendant was in police custody when he made his statements and the facts fell within the coverage of *Miranda*, the U.S. Supreme Court held that there was a "public safety" exception to the requirement that *Miranda* warnings be given before a suspect's answers may be admitted into evidence. The Court said:

> The police in this case, in the very act of apprehending a suspect, were confronted with the immediate necessity of ascertaining the whereabouts of a gun which they had every reason to believe the suspect had just removed from his empty holster and discarded in the supermarket. So long as the gun was concealed somewhere in the supermarket, with its actual whereabouts unknown, it obviously posed more than one danger to the public safety: an accomplice might make use of it, a customer or employee might later come upon it.

The Court concluded that the need for answers to questions in a situation posing a threat to the public safety outweighed the need for the prophylactic rule protecting the Fifth Amendment's privilege against self-incrimination. Furthermore, the Court held that the availability of the public safety exception does not depend upon the motivation of the individual officers involved. The Court recognized that in a spontaneous, emergency situation like the one in the *Quarles* case, most police officers act out of several different, instinctive motives—concern for their own safety and that of others, and, perhaps, the desire to obtain incriminating evidence from the suspect. A rigid adherence to the *Miranda* rules is not required when police officers ask questions reasonably prompted by a concern for the public safety.

Finally, the Court acknowledged that the public safety exception lessens the clarity of the *Miranda* rule, but expressed confidence that the police would instinctively respond appropriately in situations threatening the public safety.

> [W]e recognize here the importance of a workable rule "to guide police officers, who have only limited time and expertise to reflect on and balance the social and individual interests involved in the specific circumstances they confront." . . . But . . . we believe that the [public safety] exception . . . lessens the necessity of that on-the-scene balancing process. The exception will not be difficult for police officers to apply because in each case it will be circumscribed by the exigency which justifies it. We think police officers can and will distinguish almost instinctively between questions necessary to secure their own safety or the safety of the public and questions designed solely to elicit testimonial evidence from a suspect. ___ U.S. at ___, 104 S.Ct. at 2633, 81 L.Ed.2d at 559.

Confrontation of Suspects With Evidence

In general, it is proper for a law enforcement officer to confront a suspect with the evidence or with the other facts of the case against the suspect. Often, after such a confrontation, a suspect may confess to a crime or make damaging admissions. The question under *Miranda* is whether these statements made by the suspect are volunteered statements or the product of a form of "silent interrogation."

Courts have decided the issue both ways depending on the circumstances of individual cases. When there is no verbal interrogation and the suspect is merely confronted with evidence, an accomplice, scientific reports, etc., courts have held that damaging admissions made after the confrontation were not the products of interrogation. People v. Doss, 44 Ill.2d 541, 256 N.E.2d 753 (Illinois Supreme Court, 1970); State v. Burnett, Mo., 429 S.W.2d 239 (Missouri Supreme Court, 1968). When, however, along with such a confrontation, an officer attempts, however subtly, to get the suspect to talk, courts have found interrogation and have suppressed statements obtained without warnings. State v. LaFernier, 37 Wis.2d 365, 155 N.W.2d 93 (Wisconsin Supreme Court, 1967). Again, the crucial question under *Rhode Island v. Innis* is whether the officer's words or actions are reasonably likely to elicit an incriminating response. Toliver v. Gathright, 501 F.Supp. 148 (U.S. District Court for the Eastern District of Virginia, 1980).

Statements Responding to Statements by Officers

An officer will often receive an incriminating reply to a mere comment or statement that is not a question. Since there is usually no intent to elicit incriminating information by officers in this situation, these statements by suspects are usually held not to be the product of interrogation. United States v. Pellegrini, 309 F.Supp. 250 (U.S. District Court, Southern District of N.Y., 1970). If, however, officers' statements are deliberately directed toward obtaining incriminating information, courts will consider the statements as tantamount to interrogation. Brewer v. Williams, 430 U.S. 387, 97 S.Ct. 1232, 51 L.Ed.2d 424 (U.S. Supreme Court, 1977). The facts of the *Brewer v. Williams* case are presented later in this chapter under "Statements Obtained After Defendant Formally Charged."

Interrogation by Private Citizens

The warnings requirements of *Miranda* apply only to custodial interrogations conducted by *law enforcement officers*. Therefore, damaging admissions made by a suspect in response to interrogation by a private citizen will be admissible in court despite a lack of warnings. Yates v. United States, 384 F.2d 586 (5th Circuit Court of Appeals, 1967). However, law enforcement officers may not use private citizens as their agents in order to escape the *Miranda* rule. Commonwealth v. Bordner, 432 Pa. 405, 247 A.2d 612 (Pennsylvania Supreme Court, 1968).

WARNING

The warnings that must be given before questioning persons in custody or deprived of their freedom of action in a significant way have been stated earlier in this chapter, but will be stated again for emphasis.

1. They must be informed clearly and unequivocally that they have the right to remain silent.

2. They must be told that any statement they make can and will be used against them in court.

3. They must be informed that they have the right to consult with a lawyer and to have the lawyer with them during interrogation.

4. They must be told that if they are indigent and cannot afford a lawyer, a lawyer will be appointed to represent them.

Manner of Giving Warnings

Miranda warnings must be stated clearly and in an unhurried manner—so that the persons warned understand their rights and feel free to claim them without fear. The warnings should not be given in a careless, indifferent, and superficial manner.

When warnings are given to immature, illiterate, or mentally impaired persons, they must be given in language that they can comprehend and on which they can knowingly act. This may involve taking extra pains to explain and interpret the warnings. The crucial test is whether the words used by the officer, in view of the age, intelligence, and demeanor of the individual being interrogated, convey a clear understanding of all *Miranda* rights. Anderson v. State, 6 Md.App. 688, 253 A.2d 387 (Maryland Court of Special Appeals, 1969).

Does the Suspect Require Warnings?

Suspect Knows His Rights The *Miranda* opinion made it very clear that law enforcement officers are not to assume that any suspect knows his or her rights:

> The Fifth Amendment privilege is so fundamental to our system of constitutional rule and the expedient of giving an adequate warning as to the availability of the privilege so simple, we will not pause to inquire in individual cases whether the defendant was aware of his rights without a warning being given. Assessments of the knowledge the defendant possessed, based on information as to his age,

education, intelligence, or prior contact with authorities, can never be more than speculation: a warning is a clearcut fact. More important, whatever the background of the person interrogated, a warning at the time of the interrogation is indispensable to overcome its pressures and to insure that the individual knows he is free to exercise the privilege at that point in time. 384 U.S. at 468–69, 86 S.Ct. at 1625, 16 L.Ed.2d at 720.

Suspect Is Not Indigent If a suspect is known to be financially able to afford a lawyer, officers need not give the warning that a lawyer will be appointed in case of indigency. The suspect must, however, be given all the other warnings.

The law enforcement officer may not always be able to determine a person's financial status. But, as the *Miranda* Court stated, "the expedient of giving a warning is too simple and the rights involved too important to engage in *ex post facto* inquiries into financial ability when there is any doubt at all on that score." (emphasis supplied) 384 U.S. at 473, 86 S.Ct. at 1627, 16 L.Ed.2d at 723. Therefore, it is recommended that the complete set of warnings be given when warnings are required.

Suspect Has an Attorney Present The *Miranda* opinion seems to say that the warnings are not required to be given to persons who have an attorney present with them:

> The presence of counsel . . . would be the adequate protective device necessary to make the process of police interrogation conform to the dictates of the privilege. His presence would insure that statements made in the government-established atmosphere are not the product of compulsion. 384 U.S. at 466, 86 S.Ct. at 1623, 16 L.Ed.2d at 719.

Again, however, as a practical matter, it is a wiser and safer policy for the law enforcement officer to give the warnings anyway. The suspect may later claim that the lawyer was incompetent or had not been officially retained.

WAIVER

A waiver is a voluntary and intentional relinquishment of a known right. The determination of whether or not a suspect has fully and effectively waived *Miranda* rights presents many problems for the law enforcement officer. The only definite rule is that a waiver cannot be inferred from silence. As stated by the Supreme Court in *Miranda*. "a valid waiver will not be presumed simply from the silence of the accused after warnings are given." 384 U.S. at 475, 86 S.Ct. at 1628, 16 L.Ed. 2d at 724. This rule has been followed closely by the lower courts. Moore v. United States, 401 F.2d 533 (9th Circuit Court of Appeals, 1968). Outside of this, however, there are few concrete guidelines to aid law enforcement officers in determining whether or not they have obtained a valid waiver from a suspect and can begin questioning the suspect.

After the *Miranda* warnings have been given, the officer should ask the suspect, "Do you understand the rights that have been explained to you?" Then the officer should ask the suspect, "Do you wish to talk without consulting a lawyer or having a lawyer present during questioning?"   If affirmative answers are given to both questions, the officer should carefully note the exact language in which the answer was given in order to preserve it for possible future use in court.   The officer may then proceed with the interrogation of the suspect.

If possible, officers should always try to obtain a written waiver of rights from the suspect before questioning.   A written waiver is almost always held to be sufficient if the suspect is literate and there is no evidence of police overbearance.   Menendez v. United States, 393 F.2d 312 (5th Circuit Court of Appeals, 1968).   The form entitled "Waiver of Rights" is suggested for this purpose.

Waiver of Rights

I have had my rights explained to me and I understand what my rights are.

I am willing to answer questions and make a statement.

I do not want a lawyer at this time.

I understand and know what I am doing.

No promises or threats have been made to me and no pressure or coercion of any kind has been used against me.

Signed

Time   Date

Witness

Witness

If a written statement is obtained as a result of questioning, it should also be signed by the suspect and witnesses.   The statement should indicate the place, date, and time the taking of the statement began and the place, date, and time the statement was signed by the suspect.   As a further substantiation of the validity of the waiver, it is also suggested that the law enforcement officer ask the suspect to sign the form entitled "Reaffirmation of Waiver" after a written statement is obtained.

It is sometimes impossible for the law enforcement officer to obtain written waivers or unequivocal oral waivers.   Suspects may express themselves through an infinite variety of words and actions, some of which may be held by a court to be a valid waiver of rights and some not.   Often suspects will be indecisive and never quite get to the point of either claiming or waiving rights.   Moreover, in Tague v.

Reaffirmation of Waiver

The entire statement I have just made and signed consisting of _____ pages was made by me after I carefully considered the rights I was giving up in making the statement.

At no time while I was making the statement did I decide to or indicate any desire to reclaim any of those rights.

Signed

Time   Date

Witness

Witness

Louisiana, 444 U.S. 469, 100 S.Ct. 652, 62 L.Ed.2d 622 (1980), the U.S. Supreme Court held that the state has the burden of proving that the defendant waived his *Miranda* rights and that in the absence of any evidence of waiver, any statement obtained is inadmissible. Therefore, when no concrete written or oral waiver can be obtained, officers should take careful notes of all circumstances attending the waiver, so that they will be able to provide evidence that the waiver was knowing and intelligent, when called upon to do so. The following discussion will assist officers in determining what circumstances are important in deciding the issue of waiver.

Words and Actions Indicating Waiver

When a defendant has been fully informed of his or her rights, any reasonable oral statement of understanding and willingness to speak is usually acceptable as a waiver of rights. Examples of valid waivers are cases in which, after warnings, a suspect said, I "might as well tell you about it."—United States v. Boykin, 398 F.2d 483, 484 (3d Circuit Court of Appeals, 1968); "I'll tell you."—State v. Kremens, 52 N.J. 303, 307, 245 A.2d 313, 315 (New Jersey Supreme Court, 1968); or "I know all that."—State v. Brown, 250 La. 1125, 1140, 202 So.2d 274, 279 (Supreme Court of Louisiana, 1967). Courts have also approved non-verbal waivers such as nods and shrugs. Mullaney v. State, 5 Md.App. 248, 246 A.2d 291 (Maryland Court of Appeals, 1968). After receiving a waiver in any of these forms, the law enforcement officer may begin questioning the suspect.

Often a suspect will indicate an understanding of *Miranda* rights and then simply begin to make a statement without any other verbal or non-verbal indication of willingness to waive the rights and speak. Most courts have held that once the suspect has been informed of *Miranda* rights and indicates an understanding of those rights, choosing to speak without a lawyer present is sufficient evidence of a knowing and voluntary waiver of the rights. People v. Johnson, 70 Cal.2d 541, 75 Cal.Rptr. 401, 450 P.2d 865 (California Supreme Court, 1969); United States v. Osterburg, 423 F.2d 704 (9th Circuit Court of Appeals, 1970). However, this rule is probably valid only if the statement of the suspect follows closely after indicating an understanding of the warnings. Billings v. People, 171 Colo. 236, 466 P.2d 474 (Colorado Supreme Court, 1970).

A suspect who indicates a desire to talk to a lawyer at some time in the future but who agrees to answer questions without a lawyer has waived the right to counsel. Thompson v. State, 235 So.2d 354 (District Court of Appeal of Florida, 1970). Also, a request to see someone other than a lawyer is not considered to be an assertion of rights under *Miranda,* although a denial of such a request may have some bearing on the voluntariness of the statements. For example, in Fare v. Michael C., 442 U.S. 707, 99 S.Ct. 2560, 61 L.Ed.2d 197 (1979), the U.S. Supreme Court held that a juvenile waived his *Miranda* rights even though he had been denied a request to speak with his probation officer. The Court found that the request, by an experienced older juvenile with an extensive prior record, did not per se constitute a request to remain silent nor was it tantamount to a request for an attorney. Similarly, a request for counsel made by a suspect to a friend or relative is not the same as a request to the police. Therefore, even if the police are aware of such a request, it does not operate as an exercise of *Miranda* rights. People v. Smith, 108 Ill.App.2d 172, 246 N.E.2d 689 (Appellate Court of Illinois, 1969). The California Supreme Court held, however, that a minor's request to see his or her parents is equivalent to an adult's request to see an attorney under *Miranda.* People v. Burton, 6 Cal.3d 375, 99 Cal.Rptr. 1, 491 P.2d 793 (1971). Officers should cease questioning a minor who has made such a request until the minor's parents or an attorney is present. Otherwise, any statements taken may be held inadmissible.

Suspect Refuses to Sign Written Statements or Waivers

A suspect's refusal to sign either a written waiver or a written statement has generally been held not to affect the validity of the suspect's waiver with respect to the admissibility of the suspect's oral statements. Cummings v. United States, 398 F.2d 377 (8th Circuit Court of Appeals, 1968); Pettyjohn v. United States, 419 F.2d 651 (District of Columbia Circuit Court of Appeals, 1969). This assumes of course that a valid oral waiver has been obtained.

However, when a suspect indicates, after giving a valid written or oral waiver, a desire not to have any notes taken, this may suggest that the suspect erroneously believes that oral statements cannot be used as evidence in court. In this case, the law enforcement officer should make it clear that oral statements can be used against the suspect in court. Otherwise, a court might hold the waiver invalid. Frazier v. United States, 419 F.2d 1161 (District of Columbia Circuit Court of Appeals, 1969).

Denial of Access to Retained Counsel

If officers fail to notify an attorney retained by a suspect before they interrogate the suspect, any admission or confession obtained may be inadmissible in court even though the suspect was given warnings and waived the right to counsel:

> Under these circumstances, the interrogation was made without an informed waiver of the defendant's right to the assistance of counsel and to remain silent. When counsel has been retained to represent a prisoner, the governmental authorities cannot deny the lawyer reasonable access to his client, nor may they ignore his request that he be allowed to confer with his client prior to, if not during, the interrogation. State v. Jackson, La., 303 So.2d 734, 737 (Louisiana Supreme Court, 1974).

Competency of Suspect

A common issue with respect to waiver is whether or not the suspect is competent or capable of understanding *Miranda* rights and of waiving them. Persons who might not be considered competent to waive their rights are those in pain from injury or illness, those in shock, the mentally impaired, those under the influence of alcohol, drugs, or medicine, or the very young or old. Courts usually look at the totality of the circumstances in each case to determine whether a suspect was capable of understanding the rights and capable of voluntarily waiving them. Mossbrook v. United States, 409 F.2d 503 (9th Circuit Court of Appeals, 1969). Therefore, no single factor would ordinarily be determinative of the issue.

Since there are no definite guidelines for law enforcement officers on this issue, they must proceed with caution. If a suspect falls within any of the categories mentioned above, officers should take extra pains in explaining the meaning of the warnings. It is probably better to wait until a sick person or a person under the influence of drugs or alcohol is back to normal before attempting to warn and question the person. Officers should also delay the questioning of persons who are emotionally upset. In Sample v. Eyman, 469 F.2d 819, 821 (9th Circuit Court of Appeals, 1972), the court held that "once it has been determined that a person taken into custody is too upset to assert or waive his rights knowingly and intelligently under *Miranda,* all questioning should cease until such time as that person is clearly capable of so responding."

Juveniles are usually competent to waive their rights, but officers are advised to try and obtain the waiver in the presence of and with the advice and consent of a parent or guardian. The Indiana Supreme Court held that a juvenile's waiver of his *Miranda* rights was invalid because he was not given an opportunity to have his parents or guardian present. The court said:

> We hold therefore that a juvenile's statement or confession cannot be used against him at a subsequent trial or hearing unless both he and his parents or guardian were informed of his rights to an attorney and to remain silent. Furthermore, the child must be given an opportunity to consult with his parents, guardian or an attorney representing the juvenile as to whether or not he wishes to waive those rights. After such consultation the child may waive his rights if he so chooses, provided, of course, that there are no elements of coercion, force, or inducement present. Lewis v. State, 259 Ind. 431, 439, 288 N.E.2d 138, 142 (1972).

Unless the officer is positive that the suspect is incapable of understanding and waiving *Miranda* rights, the officer should not refrain from trying to obtain a lawful confession. It is the duty of the courts, not the law enforcement officer, to finally determine whether or not there was an intelligent and knowing waiver and a voluntary and trustworthy confession.

OTHER MIRANDA ISSUES

Fourth Amendment Violations

Even though a law enforcement officer has satisfied all the *Miranda* requirements discussed in this chapter, a statement may still be inadmissible in court if it is taken in violation of a person's Fourth Amendment rights. The leading case on this subject is Katz v. United States, 389 U.S. 347, 88 S.Ct. 507, 19 L.Ed.2d 576 (1968), in which the defendant was eavesdropped on in a telephone booth by federal agents, who had attached an electronic listening and recording device to the outside of the booth. The Court held that despite the lack of an intrusion into a constitutionally protected area, the defendant's statements were inadmissible in court because they were taken in violation of his reasonable expectation of privacy. The Court said:

> [O]nce it is recognized that the Fourth Amendment protects people—and not simply "areas"—against unreasonable searches and seizures, it becomes clear that the reach of that Amendment cannot turn upon the presence or absence of a physical intrusion into any given enclosure. 389 U.S. at 353, 88 S.Ct. at 512, 19 L.Ed.2d at 583.

The *Katz* "reasonable expectation of privacy" standard has been applied to a great variety of cases involving the Fourth Amendment, some of which are discussed elsewhere in this book. For purposes of this chapter, officers must not violate a person's reasonable expectation of privacy when obtaining statements from the person. Otherwise the statements may be inadmissible in court, even though *Miranda* requirements have been fulfilled.

Examples of court applications of the "reasonable expectation of privacy" test will be presented to give officers a clearer idea of their rights and duties. In Halpin v. Superior Court, 6 Cal.3rd 885, 101 Cal.Rptr. 375, 495 P.2d 1295 (California Supreme Court, 1972), the incarcerated defendant's wife visited him at the jail during regular visiting hours. A detective allowed the defendant and his wife to use his office to converse, and the detective left the office. The conversation was secretly taped and was used in court against the defendant. The court ruled the tapes inadmissible, stating that law enforcement officers may not deliberately create an expectation of privacy so that the prisoner and his visitor will be "lulled" into believing their conversations will be confidential.

In United States v. Fisch, 474 F.2d 1071 (9th Circuit Court of Appeals, 1973), law enforcement officers were investigating a narcotics smuggling operation. The officers obtained a motel room adjacent to that of the suspects and, by listening at the door, the officers heard a discussion of criminal acts. They used no electronic devices and committed no trespass. The court ruled that the statements were admissible, holding that the defendants had no justifiable expectation of privacy in their conversations. The court emphasized that the individual's interest in privacy must be balanced against the public's interest in the investigation and prosecution of crime:

> Upon balance, appraising the public and private interests here involved, we are satisfied that the expectations of the defendants as to their privacy, even were such expectations to be considered reasonable despite their audible disclosures, must be subordinated to the public interest in law enforcement. In sum, there has been no justifiable reliance, the expectation of privacy not being "one that society is prepared to recognize as 'reasonable.'" 474 F.2d at 1078–79.

Multiple Attempts at Interrogation

In the *Miranda* opinion, the Court said:

> Once warnings have been given, the subsequent procedure is clear. If the individual indicates in any manner, at any time prior to or during questioning, that he wishes to remain silent, the interrogation must cease. At this point he has shown that he intends to exercise his Fifth Amendment privilege; any statement taken after the person invokes his privilege cannot be other than the product of compulsion, subtle or otherwise. Without the right to cut off questioning, the setting of in-custody interrogation operates on the individual to overcome free choice in producing a statement after the privilege has been once invoked. If the individual states that he wants an attorney, the interrogation must cease until an attorney is present. At that time the individual must have an opportunity to confer with the attorney and to have him present during any subsequent questioning. If the individual cannot obtain an attorney and he indicates that he wants one before speaking to police, they must respect his decision to remain silent. 384 U.S. at 473–74, 86 S.Ct. at 1627–28, 16 L.Ed.2d at 723.

The quoted language commands that once a suspect indicates either a desire to remain silent or a desire for an attorney, all questioning must stop, at least until the suspect confers with an attorney. Despite this seeming clarity, under certain circumstances, some courts have allowed second attempts to question after a suspect has claimed the rights.

Attempts After Right to Silence Invoked The U.S. Supreme Court has allowed, under limited conditions, a second interrogation of a suspect who exercised the *Miranda* right of silence after being given warnings. In Michigan v. Mosley, 423 U.S. 96, 96 S.Ct. 321, 46 L.Ed.2d 313 (1975), the defendant was arrested early in the afternoon in connection with certain robberies and given the *Miranda* warnings by a police detective. After indicating that he understood the warnings, the defendant declined to discuss the robberies, and the detective ceased the interrogation. Shortly after 6:00 P.M. the same day, after giving the *Miranda* warnings, a different police detective questioned the defendant about a murder that was unrelated to the robberies. The defendant made an incriminating statement that was used against him at his trial. He was convicted of the murder.

The Court held that the admission into evidence of the defendant's statement did not violate *Miranda* principles. Even though the *Miranda* opinion states that the interrogation must cease when the person in custody indicates a desire to remain silent, the Court in the *Mosley* case held that "neither this passage nor any other passage in the *Miranda* opinion can sensibly be read to create a per se proscription of indefinite duration upon any further questioning by any police officer on any subject, once the person in custody has indicated a desire to remain silent." 423 U.S. at 102–03, 96 S.Ct. at 326, 46 L.Ed.2d at 320–21. The Court then gave several reasons why it allowed the second interrogation in the *Mosley* case. The defendant's right to cut off questioning had been "scrupulously honored" by the first detective. The first detective ceased the interrogation when the defendant refused to answer and did not try to wear down his resistance by repeated efforts to make him change his mind. The second interrogation was directed toward a different crime with a different time and place of occurrence. Also the second interrogation began after a significant time lapse and after the defendant had been given a fresh set of warnings.

In U.S. v. Olof, 527 F.2d 752 (9th Circuit Court of Appeals, 1975), the court held that a second interrogation by federal agents, three hours after the defendant had refused to make a statement after being given the *Miranda* warnings, violated the defendant's rights. Although the agents gave the defendant fresh warnings, they pressured him to cooperate and they questioned him about the same crime for which the first warnings were given.

These cases suggest the following guidelines for custodial interrogation of a person who has exercised the *Miranda* right to remain silent:

1. The person's right to terminate questioning at the initial interrogation should be promptly honored;

2. A significant amount of time should separate the first and second interrogation attempts;

3. The person should be given complete *Miranda* warnings again; and

4. No pressure to cooperate or other illegal tactics should be employed.

Attempts After Right to Counsel Invoked As the quotation at the beginning of this section indicates, *Miranda* created a rigid rule that an accused's request for an attorney is per se an invocation of Fifth Amendment rights, requiring that all interrogation cease. This rigid rule is based on an attorney's unique ability to protect the Fifth Amendment rights of a client undergoing custodial interrogation. Once an accused person expresses the view that he or she is not competent to deal with the authorities without legal advice, courts will examine closely any later choice to make a decision without counsel's presence. Therefore, although an accused may waive *Miranda* rights and submit to interrogation, the U.S. Supreme Court has recognized that additional safeguards are necessary after an accused has exercised the right to counsel.

The Court established these safeguards in the case of Edwards v. Arizona, 451 U.S. 477, 101 S.Ct. 1880, 68 L.Ed.2d 378 (1981). In that case, the defendant had voluntarily submitted to questioning but later stated that he wanted an attorney before the discussions continued. The following day detectives accosted the defendant in the county jail, and when he refused to speak with them he was told that "he had" to talk. The Court held that subsequent incriminating statements made without his attorney present violated the rights secured to the defendant by the Fifth and Fourteenth Amendments. The Court stated:

> [W]hen an accused has invoked his right to have counsel present during custodial interrogation, a valid waiver of that right cannot be established by showing only that he responded to further police-initiated custodial interrogation even if he has been advised of his rights. We further hold that an accused, such as [the defendant], having expressed his desire to deal with the police only through counsel, is not subject to further interrogation by the authorities until counsel has been made available to him, unless the accused himself initiates further communication, exchanges, or conversations with the police. 451 U.S. at 484–85, 101 S.Ct. at 1884–85, 68 L.Ed.2d at 386.

In Oregon v. Bradshaw, —— U.S. ——, 103 S.Ct. 2830, 77 L.Ed.2d 405 (1983), the U.S. Supreme Court attempted to explain what would constitute the initiation of further communication with the police:

> [T]here are undoubtedly situations where a bare inquiry by either a defendant or by a police officer should not be held to "initiate" any conversation or dialogue. There are some inquiries, such as a request for a drink of water or a request to use a telephone that are so routine that they cannot be fairly said to represent a desire on the part of an accused to open up a more generalized discussion relating directly or indirectly to the investigation. Such inquiries or statements, by either an accused or a police officer, relating to routine incidents of the custodial relationship, will not generally "initiate" a conversation in the sense in which that word was used in *Edwards*. —— U.S. at ——, 103 S.Ct. at 2835, 77 L.Ed.2d at 412.

In the *Bradshaw* case, the Court found that the defendant's question to a police officer, after he had asked for an attorney, as to what was going to happen to him now "evinced a willingness and a desire for a generalized discussion about the investigation; it was not merely a necessary inquiry arising out of the incidents of the custodial relationship." —— U.S. at ——, 103 S.Ct. at 2835, 77 L.Ed.2d at 412.

The *Edwards* case also established a second prerequisite to police interrogation of an accused who has requested an attorney. Once it is established that the accused "initiated" further conversation or dialogue with the police, the next inquiry is "whether a valid waiver of the right to counsel and the right to silence had occurred, that is, whether the purported waiver was knowing and intelligent and found to be so under the totality of the circumstances, including the necessary fact that the accused, not the police, reopened the dialogue with the authorities." 451 U.S. at 486, n.9, 101 S.Ct. at 1885, n.9, 68 L.Ed.2d at 387, n.9. In the *Bradshaw* case, the Court found a knowing waiver where the police made no threats, promises, or inducements to talk, the defendant was properly advised of his rights and understood them, and within a short time he changed his mind and decided to talk without any impropriety on the part of the police. In Wyrick v. Fields, 459 U.S. 42, 44, 103 S.Ct. 394, 396, 74 L.Ed.2d 214, 218 (1982), the U.S. Supreme Court held that by waiving his right to counsel at a polygraph examination, the accused also validly waived his right to have counsel present at "post-test" questioning, "unless the circumstances changed so seriously that his answers no longer were voluntary, or unless he no longer was making a 'knowing and intelligent relinquishment or abandonment' of his rights."

To summarize, before a suspect in custody can be subjected to further interrogation after requesting an attorney there must first be a showing that the suspect initiated communication with the authorities. Once this is established, it is still necessary to establish as a separate matter the existence of a knowing and intelligent waiver of the right to counsel and the right to silence. Once a valid waiver is made, interrogation may continue until the circumstances change so seriously that the answers are no longer voluntary or until the accused revokes the waiver.

Attempts After Rights Waived Often, a suspect may waive *Miranda* rights, submit to interrogation, and after an interval of time, police may wish to interrogate the suspect again. The general rule is that warnings need not be repeated at the second interrogation. People v. Hill, 66 Cal.2d 536, 58 Cal.Rptr. 340, 426 P.2d 908 (California Supreme Court, 1967). However, a few courts have required a repetition of the warnings under certain circumstances, and since it is such a simple procedure, it is recommended that the law enforcement officer repeat the warnings before each questioning session just to be safe. The Supreme Court of Pennsylvania listed five significant factors in determining whether an accused must be reinformed of his constitutional rights:

> (1) the time lapse between the last *Miranda* warnings and the accused's statement; (2) interruptions in the continuity of the interrogation; (3) whether there was a change of location between the place where the last *Miranda* warnings were given and the place where the accused's statement was made; (4) whether the same officer who gave the warnings also conducted the interrogation resulting in the accused's statement; and (5) whether the statement elicited during complained of interrogation differed significantly from other statements which had been preceded by *Miranda* warnings. Commonwealth v. Wideman, 460 Pa. 699, 706–08, 334 A.2d 594, 598 (1975).

Misdemeanors and Other Proceedings

Miranda has been held inapplicable to misdemeanors involving only fines or small jail penalties. This includes most minor traffic offenses. State v. Zucconi, 93 N.J. Super. 380, 226 A.2d 16 (Superior Court of New Jersey, 1967); State v. Pyle, 19 Ohio St.2d 64, 249 N.E.2d 826 (Supreme Court of Ohio, 1969). The New Jersey Supreme Court stated the reasons why *Miranda* rules are inapplicable to motor vehicle violations:

1. The type of police questioning used in motor vehicle violations is not ordinarily the lengthy incommunicado interrogation at which *Miranda* was aimed. Usually the questions are simple, standard, and directed toward filling out routine police reports.

2. Usually traffic violations are not serious enough to warrant the time-consuming inconvenience to the administration of justice.

3. It would be impossible to provide sufficient numbers of lawyers for all the motor vehicle violators who would be likely to request legal advice. State v. Macuk, 57 N.J. 1, 268 A.2d 1 (Supreme Judicial Court of New Jersey, 1970).

However, where the suspect may be exposed to a substantial term of imprisonment for a misdemeanor, *Miranda* has been held to be applicable. Commonwealth v. Bonser, 215 Pa.Super. 452, 258 A.2d 675 (Superior Court of Pennsylvania, 1969).

Other proceedings to which *Miranda* has been held inapplicable are customs procedures, civil commitments, extradition proceedings, license revocation proceedings, and interviews between probation officer and probationer. It is fairly safe for the law enforcement officer to assume that, unless the suspect is subject to a possible substantial criminal penalty, *Miranda* warnings are not necessary.

Statements Obtained After Defendant Formally Charged

In Massiah v. United States, 377 U.S. 201, 84 S.Ct. 1199, 12 L.Ed.2d 246 (U.S. Supreme Court, 1964), after the defendant was indicted, federal agents obtained incriminating statements from him in the absence of his counsel. While the defendant was free on bail, his co-defendant, in cooperation with the federal agents, engaged the defendant in conversation in the presence of a hidden radio transmitter. The Court held that the statements were inadmissible because the defendant was denied the basic protection of the right to assistance of counsel.

The *Massiah* decision has become less significant in recent years because the *Miranda* decision has resulted in courts shifting their emphasis from the Sixth Amendment to the Fifth Amendment. Nevertheless, as stated by the Fifth Circuit Court of Appeals:

> [I]t [*Massiah*] retains its vitality and stands as a supplement to *Miranda: Massiah* teaches that although the government may properly continue to gather evidence against a defendant after he has been indicted, it may not nullify the protection *Miranda* affords a defendant by using trickery to extract incriminating statements from him that otherwise could not be obtained without first giving the required warnings. Today *Massiah* simply means that after indictment and counsel has been retained the Fifth Amendment prevents law enforcement authorities from deliberately eliciting incriminating statements from a defendant by the surreptitious methods used in that case. United States v. Hayles, 471 F.2d 788, 791 (1973).

The U.S. Supreme Court affirmed the continuing validity of the *Massiah* case in Brewer v. Williams, 430 U.S. 387, 97 S.Ct. 1232, 51 L.Ed.2d 424 (1977). In that case, the defendant, who had been arrested, arraigned, and jailed in Davenport, Iowa, for abducting a ten-year old girl in Des Moines, Iowa, was being transported by police to Des Moines to talk to his lawyer there. Both his Des Moines lawyer and the lawyer at his Davenport arraignment advised him not to make any statements until after consulting with his Des Moines lawyer. The police officers who were to accompany him on the trip agreed not to question him during the trip. Nevertheless, one of the police officers, who knew that the defendant was a former mental patient and was deeply religious, suggested that the defendant reveal the location of the girl's body because her parents were entitled to a Christian burial for the girl who was taken away from them on Christmas Eve. The defendant eventually made several incriminating statements during the trip and finally directed the police to the girl's body.

The U.S. Supreme Court, citing *Massiah,* held that a person against whom adversary proceedings have commenced has a right to legal representation when the government interrogates him.   Since the officer's "Christian burial" speech was tantamount to interrogation and the defendant had been formally charged, the defendant was entitled to the assistance of counsel at the time he made the incriminating statements.   The Court found that the defendant did not waive his right to counsel, and therefore held any evidence relating to or resulting from his statements inadmissible.

In United States v. Henry, 447 U.S. 264, 100 S.Ct. 2183, 65 L.Ed.2d 115 (1980), the U.S. Supreme Court held inadmissible statements made by an indicted and imprisoned defendant to a paid undisclosed government informant who was in the same cell block.   Although the informant was instructed not to initiate conversations with the defendant, his instructions to pay attention to information furnished by the defendant created a situation likely to induce the defendant to make incriminating statements without the assistance of counsel.   This indirect and surreptitious type of interrogation was an impermissible interference with the defendant's right to the assistance of counsel in violation of *Massiah.*   The Court emphasized the potential susceptibility of an incarcerated person to subtle influences of government undercover agents.   The *Henry* case illustrates that courts will carefully examine any attempts to obtain statements from persons against whom adversary proceedings have commenced, in the absence of counsel, especially if the person is incarcerated.

EFFECT OF MIRANDA IN COURT

As stated earlier, statements taken in violation of *Miranda* requirements will be inadmissible in court to prove the defendant's guilt of crime.   In recent years, however, courts have allowed the use of statements taken in violation of *Miranda* for purposes other than the proof of the defendant's guilt.   In Harris v. New York, 401 U.S. 222, 91 S.Ct. 643, 28 L.Ed.2d 1 (U.S. Supreme Court, 1971), and Oregon v. Hass, 420 U.S. 714, 95 S.Ct. 1215, 43 L.Ed.2d 570 (U.S. Supreme Court, 1975), the Court admitted testimony of previous inconsistent statements taken from a defendant in violation of his *Miranda* rights solely for the purpose of impeaching the defendant's testimony at trial.   Stressing that the trustworthiness of the defendant's earlier conflicting statements must satisfy legal standards, the Court in *Harris* said:

> The shield provided by *Miranda* cannot be perverted into a license to use perjury by way of a defense, free from the risk of confrontation with prior inconsistent utterances.   We hold, therefore, that petitioner's credibility was appropriately impeached by use of his earlier conflicting statements.   401 U.S. at 226, 91 S.Ct. at 646, 28 L.Ed.2d at 5.

Officers should not interpret the *Harris* and *Hass* cases as providing an opportunity to get around the requirements of the *Miranda* case.   An admission or confession obtained in compliance with *Miranda* is much more valuable to the prosecution than an illegally obtained statement to be used only for impeachment.   Therefore, officers should carefully comply with the *Miranda* requirements in order to obtain convincing evidence of guilt in the form of an admissible confession. Also, it should be reemphasized that *involuntary* statements obtained from a defendant cannot be used for any purpose in a criminal trial. The U.S. Supreme Court has stated that "*any* criminal trial use against a defendant of his *involuntary* statement is a denial of due process of law, 'even though there is ample evidence aside from the confession to support the conviction.' " Mincey v. Arizona, 437 U.S. 385, 398, 98 S.Ct. 2408, 2416, 57 L.Ed.2d 290, 303 (1978).

In United States v. Hale, 422 U.S. 171, 95 S.Ct. 2133, 45 L.Ed.2d 99 (1975), and Doyle v. Ohio, 426 U.S. 610, 96 S.Ct. 2240, 49 L.Ed.2d 91 (1976), the U.S. Supreme Court held that a defendant's silence after receiving the *Miranda* warnings could not be used against him at trial for the purpose of impeaching his trial testimony. The Court quoted the *Hale* case in the *Doyle* case as follows:

> "[W]hen a person under arrest is informed as *Miranda* requires, that he may remain silent, that anything he says may be used against him, and that he may have an attorney if he wishes, it seems to me that it does not comport with due process to permit the prosecution during the trial to call attention to his silence at the time of arrest and to insist that because he did not speak about the facts of the case at that time, as he was told he need not do, an unfavorable inference might be drawn as to the truth of his trial testimony .   .   . ." 426 U.S. at 619, 96 S.Ct. at 2245, 49 L.Ed.2d at 98.

Another effect of a *Miranda* violation is that it may cause evidence obtained in a subsequent search and seizure to be held inadmissible. In People v. Superior Court (Keithley), 13 Cal.3d 406, 118 Cal.Rptr. 617, 530 P.2d 585 (California Supreme Court, 1975), the court held that consent to search obtained after questioning conducted in violation of *Miranda* was the product of illegal conduct. The consent search was declared invalid. Officers, therefore, should strictly follow the *Miranda* requirements or risk the exclusion not only of statements obtained but also of evidence seized in a subsequent search. United States v. Cassell, 452 F.2d 533 (7th Circuit Court of Appeals, 1971).

SUMMARY

An admission or confession obtained by a law enforcement officer will be inadmissible in court unless (1) it is voluntary and (2) the requirements of the Supreme Court case of *Miranda v. Arizona* are satisfied. An involuntary statement—one that is coerced by police or is otherwise not the free and rational choice of the defendant— is likely to be unreliable and violates the due process clause of the Fourteenth Amendment to the Constitution. Courts will find a statement involuntary if it is the product of any kind of police coercion, whether by force or threat of force, or by subtler forms of coercion such as promises of leniency or trickery. In making this determination, courts will also consider the personal characteristics of the defendant, such as age, mental capacity, physical or mental impairment, and prior experience with the police, in establishing the setting in which coercion might operate to overcome the will of the defendant. This approach is called the "totality of the circumstances" test for determining voluntariness of a statement.

The *Miranda* case held that the prosecution may not use a statement, whether exculpatory or inculpatory, stemming from a custodial interrogation of the defendant, unless it demonstrated the use of procedural safeguards effective to secure the privilege against self-incrimination. Those procedural safeguards are the giving of warnings of rights and the obtaining of a valid waiver of those rights before an interrogation is begun. Therefore, the major issues of *Miranda* can be broken down into four categories: custody, interrogation, warning, and waiver.

A person is in custody if the person is under arrest or is restrained so that he or she is deprived of freedom of action in any significant way. Custody is determined by examining the totality of facts and circumstances surrounding an encounter between a person and law enforcement authorities, including the place, the time, the presence of family, friends, or other persons, the nature and duration of questioning, and the conduct and number of police officers. The determination of custody requires a balancing of the needs of effective law enforcement against the need to protect persons from the coercion inherent in a compelling, police-dominated atmosphere.

Interrogation refers not only to express questioning but also to any words or actions on the part of police that the police should know are reasonably likely to elicit an incriminating response. Nevertheless, clarifying questions, spontaneous questions, and other brief and routine questions are not considered to be interrogation for *Miranda* purposes. Also, volunteered statements are not the product of interrogation and are not subject to the *Miranda* requirements.

Before persons in "custody" may be subjected to "interrogation," they must be given the familiar *Miranda* warnings.

1. They must be informed clearly and unequivocally that they have the right to remain silent.

2. They must be told that any statement they make can and will be used against them in court.

3. They must be informed that they have the right to consult with a lawyer and to have the lawyer with them during interrogation.

4. They must be told that if they are indigent and cannot afford a lawyer, a lawyer will be appointed to represent them.

These warnings must be recited clearly and unhurriedly and must be carefully explained to immature, illiterate, or mentally impaired persons.

If the person waives the *Miranda* rights to remain silent and to have an attorney, the person may be questioned. Waiver will not be inferred from mere silence, but may be expressed by a great variety of words and gestures. If possible, an officer should obtain a written waiver of rights, because it provides the best evidence of a voluntary and intentional relinquishment of a known right.

Even though the voluntariness and *Miranda* requirements have been met, a statement may still be inadmissible if the officer violates a person's reasonable expectation of privacy in obtaining it. Multiple attempts at interrogation are permitted, but the defendant's right to cut off questioning must be scrupulously honored, fresh warnings must be given, and no coercion or other pressures may be employed. If the defendant has exercised the right to counsel, further interrogation without counsel may be conducted only upon the initiation of the defendant and the waiver of *Miranda* rights. After a defendant has been formally charged and has retained counsel, law enforcement authorities are prohibited from using any methods, however surreptitious or indirect, to elicit incriminating evidence from the defendant in the absence of counsel. Finally, *Miranda* is inapplicable to minor misdemeanors, traffic offenses, and other proceedings in which the defendant is not potentially subject to a substantial term of imprisonment.

REVIEW AND DISCUSSION QUESTIONS

1. Would any of the following cause a statement of a suspect to be involuntary?
a. An appeal to the suspect's moral or religious beliefs.
b. Confronting the suspect with the deceased or seriously injured victim of the crime in question.
c. Starting an argument with, challenging, or baiting the suspect.

2. Practically speaking, doesn't a person need a lawyer to help decide whether or not to waive *Miranda* rights? Isn't the compelling atmosphere of a custodial setting just as likely to influence a person's decision to waive rights as it is to influence the decision to confess?

3. Is a person's giving of consent to search an inculpatory or exculpatory statement? Should a person in custody by given *Miranda* warnings before being asked for consent to search?

4. If a person is in custody for *Miranda* purposes, does this constitute a seizure tantamount to arrest requiring probable cause under the rationale of *Dunaway v. New York?* (See Chapter 4.)

5. It is reasonable to assume that a person under investigation for a crime might think that complete silence in the face of an accusation might not look good to a judge or a jury. Should the *Miranda* warnings include a statement that a person's silence may not be used against the person in any way?

6. Should suspects be told the nature and seriousness of the offense for which they are being interrogated? What if a person believes that he is being investigated for an accident caused by his driving while intoxicated, but he does not know that a person in the other vehicle has died?

7. What would be the advantages and disadvantages of requiring law enforcement officers to tape record the entire process of administration of *Miranda* warnings and the suspect's invocation or waiver of rights?

8. Is it proper for a law enforcement officer to inform a suspect who has just invoked the *Miranda* right to counsel that the case against the suspect is strong and that immediate cooperation with the authorities would be beneficial in the long run? If the suspect says, "What do you mean?" would it be considered an initiation of further communication by the suspect and a waiver of the right to counsel?

9. Considering the confusion and pressures associated with being arrested and transported to a police station, should arrested persons be advised, in addition to the *Miranda* warnings, of where they are being taken, what is going to happen to them, how long they will be held, and with whom they may communicate?

10. Would the *Massiah* rule be violated if conversations of an indicted and imprisoned person were obtained by means of a listening device installed in the person's cell?

14

Pre-trial Identification Procedures

Pre-trial confrontation of a suspected criminal with witnesses to or victims of the crime has long been an accepted law enforcement technique to identify perpetrators of crime and also to clear from suspicion those who are innocent. In 1967 the U.S. Supreme Court handed down three major decisions governing this area of the law—*United States v. Wade,* 388 U.S. 218, 87 S.Ct. 1926, 18 L.Ed.2d 1149; *Gilbert v. California,* 388 U.S. 263, 87 S.Ct. 1951, 18 L.Ed.2d 1178; and *Stovall v. Denno,* 388 U.S. 293, 87 S.Ct. 1967, 18 L.Ed.2d 1199. These decisions provide the groundwork for most of the law applicable to pre-trial identification procedures today.

The discussion of the *Wade, Gilbert,* and *Stovall* cases will use the terms *showup, lineup,* and *confrontation* throughout and, therefore, these terms will be defined at the outset. A *showup* is the presentation of a single suspect to a victim or witness of a crime for the purpose of identifying the perpetrator of the crime. A *lineup* is the presentation at one time of several persons including a suspect to a victim or witness of a crime for the purpose of identifying the perpetrator of the crime. A lineup gives the victim or witness several alternate choices. A *confrontation* includes both showups and lineups and is any presentation of a suspect to a victim or witness of a crime for the purpose of identifying the perpetrator of the crime. These terms are also sometimes used in connection with photographic or voice identifications. Thus, for example, a photographic showup would be a presentation of a single photograph of a suspect to a victim or witness of a crime.

REQUIREMENT OF COUNSEL—THE WADE–GILBERT RULE

In the *Wade* and *Gilbert* decisions, the Supreme Court decided that a pre-trial confrontation of a suspect of a crime with witnesses or victims of the crime was a critical stage in the legal proceedings against the suspect. As such, the Court ruled that a suspect has a right to the presence of a lawyer at the confrontation if so desired. Furthermore, if unable to afford a personal lawyer, the suspect is entitled to have one appointed by the court. This ruling is an extension of the right of all accused persons to have the assistance of counsel for their defense at all critical stages of their criminal prosecution as guaranteed by the Sixth Amendment to the Constitution.

Basis of Court's Decision

The Supreme Court's reasoning in these cases was based on (1) the inherent unreliability of eyewitness identifications and (2) the possibility of improper suggestions being made to witnesses during the confrontation procedure. The Court said:

> 'The vagaries of eyewitness identification are well-known; the annals of criminal law are rife with instances of mistaken identification . . . . The identification of strangers is proverbially untrustworthy . . . . A major factor contributing to the high incidence of miscarriage of justice from mistaken identification has been the degree of suggestion inherent in the manner in which the prosecution presents the suspect to witnesses for pretrial identification. A commentator has observed that "[t]he influence of improper suggestion upon identifying witnesses probably accounts for more miscarriages of justice than any other single factor—perhaps it is responsible for more such errors than all other factors combined." . . . Suggestion can be created intentionally or unintentionally in many subtle ways. And the dangers for the suspect are particularly grave when the witness's opportunity for observation was insubstantial, and thus his susceptibility to suggestion the greatest.' 388 U.S. at 228–29, 87 S.Ct. at 1933, 18 L.Ed.2d at 1158–59.

The Court believed that the presence of counsel at the pre-trial confrontation with witnesses would prevent misconduct by those conducting the confrontation. Also, the attorney would have first-hand knowledge of events at the confrontation and could, therefore, conduct an intelligent cross-examination of witnesses at a later suppression hearing or trial and point out any improprieties that might have occurred. The Court said:

> Since it appears that there is grave potential for prejudice, intentional or not, in the pretrial lineup, which may not be capable of reconstruction at trial, and since presence of counsel itself can often avert prejudice and assure a meaningful confrontation at trial, there can be little doubt that for Wade the post-indictment lineup was a critical stage of the prosecution at which he was "as much entitled to such aid [of counsel] . . . as at the trial itself." . . . Thus both Wade and his counsel should have been notified of the impending lineup, and counsel's presence should have been a requisite to conduct of the lineup, absent an "intelligent waiver." 388 U.S. at 236–37, 87 S.Ct. at 1937, 18 L.Ed.2d at 1162–63.

Waiver of Right to Counsel

As the preceding quotation indicates, suspects may waive their right to the presence of counsel at a pre-trial confrontation. Before suspects can intelligently and understandingly waive their right to presence of counsel, they should be clearly advised of their rights. The suggested "Pre-trial Identification Warning and Waiver" form should effectively satisfy the standards of the U.S. Supreme Court.

Substitute Counsel

If a suspect requests the advice and presence of a personal lawyer and that lawyer is not immediately available, a substitute lawyer may sometimes be called for the purpose of the confrontation. Zamora v. Guam, 394 F.2d 815 (9th Circuit Court of Appeals, 1968). As stated in *United States v. Wade:*

> Although the right to counsel usually means a right to the suspect's own counsel, provision for substitute counsel may be justified on the ground that the substitute counsel's presence may eliminate the hazards which render the lineup a critical stage for the presence of the suspect's *own* counsel. 388 U.S. at 237 n. 9, 87 S.Ct. at 1938 n. 9, 18 L.Ed.2d at 1163–64 n. 27.

CHECKLIST FOR LINEUP IDENTIFICATIONS

The following guidelines may be helpful in conducting a lineup identification after the suspect has been advised of the right to counsel and counsel has been retained or waived.

Before the Lineup

1. No lineup identification should be conducted by a law enforcement officer without discussing the legal advisability of it with the prosecuting attorney.

2. A person in custody may be compelled to participate in a lineup without violating Fourth or Fifth Amendment rights. Most courts have reasoned that once a person is in custody, the person's liberty is not further infringed by being presented in a lineup for witnesses to view. People v. Hodge, 186 Colo. 189, 526 P.2d 309 (Supreme Court of Colorado, 1974). Also, the right against compulsory self-incrimination is not violated by a lineup, because no one is compelled to utter any words of a testimonial or communicative nature.

Compelling persons who are not in custody to appear in a lineup involves a much greater intrusion on liberty and is usually only done by order of the court or the grand jury, or by authority of statute in some states. Some courts have upheld the ordering of a person not in custody to appear in a lineup in serious cases in which the public interest in law enforcement outweighed the privacy interests of the person. Wise v. Murphy, D.C.App., 275 A.2d 205 (District of Columbia Court of Appeals, 1971). Other courts have held that a person not in custody cannot be ordered to participate in a lineup without probable cause to arrest. Alphonso C. v. Morgenthau, 50 A.D.2d 97, 376 N.Y.S.2d 126 (Supreme Court of New York, Appellate Division, 1975).

Pre-Trial Identification Warning and Waiver

Name   Address

Age   Place

Date   Time

Warning

Before appearing at any confrontation with any witnesses being conducted by (Name of Police Department) in relation to (Description of Offense), you must understand your legal rights.

The results of the confrontation can and will be used against you in court.

You have the right to the presence and advice of an attorney of your choice at any such confrontation.

If you cannot afford an attorney and you want one, an attorney will be appointed for you at no expense, before any confrontation is held.

Waiver

I have been advised of my right to the advice of an attorney and to have an attorney present at any confrontation with witnesses, and that if I cannot afford a lawyer, one will be appointed for me before any such confrontation occurs. I understand these rights.

I do not want a lawyer and I understand and know what I am doing.

No promises have been made to me and no pressures of any kind have been used against me.

_____

Signature of Suspect

Certification

I, (Name of Officer), hereby certify that I read the above warning to (Name of Suspect) on (Date), that he indicated that he understood his rights, and signed the WAIVER form in my presence.

_____

Signature of Officer

_____

Witness

3. A record should be made of the suspect's waiver of the right to counsel and voluntary participation in the lineup. If counsel is present, counsel's name should be recorded.

4. If the suspect has chosen to have an attorney present at the lineup proceedings, the attorney should be given every opportunity to observe all the proceedings, to take notes, and to tape record the identification process in whole or part. If the attorney has any suggestions that might improve the fairness of the proceedings, the officer in charge may follow them if they are reasonable and practicable. However, the attorney should not be allowed to control the proceedings in any way.

The suspect's attorney must be made aware that an identification is taking place. The attorney's mere presence will not satisfy the *Wade-Gilbert* rule. In a case in which the suspect and his attorney were unaware that witnesses had identified the suspect during his arraignment, the suspect's right to counsel was held to be violated. Mason v. United States, 414 F.2d 1176 (District of Columbia Circuit Court of Appeals, 1969). Counsel's purpose is to ensure that the identification is conducted fairly and to reconstruct the procedures at trial. Counsel can do neither if unaware that an identification is taking place.

5. Even when the suspect's counsel is not required at a lineup (See the next section on "Exceptions to the Wade-Gilbert Rule"), officers should allow counsel to be present in order to minimize subsequent challenges to the fairness of the lineup. State v. Taylor, 60 Wis.2d 506, 210 N.W.2d 873 (Wisconsin Supreme Court, 1973).

6. The names of all persons participating in the lineup and the names of the officers conducting the lineup should be recorded and preserved.

7. The witness or victim viewing the lineup should be advised of the purpose for which it is being conducted, but the officer should not suggest that the suspect is one of those in the lineup or even that the suspect is in police custody.

8. All witnesses who are to view the lineup should be prevented from seeing the suspect in custody, particularly in handcuffs, or in any other circumstances that would indicate the identity of the suspect in question.

9. If possible, witnesses should not be allowed to view photographs of the suspect prior to the lineup. If a witness has viewed photographs prior to a lineup, the officer conducting the lineup should inform the suspect's counsel and the court of any identification of the suspect's photograph, any failure to identify the suspect's photograph, and any identification of the wrong photograph.

10. Before viewing the lineup, each witness should be required to give a written description of the perpetrator of the crime to the officer in charge of the lineup. A copy should be made available to defense counsel.

During the Lineup

1. Insofar as possible, all persons in the lineup should be of the same general weight, height, age, and race, and have the same general physical characteristics. Also, they should be dressed similarly. A defendant may be required to wear distinctive clothing at the lineup. United States v. King, 433 F.2d 937 (9th Circuit

Court of Appeals, 1970). Also a defendant may be required to shave, trim his hair, or even grow a beard before participating in a lineup. United States v. O'Neal, 349 F.Supp. 572 (U.S. District Court, Northern District of Ohio, 1972). If suspects fail to cooperate with identification procedures or attempt to change their appearance, the officer conducting the lineup should keep a careful record of this behavior.

2. Should any body movement, gesture, or verbal statement be necessary, it should be made one time only by each person in the lineup, and repeated only at the express request of the observing witness or victim. Again, the officer conducting the lineup should keep a careful record of a suspect's failure to cooperate.

3. A color photograph of the lineup should be taken and developed as soon as possible. A copy of the photograph should be made available immediately to the suspect's counsel.

4. If more than one witness is called to view a lineup, the persons who have already viewed it should not be allowed to converse with the persons who have not yet viewed the lineup. It is good practice to keep witnesses who have viewed the lineup in a room separate from witnesses who have not yet viewed the lineup. Also, only one witness at a time should be present in the room where the lineup is being conducted.

5. The officer in charge of the lineup should not engage in unnecessary conversation with witnesses.

6. The officer in charge of the lineup should not allow unnecessary persons in the lineup room. A suggested group of people to include would be the witness, the officer conducting the lineup, the prosecuting attorney, the suspect's attorney, and possibly an investigator.

7. Each witness, upon entering the room in which the lineup is being conducted, should be handed a form for use in the identification. The form should be signed by the witness, the defense attorney, and the law enforcement officer conducting the lineup. A suggested form appears on page 349.

8. A copy of this identification form should be given to the suspect's attorney at the completion of the viewing of the lineup by each individual witness.

9. Use of a one-way mirror in a lineup, so that the suspect is unable to know what occurs on the other side of the mirror, has been held to be a prima facie violation of constitutional due process. This means that a lineup identification in which a one-way mirror is so used will be illegal, unless the officer in charge of the lineup can show that particularly compelling or exigent circumstances made the practice necessary. State v. Northup, 303 A.2d 1, 5 (Supreme Judicial Court of Maine, 1973). When the suspect's counsel is present, one-way mirrors may be permitted because counsel can observe the conduct of the lineup and preserve the suspect's rights. A one-way mirror may also be used to protect witnesses who fear retaliation. Commonwealth v. Lopes, 362 Mass. 448, 287 N.E.2d 118 (Massachusetts Supreme Court, 1972).

Witness Lineup Identification Form

The positions of the persons in the lineup will be numbered left to right, beginning with 1 on your left.

    A. If you have previously seen one or more of the persons in the lineup, place an X in the appropriate square (or squares) corresponding to the number of the person in the lineup.

    B. Then sign your name and fill in the date.

    C. When completed, hand this sheet to the officer.

1	2	3	4	5	6	7
☐	☐	☐	☐	☐	☐	☐

_____
Signature of Witness

_____
Date and Time

_____
Signature of Law Enforcement Officer

_____
Signature of Attorney for Suspect

After the Lineup

1. The officer in charge of the lineup should make complete notes of everything that takes place at the lineup and then make an official report of all the proceedings to be filed in the department's permanent records. A copy should be made available to the suspect's attorney.

2. Law enforcement officers must disclose to the court reviewing the lineup any evidence that might affect the accuracy of the identification whether occurring before, during, or after the lineup. Failure to do so may be a violation of the suspect's due process rights.

EXCEPTIONS TO THE WADE–GILBERT RULE

The *Wade* and *Gilbert* decisions have caused much controversy and have generated many conflicting opinions in subsequent court decisions. Some lower courts have limited *Wade* and *Gilbert* to their particular facts. Others have created exceptions to the broad holdings implicit in the decisions. An attempt to indicate some of these exceptions follows.

Identifications Conducted Before the Initiation of Adversary Judicial Proceedings

Kirby v. Illinois   The *Wade* and *Gilbert* decisions generated various lower court interpretations on the issue—at what stage of a criminal proceeding does a suspect have a right to counsel at an identification procedure. Both the *Wade* and *Gilbert* decisions dealt with identification procedures that took place after the suspect had already been indicted. Some lower courts, interpreting these decisions literally, restricted the right to counsel only to lineups and showups occurring after the formal filing of charges. People v. Palmer, 41 Ill.2d 571, 244 N.E.2d 173 (Supreme Court of Illinois, 1969). Other courts, however, reasoned that since the purpose of counsel's presence is to prevent prejudice to the suspect and assure meaningful cross-examination of witnesses at trial on the issue of identification, counsel should be required whether the lineup or showup occurs before or after the formal filing of criminal charges. People v. Fowler, 1 Cal.3d 335, 82 Cal.Rptr. 363, 461 P.2d 643 (Supreme Court of California, 1969).

The U. S. Supreme Court cleared up the controversy in Kirby v. Illinois, 406 U.S. 682, 92 S.Ct. 1877, 32 L.Ed.2d 411 (1972). In the *Kirby* case, the Court held that the right to counsel attaches to lineups and showups held "at or after the initiation of adversary judicial criminal proceedings—whether by way of formal charge, preliminary hearing, indictment, information or arraignment." 406 U.S. at 689, 92 S.Ct. at 1882, 32 L.Ed.2d at 417. Therefore, a law enforcement officer need not warn a suspect of the right to counsel at a confrontation with witnesses nor provide the suspect with counsel at the confrontation, if the suspect has not been formally charged with a crime.

Courts differ, however, in their interpretations of when a suspect has been formally charged with a crime. The Supreme Court of Pennsylvania, for example, affords an accused a right to counsel at all lineups held after arrest. Commonwealth v. Richman, 458 Pa. 167, 320 A.2d 351 (1974). In People v. Blake, 35 N.Y.2d 331, 361 N.Y.S.2d 881, 320 N.E.2d 625 (Court of Appeals of New York, 1974), the court concluded that a complaint for an arrest warrant triggers the right to counsel since it is an "accusatory instrument." Other courts have held that the issuance of an arrest warrant triggers the right to counsel. United States ex rel. Robinson v. Zelker, 468 F.2d 159 (2d Circuit Court of Appeals, 1972). Each officer must determine at what point in the criminal justice process the right to counsel at pre-trial identification procedures attaches under state law.

Even though a suspect has no right to counsel at a confrontation with witnesses, the right to have the identification procedure conducted in a fair and impartial manner is retained. The Court in the *Kirby* case said:

> What has been said is not to suggest that there may not be occasions during the course of a criminal investigation when the police do abuse identification procedures. Such abuses are not beyond the reach of the Constitution. As the Court

pointed out in *Wade* itself, it is always necessary to "scrutinize *any* pretrial confrontation. . . ." 388 U.S. at 227, 87 S.Ct. at 1932. The Due Process Clause of the Fifth and Fourteenth Amendments forbids a lineup that is unnecessarily suggestive and conducive to irreparable mistaken identification. Stovall v. Denno, 388 U.S. 293, 87 S.Ct. 1967, 18 L.Ed.2d 1199; Foster v. California, 394 U.S. 440, 89 S.Ct. 1127, 22 L.Ed.2d 402. When a person has not been formally charged with a criminal offense, *Stovall* strikes the appropriate constitutional balance between the right of a suspect to be protected from prejudicial procedures and the interest of society in the prompt and purposeful investigation of an unsolved crime. 406 U.S. at 690–91, 92 S.Ct. at 1883, 32 L.Ed.2d at 418–19.

Stovall v. Denno   The case of Stovall v. Denno, 388 U.S. 293, 87 S.Ct. 1967, 18 L.Ed.2d 1199 (U. S. Supreme Court, 1967), mentioned in the above quote from the *Kirby* case, is of vital importance to law enforcement officers and deserves further discussion here. The basic holding of the case is that the Due Process Clause of the Fifth and Fourteenth Amendments to the Constitution forbids any pre-trial identification procedure that is unnecessarily suggestive and conducive to irreparable mistaken identification. For the law enforcement officer, this simply means that *all* lineups and showups must be conducted in a fair and impartial manner. The word *all* is emphasized because the *Stovall* test applies whether or not a suspect is represented by an attorney at the identification procedure.

The *Stovall* case is particularly important to law enforcement officers with respect to confrontations occurring *before* the initiation of adversary judicial criminal proceedings against a suspect. Courts will carefully scrutinize identification procedures for fairness and impartiality in these instances because suspects are without the benefit of an attorney to protect their rights. Therefore, when a law enforcement officer conducts a *lineup* to identify a suspect, before the suspect has been formally charged, the officer should follow carefully the recommended procedures in the Checklist for Lineup Identifications. When a *showup* rather than a lineup is used the officer must be extra careful to ensure that identification procedures are fair and impartial. A common type of showup is the on-the-scene showup in which the suspect is arrested or apprehended at or near the scene of the crime and is immediately brought before victims or witnesses by a law enforcement officer for identification purposes. Clearly, so long as adversary judicial criminal proceedings have not been initiated, the suspect has no right to counsel at this type of confrontation. However, does an on-the-scene showup satisfy the *Stovall* requirements of fairness and impartiality?

Although courts differ on this question, the prevailing view is that practical considerations may justify a prompt on-the-scene showup under the *Stovall* test. In Russell v. U.S., 408 F.2d 1280 (District of Columbia Circuit Court of Appeals, 1969), the court said that the delay required to assemble a lineup "may not only cause the detention of an innocent suspect; it may also diminish the reliability of any identification obtained." 480 F.2d at 1284. Immediate identifications are desirable because memories are fresh and the suspect has no opportunity to change clothes or appearance. Furthermore, if a suspect is innocent, a prompt on-the-scene showup enables the police to continue their search for the real offender unhampered by delay. The court in the *Russell* case suggested that only "fresh" on-the-scene identifications that occur within mintues of the witnessed crime would satisfy the *Stovall* standard. The District of Columbia Circuit Court of Appeals discussed "on-the-scene" showups in the case of Bates v. United States, 405 F.2d 1104 (1968):

> There is no prohibition against a viewing of a suspect alone in what is called a "one-man showup" when this occurs near the time of the alleged criminal act; such a course does not tend to bring about misidentification but rather in some circumstances to insure accuracy. The rationale underlying this is in some respects not unlike that which the law relies on to make an exception to the hearsay rule, allowing spontaneous utterances a standing which they would not be given if uttered at a later point in time. An early identification is not error. Of course, proof of infirmities and subjective factors, such as hysteria of a witness, can be explored on cross-examination and in argument. Prudent police work would confine these on-the-spot identifications to situations in which possible doubts as to identification needed to be resolved promptly; absent such need the conventional lineup viewing is the appropriate procedure. 405 F.2d at 1106.

Therefore, law enforcement officers should only use on-the-scene showups when the suspect can be shown to the witness minutes after the crime has occurred. Also, officers should not coach the witness or add in any way to the already inherent suggestiveness of the on-the-scene identification. If there is a significant delay between the commission of the crime and the confrontation, officers should take the suspect to the station and conduct a lineup in accordance with suggested procedures in the Checklist for Lineup Identifications.

Neil v. Biggers   Despite the advice in the previous paragraph, law enforcement officers have often conducted showups several days, weeks, or even months after a crime has occurred. Before 1972, most courts, applying the standards of *Stovall v. Denno,* held that delayed one-on-one confrontations were impermissibly suggestive and violative of due process. Evidence of identifications made under these circumstances was held inadmissible in court.

In 1972, however, the U. S. Supreme Court decided the case of Neil v. Biggers, 409 U.S. 188, 93 S.Ct. 375, 34 L.Ed.2d 401, in which the Court focused on whether the identification was accurate or reliable despite the suggestiveness of the identification procedure. *Neil v. Biggers* involved a defendant who had been convicted of rape on evidence consisting in part of the victim's visual and voice identification of him at a station-house showup seven months after the crime. At the time of the crime, the victim was in her assailant's presence for nearly one-half hour and directly observed him indoors and under a full moon outdoors. She testified at trial that she had no doubt that the defendant was her assailant. She gave the police a thorough description of the assailant immediately after the crime that matched the description of the defendant. And she had made no identification of others presented at previous showups or lineups, or through photographs.

The Court, despite its concern about the seven-month delay between the crime and the confrontation, held that the central question was "whether under the 'totality of the circumstances' the identification was reliable even though the confrontation procedure was suggestive." 409 U.S. at 199, 93 S.Ct. at 382, 34 L.Ed.2d at 411.

The Court listed the following five factors to be considered in evaluating the likelihood of misidentification:

1. The opportunity of the witness to view the criminal at the time of the crime;

2. The witness's degree of attention;

3. The accuracy of the witness's prior description of the criminal;

4. The level of certainty demonstrated by the witness at the confrontation; and

5. The length of time between the crime and the confrontation.

Applying these facts to the facts of the case, the Court found no substantial likelihood of misidentification and held the evidence of the identification admissible in court.

Manson v. Brathwaite   In the case of Manson v. Brathwaite, 432 U.S. 98, 97 S.Ct. 2243, 53 L.Ed.2d 140 (U.S. Supreme Court, 1977), the Court added an additional factor to be considered by courts in determining the admissibility of identification evidence—the corrupting effect of the suggestive identification itself. The *Brathwaite* case involved an undercover drug officer's viewing of a single photograph of a drug crime suspect that had been left in his office by a fellow officer. Two days had elapsed between the crime and the viewing of the photograph. After finding that the single photographic display was unnecessarily suggestive the Court considered the five factors affecting the reliability of an identification set out in *Neil v. Biggers*. The Court found that the undercover officer was no casual observer, but a trained police officer; that he had sufficient opportunity to view the suspect for two or three minutes in natural light; that he accurately described the suspect in detail within minutes of the crime; that he positively identified the photograph in court as that of the drug seller; and that he made the photographic identification only two days after the crime.

The Court's analysis of the five factors indicated that the undercover drug officer was able to make an accurate identification of the defendant. The Court did not end its discussion at this stage as it did in the *Biggers* case, however. Instead, the Court took the additional step of analyzing the corrupting effect of the suggestive identification and then weighing that against the factors indicating reliability. The Court said:

> Although identifications arising from single-photograph displays may be viewed in general with suspicion, . . . we find in the instant case little pressure on the witness to acquiesce in the suggestion that such a display entails. D'Onofrio had left the photograph at Glover's office and was not present when Glover first viewed it two days after the event. There thus was little urgency and Glover could view the photograph at his leisure. And since Glover examined the photograph alone, there was no coercive pressure to make an identification arising from the presence of another. The identification was made in circumstances allowing care and reflection. 432 U.S. at 116, 97 S.Ct. at 2254, 53 L.Ed.2d at 155.

Under the totality of the circumstances, the Court held that the identification was reliable and that evidence of the identification was admissible in court.

The following quotation from the *Brathwaite* case sets out the basic test for determining the admissibility of evidence of identifications that take place before the initiation of adversary criminal proceedings:

> We therefore conclude that reliability is the linchpin in determining the admissibility of identification testimony for both pre- and post-*Stovall* confrontations. The factors to be considered are set out in *Biggers*. 409 U.S. at 199–200, 93 S.Ct. at 382. These include the opportunity of the witness to view the criminal at the time of the crime, the witness' degree of attention, the accuracy of his prior description of the criminal, the level of certainty demonstrated at the confrontation, and the time between the crime and the confrontation. Against these factors is to be weighed the corrupting effect of the suggestive identification itself. 432 U.S. at 114, 97 S.Ct. at 2253, 53 L.Ed.2d at 154.

The lesson of the *Biggers* and *Brathwaite* cases is that even though an officer conducts an unnecessarily suggestive identification procedure, all is not lost, because evidence of the identification may still be admitted in court if the identification is otherwise reliable. Officers, however, should not interpret these cases to mean that they need no longer be concerned about conducting fair and impartial identification procedures. As the Court stated in the *Brathwaite* case:

> [I]t would have been better had D'Onofrio presented Glover with a photographic array including "so far as practicable . . . a reasonable number of persons similar to any person then suspected whose likeness is included in the array." . . . The use of that procedure would have enhanced the force of the identification at trial and would have avoided the risk that the evidence would be excluded as unreliable. 432 U.S. at 117, 97 S.Ct. at 2254, 53 L.Ed.2d at 155.

Since officers have control over the conduct of the identification procedures, but have little or no control over the five factors determining the reliability of the identification, they should conduct all identification procedures fairly and impartially. Therefore, in order to avoid the risk that identification evidence will be excluded as unreliable, officers should follow as closely as possible the checklists for lineup identifications set out earlier in this chapter or, when photographs are used, the guidelines on photographic identifications appearing later in this chapter.

Emergency Identifications

In an emergency (e.g., a witness believed to be dying), a relaxation of the right to counsel rule and the *Stovall* "fairness" rule may be allowed when necessary to prevent the loss of vital evidence. In an illustrative case, a defendant who was being held in jail on a charge of robbing a store was presented to a hospitalized victim of a separate assault and robbery offense that was under investigation. There was uncertainty whether the defendant had retained a lawyer on the store robbery charge, but no lawyer was contacted for the identfication proceeding in the separate assault and robbery crime. The defendant was transported to the hospital by a deputy sheriff. The victim spontaneously and positively identified the defendant as his assailant. The defendant claimed that he should have been represented by a lawyer at this pre-trial confrontation with the victim.

The court applied the *Stovall* test and decided that a claimed violation of constitutional rights in the conduct of a confrontation with a witness depends on the totality of the circumstances surrounding it.   In this case, the circumstances surrounding the identification were not unnecessarily suggestive and conducive to irreparable mistaken identification: (1) No preliminary statements were made to the victim; (2) The victim's words of identification were spontaneous and positive; (3) The defendant said nothing in the presence of the victim; (4) The case was merely in the investigatory stage; (5) The critically injured victim (thought to be dying) was about to be moved to a distant hospital.   Under these emergency conditions, the fact that a lawyer was not present did not void the identification.   Trask v. Robbins, 421 F.2d 773 (1st Circuit Court of Appeals, 1970).

It should be noted that the *Trask* case was decided before the 1972 U. S. Supreme Court decision in *Kirby v. Illinois*.   Under the rule of the *Kirby* case, the defendant in the *Trask* case would not have been entitled to a lawyer at the showup even absent an emergency, because the showup was conducted before formal charges were brought against the defendant.   Nevertheless, the showup would still have had to satisfy the *Stovall* fairness test.   Furthermore, even if formal charges had been brought against the defendant, it is very likely that, in the genuine emergency that existed, the court still would have allowed an exception to the rule requiring presence of counsel at confrontations.   Therefore, when there is a genuine emergency, accompanied by a strong risk that identification evidence will be lost forever if a showup is not conducted immediately, the law enforcement officer should conduct the showup immediately and take careful notes of all the surrounding circumstances.

PHOTOGRAPHIC IDENTIFICATIONS

A common and accepted method of police investigation is the showing of mug shots or photographs to witnesses to aid in identifying or eliminating criminal suspects.   The U. S. Supreme Court in Simmons v. United States, 390 U.S. 377, 88 S.Ct. 967, 19 L.Ed.2d 1247 (1968), approved this procedure, subject to the same standards of fairness set out in *Stovall v. Denno.*   Furthermore, the U. S. Supreme Court held that there is no right to counsel at any photographic identification procedure, whether held before or after the initiation of adversary judicial criminal proceedings.   United States v. Ash, 413 U.S. 300, 93 S.Ct. 2568, 37 L.Ed.2d 619 (1973).

Each case, therefore, must be decided on the totality of the circumstances surrounding it and the identification evidence will be excluded in court "only if the photographic identification procedure was so impermissibly suggestive as to give rise to a very substantial likelihood of irreparable misidentification."   390 U.S. at 384, 88 S.Ct. at 971, 19 L.Ed.2d at 1253.   The following guidelines, based on the *Simmons* case, are suggested for photographic identifications.

1. More than one photograph should be shown to a witness.   In the *Simmons* case, six photographs were shown to several witnesses, and the Supreme Court suggested that even more than six would be preferable.

2. The people appearing in the photographs should be of the same general age, height, weight, and color of hair and skin.

3. No group of photographs should be arranged in such a way that the photograph of a single person reoccurs or is in any way emphasized.

4. If there are two or more suspects, no two should appear together in a group photo.

5. Witnesses should be handled in a manner similar to that suggested in the Checklist for Lineup Identifications (above).

6. If there are several witnesses, only some of them should be shown the photographs, in order to obtain an initial identification. Then the suspect could later be displayed to the remaining witnesses in a more reliable lineup and those witnesses' perceptions would not be influenced by a viewing of the photographs.

7. The officer in charge should keep careful notes of all remarks of witnesses while viewing photos, and of all identifications and mistakes in identification.

8. After the photographs have been shown to the witnesses, they should be numbered and preserved as evidence.

9. After a witness selects a photograph from a photographic display, that witness should not be shown the same photograph in later photographic displays. Such a procedure would tend to fix the image of the photograph in the witness's mind and blur the image actually perceived at the crime. United States v. Eatherton, 519 F.2d 603 (1st Circuit Court of Appeals, 1975).

10. Photographs of suspects in the act of committing the crime (such as bank robbery surveillance photographs) do not present any problems of suggestiveness and mistaken identification. Courts have held that presenting such photographs to witnesses shows the actual perpetrator of the crime in the act rather than suggesting a number of possible perpetrators. The photographs refresh the witness's memory of the actual crime and thereby strengthen the reliability of the witness's in-court identification. United States v. Evans, 484 F.2d 1178 (2nd Circuit Court of Appeals, 1973).

11. Mug shots should not be used together with other photographs for identification purposes. Mug shots may prejudice suspects by implying that they have a criminal record.

12. Photographic identification should not be used once a suspect's identity is known and the suspect is in police custody. A lineup should be used in these circumstances because lineups are more accurate than photographic identifications. State v. Wallace, 285 So.2d 796 (Louisiana Supreme Court, 1973).

These guidelines are only suggested and different circumstances may require different identification procedures. The law requires that the totality of the circumstances surrounding the identification must not be so overly suggestive as to cause a substantial likelihood of irreparable misidentification. Of course, as indicated in the case of *Manson v. Brathwaite,* discussed earlier in this chapter, courts will look beyond the mere fact of a suggestive photographic identification procedure in determining whether there was a substantial likelihood of irreparable misidentification. Courts will analyze each case with respect to the five factors determining the reliability of the identification as set out in *Neil v. Biggers.* Courts will then weigh those factors against the corrupting effect of the suggestive identification as was done in *Manson v. Brathwaite.* Law enforcement officers should follow the guidelines for photographic identifications set out in this section to minimize the suggestiveness of identification procedures and to ensure that identification evidence will not be excluded as unreliable.

EFFECT OF IMPROPER IDENTIFICATION PROCEDURE

In order to enforce the standards set out by the U. S. Supreme Court with respect to pre-trial identifications, certain rules have been established for the admission of identification evidence in court. If a pre-trial identification is made in violation of a defendant's right to counsel or if the identification is unreliable and thereby violates a defendant's due process rights, the court must exclude at trial:

1. Any evidence of the pre-trial identification presented as a part of the prosecution's direct case; and

2. Any identification of the perpetrator of the crime made by a witness in court.

If, however, the prosecution can establish by clear and convincing evidence that a witness had a source independent from the illegal confrontation for identifying the perpetrator of the crime, the court may allow in-court identification testimony. A judge will find that an in-court identification has an independent source when convinced that the identifying witness, by drawing on personal memory of the crime and observations of the defendant during the crime, has such a clear and definite image of the defendant that the witness can make an identification unaffected by the illegal confrontation. Some of the factors considered by judges in determining independent source are:

1. Opportunity for observation during the crime;

2. Prior knowledge of the identity of the perpetrator of the crime;

3. Accuracy of the witness's description of the perpetrator given to the police;

4. Failure of the witness to identify the defendant at prior confrontations;

5. Identification of a person other than the defendant prior to the confrontation;

6. Lapse of time between the crime and the confrontation; and

7. Differences of opinion among witnesses.

Law enforcement officers should obtain information on these factors from witnesses and record the information in their reports. Officers should obtain as much detail as possible because strong evidence of an independent source for identification of a criminal can salvage an improperly conducted identification procedure. Such evidence can often mean the difference between winning and losing a case.

SUMMARY

A criminal suspect has a right to counsel at all lineups and showups *after* the initiation of adversary judicial proceedings against the suspect. The emergency showup is the only possible exception to this rule. In every other case, the suspect should be warned of the right to counsel in accordance with the form provided. All formal confrontations should be conducted in accordance with the guidelines in the Checklist for Lineup Identifications.

If a lineup or showup is conducted *before* adversary judicial proceedings are initiated against a suspect, the suspect is *not* entitled to the presence or advice of counsel. Nevertheless, *all* pre-trial identification procedures, whether lineups or showups, must be conducted in accordance with due process, which forbids any pre-trial identification procedure that is unnecessarily suggestive and conducive to irreparable mistaken identification. As further interpreted by the U.S. Supreme Court, the due process test can be simply stated as requiring that all pre-trial identifications be reliable in the totality of the circumstances or evidence of the identification will be inadmissible in court. Factors to be considered in determining reliability are the opportunity of the witness to view the criminal at the time of the crime, the witness's degree of attention, the accuracy of the witness's prior description of the criminal, the level of certainty demonstrated at the confrontation, and the time between the crime and the confrontation. These factors are to be weighed against the corrupting effect of any suggestive identification.

To ensure reliable identifications, law enforcement officers must conduct all confrontations as fairly and impartially as possible. Officers are again advised to follow the guidelines in the Checklist for Lineup Identifications.

A criminal suspect is *not* entitled to the presence or advice of counsel at *photographic* identification procedures no matter when they are held. Nevertheless, such procedures must also be conducted as fairly and impartially as possible. Officers are advised to follow the guidelines for photographic identifications provided in this chapter.

REVIEW AND DISCUSSION QUESTIONS

1. What circumstances might justify the use of a one-way mirror during a lineup procedure? What if a witness or victim refuses to participate in a lineup unless a one-way mirror is used?

2. Why shouldn't a person have a right to demand an immediate lineup to clear himself or herself and avoid the many inconveniences associated with being arrested?

3. State three ways in which a law enforcement officer conducting a lineup can decrease the suggestibility of the lineup. State three ways in which a law enforcement officer can decrease the suggestibility of a one-man showup.

4. Assume that a suspect is about to be placed in a lineup and is told by a law enforcement officer that he has a right to counsel at the lineup. If the suspect asks, "Why do I need a lawyer?" what should the officer tell him?

5. Why should photographic identification procedures not be used when a physical lineup is contemplated? What arguments would a defense attorney make at a suppression hearing under the following circumstances?

a. The witness identified the defendant's photograph at a pre-trial photographic display, but failed to identify the defendant at a later physical lineup.

b. The witness failed to identify the defendant's photograph at a pre-trial photographic display, but identified the defendant at a later physical lineup.

c. The witness identified the defendant's photograph at a pre-trial photographic display and also identified the defendant at a later physical lineup.

6. Is it possible to conduct a fair lineup when the suspect is unusually tall or short or has very distinctive features or deformities?

7. Would an emergency one-person showup be justified if the suspect and not the victim were seriously injured? In what ways could the suggestibility of the showup be decreased?

8. Would certain suggestive pre-trial identification procedures be excusable in a small rural police department as opposed to a large urban police department? What procedures might be excusable and why?

9. Discuss the following quotation from Justice Brennan's dissenting opinion in United States v. Ash, 413 U.S. 300, 344, 93 S.Ct. 2568, 2591, 37 L.Ed.2d 619, 646–47 (1973), in which the U.S. Supreme Court held that there is no right to counsel at any photographic identification procedure:

> There is something ironic about the Court's conclusion today that a pretrial lineup identification is a "critical stage" of the prosecution because counsel's presence can help to compensate for the accused's deficiencies as an observer, but that a pretrial photographic identification is not a "critical stage" of the prosecution because the accused is not able to observe at all.

10. Would there be any need for counsel at a lineup if the entire lineup procedure were recorded on both audio and video tape?

15

Electronic Surveillance

Electronic surveillance through the use of wiretaps, bugs, or other devices to overhear conversations or obtain other kinds of information is a relatively recent concern of criminal and constitutional law. Certainly the Founding Fathers could not have even imagined the possibilities for gathering information on crime created by the marvels of twentieth-century technology. Nor could they have contemplated the potential invasions of privacy brought about by the new technology when they drafted the Constitution. It is not surprising, then, that the Constitution gives little guidance for balancing privacy interests against the need for effective law enforcement in the area of electronic surveillance. On the one hand, electronic listening, tracking, and recording devices provide a very powerful tool for law enforcement officials in investigating and prosecuting crime. On the other hand, the potential for abuse of individual rights can be far greater than that of any ordinary search or seizure. As will be revealed in this chapter, the task of resolving these competing interests has fallen on state legislatures, the United States Congress, and, ultimately, on the courts. This chapter will trace the early development of the law of electronic surveillance, will examine legislative responses to the problem, and will analyze court decisions in this area.

HISTORY

Although electronic eavesdropping had been used as an information-gathering technique since the mid-1800s, the U.S. Supreme Court did not decide its first electronic eavesdropping case until 1928. In Olmstead v. United States, 277 U.S. 438, 48 S.Ct. 564, 72 L.Ed. 944, a case involving interception of telephone conversations by means of a wiretap, the Court held that wiretapping was not covered by the Fourth Amendment. One of the reasons for this decision, as discussed in Chapter 3 under "Privacy," was that there was no search so long as there was no physical trespass into the defendant's premises. The other reason was that all the evidence had been obtained by hearing only, and since the Fourth Amendment referred only to the seizure of tangible items, the interception of a conversation could not qualify as a seizure. As we have seen in Chapter 3, the *Katz* case rendered invalid the first rationale of the *Olmstead* decision by changing the focus of Fourth Amendment analysis from a "property" approach to a "privacy" approach. The second rationale of the *Olmstead* decision has also been disposed of by Berger v. New York, 388 U.S. 41, 87 S.Ct. 1873, 18 L.Ed.2d 1040 (1967), which will be discussed later in this chapter.

In the *Olmstead* opinion, the Court noted that "Congress may of course protect the secrecy of telephone messages by making them when intercepted, inadmissible in evidence in federal criminal trials, by direct legislation, and thus depart from the common law of evidence." 277 U.S. at 465–66, 48 S.Ct. at 568, 72 L.Ed. at 951. Six years later, Congress did just that with the passage of Section 605 of the Federal Communications Act of 1934, which read in part:

> [N]o person not being authorized by the sender shall intercept any communication and divulge or publish the existence, contents, substance, purport, effect, or meaning of such intercepted communication to any person .   .   .   .

In Nardone v. United States, 302 U.S. 379, 58 S.Ct. 275, 82 L.Ed.2d 314 (1937), the U. S. Supreme Court held that section 605 applied to federal law enforcement officers and that testimony of federal officers in court about the contents of intercepted conversations was a form of divulgence prohibited by the act and was therefore inadmissible. Wiretapping was not illegal under the Court's interpretation, however, if the information was not used outside the governmental agency. Weiss v. United States, 308 U.S. 321, 60 S.Ct. 269, 84 L.Ed. 298 (1939), held that section 605 applied to intrastate as well as interstate communications. Therefore, wiretap evidence obtained by state law enforcement officers was inadmissible in a federal prosecution, but, under the decision in Schwartz v. Texas, 344 U.S. 199, 73 S.Ct. 232, 97 L.Ed. 231 (1952), was admissible in a state prosecution because the exclusionary rule had still not yet been applied to the states. It was not until 1968, seven years after *Mapp v. Ohio* and after wiretapping itself had been made subject to the Fourth Amendment, that the *Schwartz* decision was overruled by Lee v. Florida, 392 U.S. 378, 88 S.Ct. 2096, 20 L.Ed.2d 1166 (1968), and wiretap evidence obtained by state officials was made inadmissible in state prosecutions. It is noteworthy that the *Lee* case was decided just two days before the enactment by Congress of Title III of the Omnibus Crime Control and Safe Streets Act of 1968, 18 U.S.C.A. §§ 2510–2520, which superceded section 605 of the 1934 Act. Most of the rest of this chapter will deal with the enactment, content, and interpretation of Title III. But, first, it is worthwhile to provide some background on the constitutionality of electronic surveillance to set the stage for the discussion of Title III.

THE CONSTITUTIONALITY OF ELECTRONIC SURVEILLANCE

As we have seen, in the 1960s the U.S. Supreme Court clearly established that electronic surveillance is a "search and seizure" within the meaning of the Fourth

Amendment. Given that premise, it became necessary for the Court to decide what kinds of electronic surveillance the Fourth Amendment allows, to what extent it is allowed, and what kinds are prohibited, if any. The guidelines for these constitutional limits on electronic surveillance were worked out in a series of decisions in the mid-1960s.

It is worthwhile to begin the discussion with Justice Brennan's dissent in Lopez v. United States, 373 U.S. 427, 83 S.Ct. 1381, 10 L.Ed.2d 462 (1963). In that dissent, Justice Brennan echoed the fears of law enforcement officials that if wiretaps were subjected to Fourth Amendment analysis, they would be completely prohibited, because they would be seen as inherently unreasonable searches. Brennan stated, "For one thing, electronic surveillance is almost inherently indiscriminate, so that compliance with the requirement of particularity in the Fourth Amendment would be difficult." 373 U.S. at 463, 83 S.Ct. at 1401, 10 L.Ed.2d at 485. He continued:

> If in fact no warrant could be devised for electronic searches, that would be a compelling reason for forbidding them altogether. The requirements of the Fourth Amendment . . . are the bedrock rules without which there would be no effective protection of the right to personal liberty . . . . Electronic searches cannot be tolerated in the name of law enforcement if they are inherently unconstitutional. 373 U.S. at 464, 83 S.Ct. at 1401, 10 L.Ed.2d at 485.

Despite his strong language, it is clear that Brennan left open the possibility that some forms of electronic surveillance might be constitutionally permissible.

The U.S. Supreme Court first explicitly considered the constitutionality of electronic surveillance conducted under authority of a warrant three years later in Osborn v. United States, 385 U.S. 323, 87 S.Ct. 429, 17 L.Ed.2d 394 (1966). In that case, federal law enforcement officials had information that labor leader Jimmy Hoffa's attorney was trying to bribe a prospective juror. The officials obtained a warrant authorizing an undercover agent with a concealed tape recorder to record a specific conversation with the attorney. The tape of the conversation was admitted at trial and the attorney was convicted of attempting to bribe a juror. The U.S Supreme Court upheld the conviction emphasizing that "[t]he issue here is . . . the permissibility of using such a device under the most precise and discriminate circumstances . . . ." 385 U.S. at 329, 87 S.Ct. at 432–33, 17 L.Ed.2d at 399.

The Court's limited grant of constitutional permissibility for electronic surveillance was tested again the next year in Berger v. New York, 388 U.S. 41, 87 S.Ct. 1873, 18 L.Ed.2d 1040 (1967). In Berger, the issue was the constitutionality of a New York statute that authorized electronic surveillance pursuant to a judicial warrant. The New York law provided:

> An ex parte order for eavesdropping . . . may be issued by any justice . . . or judge . . . upon oath or affirmation of a district attorney, or of the attorney-general or of an officer above the rank of sergeant of any police department of the state . . . that there is reasonable ground to believe that evidence of crime may be thus obtained, and particularly describing the person or persons whose communications, conversations or discussions are to be overheard or recorded and the purpose thereof, and, in the case of a telegraphic or telephonic communication, identifying the particular telephone number or telegraph line involved. In connection with the issuance of such an order the justice or judge may examine on oath

the applicant and any other witness he may produce and shall satisfy himself of the existence of reasonable grounds for the granting of such application. Any such order shall be effective for the time specified therein but not for a period of more than two months unless extended or renewed by the justice or judge who signed and issued the original order upon satisfying himself that such an extension or renewal is in the public interest . . . .

The U.S. Supreme Court first held that conversations were protected by the Fourth Amendment and that the use of electronic devices to capture conversations was a search within the meaning of the Fourth Amendment. The Court then held this statute unconstitutional, primarily because it did not properly limit the nature, scope, or duration of the electronic surveillance. In so holding, the Court emphasized that the availability of an initial two-month surveillance period was "the equivalent of a series of intrusions, searches, and seizures pursuant to a single showing of probable cause." 388 U.S. at 59, 87 S.Ct. at 1883, 18 L.Ed.2d at 1052. The Court also stressed that the statute placed no termination requirement on the eavesdrop, even after the desired conversations had been obtained. Furthermore, the statute had two major deficiencies with respect to probable cause. First, an eavesdropping warrant could be issued without probable cause that a particular crime had been committed and without a particular description of the "property" (conversations in this context) to be seized. Secondly, an eavesdropping order could be extended or renewed without a showing of probable cause for continuation of the eavesdrop. Finally, in contrast to conventional search warrant procedures, the statute permitted electronic eavesdropping without prior notice or without requiring a showing of exigency excusing notice.

The Court's concern with the overbroad authorization of the New York statute is reflected in its comparison of the electronic search in the *Berger* case with the search in the *Osborn* case discussed earlier:

> The invasion [in *Osborn*] was lawful because there was sufficient proof to obtain a search warrant to make the search for the limited purpose outlined in the order of the judges. Through these "precise and discriminate" procedures the order authorizing the use of the electronic device afforded similar protections to those that are present in the use of conventional warrants authorizing the seizure of tangible evidence. Among other safeguards, the order described the type of conversation sought with particularity, thus indicating the specific objective of the Government in entering the constitutionally protected areas and the limitations placed upon the officer executing the warrant. Under it the officer could not search unauthorized areas; likewise, once the property sought, and for which the order was issued, was found the officer could not use the order as a passkey to further search. In addition, the order authorized one limited intrusion rather than a series or a continuous surveillance. And, we note that a new order was issued when the officer sought to resume the search and probable cause was shown for the succeeding one. Moreover, the order was executed by the officer with dispatch, not over a prolonged and extended period. In this manner no greater invasion of privacy was permitted than was necessary under the circumstances. Finally the officer was required to and did make a return on the order showing how it was executed and what was seized. Through these strict precautions the danger of an unlawful search and seizure was minimized. 388 U.S. at 57, 87 S.Ct. at 1882–83, 18 L.Ed.2d at 1051.

Despite the Court's disapproval of the New York statute in the *Berger* case, the possibility that a properly circumscribed warrant procedure for electronic surveillance could be created was left open. This possibility was given further credence by the landmark case of *Katz v. U.S.,* discussed in Chapter 3. In that case, FBI agents attached an electronic listening device to a public telephone booth and recorded the defendant's calls. The Court held that the interception was an unlawful search and seizure because there was no warrant. In discussing the warrant requirement, the Court said:

> [T]he surveillance was limited, both in scope and in duration, to the specific purpose of establishing the contents of the petitioner's unlawful telephonic communications. The agents confined their surveillance to the brief periods during which he [Katz] used the telephone booth, and they took great care to overhear only the conversations of the petitioner himself.
> Accepting this account of the Government's actions as accurate, it is clear that this surveillance was so narrowly circumscribed that a duly authorized magistrate, properly notified of the need for such investigation, specifically informed of the basis on which it was to proceed, and clearly apprised of the precise intrusion it would entail, could constitutionally have authorized, with appropriate safeguards, the very limited search and seizure that the Government asserts in fact took place. 389 U.S. 347, 354, 88 S.Ct. 507, 512–13, 19 L.Ed.2d 576, 583–84.

This possibility that a constitutionally permissible warrant procedure for electronic surveillance could be set up paved the way for congressional action in this area. In the year following the *Berger* and *Katz* opinions, Congress enacted the Omnibus Crime Control and Safe Streets Act of 1968. Title III of that act superceded the prohibition against wiretapping in Section 605 of the Federal Communications Act of 1934 and provided authorization for electronic surveillance pursuant to warrant.

As a background for discussion of Title III, it is worthwhile to summarize the constitutional principles established by the *Lopez, Osborn, Berger,* and *Katz* cases. First, electronic surveillance by agents of the government is a search and seizure governed by the Fourth Amendment. Secondly, it is permissible only if conducted pursuant to the authority of a warrant affording similar protections to those that are present in the use of conventional warrants authorizing the seizure of tangible evidence. Finally, a warrant procedure authorizing electronic surveillance must carefully circumscribe the search in nature, scope, and duration and must not permit "a trespassory invasion of the home or office, by general warrant, contrary to the command of the Fourth Amendment." 388 U.S. at 64, 87 S.Ct. at 1886, 18 L.Ed.2d at 1055.

TITLE III OF THE OMNIBUS CRIME CONTROL AND SAFE STREETS ACT OF 1968

The passage of Title III of the Omnibus Crime Control and Safe Streets Act of 1968, following so closely on the heels of the *Berger* and *Katz* decisions, was not simply a result of Congress enacting legislation in response to the constitutional guidelines set out in those decisions. There had long been concern about the inadequacy of existing electronic surveillance legislation. Besides the issues raised in various Supreme Court cases, defense lawyers and civil libertarians complained of Justice Department abuses under Section 605 of the Federal Communications Act of 1934 and other violations of the privacy rights of American citizens. On the other side, proponents of electronic surveillance argued that wiretapping and bugging were essential tools for law enforcement officials to combat the modern sophisticated criminal, especially in the area of organized crime. In fact, the belief that electronic surveillance was the only way to deal with the unique problems of investigating and prosecuting organized crime prompted the President's Crime Commission to recommend legislation authorizing electronic surveillance. Other impetuses to the passage of Title III in 1968 were the political pressures exerted in the context of a national climate of fear brought about by intense social unrest and the assassinations of Martin Luther King, Jr. and Robert F. Kennedy, and exemplified by the "law and order" presidential campaign of Richard M. Nixon. The result was a bipartisan effort to balance modern society's conflicting demands for privacy and for more effective law enforcement.

We turn now to a detailed discussion of Title III and cases interpreting it. Because of the length of the law, it is not possible to reproduce its provisions verbatim. Therefore, the discussion will be necessarily general in nature.

Judicial Supervision

One of the most important characteristics of Title III, designed to protect against governmental abuses of citizens' privacy rights, is its provision for judicial supervision of all aspects of electronic surveillance. Federal law enforcement officials may not intercept wire or oral communications without prior judicial approval. A court may issue a surveillance order only for specified crimes including espionage, treason, labor racketeering, murder, kidnapping, robbery, extortion, bribery of public officials, gambling, drug trafficking, and counterfeiting. Before issuing a surveillance order, however, the court must find:

1. Probable cause to believe that the person whose communication is to be intercepted has committed, is committing, or is about to commit one of the specified crimes;

2. Probable cause to believe that particular communications concerning that offense will be obtained through the interception;

3. That normal investigative procedures have been tried and have failed or reasonably appear to be unlikely to succeed if tried or to be too dangerous; and

4. Probable cause to believe that the facilities from which, or the place where, the wire or oral communications are to be intercepted are being used, or are about to be used, in connection with the commission of the specified offense, or are leased to, listed in the name of, or commonly used by the suspect.

Other aspects of judicial supervision of electronic surveillance are the court's power to require, at any time, reports on the progress of the interception toward the achievement of authorized objectives, the requirement of court approval for any extension of the surveillance, and the requirement that the court seal the recordings of any communications immediately upon the expiration of the order. Judicial sanctions for violations of Title III include penalties for contempt of court, suppression of evidence, awards of civil damages, and criminal penalties.

Procedures

Title III establishes specific procedures for the application for, the issuance of, and the execution of court orders for the interception of wire or oral communications.

Application Application procedures for interception orders are governed by 18 U.S.C.A. § 2518(1) which is quoted below:

> § 2518. Procedure for interception of wire or oral communications
>
> (1) Each application for an order authorizing or approving the interception of a wire or oral communication under this chapter shall be made in writing upon oath or affirmation to a judge of competent jurisdiction and shall state the applicant's authority to make such application. Each application shall include the following information:
>
> (a) the identity of the investigative or law enforcement officer making the application, and the officer authorizing the application;
>
> (b) a full and complete statement of the facts and circumstances relied upon by the applicant, to justify his belief that an order should be issued, including (i) details as to the particular offense that has been, is being, or is about to be committed, (ii) a particular description of the nature and location of the facilities from which or the place where the communication is to be intercepted, (iii) a particular description of the type of communications sought to be intercepted, (iv) the identity of the person, if known, committing the offense and whose communications are to be intercepted;
>
> (c) a full and complete statement as to whether or not other investigative procedures have been tried and failed or why they reasonably appear to be unlikely to succeed if tried or to be too dangerous;
>
> (d) a statement of the period of time for which the interception is required to be maintained. If the nature of the investigation is such that the authorization for interception should not automatically terminate when the described type of communication has been first obtained, a particular description of facts establishing probable cause to believe that additional communications of the same type will occur thereafter;
>
> (e) a full and complete statement of the facts concerning all previous applications known to the individual authorizing and making the application, made to any judge for authorization to intercept, or for approval of interceptions of, wire or oral communications involving any of the same persons, facilities or places specified in the application, and the action taken by the judge on each such application; and
>
> (f) where the application is for the extension of an order, a statement setting forth the results thus far obtained from the interception, or a reasonable explanation of the failure to obtain such results.

Only the United States Attorney General or a specially designated Assistant Attorney General may authorize an application for a federal interception order. Only a federal investigative or law enforcement officer, as defined by the Act, or an attorney authorized to prosecute Title III offenses, may make an application for a federal interception order. With respect to the requirement of identifying the person whose communications are to be intercepted, the U.S. Supreme Court held that the applicant must name all persons who the government has probable cause to believe are committing the offense for which the application is made. United States v. Donovan, 429 U.S. 413, 97 S.Ct. 658, 50 L.Ed.2d 652 (1977). The *Donovan* case also held, however, that failure to comply with this identification requirement did not require the exclusion of evidence obtained by the interception.

Issuance of Interception Order   If, on the basis of the application, the judge makes the required findings, the judge may issue an order authorizing or approving the interception of wire or oral communications.   Each order must specify:

1. The identity, if known, of the person whose communications are to be intercepted;

2. The nature and location of the communications facilities as to which, or the place where, authority to intercept is granted;

3. A particular description of the type of communications sought to be intercepted, and a statement of the particular offense to which it relates;

4. The identity of the agency authorized to intercept the communications, and of the person authorizing the application; and

5. The period of time during which the interception is authorized, including a statement as to whether or not the interception shall automatically terminate when the described communication has been first obtained.

Execution of Interception Order   Every order to intercept wire or oral communications must be executed "as soon as practicable."   In United States v. Martino, 664 F.2d 860 (2d Circuit Court of Appeals, 1981), however, the court held that delay in the execution of an interception order did not require the suppression of evidence obtained if the delay was not willful and if the information upon which probable cause was based had not become stale.

Title III requires that authorized interceptions be conducted in such a way as to minimize the interception of communications not otherwise subject to interception under Title III.   This minimization effort must be objectively reasonable under the circumstances.   In Scott v. United States, 436 U.S. 128, 98 S.Ct. 1717, 56 L.Ed.2d 168 (1978), the U.S. Supreme Court held an interception reasonable although only forty percent of the intercepted conversations related to crimes specified in the order because the remaining conversations were ambiguous and were of brief duration.

Authorized interceptions must terminate upon attainment of the authorized objective, or in any event in thirty days.   Extensions of an interception order may be granted, but only upon reapplication in accordance with the same procedures as an original application.

Finally, after the denial of an application for an interception order or after the termination of the period of an order, an "inventory" must be served upon the persons named in the order and upon such other parties to intercepted communications as the judge may determine in the interest of justice.   The inventory must include notice of the fact of the application or order, the date of the approval or denial of the application, the period of an authorized interception, and whether or not wire or oral communications were or were not intercepted during the period. Failure to serve the inventory, however, is not grounds for suppression, unless the failure causes actual, incurable prejudice.   United States v. Harrigan, 586 F.2d 860, 865 (1st Circuit Court of Appeals, 1978).

Title III authorizes communication common carriers, landlords, custodians, and others to provide information, facilities, or technical assistance to persons authorized by law to intercept wire or oral communications. Before rendering assistance, however, the person must be provided with a court order directing the assistance or a certification in writing from an authorized official that no court order is required by law, that all statutory requirements have been met, and that the specified assistance is required.

Individual Rights

As stated earlier, Title III was the result of a bipartisan congressional effort to balance the need for more effective law enforcement against the need to protect constitutional rights. It is worthwhile to point out specific ways in which Title III provides for the protection of individual rights. First, a person who was a party to any intercepted communication or against whom the interception was directed has a limited right to inspect such portions of the intercepted communications, applications, and orders as the judge determines to be in the interest of justice. The prosecution may not use as evidence the contents of an intercepted communication unless each party has been furnished with a copy of the application and the interception order not less than ten days before the trial, hearing, or proceeding. This ten-day notice period is designed to provide a person the opportunity to make a motion to suppress.

Second, a person's privacy rights are protected by the provision that applications and orders granted under Title III may be disclosed only upon a showing of good cause before a judge. In *In re Applications of Kansas City Star,* 666 F.2d 1168 (8th Circuit Court of Appeals, 1981), the court held that in determining whether there is good cause for disclosure, courts must consider what effect disclosure of applications and orders has on a person's privacy when there is no suppression hearing and no governmental need to disclose the documents. The court held that there was not good cause to disclose to the news media affidavits relating to wiretaps on third parties that had been released to the defendant. Also, the First Circuit Court of Appeals held that the Freedom of Information Act (5 U.S. C.A. § 552) could not be used to gain access to records of electronic surveillance made in violation of the Fourth Amendment. Providence Journal Co. v. FBI, 602 F.2d 1010 (1st Cir.1979).

A third individual right under Title III arises when the victim of an illegal interception is called as a witness before a grand jury and asked questions based upon that interception. In Gelbard v. United States, 408 U.S. 41, 92 S.Ct. 2357, 33 L.Ed.2d 179 (1972), the U.S. Supreme Court held that a grand jury witness may invoke a violation of Title III as a defense to charges of contempt for refusing to answer questions. Generally, if the witness makes a preliminary showing that the government's questions were based on illegally obtained information, the burden shifts to the government to prove otherwise. If the government fails, the witness may refuse to testify without penalty.

Another individual right under Title III is the right of a person whose communications have been intercepted, disclosed, or used in violation of Title III to bring a civil action against the person who caused the violation. Defendants in such an action may avoid liability by establishing that they relied in good faith on a court order or legislative authorization and that their actions were objectively reasonable. In Kilgore v. Mitchell, 623 F.2d 631 (9th Circuit Court of Appeals, 1980), the court held that the actions of governmental investigators were objectively reasonable where the surveillance was conducted pursuant to a court order, it was consistent with Department of Justice policies, and it was conducted before Title III was interpreted by the courts.

Finally, Title III permits any person who was a party to any intercepted communication or a person against whom the interception was directed to move to suppress the contents of the communication or evidence derived from it. The U.S. Supreme Court, in Alderman v. United States, 394 U.S. 165, 89 S.Ct. 961, 22 L.Ed. 2d 176 (1969), held that the owner of premises where allegedly illegal electronic surveillance occurred also may move to suppress such evidence on Fourth Amendment grounds. Grounds for suppression under Title III are:

1. The communication was unlawfully intercepted;

2. The order of authorization or approval under which it was intercepted is insufficient on its face; or

3. The interception was not made in conformity with the order of authorization or approval.

Generally, courts have been reluctant to suppress evidence for violations of Title III unless the violation was central to the statutory scheme. For example, in United States v. Giordano, 416 U.S. 505, 94 S.Ct. 1820, 40 L.Ed.2d 341 (1974), the U.S. Supreme Court ordered suppression where an executive assistant of the U.S. Attorney General, rather than the Attorney General himself or a specially designated assistant, had authorized an application for an interception order. The court considered authorization by the Attorney General or a specially designated assistant central to the statutory scheme of promoting restraint by centralizing eavesdropping responsibility in a politically accountable government official. In United States v. Chavez, 416 U.S. 562, 94 S.Ct. 1849, 40 L.Ed.2d 380 (1974), however, the Justice Department contended that the Attorney General had in fact personally approved the surveillance request, but the application had misrepresented the authorizing official to be his executive assistant. The Court, despite the technical violation, denied suppression because the violation was not considered central to the statutory scheme. The Court said, "No role more significant than a reporting function designed to establish on paper that one of the major procedural protections of Title III had been properly accomplished is apparent." 416 U.S. at 579, 94 S.Ct. at 1858, 40 L.Ed.2d at 394.

Applicability to the States

Title III specifically authorizes state law enforcement officials to apply for, obtain, and execute orders authorizing or approving the interception of wire or oral communications. The procedures are similar to those governing federal interception orders. The primary difference is that the state procedure must be authorized by a separate state statute. If a state statute so authorizes, the principal prosecuting attorney of the state, or of a political subdivision of the state, may apply to a state court judge of competent jurisdiction for an interception order. The judge, in granting the order, must comply with both the applicable state statute and with Title III. The interception order may be granted only when the interception may provide

> evidence of the commission of the offense of murder, kidnapping, gambling, robbery, bribery, extortion, or dealing in narcotic drugs, marihuana or other dangerous drugs, or other crime dangerous to life, limb, or property, and punishable by imprisonment for more than one year, designated in any applicable State statute authorizing such interception, or any conspiracy to commit any of the foregoing offenses.   18 U.S.C.A. § 2516(2).

State legislation may not authorize interceptions that fall short of the requirements of Title III. States may, however, enact laws that place stricter limits on electronic surveillance than those in Title III. Federal courts are not obliged to adhere to more restrictive state laws and will generally admit evidence that violates such a law, so long as the evidence was not obtained in violation of Title III. For example, in United States v. Daniel, 667 F.2d 783 (9th Circuit Court of Appeals, 1982), an interception of a conversation without a search warrant violated state law. Nevertheless, the evidence was held admissible in federal court because Title III does not require a warrant when one of the parties to the intercepted conversation consents to the interception.

Exceptions to Title III

Many types of interceptions of wire or oral communications are either not covered by the provisions of Title III or are specifically excepted from coverage. Because these exceptions are numerous, they will be discussed in general terms only.

A party to a conversation who has no reasonable expectation of privacy with respect to the conversation is not protected either by Title III or by the Fourth Amendment. Title III defines an oral communication as "any oral communication uttered by a person exhibiting an expectation that such communication is not subject to interception under circumstances justifying such expectation." 18 U.S. C.A. § 2510(2). In State v. Salisbury, 662 F.2d 738 (11th Circuit Court of Appeals, 1981), the court held that a person has no legitimate expectation that another party to the conversation will not record the conversation or reveal its contents to authorities.

Similarly, when one party to a conversation consents to the interception of the conversation, neither Title III nor the Fourth Amendment prevents the use of the conversation in court against another party to the conversation. Thus, a law enforcement officer, an informant, or a private citizen who is a party to a conversation may record or permit a law enforcement official to record the conversation without violating Title III or the Fourth Amendment. For example, in United States v. Capo, 693 F.2d 1330 (11th Circuit Court of Appeals, 1982), the government's interception of a conversation between a consenting informant and the defendant was held not to be a violation of the Fourth Amendment since the defendant willingly projected his voice outside the privacy of his home and it was intercepted at the other end.

Under Title III, an operator of a switchboard or an officer, employee, or agent of any communication common carrier may intercept, disclose, or use a wire communication in the normal course of business if necessary to the rendition of service or the protection of the rights or property of the carrier. Communication common carriers may not, however, use service observing or random monitoring except for mechanical or service quality control checks. Also, under Title III, an employee of the Federal Communications Commission may intercept, disclose, or use radio communications if done in the normal course of employment and pursuant to FCC monitoring responsibilities.

Title III exempts from its coverage any interception conducted by investigative or law enforcement officers using telephone or telegraph facilities in the ordinary course of their duties. In Campiti v. Walonis, 611 F.2d 387 (1st Circuit Court of Appeals, 1979), the court held that this exemption did not apply when an unusual method of surveillance was used to monitor a prison inmate's telephone conversations. In that case, an officer's listening to an inmate's conversation on an extension phone without the inmate's knowledge was found not to be within the ordinary course of the officer's duties, since the usual method of monitoring conversations was to stand close enough to hear the inmate's part of the conversation.

Another exception to Title III appears in 18 U.S.C.A. § 2511(3) which states that none of the electronic surveillance requirements of Title III shall limit the constitutional power of the President to take such measures as are deemed necessary "to protect the Nation against actual or potential attack or other hostile acts of a foreign power, to obtain foreign intelligence information deemed essential to the security of the United States . . . to protect national security information against foreign intelligence activities, [or] to protect the United States against the overthrow of the government by force or other unlawful means, or against any other clear and present danger to the structure or existence of the Government."

The case of United States v. United States District Court, 407 U.S. 297, 92 S.Ct. 2125, 32 L.Ed.2d 752 (1972) involved a conspiracy to destroy property of the federal government. The government relied on § 2511(3) to justify the wiretapping of an American citizen that was conducted without a court order. The U.S. Supreme Court held that § 2511(3) "merely provides that the Act shall not be interpreted to limit or disturb such power as the President may have under the Constitution. . . . Congress simply left presidential powers where it found them. . . . Congress only intended to make clear that the Act simply did not legislate with respect to national security surveillances." 407 U.S. at 303–06, 92 S.Ct. at 2130–31, 32 L.Ed.2d at 758–60. The Court went on to say that "Fourth Amendment protections become the more necessary when the targets of official surveillance may be those suspected of unorthodoxy in their political beliefs. The danger to political dissent is acute where the Government attempts to act under so vague a concept as the power to protect 'domestic security.' " 407 U.S. at 314, 92 S.Ct. at 2135, 32 L.Ed.2d at 764. In conclusion, the Court stated that "the Government's concerns do not justify departure in this case from the customary Fourth Amendment requirement of judicial approval prior to initiation of a search or surveillance." 407 U.S. at 321, 92 S.Ct. at 2139, 32 L.Ed.2d at 768.

Title III does not apply to electronic surveillance conducted outside the territorial jurisdiction of the United States. For example, Stowe v. Devoy, 588 F.2d 336 (2d

Circuit Court of Appeals, 1978), held that neither Title III nor the Fourth Amendment applied to evidence obtained in Canada by Canadian officials in compliance with Canadian law.

Because Title III regulates only the interception of oral and wire communications, it does not apply to the use of electronic devices emitting signals that enable law enforcement officials to track the location of objects and persons. Use of these devices, sometimes called transmitters or beepers, is governed solely by the Fourth Amendment. Since most of the legal issues involving these devices relate to the attachment of the devices to vehicles and containers, discussion of these issues appears in Chapter 10 dealing with the warrantless search of vehicles and containers. Similarly, Title III does not apply to tracers and pen registers. A tracer is a device that traces the source of calls made to a particular number. A pen register records all numbers dialed from a particular number. Neither of these devices intercepts the contents of a wire or oral communication. In Smith v. Maryland, 442 U.S. 735, 99 S.Ct. 2577, 61 L.Ed.2d 220 (1979), the U.S. Supreme Court held that the installation and use of a pen register is not a search and is therefore not subject to the Fourth Amendment. The Court reasoned that the defendant had no reasonable expectation of privacy in the destination of his outgoing phone calls because the telephone company routinely monitors these calls to check billing, to detect fraud, and to prevent other violations of law. Federal courts have not yet addressed the Fourth Amendment implications of the use of tracers. Because telephone companies do not routinely monitor incoming calls, the rationale of the Smith case may not apply to the use of tracers.

Although law enforcement officials must obtain a judicial order to intercept wire or oral communications, neither Title III nor the Fourth Amendment requires them to obtain judicial authorization to covertly enter premises to install a listening device. In Dalia v. United States, 441 U.S. 238, 99 S.Ct. 1682, 60 L.Ed.2d 177 (1979), a federal court authorized the interception of all oral communications concerning an interstate stolen goods conspiracy at the defendant's office. Although the interception order did not explicitly authorize entry into the defendant's office, FBI agents secretly entered the office and installed a listening device in the ceiling. Six weeks later, after the surveillance had terminated, the agents reentered the office and removed the device. The defendant was convicted, partly on the basis of intercepted conversations. The U.S. Supreme Court considered the legislative history of Title III and concluded as follows:

> [O]ne simply cannot assume that Congress, aware that most bugging requires covert entry, nonetheless wished to except surveillance requiring such entries from the broad authorization of Title III, and that it resolved to do so by remaining silent on the subject. On the contrary, the language and history of Title III convey quite a different explanation for Congress' failure to distinguish between surveillance that requires covert entry and that which does not. Those considering the surveillance legislation understood that, by authorizing electronic interception of oral communications in addition to wire communications, they were necessarily authorizing surreptitious entries. 441 U.S. at 252, 99 S.Ct. at 1691, 60 L.Ed.2d at 189.

With respect to the Fourth Amendment, the Court found that nothing in the language of the Fourth Amendment or the Court's decisions suggested that search warrants must include a specification of the precise manner in which they must be executed. "On the contrary, it is generally left to the discretion of the executing officers to determine the details of how best to proceed with the performance of a search authorized by warrant—subject of course to the general Fourth Amendment protection 'against unreasonable searches and seizures.'" 441 U.S. at 257, 99 S.Ct. at 1693, 60 L.Ed.2d at 192.

Finally, Title III specifically provides authority for designated federal or state officials to intercept wire or oral communications without a court order in certain emergency situations. An emergency must exist with respect to conspiratorial activities threatening the national security interest or to conspiratorial activities characteristic of organized crime requiring a communication to be intercepted. An application for an interception order must be made within forty-eight hours of the occurrence of the interception and, if an order is not obtained, the interception must immediately terminate when the sought communication is obtained or when the application is denied, whichever is earlier.

Constitutionality of Title III

Our discussion of Title III of the Omnibus Crime Control and Safe Streets Act of 1968 has centered around the specific provisions of the Act and court interpretation of those provisions. By and large, these decisions have eroded the limited protections provided by the Act and have provided little support for the constitutional principles established in the *Osborn, Berger,* and *Katz* decisions discussed earlier. Although Title III has survived constitutional challenges in several lower federal courts, the U.S. Supreme Court has yet to decide on the constitutionality of the Act. It remains to be seen whether Title III, as interpreted, can withstand a challenge based upon the Fourth Amendment's prohibition against general searches.

SUMMARY

Electronic surveillance was originally considered beyond the coverage of the Fourth Amendment because it involved no trespass into the defendant's premises and because it involved no seizure of tangible items. In a series of U.S. Supreme Court decisions in the mid-1960s, the Court reversed this approach and held that electronic surveillance by agents of the government is a search and seizure governed by the Fourth Amendment. The leading case adopting this new approach was *Katz v. U.S.,* which held that the Fourth Amendment protects people not places, thereby shifting the focus of the Fourth Amendment from property to privacy. In addition, the Court held that electronic surveillance is permissible only if conducted pursuant to a warrant that carefully limits the surveillance in nature, scope, and duration.

In 1968, Congress enacted Title III of the Omnibus Crime Control and Safe Streets Act which attempted to balance the need to use electronic surveillance for more effective law enforcement against the need to protect the privacy rights of individuals. Title III provided for judicial supervision of all aspects of electronic surveillance and established warrant procedures similar to those required for the search and seizure of tangible objects. These procedures were designed to limit who could authorize an application for an electronic surveillance order, who could apply for an order, the duration of electronic surveillance allowed, and various aspects of the execution of an electronic surveillance order. Individual rights provided under Title III included a limited right to inspect intercepted communications, restrictions on the disclosure of applications and orders, and rights to bring civil actions and motions to suppress for violations. Title III also specifically provides that state law enforcement officials may apply for, obtain, and execute electronic surveillance orders if authorized by a separate state statute.

There are many exceptions to the coverage of Title III. Title III does not protect a party to a conversation who has no reasonable expectation of privacy with respect to that conversation. Also, if one party to a conversation consents to the interception of a conversation, the conversation may be used against the other party. Any interception conducted by investigative or law enforcement officers using telephone or telegraph facilities in the ordinary course of their duties is exempted. And certain electronic surveillance related to national security and foreign intelligence is exempted. Finally, Title III does not apply to the use of electronic devices that do not intercept oral or wire communications, such as beepers, tracers, and pen registers.

Although a warrant is required to intercept wire or oral communications, judicial approval is not required to covertly enter premises to install a listening device. Neither is a warrant required to intercept wire or oral communications in emergencies involving conspiracies threatening national security or conspiracies involving organized crime, although an interception order must be applied for within forty-eight hours of the interception.

In general, court decisions interpreting the specific provisions of Title III have tended to erode the limited protections to individual rights provided in the Act by refusing to suppress evidence for violations of Title III unless the violation was central to the statutory scheme or unless there was incurable prejudice to the defendant. The constitutionality of Title III has yet to be determined by the U.S. Supreme Court.

REVIEW AND DISCUSSION QUESTIONS

1. Would an amendment to the Constitution dealing with modern-day intrusions on privacy have been a better way to deal with the problems posed by electronic surveillance than stretching the interpretation of the Fourth Amendment? Draft such an amendment.

2. Describe three ways in which court decisions have eroded the limited protections to individual rights provided in Title III of the Omnibus Crime Control and Safe Streets Act of 1968.

3. Although a physical trespass to property is no longer required to invoke the protections of the Fourth Amendment in electronic eavesdropping cases, is it safe to say that if there is a physical trespass, the Fourth Amendment's protections are automatically invoked?

4. Is the installation of a listening device in someone's home the same as hiding a police officer in a closet in the home? How does the police officer's ability to look through a keyhole in the closet affect the comparison?

5. Since Title III does not require judicial authority to covertly enter premises to install a listening device, is it correct to say that a person's conversations are no more protected in his or her home than they are in a telephone booth?

6. Under Title III, should the allowable duration of an interception order depend on the nature of the crime? Give examples.

7. How can a law enforcement officer ensure that authorized interceptions are conducted in such a way as to minimize the interception of communications not otherwise subject to interception under Title III? Should compliance with this requirement of Title III depend on the subjective intention of the officers conducting the surveillance?

8. Give some examples of ways in which a law enforcement official applying for an interception order might indicate that normal investigative procedures have failed, appear unlikely to succeed, or would be too dangerous.

9. What are some potential problems in determining when the authorized objective of an interception order under Title III has been attained?

10. Give some examples of conversations that would not be protected by Title III or by the Fourth Amendment because a party to the conversation has no reasonable expectation of privacy with respect to the conversation.

TABLE OF CASES

References are to pages

W

Y

Z

Index

References are to Pages

ABANDONED PROPERTY
See also Open Fields; Plain View.
Generally, 257–258, 269–280.
Abel v. United States, 271–273.
Curtilage, 271.
Determination,
    Generally, 270–280.
    Expectation of privacy, 278–280.
    Intent,
        Generally, 272–276.
        Motor vehicles, 275–276.
        Objects, 274–275.
        Premises, 272–274.
    Place property left, 270–272.
    Police behavior, 271, 274–275, 276–278.
Fourth Amendment, 257, 269.
Hester v. United States, 257–258, 270.
Plain view, 269.
Search, 269.
Seizure, 269–270.
Voluntariness, 269–278.

ABEL v. UNITED STATES
Seizure of abandoned property, hotel room, 271–272.

ACQUITTAL
Motion for judgment of, 40–41, 44.

ADMINISTRATIVE SEARCH
See Search Warrant.

ADMISSIBILITY
Evidence, see Evidence.

ADMISSIONS
See also Confessions; Evidence.
Miranda, see Miranda.
Probable cause, 148–149.

AFFIDAVIT
See also Complaint; Criminal Court Procedure; Magistrate; Probable Cause; Search Warrant.
Generally, 111–174.
Anticipatory search warrant, 123–124.
Arrest warrant, 30, 74–77.
Definition, 30, 111.
Description of place or person,
    Generally, 117–119.
    Beeper, 119.
    Mail, 119.
    Multiple occupancy dwelling, 117–118.
    Person, 118.
    Premises, 117–118.
    Surgery, 118.
    Vehicles, 118–119.
Description of things, 119–121.
False statements, 111–113.
Form, 112.
Grounds, 111–124.
Incorporation, 121–122.
Informants, see Informants.
Items subject to seizure,
    Contraband, 115.
    Instrumentalities, 115.
    "Mere evidence,"
        Bank records, 116.
        Business records, 115–116.
        Limitations on seizure, 115–116.
        Personal papers, 115–116.
    Stolen property, 115.
Multiple, 121–122.
Supplemental, 121–122.

AGUILAR v. TEXAS
Informants, 153–174.
Probable cause to search, hearsay method, 153–174.
Warrants, preference, 73, 179.

385

†